S0-AKZ-240

READING GREEK TRAGEDY

READING GREEK TRAGEDY

Simon Goldhill
Fellow of King's College, Cambridge

CAMBRIDGE
UNIVERSITY PRESS

Published by the Press Syndicate of the University of Cambridge
The Pitt Building, Trumpington Street, Cambridge CB2 1RP
40 West 20th Street, New York, NY 10011-4211 USA
10 Stamford Road, Oakleigh, Melbourne 3166, Australia

© Cambridge University Press 1986

First published 1986
Reprinted 1988, 1990, 1992, 1994

Translations from the Greek tragedians are taken from the series
edited by D. Grene and R. Lattimore and published by the University
of Chicago Press, and, with the exception of *Medea*, are reproduced
by the permission of the University of Chicago Press. *Medea* is
reproduced by permission of The Bodley Head Ltd. The plays in
question are: Aeschylus, *Agamemnon* and *Choephoroi* translated by R.
Lattimore © 1953 by the University of Chicago. Euripides, *Bacchae*
translated by W. Arrowsmith © 1958 by the University of Chicago;
Electra translated by E. T. Vermeule © 1958 by the University of
Chicago: *Hippolytos* translated by D. Grene © 1942 by the University
of Chicago: *Medea* translated by Rex Warner © 1944; *Troades*
translated by R. Lattimore © 1958 by the University of Chicago.
Sophocles, *Ajax* translated by J. Moore © 1957 by the University of
Chicago; *Antigone* translated by E. Wyckoff © 1954 by the University
of Chicago; *Oedipus Tyrannos* translated by D. Grene © 1942 by the
University of Chicago

Printed in Great Britain by Athenæum Press Ltd,
Gateshead, Tyne & Wear

British Library cataloguing in publication data

Goldhill, Simon
Reading Greek tragedy.
1. Greek drama (Tragedy) – History and criticism
I. Title
882'.01'09   PA3131

Library of Congress cataloguing in publication data

Goldhill, Simon
Reading Greek tragedy.
Bibliography: p.
Includes index.
1. Greek drama (Tragedy) – History and criticism.
I. Title
PA3131.G54 1986   882'01   85-19004

ISBN 0 521 30583 7 hardback
ISBN 0 521 31579 4 paperback

CE

For Shoshana Shira,
my flower, my song

A strong song tows
us, long earsick.
Blind, we follow
rain slant, spray flick
to fields we do not know.

BUNTING

CONTENTS

PREFACE

I would advise in addition the eschewal of overt and self-conscious discussion
of the narrative process. I would advise in addition the eschewal of overt and
self-conscious discussion of the narrative process.

JOHN BARTH

This book is designed as an advanced critical introduction to Greek tragedy,
primarily for the reader who has little or no Greek. I aim to provide a
combination of powerful readings of individual plays with an understanding
of the complex difficulties involved in the analysis of the workings of Greek
tragic texts, in the light of modern literary critical studies.

For Greek tragedy, the best available critical material – on which I have
drawn liberally – is based on a close reading of the Greek text, and even where
an attempt is made to help the Greekless reader by transliteration or
translation, insufficient assistance is provided for the reader without an
extensive knowledge of fifth-century Athenian culture. It is little help to
translate *polis* as 'city' or 'city-state', or to leave it in a transliterated form, if
the reader has no understanding of the nature of civic ideology in the fifth
century and its importance for tragedy in particular.[1]

There have been works attempting such a wider introduction, but they are
in general pitched, often with schools in mind, far below the level of critical
awareness or sophistication required by the modern reader who approaches
these plays from disciplines other than classics.[2] This book is composed
specifically for the reader who does not know Greek but who wishes to read
Greek tragedy with some critical awareness, and to appreciate and discuss in
all their complexities the problems raised by these texts.

The book is divided into four sections, each of two chapters: 1–2, language
and the city; 4–5, people and the city; 7–8, knowledge and mind; 10–11,
theatre as theatre. Each of these eight chapters has a similar form, and consists
of a general introduction to the range of questions and material involved in a
particular key topic in the study of Greek tragedy, together with a reading of

---

[1] This is a common problem particularly with collections of essays by classicists, such as Segal
ed. 1968, and especially Segal ed. 1983.
[2] E.g. Arnott 1959; Baldry 1981; and most recently Walton 1984.

certain plays in the light of the more general discussion. So, for example, the chapter 'Sexuality and difference' considers the various critical attitudes that have been taken in the discussion of sexual roles in Athenian culture and in particular in the tragic texts, and then develops a reading of the *Medea* and in far greater detail the *Hippolytus* specifically in terms of the questions of sexuality and difference. This allows the construction of detailed critical readings of the most commonly discussed individual plays with regard to a general and more widely relevant topic. Naturally, one cannot hope to give in a single chapter of such length an exhaustive treatment of a topic as complex as sexuality and difference, but this format not only offers access to the range and force of a modern critical debate and how it relates to particular plays, but also attempts to provide the means through which other plays of the tragic corpus may be approached and read.

The four sections are linked by three more general chapters (3, 6, 9), each of which deals with an essential element of background to the understanding of tragedy – the city and its ideology, Homer and his influence, the upheavals of the fifth-century enlightenment associated with the sophists. In these chapters, the social, literary and intellectual aspects of tragedy are put into a wider context.

I have called the book *Reading Greek Tragedy* not because I believe tragedy should not be performed, nor because most of us first approach these plays through the printed page, but because of certain contemporary critical associations with the term 'reading', which will become clear through the course of the book, and which will serve to distinguish this work from the major traditions of classical scholarship through which tragedy is most often approached. It is a somewhat polemical title for what is self-consciously a challenging book.

I have in general quoted from the Chicago Press series of translations under the editorship of David Grene and Richard Lattimore. Overall it has seemed more convenient to keep to a single, justifiably popular translation, than to seek out what I regard as the best translation for each play or set of lines. However, I have also often needed to adapt the translation to make my points more clearly or directly. I have only rarely indicated in the text where I have made such alterations.

I have not included such standard information as the dating of the plays, the lives of the poets, the construction of the theatre, the number of the actors etc., which is readily available elsewhere. It may be worth stating here, however, that all our extant plays were produced in public festivals in Athens and its territory Attica in the latter part of the fifth century B.C. Greek tragedy is Athenian tragedy, specifically Attic drama, from a remarkably brief span of years.

Although the book may be read with any translation, it is assumed that the plays in question have been read: there are no plot summaries or cribs. All Greek is, of course, transliterated, and to avoid confusion for readers unused to a highly inflected language, I have often given simply the base of the word quoted, when it is not in the nominative singular, for nouns and adjectives, or infinitive for verbs. So *philein* and *phil-* are normally used to cover all parts of the verb *philein*. Classicists may easily refer to the Greek text for any necessary clarification. The notes have been used almost exclusively for references, often to further reading on points of interest or further discussion of specific issues. They are not intended to be exhaustive, but helpful to the student or scholar wishing to continue the debates of this book into more detailed areas of scholarship.

It is a pleasure to be able to thank here the many friends and colleagues who have helped me on this book. Dr Robin Osborne and Dr Norman Bryson, read chapters and offered extremely useful comments and encouragement for the project. Dr Robin Osborne, Dr Richard Hunter, Mrs Patricia Easterling kindly showed me work in progress of which I have made liberal use. Professor Froma Zeitlin's influence from shared conversations, ideas and work has been constant: her encouragement and support can be thanked properly only here and not in the many relevant places in my text. Professor Geoffrey Lloyd read many of the chapters and particularly on questions of social and intellectual background offered essential advice and the benefit of his great understanding. Pat Easterling read all the chapters in draft: her astute criticisms and careful scholarship on all matters have been invaluable. John Henderson read the whole book as it progressed with sustaining patience and humour, as well as encouragement and criticism. And a special word of thanks to Jon, Flora, Lizzie and Sho – who convinced me in the first place that it should be possible.

Thanks are also due to the officers of the Press, Pauline Hire and Susan Moore, for their skill and efficiency.

S.D.G.
Cambridge 1985

PREFACE TO SECOND PRINTING

I wish to thank the many readers and reviewers, especially Paul Cartledge, who have helped with the revisions of this second printing.

S.D.G.
Cambridge 1988

1 · THE DRAMA OF LOGOS

The Linguistic Turn
                    R. RORTY, book title

Like so many modern philosophers, literary critics and novelists – heirs to ancient questions – fifth-century B.C. writers show an 'intense interest in the limits and possibilities of language'.[1] This interest connects numerous writers across numerous genres and disciplines. In the texts of philosophy, the concern with language not only gives rise to the development of linguistic study itself, but also is reflected in the prime place of *logos*, dialectic, rhetoric – the role of language itself – in the development of philosophical systems from Heraclitus to Aristotle. Modern occidental philosophy, for all its historical turns, is still working through Aristotelian linguistic categories and distinctions. It is the fifth century too that offers the first formal studies in rhetoric, the teaching and practice of which dominated education for two thousand years and more, and has recently been the focus of much of the most iconoclastic modern philosophical and literary criticism.[2]

In a society dominated institutionally by the assembly and the lawcourts, the discussion of the best way to use language (persuasion, argumentation, rhetoric) is an issue of considerable social and political importance, an issue brought into sharp focus under the pressure of the sophists' new methods of manipulative argumentation.[3] When the comic poet, Aristophanes, in the *Clouds*, his satire on modern thought and education, wishes to mock the processes of contemporary intellectual debate, he composes a dramatic exchange between personifications of the old, just *logos* ('argument', 'way or system of thinking', 'reason') and the new, unjust *logos* which focuses particularly on the ability of the new *logos* to make the weaker case appear stronger. So too his characters make fun of the philosophers' search for correct usage, linguistic purity and etymologies, with the less than serious test case of the word 'chicken'.

[1] Guthrie 1962–81, Vol. III, 219.
[2] I am thinking especially of Paul de Man and Jacques Derrida. For the development of rhetorical study see Kennedy 1963; Pfeiffer 1968; Russell 1983.
[3] See below, Chapter 9.

For the historian Thucydides, one of the most telling crisis points in the city under the abnormal stress of plague and overcrowding is the shifting and distortion of words away from traditional senses and values: language itself is an object of study among the symptoms of the city in turmoil.[4] The texts of the orators themselves – Demosthenes, Lysias, Isocrates and others – form a corpus fascinating not only for their various insights into Greek social and legal attitudes but also for the development of rhetoric in practice. All these areas of writing demonstrate a recognition of language as something to be studied, utilized, considered in and for itself. Language is not just treated as if it were a transparent medium, offering instant or certain access to meaning or thought or objects; rather, the role of language in the production of meaning, in the development of thought, in the uncertainties of reference, is a regular source of debate not only at the level of philosophical enquiry or literary self-consciousness but also in the more general awareness of the possibilities and dangers of the tricks and powers of words. The fifth century underwent 'a linguistic turn'.

Tragedy offers a particularly valuable insight into this important topic. Language as a specific mark of the civilized quality of being human, comes under the scrutiny of a tragic critique that questions the terms and attitudes of such self-definition of culture. As much as the shifting of language for Thucydides is a sign and symptom of the city at breaking-point, so the tragic texts, which depict and analyse the tensions, uncertainties and collapse of social order, return again and again to the shifting, distorting qualities of language – the ambiguities of the normative terms of society, the tensions in the civic and familial vocabulary and discourse, the twisting manipulations and over-rigid assertions of agonistic debate. When A. E. Housman brilliantly parodies a tragic dialogue, with characteristic insight he has his chorus ask 'What? For I know not yet what you will say.' Housman is poking fun, of course, but in a precise way he recalls the recurring questions in Greek tragedy about the functioning of language; the repeated doubts and misgivings about the sense and usage of words. Such comments and questions about what is being said in the course of tragic exchanges are not meaningless or undirected fillers, as is sometimes suggested by more banal critics – or in jest by Housman – nor are they simply ways of having a character repeat a story or remark for dramatic clarity or because characters and audience would not be typically 'Greek if [they] did not enjoy listening as long as possible to a fine tale beautifully told'.[5] Rather such comments and questions about language or meaning in the process of communication indicate the interest and uncertainty with regard to the sense, control and manipulation of words. Lack of security

[4] Thuc. 3.82.   [5] Fraenkel 1950, Vol. II, 182.

and misplaced certainty in and about language form an essential dynamic of the texts of tragedy.[6]

To an audience with solely modern expectations, it may appear that it is the dramatic conventions of tragedy which place a special emphasis on the spoken word. The extreme physical violence and destructiveness of the ancient myths are usually described by such devices as messenger speeches rather than depicted in explicit staging, and the most climactic scenes are often the clashing rhetorical arguments of different views and attitudes – the *agon*. Indeed, although Aristotle described tragic drama as the imitation of an action – *drama* in Greek means 'doing', 'a deed' – to the modern reader these plays have often seemed less than 'action-packed'. 'Static', 'statuesque' are common (if misleading) evaluations. But when I say there is a special focus on language in these plays, I do not mean to compare anachronistically the conventions of ancient tragedy with the conventions of modern drama and I certainly do not wish to imply that the context or particulars of performance or stage-action can be disregarded. It would be foolish to maintain that the *Oresteia*, in particular, with the final procession of torch-bearers, the entrance of the Erinyes, the carpet scene, does not involve visual, dramatic action essential to the trilogy's working. Under the influence of the lengthy tradition of philological study and the modern critical concern with the self-reflexive qualities of literature it is indeed all too easy to forget that these texts have come down to us without the stage-directions, music, dancing and costume that contribute so much to a performance. The religious, social, political context and implications of the institution of the dramatic festivals will also be a recurring interest of this book.

But there is considerably more involved in the assertion that this drama demonstrates a concern with language than the somewhat tautologous statement that a script in performance dramatizes the exchange of words, or, to be more specific, that a messenger-scene dramatizes the process of message-sending. For not only does a masterpiece such as the *Oresteia* utilize such conventional scenic devices as the arrival of a messenger to new and startling effect with particular significance for the understanding of the trilogy – as we shall see, it is simply insufficient to regard the messenger scene of the *Agamemnon* as merely conventional – but also the explicit comments of the play's characters draw further attention to the role of language itself in the process of the communication on stage. It is the way in which what one does with words becomes a thematic consideration of the *Oresteia* that makes this trilogy a 'drama of logos'.

The trilogy opens with a watchman waiting for a beacon-signal, which duly

[6] For studies of this, see Goldhill 1984a; Zeitlin 1982a; Podlecki 1966a, Segal 1982, 1983.

arrives. The first scene is an extended discussion between the queen and the chorus of what this light means and how it comes to have such meaning. The chorus remains not completely convinced by the queen's explanation of the mechanics and code of her signal system. Can this light really work as Clytemnestra described? The scene of message-sending and interpreting is followed by the arrival of a human messenger. The two scenes are explicitly linked (as well as juxtaposed) in the text. Rather than the mechanical model of communication, now there is a man with words. The ironies and uncertainties of this messenger scene mark the different difficulties involved in using words as opposed to sending a beacon-signal. Language cannot be fitted into a mechanistic model of signal-sending and receiving.[7] The queen, indeed, sends the messenger back to the king with a palpably false message which prepares the way for her plot. The messenger's next delivery will show all too clearly the possible dangers in the exchange of language when Clytemnestra is involved. This danger of the misuse of language is vividly depicted in the carpet scene, where the queen's powerful, manipulative persuasion leads Agamemnon to his death. Like Iago or Richard III, the queen's strength and transgressive power stem from her ability to weave a net of words around a victim. It is her verbal deceits that enable her to overthrow order. The Cassandra scene, which follows, offers two more important views on the process of communication. First, the scenario of the persuasive female speaker is reversed. Unlike Clytemnestra, whose lies were all too persuasive and effective, the inspired prophetess's truth persuades no-one and cannot be understood. Secondly, the prophetess's insight into the future and her true language not only express her awareness of the complexity of events but also develop the important theme of finding the right words, or name, which recurs throughout the trilogy. The search to control the future through accurate and powerful language links the many prayers, prophecies and curses of this play. Language, when used rightly, can have a direct and binding effect.

The search to find the correct language of prayer is important for the opening scenes of the *Choephoroi*, which place in parallel the prayers of the son and daughter of Clytemnestra for divine help. Together with the chorus in the lyric *kommos*, the children invoke the gods and their father. Before and after the *kommos*, there are two complex scenes revolving around the process of sign-reading – the recognition scene and Orestes' prophetic interpretation of the sign of Clytemnestra's dream. Like the scene of the beacon-signal discussion, and the many scenes of prophecy, these two scenes of sign-reading

---

[7] As many linguists have attempted to prove or disprove: cf. e.g. Jakobson and Halle 1956, as discussed e.g. in Culler 1975, for an influential model of language based on message-sending. Eco 1976 offers the most developed view of signal-sending and language. The *Oresteia* is illuminated by these studies as it illuminates them!

further develop the theme of interpretation and (mis)understanding. This development is important to the manner in which Orestes effects the revenge. For, like his mother, he depends on the manipulative power of deceitful persuasion to elude the interpretation of a hearer. He arrives disguised as a messenger with a false tale told in a foreign accent. Aegisthus too, is summoned to the palace by the nurse, who is persuaded to falsify her message. It is right for the chorus to pray to 'deceitful persuasion' when Orestes is in the palace. For the revenge is performed with a parallel reliance on deceit and misrepresentation.

As much as the earlier transgressions of the trilogy are committed through the misuse of language, the ending of the *Eumenides* attempts to right that disorder through the powers of the word. The final act of persuasion comes from the divine lips of Athene, who convinces the Erinyes to give up their anger, and turn from curse to blessing (again the power of language to affect the future course of things is basic to the narrative). The institution of the court, which is also essential to the ending of the trilogy, introduces the mediation of words – speech-making, the jurors' decision – between the violent antagonists of the case. The establishment and rule of law, which formalizes and consecrates social relations of order, marks the necessary involvement of *ideology* in the use of language in a social setting. The control of language, the awareness of the dangers of the misues of language are essential to the security of the social discourse in which social order is formed. From the signal to law . . . the *Oresteia* charts the social functioning of language in the city.

In this extremely brief and, for sure, selective run-through of the narrative of the *Oresteia* (which I will develop in more detail shortly) it is none the less clear how the use of language constitutes one of the important themes of the trilogy. The powers and dangers of language are essential to the narrative of revenge through the repeated acts of deceitful persuasion. The workings of language are traced and discussed through the different scenes of message-sending, sign-reading, interpretation and manipulation. The search for the right word, the desire for accurate prediction and prophecy, the effects of blessing, curse and invocation are all linked to the understanding of the workings of language. The word of the law and Athene's divine persuasion are the means by which reconciliation is sought.

Now the *Oresteia* is one of the most complex works of Greek literature: its highly involved lyric choruses, intense action and extended, interwoven imagery have prompted study after study that testify to this work's inexhaustibility. Its influence has been as immense as its continuing popularity. As with each Greek tragedy (but especially in the case of such complex poetic utterance) translation becomes a rewriting, a reselection of connections, echoes, meanings. Moreover, to talk about language will involve us in a wide series of other topics and themes which I can sketch only in broadest fashion here, but which bear significantly on our discussion. My treatment of one of the play's complex themes must constantly be qualified by an awareness of the necessary limitations of such a reading of the text.

I want to open my detailed analysis of the trilogy with the investigation of the sending and receiving of messages as a model of the exchange of language. A good place to begin is with the messenger scene of the *Agamemnon*.

The messenger scene comes at an earlier point in this play than in most other tragedies and the structure of the scene is markedly more complex than in many others. For rather than a single extended speech on a single disastrous event, the messenger delivers three long speeches, an address of welcome and two speeches describing what happened at Troy and on the journey home, and in between these latter two speeches Clytemnestra herself delivers a long address in which she gives a message to be taken back to Agamemnon. The herald moves from the confident optimism of his first joyful announcements of return and victory to the sad uncertainties of his second tale of the storm at sea, and between these two speeches Clytemnestra advances her plot of murder by sending a hypocritical welcoming message to her husband. The scene moves from the possibility of the happy return of the conquering hero to dread and foreboding for the lost fleet and the returning king: a considerable factor in this movement away from initial joy and certainty is the progressive undercutting of the secure exchange of language, not just in the juxtaposition of Clytemnestra's hypocrisy and the messenger's shift from rejoicing to foreboding, but also in the way in which the clarity and certainty of the messenger's language seem to be questioned. For a messenger in tragedy is normally treated by critics and characters alike as if he brought a clear and certain record of events – if in somewhat heightened language. But both the content of this messenger's message and his lack of awareness of the possibly dangerous misunderstandings that can arise in the exchange of language undermine any assumed straightforwardness in the process of giving and receiving a message. The first hints of this movement can be seen in the messenger's opening proud boast of the successful destruction of Troy (527–8):

> Gone are their altars, the sacred places are gone.

This destruction of religious sites is exactly what Clytemnestra earlier had prophesied could lead the Greeks to their doom (338–40):

> And if they reverence in the captured land the gods who hold the city
> and all the sacred places of the gods
> they, the despoilers might not be despoiled in turn.

The messenger's use of exactly the same phrase 'the sacred places of the gods' in the same metrical position expresses the fulfilment of the queen's fear; the messenger fails to realize the ominous impact of the message he conveys. In his unawareness of the foreboding his words give rise to, the messenger's statement marks the possibility of a dangerous unawareness of the implications of the use of language. His message already conveys more than he knows.[8]

This lack of awareness is seen markedly at the beginning and end of his second long speech. The chorus have been trying to hint that something disastrous has been happening at home in the absence of the army and king. They pick up the messenger's earlier expression of joy that he'd willingly die now that he's home at last (539), but they turn his expression to a grim willingness to greet death rather than continue in their present woes (550):

> So much, that as you said now, even death were grace.

But the messenger completely fails to appreciate the chorus' new despairing use of his own words, and with an extraordinary *non sequitur* replies as if they had merely reiterated his happiness (551):

> Yes, for things have been well done.

This odd reply, his apparent inability to understand the words spoken to him or to respond to them, seemes to stress the uncertainties in the process of communication, the gaps and misunderstandings between a speaker and listener in the exchange of language – just as he begins to deliver his message.

This message depicts the labours of the Greek soldiers, and he sums up the first part of his speech rhetorically with a question (567):

> But why live such grief again? Toil is over.

The word for 'toil' is *ponos*, which recurs throughout the trilogy from the first line as an expression – almost a leitmotif – for the turmoil in the house of Atreus. If the Argives' toil in one sense is over, in another way it is being further prepared in this scene by Clytemnestra's plotting – in which this messenger will play his part. Once again, the language of the messenger exceeds his apparent immediate intention.

The herald concludes his speech with a standard sounding phrase (582):

> You have the whole story.

The fact that his last speech of the bad news of the storm at sea is yet to be told, as well as his lack of awareness of the relevance of his own and the chorus' words make this messenger's certainty in the giving and receiving 'the whole

---

[8] Fraenkel deletes the messenger's comment precisely because he could not believe the messenger would speak so naively. As we will see, this is not the only example of such behaviour from the messenger – or other characters.

story' ironic. As so often in the *Oresteia*, faith in the clear and assured exchange of language is to be set against the misunderstandings and uncertainties of the surrounding verbal communications.

Indeed, Clytemnestra follows this message-giving with a message-sending of her own (604–8):

> Take this message to the king.
> Come and with speed back to the city that longs for him,
> and may he find a wife within the house as true
> as on the day he left her, watchdog of the house,
> gentle to him alone, fierce to his enemies . . .

His present tale seems veined with unrecognized ironies and misunderstandings, but the next message the herald will take will be a specific act of deceit. The queen's powerful manipulation both of language and of the process of sending messages is in direct contrast with the messenger's naive faith in simply transmitting 'the whole story'. Indeed, Clytemnestra echoes precisely those last words of the messenger in dismissing his usefulness (598–9):

> Why should you tell me then the long tale at length
> when from my lord himself I shall hear the whole story.

'Hearing the whole story' is an extremely disingenuous description both of her verbal exchanges with Agamemnon and of the more physical welcome she is preparing. Clytemnestra is using her words and the process of sending a message to weave a web of dissimulation and deceit, manipulating language as an opportunity for furthering her plot. The repetition of the messenger's phrase 'the whole story' in her mouth marks the difference in its possible connotations and implications. The juxtaposition of the optimism of the returning soldier – optimism in the end of toil and in his role as simple message conveyor – and the deceitful, message-sending queen, manipulating words to her own murderous ends, creates a significant tension which marks the danger of the power of language in the mouth of the waiting adulteress.

The specific nature of the queen's verbal deceit is hinted at in her final remarks to the messenger.[9] The hypocritical adulteress's vaunt that 'with no man else have I known delight, nor any shame of evil speech', is, she claims 'loaded with truth'. Particularly after such a notably precise reversal of the truth, this image suggests the marked possibility of its opposite, that words can be emptied, unloaded of truth. If words can be so loaded and unloaded with truth, can language give direct access to a speaker's intention? The model of language suggested by this phrase implies a gap at the heart of communi-

---

[9] Lattimore gives these lines to the messenger. This does not substantially alter the point I am making about the imagery.

cation between signifiers and what they signify, as if in a message form could be separated from content. In the misrepresentations of Clytemnestra's boast, it is easy indeed to discern the possibility of words being loaded with and emptied of truth.

This suggestion that Clytemnestra's hypocrisy implies a separation between a signifier and what it signifies is particularly important for the scenes preceding the messenger scene, which are also largely concerned with the arrival and understanding of a message, or rather, of a signal, the beacon-light whose anticipation opens the play. Indeed, the beacon-speeches scene, the first scene in which Clytemnestra speaks, is important to the development of the play's view of the processes of communication. For by Aeschylus' invention of the beacon and its discussion, and by the early placing of the messenger scene, the action leading up to the carpet scene and the deception of Agamemnon is dominated by the images, discussion and process of message-sending and receiving, a complex model of language exchange and interpretation. The beacon-speeches scene, which has all too rarely been treated with any analytic rigour or insight by critics, has a major role not just in the system of imagery connected with 'light', 'fire', but also in developing our understanding of Clytemnestra's power in terms of her control over the processes of communication and exchange.

The chorus, who have come to hear what the strange beacon-light may mean, are told by Clytemnestra that it indicates the successful completion of the Trojan war in a victory for the Greek host. The chorus remain somewhat mistrustful of the queen's news and they request proof, and she delivers two long speeches to convince them. After the first, the chorus call her 'lady' and say that they will thank the gods, but would like to hear the proof again. They are amazed. After the second, the chorus call her 'lady' again but add 'you speak like a sensible man with good feeling. I have listened to the proofs of your tale and I believe . . . ' They now accept that they have been given the proof that they requested. Is there, then, a difference between the two speeches? Why does the second speech find the chorus' agreement? Is it just the accumulation of rhetorical force, as critics have generally asserted? Is it convincing because it is a proof twice told?

There is indeed a highly significant and emphatic difference between the two speeches of proof, which even when noted by critics has led to bafflement.[10] In the first proof, Clytemnestra describes in detail the passage of the beacon-light from place to place in its route from Troy to Argos. She describes how the fire is passed along the chain, she explains how the flame travels. She concludes (315–16):

[10] Cf. Verrall's remarks as repeated and discussed by Fraenkel 1950 ad loc.

> By such proof and such symbol I announce to you
> my lord at Troy has sent his messengers to me.

The word 'has sent his messengers to me' is the technical word in Greek for 'to pass the password', 'give the watchword', and the verb in Greek is used somewhat strangely here without a direct object. The sense of 'passing a password' is particularly apposite for the first proof that Clytemnestra has constructed, not only because the light is passed from site to site along a chain, but also because it is precisely like a password in that the beacon-light is a marker without connotation. It is a signifier which has meaning only in terms of a pre-arranged and pre-established system, a 'code'. Like a password, the beacon can only indicate in a binary way: it either signals or it does not; and it can only signify in that manner. It cannot, as a man with words can, communicate madly/stupidly/deceitfully. The meaning of the signal depends on the pre-agreed and unchanging system of markers. It is the mere presence of such a signal and such a system that Clytemnestra seeks to explain by her proof of the passage of light from place to place. In demonstrating the linkages of the system from Troy to Argos, Clytemnestra only shows how the message comes to signal its light. She demonstrates the establishment of the closed system, her 'code'.

In the second speech, however, Clytemnestra, in a quite different fashion, describes what the light might mean, its message and connotations. She delivers an extended description of how Troy was sacked, which as has often worried critics, she could not possibly have known.[11] This forceful description is not, however, just another purple passage for the queen. Rather, the two speeches markedly separate the form and possible content, the signifier (beacon-light) and the signified (a message) in the communication of the beacon-chain. The fact that the message Clytemnestra provides for the light is so markedly a fictitious, imaginative weaving of words emphasizes the arbitrary connection of signifier and signified in the process of message-sending and receiving.

The first two major scenes in which Clytemnestra appears, then, both demonstrate the queen's ability to manipulate the relation between signal and sense. Regarded together in the development of the play, they act as a highly significant prelude to the carpet scene, where it will be the queen's manipulative persuasion which deceives Agamemnon and leads him to step on the tapestries towards his death. The beacon-speeches scene is not merely demonstrative of the queen's powerful force or an exhibition of rhetoric. It offers also a specific indication of the nature of the force of her power in her manipulation of the exchanges of communication.

[11] See note 10.

Few scenes in the corpus of Greek tragedy have excited critics' imagination and disagreements as much as the carpet scene. The king returning home in triumph from the Trojan war is confronted before the palace and the Argive elders by his wife, who bars his way to the palace doors by a path of purple tapestries. Clytemnestra's first speech to the king is a fascinating prelude to the exchange in which he finally yields to her wishes. It is a speech of greeting and, like the message of welcome she sent before, it is full of hypocrisy. Her present joy, she enthuses, is in contrast to her past fear, where rumour after rumour of Agamemnon's death reached her. The queen dwells for some thirty lines on the misinformation she received, stressing again and again the vocabulary of 'speaking', 'messages', 'lies', as she herself weaves her misrepresentations around her husband. 'As if she were challenging Agamemnon to see the truth', writes Kitto.[12] But it is more than that. We are watching Clytemnestra's false language describing itself in the tales of lies that she is constructing. Self-referentially, Clytemnestra's lying speech is about lying speeches.

Agamemnon at first refuses to step on the cloths spread for him. He recognizes a meaning in the act of stepping on the tapestries which is not befitting his status as a mortal, Greek male. He cannot tread that path 'without fear'. This reluctance has been well analysed in terms of traditional Greek attitudes.[13] The wanton destruction of the household property that his trampling of 'these tinted splendours' represents, is in absolute opposition to the normal ethos of the household, which aims at continuity and stability of wealth and possessions.[14] Even as he steps down Agamemnon says 'Great the extravagance and great the shame I feel to spoil such treasure and such silver's worth of webs' (948–9). Clytemnestra replies in famous lines with an arrogance and confident assurance of permanent wealth that flies in the face of the common Greek awareness of the vicissitudes of fortune and the dangers of excess (958–62):

> The sea is there. Who can drain its yield? It breeds
> precious as silver, ever of itself renewed,
> the purple ooze wherein our garments can be dipped.
> And by God's grace this house keeps full sufficiency
> of all. Poverty is a thing beyond its thought.

In contrast with this hubristic boast, Agamemnon's fear of the gods is the more common Greek reaction not only to conspicuous rejoicing at success but even to success itself. It would seem the king's fear is well placed. Why, then, does he step down?

[12] 1956, 23.   [13] Cf. especially Jones 1962, 72–137.
[14] On this ethic, see below, Chapter 3.

The traditional answer to this traditional question is to look for justification or motivation in the character of Agamemnon. Is he really arrogant and delighted to have this opportunity to take such vain, glorious, prideful steps?[15] Or is he too much of a gentleman to refuse his wife?[16] Or is he too tired and war-weary to fight again?[17] In the absence of any explicit motivation, every line has been combed to prove one mental state or another. Rather than follow this line of interpretation,[18] I want to consider the argumentation by which Clytemnestra achieves her end to see what light the analysis of the role of language itself can shed on this question. Unfortunately, Lattimore's translation here is less than satisfactory for my purposes, and I shall have to modify it somewhat to render the Greek more precisely. It is a short, but highly complex dialogue.

First Clytemnestra simply requests that Agamemnon should not cross her will or opinion in what he says. He asserts the fixedness of his intention. The queen then begins a process of questioning which seeks to undermine that fixed intention by undercutting the certainty of the context in which the meaning of the act of stepping on the tapestries has been defined. She asks first 'Would you in fear have vowed to the gods to do this in this way?' It was customary in the ancient world in times of stress or danger for a person to vow an expensive propitiatory offering to the gods.[19] In such circumstances, it is normal and right to destroy or sacrifice a part of the household's wealth. Clytemnestra asks Agamemnon if he would be prepared to trample the tapestries were he to have vowed to the gods in a moment of fear to do so. Agamemnon confesses that if he took such a vow on good religious advice, then it would be correct to fulfil it by walking on the tapestries: 'If someone who knew well enjoined that task to me.' Clytemnestra then asks 'If Priam had won as you have what would he have done?' Would another person be reasonably expected to do as she asked? Agamemnon confesses that the Trojan king might well have walked on such cloths, though he had asked not to be treated like a barbarian. Clytemnestra now turns to Agamemnon's expressed fear of the envy that would come with such ostentatious display. She advises him not to be ashamed before the reproach of his fellow men – note she leaves out any mention of the gods. Agamemnon recalls, however, the strength of such public opinion. Clytemnestra with a neat turning of the argument replies that a person without envy is a person without admiration – a double negative which does not, of course, prove that it is positively right to act in such a way as to cause envy. Agamemnon turns here to the attack: he reminds his wife

---

[15] Denniston–Page's opinion.   [16] Fraenkel's opinion.   [17] Fraenkel's opinion, also.
[18] I have discussed it elsewhere, in Goldhill 1984a, 69–74 and 167–9.
[19] Offers of such sacrifices, particularly of hecatombs, are common in Homer.

that it is unsuitable for a woman to desire battle. An ironic enough rejoinder, not only as he is rapidly losing the battle of words but also because he will shortly be killed in a travesty of battle – naked, in the bath, by an axe-wielding woman. Clytemnestra again turns his remark to her favour, suggesting that even yielding is a fitting gesture for the powerful: 'for the mighty even to give way is grace'. The verb 'give way' is the normal Greek expression for to be defeated in battle. She picks up the battle-imagery of her husband but deflects the negative implications of his remark: once more the manipulation of language towards a specific victory. Agamemnon finally asks if such a victory means so much to the queen and she replies (943):

> Be persuaded; willingly yield your power to me.

This dialogue suitably concludes with the exhortation to be persuaded. It is the manipulative force of persuasion that we have been watching in Clytemnestra's struggle to have the power over the house yielded to her female control. When Agamemnon sought to define the meaning of the act of stepping on the carpet in one way, Clytemnestra demonstrated that such a meaning was not fixed but could be shifted, manipulated, first by the postulation of different circumstances and secondly by the realignment of the moral terms Agamemnon used to describe the argument. Another occasion, another person, and the sense of the act seems different. The deprecated envy is only the accompaniment of the praised admiration of men. To be defeated in the debate is not the loss of battle but the grace of yielding from a position of power. The carpet as symbol, the figure in the carpet, under the pressure of Clytemnestra's questioning yields further meanings, and it is through this yielding of further meanings that the certainty and fixedness of Agamemnon's original position is undermined. It is not so much the weakness of Agamemnon's character, as the strength of Clytemnestra's undercutting arguments that is indicated in this dialogue. It is the dramatic staging of the power of the rhetoric of persuasion in the pursuit of dominance.

On one level, then, it may seem simply that it is the force of Clytemnestra's use of language that is acted out here. Agamemnon's lack of explicit motivation only strengthens the focus on Clytemnestra's rhetoric as it successfully works. On another level, however, Clytemnestra's persuasion can also be seen as a culmination of the earlier scenes. As in the messenger scene, we see the queen's manipulative language in her lying stories; as in the beacon-speeches scene Clytemnestra disjoins signifiers from what they signify to achieve her persuasion: as I argued above, it was relevant that Clytemnestra's analysis of the beacon-signal separated a symbol (as she calls the light) from its meaning or message; it is such separation that makes possible her manipulation of communication. So with her interpretation of Agamemnon's reluctance to step on the carpet, Clytemnestra's arguments separate the act of stepping on the carpet and a fixed meaning for such an act. The beacon-speeches scene, the messenger scene and the carpet scene show in different but related ways Clytemnestra's manipulation of the relation of signs and meaning.

Language, when Clytemnestra uses it, becomes frightening. The uncertainty she introduces is not merely verbal, but works also towards the death of her husband, the king – the overthrow of social order. As with Thucydides' view of Athens in the plague, the (in)stability of language and the (in)stability of social order are mutually implicative: 'The tapestry . . . is itself the emblem and the instrument of disruption in the sign system on which all civilized order rests.'[20]

When Clytemnestra appears with the corpses of Agamemnon and Cassandra, vaunting the success of her plotting, it is indeed precisely the power of her language which she exalts first and foremost (1372–6):

> Much have I said before to serve necessity
> but I will take no shame now to unsay it all.
> How else could I, arming hate against hateful men,
> disguised in seeming tendencies, fence high the nets
> of ruin beyond overleaping?

Shame, the bond and control of social order, has been ignored in Clytemnestra's transgressions in and of language. The chorus in reaction can only stand in fear and awe of her 'mouth so arrogant'.

Before I turn to investigate in further depth this fear of language and the various attempts to control it in the *Oresteia*, I want to look briefly at how Orestes' revenge shows a similar reliance on the deceptive powers of language. For in the *Choephoroi*, a play marked by paradoxical reversals, the attempt to right the social order thrown into disorder by Clytemnestra is explicitly described as being made – and ordered to be so by Apollo – in the same transgressive manner as the regicide was committed. Like Agamemnon and Cassandra, Orestes and Pylades come to the palace door to be greeted by Clytemnestra. But now the deceit is on the part of the guests who will kill their host. Clytemnestra welcomes them with a speech of considerable irony (688–71): 'we have all the comforts that go with a house like ours, hot baths and beds to charm away your weariness'. Certainly hot baths and beds are customarily offered to guests in the Greek world from Homer onwards, but the phrase 'house like ours', if further emphasis were necessary, helps recall in

[20] Segal 1981, 55.

the reference to 'hot baths' the place where Agamemnon was slaughtered, as the 'beds' and the 'charm' recall the specific transgressions of Clytemnestra's adultery. The term for 'weariness' moreover is *ponos*, the word so often associated with the turmoil in the house of Atreus (a turmoil specifically recalled here in the 'baths' and 'beds'). But the ironic surplus of meaning in Clytemnestra's offer, unlike the 'fences of words' she erected to conceal her machinations, seems to bring to unexpected prominence precisely the crimes she had managed to hide in their plotting. As Clytemnestra is being deceived, her language unavoidably proclaims her earlier transgressions. She won control through words; she will lose it through words.

Orestes, pretending to be a messenger, tells the false story of his own death in order to gain safe acceptance to the house, and the queen and her son enter the doors as she had with Agamemnon, but towards a different outcome. The chorus now pray to 'deceitful persuasion' and Hermes, the messenger god, divinity of lying and untrustworthy communication and exchange,[21] to help the avengers. But from the palace unexpectedly there comes now a new character, Orestes' old nurse. As with the porter in *Macbeth*, critics here write of the drop in tension, the low-life scene compared to the high palace drama of succession and revenge. But there is considerably more to this scene than that. On the one hand, there is an essential process of definition being constructed in the vocabulary of nursing and the vocabulary of maternity, which looks forward to the rejection of the ties of mother and son not only in the matricide but also and importantly in the trial-scene, where Apollo's defence of Orestes' matricide relies on the devaluation of the role of the mother in generation as merely the nurse of the male seed, as, indeed, one of the reasons Athene gives for supporting Orestes is the fact that she was not born of woman. The appearance of the nurse between the entrance of Orestes to the palace and the matricide plays an important part in this movement away from the mother. On the other hand, once again we see that the process of message-sending, manipulation and interpretation is essential to the dramatic action. For the chorus find that the nurse, Cilissa, has been sent as a messenger to fetch Aegisthus. The chorus persuade her to change her message to one more helpful to the avengers: 'it is the messenger', they say, 'who makes the bent word straight' (773). Cilissa cannot understand their reason, though she realizes it is connected to the earlier messengers: 'What is this? Have you some news that has not been told?' (778). But the chorus simply tell her 'Go on and take your message, do as you are told' (779). And like the other unwitting conveyors of dangerous words in this play, she delivers her message.

The chorus once more pray, now to Zeus and again to Hermes, to support

---

[21] See below, Chapter 3, on Hermes.

the avengers. Their twisting of Clytemnestra's message is sited between two prayers to the divinities of deceitful communication for assistance. Hermes here is addressed in his connections with the failure of communication and exchange (816–18):

> He speaks the markless word, by night hoods
> darkness on the eyes nor shows more plainly
> when the day is there.

The messenger god, divinity of deceit, to whom both Orestes and Electra had also prayed, may indeed be seen at work in the deceitful message that leads the unrecognizing Aegisthus to his death.

These scenes, then, leading to the actual murders of revenge place considerable emphasis on the exchange of language as uncertain, and dangerous – an emphasis which makes parallel Clytemnestra's plot and Orestes' revenge in their similar reliance on deceitful persuasion, misrepresenting messages in the power struggle in the house. Language is both means and matter of the transgressions of mother and son.

The dangers of language are immediately evident in the *Choephoroi* after the prayer to Hermes. Aegisthus enters and is despatched into the house and his doom in a mere seventeen lines. But once more, as so often in this trilogy, the role of language and message-sending is brought to the fore. Aegisthus announces himself with a strange periphrasis (838): 'It is not without summons that I came but called by messenger.' We are directed back to the process by which his message was prepared by the chorus and delivered by the nurse. Aegisthus goes on to talk of the messengers' news. He is unclear whether the reports are mere rumours or true accounts. The chorus offer him the ambiguous clarity of going in and learning (850) 'man to man'. He will indeed learn the answer to his enquiry 'man to man', but not as he expects. Once more, not only is the discussion about the true and misleading content of language but also it is a discussion which is (mis)leading one party to his destruction. Aegisthus accepts their advice (851–4):

> I wish to question, carefully, this messenger
> and learn if he himself was by when the man died
> or if he heard but some blind rumour and so speaks.
> The mind has eyes, not to be easily deceived.

In contradiction to Clytemnestra's immediate hospitality, Aegisthus asserts caution as in ignorance he approaches his death even more swiftly. He arrives called by a false messenger, led on by the dissembling chorus, to die at the hands of the false messenger inside. Aegisthus' lack of trust in messages is apt, if useless.

In the light of our discussion so far, it is not surprising that Aegisthus' lack of trust in the process of communication and language finds many echoes throughout the narrative of the *Oresteia*. Reaction to the dangers of language-exchange produces many expressions of a reciprocal desire for the control and order of words in communication. Aegisthus' imagery of blindness and sight points towards a thematic structure of the play that is especially relevant to our discussion of the role of language. For one of the specific constant echoes to the fear produced by the dangers of communication is the stated need for 'clarity' in language to control and eradicate that fear. 'Clarity', 'precision' in language would remove the possibility of the dangerous deceptions and misunderstandings in the exchange of words. 'Clarity' brings a certainty of knowledge.

This language of 'clarity', however, shows well the complexity that the intertwined network of images gives rise to in the *Oresteia*. The positive value of clarity depends on the hierarchical oppositions of light to dark, of sight to blindness. Aegisthus' imagery seems directly evaluative in this way. The untrustworthy language of rumour is 'blind', but the intelligent man's mind to escape deception 'has eyes'. This value-charged imagery of light and sight recurs throughout the play from the beacon-signal to the torches of the final procession of the *Eumenides*, and many critics have read in this vocabulary and imagery a teleological pattern of a search for the true light (sight) to dispel darkness (blindness), a move from ignorance and doubt towards certain knowledge. 'Movement from enigmatic utterance to clear statement, from riddle to solution, dominate the structure of the *Oresteia*.'[22] 'The light the Watchman sees blazing out of the darkness culminates, after several other false lights, in the torch-lit procession that escorts the Eumenides to their new home in Athens, and really does put within man's grasp, if he will take it, "release from misery".'[23]

The imagery of light and sight, however, as Kitto's remarks about 'several other false lights' suggest, does not only contribute to the development of the positive value of 'clarity'. It is also essentially connected to the uncertainty of visions, dreams, and the insubstantiality of perception. Consider these lines from the *Agamemnon*, which explicitly draw a parallel between the beacon-signal and the messenger's message. The herald is seen approaching from the shore (489–98):

> Now we shall understand these torches and their shining,
> the beacon and the interchange of flame and flame.
> They may be real, yet bright and dream-wise ecstasy
> in light's appearance might have deceived our minds.

[22] Lebeck 1971, 2.   [23] Kitto 1961, 67.

> I see a herald coming from the beach, his brows
> shaded with sprigs of olive and upon his feet
> the dust, dry sister of the mud, makes plain to me
> that he will find a voice, not merely kindle flame
> from mountain timber and make signals from the smoke,
> but he will speak, telling us outright . . .

The difference that is being constructed here between the beacon and the messenger opposes the mere appearance of fire (the beacon-chain) to a person with language; the 'interchange of flame and flame' to the exchange of speech. The use of words, it is assumed, will make the light's meaning clear – an ironic enough assumption considering the undercutting of the certainty of communication in the scene that follows. Light and vision are here associated negatively with 'appearance', 'dream', 'deception', unreality – the insubstantiality of seeming as opposed to being.

The sense of the instability of vision is especially marked at the end of the *Choephoroi*, a play in which the vocabulary of sight is prominent throughout. Orestes describes the terrifying appearance of the Erinyes which the chorus cannot see: he is disturbed by visions, by fancies, they suggest. He strongly rejects their inference (1053–4):

> These are no fancies of affliction. They are clear,
> and real, and here, the bloodhounds of my mother's hate.

Orestes appeals to the certain knowledge which clarity provides, at the moment at which his vision seems most doubtful. As with Aegisthus approaching his death, Orestes' assertion of clarity, of clear vision, seems a misplaced certainty, a grim irony. The hierarchical opposition of reality to dream, fancy, vision on which this scene seems to draw is thrown into confusion, however, at the beginning of the *Eumenides*, where those visions of the madman appear as the chorus of the drama, and where they are driven into action by the appearance of the dream-spirit of Clytemnestra. That dreams are both deprecated as mere insubstantial seeming but also appear to direct events, that a vision of the Erinyes is both the symptom of mental and visual disorder and can appear as the chorus of the final play of the trilogy, complicate the establishment of a coherent criterion of judgement based on the language of sight and light. In other words, when so many characters appeal to, hope for, or trust in 'clarity', it is not merely the subsequent passage of events that makes their belief seem disturbingly ironic. The very language of 'clarity', of 'seeing clearly', of 'insight', of 'seeing the light' seems to provide a dubious basis or criterion for judgement, when the same vocabulary appears to express both the certainty of sure knowledge and the insubstantiality of mere appearance.

   The language of vision and in particular that of 'clarity' brings certain difficulties with it, then, in the search for control over the shifts and tricks of communication. Rather than the attainment of 'clarity', it is the unachieved desire for it that re-echoes through the text. Indeed, even as the reconciled Erinyes approach their final torch-lit exit – Kitto's 'realization of that final light' – Athene stresses man's continuing ignorance of the passage of events even in the newly constituted civic order. As she sings of the control of the Eumenides over the 'handling entire of men's lives' she reflects how the man who experiences the heavy force of the Eumenides 'knows not whence or why came the blows of life'. The goddess seems to authorize human ignorance in the face of the vicissitudes of life. Darkness is not totally dispelled.

   The search for control over language and the passage of events is developed in numerous ways. Here the chorus of the *Agamemnon* consider the precision of naming (681–90):

> Whoever named you so, in absolute accuracy?
> Could it be someone unseen in foreknowledge
> of what had to happen using his tongue to the mark,
> who named you, spear-bride, fought-over
> Helen?
> Appropriately named, since hell for ships,
> hell for men, hell for cities. . . .

The chorus of the *Agamemnon*, after they hear the news from the herald of the fall of Troy, reflect once more on the war's origin, the adultery of Helen. Up to this point in the play, Helen has not been referred to by name, but has only been called 'woman'. A name is that by which a society's members recognize and order its relationships, and Helen's adultery is an act that transgresses the affiliations of society.[24] It is as if the chorus' language implies that because Helen has placed herself outside society by her adulterous transgression, she has lost that mark of recognition by which society places her, her name. But now that the adultery has been avenged, the chorus turn to consider the 'woman' again and explicitly reflect on the process of the giving of her name. They wonder who could have given her a name with such 'absolute accuracy'. The expression for 'accuracy', *etetumos*, is a form of the word which gives us our term 'etymology' and implies a precise fixing through exactly the sort of original naming process implied in this passage. The importance of the right name is not merely one of social categorization; through the accuracy of 'using his tongue to the mark' an insight into the future is gained. The name gives access to 'foreknowledge of what must happen'. Predication is also prediction

[24] On the protocols of using a woman's name, see Schaps 1977. On naming, adultery, and society in general, see Tanner 1980.

– nomen/omen. The connection between the name and Helen's life turns out, however, to be a verbal play, a triple pun which I have attempted to capture in my adaptation of Lattimore's translation by the expressions 'hell for ships, hell for men, hell for cities'. A closer translation of the Greek is 'ship-destroyer, man-destroyer, city-destroyer . . . ' but such a rendering misses the essential connection of the words '*Helenan* (Helen) and *Helenas* (ship-destroyer), *Helandros* (man-destroyer), *heleptolis* (city-destroyer)'. Helen's name contains an indication of the destruction she will cause. The shifting word play of a pun has significance. The meaning of the name is realized too late, however, to give the control that an earlier understanding may have provided. Helen's story indicates what's in a name.

This passage is a good example of the search for control over events through the control of language. The accurate understanding and use of a name gives an understanding of what must happen. Here the origin, the *etymon*, of the name provides a model of comprehension as the chorus attempt to explain the Trojan war. This ode will conclude with stanzas explaining the generation of sin and transgression through the imagery of childbirth and descent – another explanatory origin. These metaphors look forward to the outcome of the trial, which will also depend on relationships of origins and descent, that is, on what is the essential relation of Orestes to his two parents. It is evident in these different but connected searches for an explanation through an origin how closely intertwined in the texture of the play are the thematic concerns of language-control, control over the passage of events, and the sexual discourse which dominates so much of the action.

The sense of control offered by etymology and the right name is returned to at several important points in the narrative of the *Oresteia*. After Orestes has led his mother into the palace to kill her, an act depicted both as a god-ordered act of Justice and the most awful transgression of the dictates of Right, the chorus sing an ode attempting to explain the pattern of events leading to this paradoxical act. As they turn to the matricide, they offer an explanatory etymology of the word for Justice, or Right, as Lattimore translates (948–51):

> but in the fighting his hand was steered by the very
> daughter of Zeus : Right we call her,
> mortals who speak of her and name her well.

The term 'right', '*dikē*', is explained etymologically as 'the daughter of Zeus', *Dios korē*. That is the correct naming, the correct way to speak. At the moment of supreme tension in the concept of Justice – a concept germane to this trilogy as we will see in the next chapter – the chorus attempted to find a fixed meaning, and once more it is in the language of origin and descent; indeed, Justice can be understood by her literal origin in the father of the gods himself, whose authorization for the matricide his son Apollo will claim in the trial scene. The chorus attempt to control the narrative through the understanding of the word, and attempt to control the word by the explanatory origin of etymology.

The sense of control sought for in etymology and correct naming is in reaction to the dangers of misusing and misunderstanding words. This danger of the miscomprehension or mishandling of language is seen most clearly in the language of prayer and the related notion of cledonomancy. Cledonomancy is a way of telling the future by turning a speaker's words against the user. Here is an example (1652–3):

> Aegisthus: I too am sword-handed against you. I am not afraid of death.
> Chorus: Death you said and we accept the omen – we take up the word of fate.

Aegisthus' bravado is turned to an unintended prophecy of his own death by the chorus' acceptance of his words as an omen. Words can determine as well as predict. Cledonomancy indicates the dangers of an inability to control language, which in eluding the speaker can lead him to an unwished end.[25] As much as Agamemnon demonstrated an inability to see through Clytemnestra's manipulative language, so Aegisthus shows here an inability to prevent his language being manipulated. The reduction of the aggressive role of Aegisthus in Aeschylus' version of this story is seen in his and Clytemnestra's respective powers of language, as well as his absence from the performance of the regicide.

These dangers in the use of language are nowhere more evident than in the religious circumstances of making a prayer. Greek religious ceremonies normally begin with an exhortation to beware an improper use of language; and, as with many religious cult attitudes, a rigour towards the suitable performance of prayers is demanded. In the *Oresteia*, where there are numerous prayers to the gods as expressions of desire for control over events, numerous invocations for assistance towards particular ends, the correct language of prayer is constantly under question. Sometimes, it is as direct a request as the chorus' short prayer as Aegisthus enters the palace to the waiting Orestes (855–8):

> Zeus, Zeus, what shall I say, where make
> a beginning of prayer for the god's aid?
> My will is good
> but how shall I speak to match my need?

[25] Cf. Peradotto 1969 for this theme in the *Oresteia*.

The chorus' initial reaction to the uncertainty of a crisis point in the narrative of revenge is to turn to the gods in prayer, and they recognize the necessity and difficulty of finding the right words to gain their end. Especially when addressing a god, the power and risks of language require care.

Often, however, through more extended questioning of the language of prayer there develops a complex enquiry into the sense of important terms of the trilogy's discourse. When Electra is about to make offerings at Agamemnon's tomb, she carefully catechizes the chorus as to the correct vocabulary for such a dubious religious occasion. I quote here some lines from the end of their discussion (117–22):

> Chorus: Remember, too, those responsible for the murder.
> Electra: What shall I say? Guide and instruct my ignorance.
> Cho.: Invoke the coming of some man, or more than man.
> El.: Are you saying someone to judge or someone to punish?
> Cho.: Say simply someone who will kill in return.
> El.: I can ask this and not be wrong in the god's eyes?

This is an important piece of dialogue with many strands. I wish to concentrate here mainly on Electra's penultimate question, where she introduces a distinction between 'someone to judge', and 'someone to punish'.[26] Both words have the same stem, *dikē*, which I have already discussed briefly above, where it was translated as 'right' or 'justice'. The processes of revenge, punishment, and the lawcourt, however, as well as more abstract notions of Justice, are expressed through this complex term. Through two words formed from this stem, Electra is introducing a distinction between two sorts of reaction to the problem of transgression. Through the first term, *dikastes*, 'someone who will judge', 'juror' she implies the process of legality, judgement of cases, but through the second term, *dikēphoros*, 'one who brings justice', 'punisher', 'revenge-bringer' she implies a reciprocal act of punishment, retribution – as the chorus go on to demand 'someone who will kill in return'. As Kitto has argued forcibly (and as we will discuss in the next chapter) this distinction has been regarded as essential to the trilogy as it moves from the destructive punishment of revenge to the institution of the lawcourt. Electra's question, then, about what the chorus means, is a subtle and important contribution to our understanding of the notions of sin, transgression and punishment. But the chorus ride roughshod over any possible distinction. 'Say simply', they retort to her attempted distinction, 'someone who will kill in return.' Not merely punishment, but the revenge of a reciprocal death is required. Electra, however, questions this answer too:

---

[26] These lines are discussed further in Chapter 2.

Can she really pray for her own mother's death and be thought pious? The chorus' simple desire for revenge is for Electra a more complex issue.

This hesitation is important as Electra actually offers her prayer. Rather than praying 'simply' for someone to 'kill in return', her request is couched in the passive, that the murderess 'should die', and she qualifies this slightly less direct stance with the added adverbial expression 'with *dikē*': this may indeed be translated as Lattimore does, that they should die 'as they deserve', but the word can also imply 'in a just way', or 'by revenge', or 'as punishment'. Rather than 'simply saying' what the chorus advised, Electra prays that her mother's death should come about under the aegis of *dikē* – a qualification which recalls precisely the ambiguous nature of the matricide as an act of Justice. Despite the lengthy passage of questioning to find the right words of prayer, Electra's address restresses her uncertainty and the uncertainty of her language. Electra's prayer reflects well the need for obsessive care in religious invocation and also the developing discourse of transgression and punishment in the trilogy.

The language of prayer, then, which runs through the *Oresteia* from the opening invocation of the watchman in the *Agamemnon* to the final extended prayers of the departing procession in the *Eumenides*, reflects the belief in the efficacy of words over events and people, and also the power of words to go beyond and elude their users. Care, fear, piety 'fence' the use of language. It is against this background, too, that the brazen deceits and manipulations of Clytemnestra and her son must be viewed.

One of the specific difficulties of any discussion of the themes of language in the *Oresteia* is the complex set of interrelations between the role of language and the discourse of sexuality which so dominates the text of the trilogy (and which has been the focus of much modern criticism).[27] We have already seen how the search for the original etymological sense of words and names is connected to the narrative of child–parent relations through the shared vocabulary of generation, paternity and descent. We have also seen how the narrative progresses through a series of scenes in which members of one sex use language to assert dominance over a member of the opposite sex, and how those exchanges are seen in terms of a sexual conflict. As Cassandra expresses the narrative in her true predictions:

> When falls for me, a woman slain, another woman
> and when a man dies for this wickedly mated man . . .

Cassandra schematizes the passage of events in terms of sexual difference. Indeed, the difficulties of communication that I have been tracing seem often

[27] See especially Zeitlin 1978; Winnington-Ingram 1949; Goldhill 1984a.

to be regarded as stemming from the opposition of the sexes. When Orestes approaches the palace for the first time, he requests that someone in authority should come out (663–7): the lady of the house or more appropriately its lord;

> for then no delicacy in speaking blurs the spoken word.
> A man takes courage and speaks out to another man,
> and makes clear everything he means.

It is, of course, Clytemnestra who comes out to greet the stranger[28] and, as we have already seen, the ironies and deceptions of the dialogue between mother and son seem to fulfil Orestes' expectations of a lack of clarity in communication between members of the opposite sex.

There are many further connections between the discourse of sexuality and the role of communication. In particular, it is possible to read a specific interrelation between Clytemnestra's sexual and verbal transgressions. Her adultery, like her sister Helen's, is a corruption of the bonds of marriage, and as Tanner has argued so convincingly, it is a corruption which threatens the whole of society.[29] This is not just because adultery threatens the process of secured generational continuity and inheritance or because it shatters the institutions of the family, but also because it strikes at the heart of a relation of exchange through which society is formed and ordered.[30] Women are given and taken in marriage; they are the objects of an exchange that links homes, guarantees the control and order of sexual relations and with it the necessary continuity of society and the maintenance of the boundaries and categorizations of the social system. As she distorts the exchange of words in her deceptive communication, in choosing her own sexual partner apart from the ties of matrimony Clytemnestra corrupts her position in the system of exchange through which marriage and society are constituted. The queen transgresses the boundaries of definition and social categorizations sexually and linguistically. Clytemnestra's sexual and verbal transgressions are linked in their parallel corruptions of the essential basis of society, the relations of exchange.

Many of the ideas of the preceding paragraphs come together in the Cassandra scene of the *Agamemnon*, the longest scene of the play and one of corresponding importance. After Clytemnestra has led Agamemnon into the palace, the chorus sing of their fear, and turn to pray against their uncertain foreboding. But Clytemnestra returns to invite Cassandra to join the sacrifice –

---

28 On women coming out, see Foley 1982a, which is discussed below in Chapter 4. On these lines, see Goldhill 1984b.
29 1980, especially 24ff.
30 See the seminal work of Lévi-Strauss 1966, discussed in Tanner 1980, 79ff.

an ironic request since it will be as victim that Cassandra will stand at the altar. But Cassandra persistently refuses to answer or even acknowledge Clytemnestra's questions, and as so often in verbal exchanges in this trilogy the exchange turns to consider the process of communication itself (1047–63):

> Chorus: She's stopped speaking to you a clear expression.
> Fenced in these fatal nets wherein you find yourself,
> you should be persuaded, if you can be persuaded;
> perhaps you cannot be persuaded.
> Clytemnestra: Unless she uses speech incomprehensible,
> barbarian, wild as the swallow's song, within her
>   understanding
> I am speaking and I am persuading her with my speech . . .
> But if in ignorance you do not receive my speech
> then make a sign, not by voice, but by foreign hand.
> Cho.: I think this stranger girl needs an accurate interpreter.

The silence of Cassandra forces explicit recognition of the process of the exchange of words (signs) that makes up communication. The notable ambiguity of the chorus' first remark – she has stopped speaking and what she said was clear, or she has stopped speaking clear words – not only emphasizes the possibility of deceit in Clytemnestra's offer to join the sacrifice, but also marks specifically the process of exchange of language, or rather the apparent break in the dialogue that Cassandra's silence enforces. The chorus' triple repetition of the word for 'persuasion' in their third line – more clumsy in my English translation than in the Greek – places a strong stress on the force of Clytemnestra's language that the carpet scene has just demonstrated. Here the strength of persuasive rhetoric to dominate the listener appears to have no effect on the foreign girl. The remarks of Clytemnestra herself also emphasize the process of language exchange in the almost tautologous 'I am speaking and persuading her with my speech', as does the suggestion that Cassandra's language may not be Greek. When the queen still receives no reply, she resorts to a signal without a voice: 'make with your barbarian hand some sign', as Lattimore translates. We have already seen in the beacon-speeches scene, and in the lines announcing the herald's arrival, how the opposition of a sign in language and a sign without language has been important to the understanding of the discourse of communication and interpretation in this trilogy. The queen's expression 'if you do not receive my speech' points exactly to the model of language exchange I have been considering. The queen sends her utterance, her verbal message, but it is not received. There is a breakdown in communication, which emphasizes the gap between addressor and addressee. Clytemnestra's persuasion fails here to bridge the gap between speaker and listener. And in the face of this breakdown of communication the chorus, typically, revert to the need for accuracy and for interpretation: 'this stranger girl needs an accurate interpreter'. The interpreter is a figure who stands between addressor and addressee to facilitate communication.

This strong emphasis on the process of communication and language as a prelude to Cassandra's prophecies is particularly important. After the scenes dominated by Clytemnestra, in which we have considered the queen's manipulation of speech, where language was both the means and the matter of transgression, after the chorus' and others' repeatedly expressed hopes for a true and accurate language, now the stage will be dominated by Cassandra, the inspired princess, possessed of complete insight, an absolutely true and certain language. But ironically enough, this is language which is incapable of being understood, incapable of being received. The speaker's utterance is true and accurate and predictive but cannot be received by the listener. As often as she tells the chorus of the plot in the palace, they maintain their incomprehension: 'I can make nothing of these prophecies ... no I am lost. After the darkness of her speech I go bewildered in a mist of prophecies.'

Cassandra's language of truth, however, is not simply a scientific language of predication, as some philosophers would claim a true language would have to be. Rather, it is a heightened, metaphoric language of mantic insight (1087–92):

Cassandra: What house is this?
Chorus: The house of the Atreidae. If you are not aware of this
I tell you; and this you will not say is false.
Cass.: No, rather say it is a house God hates, guilty within
of kindred bloodshed, torture of its own,
the shambles for men's butchery, the dripping floor.

Cassandra's simple question as to where she is being led, receives the simple answer: 'the house of the Atreidae'; and the chorus go on to emphasize the process of exchange of language in their strangely periphrastic continuation. Their information is offered to the prophetess if she does not know – as we will see the status of Cassandra's knowledge is of importance to the whole scene – and, they continue with an odd double negative, Cassandra will not say that this information is false. This answer is, however, insufficient for the prophetess. She accepts but respecifies the answer (as the Greek syntax makes clear[31]); it is not quite right to call it simply the house of the Atreidae; it is a god-hated, self-consuming butcher house. Cassandra's answer shows the significance of the chorus' previous remark: for she precisely does not accept their description as truth, even if it is not enough simply to call it false. The chorus' remark can only partly be accepted.

[31] Cf. Goldhill 1984b.

The extraordinary, intertwined, metaphoric level of Cassandra's description continues throughout her language. Even when she announces that her prophecies will now be clear, the word for 'clear' is embedded in a complex structure of four similes for each of which it has a different connotation (Lattimore translates it as 'bright and strong' in an attempt to capture this multivalency) (1178–82):

> No longer shall my prophecies like some young girl,
> new-married, glance from under veils but bright and strong
> as winds blow into morning and the sun's uprise
> shall wax along the swell like some great wave to burst
> at last upon the shining of this agony.

Lampros, the word translated 'bright and strong' applies to each of the phrases surrounding it: it applies to the girl's face shining from under the veil; it applies to the keenness of the blowing; it is used for the brightness of the sun; the strength of the wave; and finally it looks forward to the 'shining of this agony'. As Silk comments, 'this intense concentration seems not merely apt for a prophetess versed in oracular equivocations, but somehow suggestive of her unique access to the complexities of events'.[32] Both the inability to predict the passage of events and the fear and uncertainty of language in describing and interpreting things are overcome in the intense metaphoric truth of Cassandra's prophecies.

It is, therefore, especially ironic that Cassandra's predictions merely lead her knowingly to her own murder. As she affirms (1299):

> Friends, there is no escape; not for any more time.

Indeed, she throws down her prophetess's wreaths and staff (1264–6) in her anger at her approaching doom. For the chorus, the elusive power of language, their elusive uncertainty about the future, made them believe that control of language, control of prediction, might offer control and mastery over events; certainly their present incapacity to understand or order the world of words sufficiently and their uncertainty about what is happening and what will happen lead to their incapacity for action that is so forcefully dramatized in their ineffective measures in reaction to the death cry of Agamemnon (1368–9):

> Yes, we should know what is true before we break our rage.
> Here is sheer guessing – far different from sure knowledge.

But for Cassandra her perfect knowledge of the future, her power to express it in language, merely lead to the inescapability of her fate. An absolute knowledge of the future means an absolutely determined world. Cassandra's

[32] 1974, 197.

evident control over language and prediction brings not mastery but merely a powerful sense of the fated universe.

As I have already mentioned, many of Cassandra's prophecies withhold the names of the characters that her narratives describe, but use rather a sexual determination – the male, the female, the man, the woman. Even this sexually charged narrative escapes the chorus. Towards the end of the scene they can still ask (1251):

> What man is it who brings about this woeful thing?

Cassandra's reply can only recognize their incomprehension of her language and its sexual narrative (1252):

> For certain, you have greatly mistaken my prophecies.

The perfect language of Cassandra with its complex metaphoric truths and the extreme misunderstandings of the chorus dramatize in the starkest form the disjunctions and distortions of the exchange of language that constitute the view of communication in this trilogy.

The narrative of the *Oresteia*, with its prayers, projections, deceits and miscomprehensions, leads towards the trial of Orestes in the Areopagus. Before a jury of the elders of Athens, the justice of Orestes' action will be debated and determined in the newly constituted institution of justice, the lawcourt. The defence speaker will be Apollo; the prosecution, the Erinyes. The grand scale of the work, performed before the whole city, continues. The oppositions of the trial have been discussed by many, and we will discuss them further in the next chapter. With Apollo are lined Orestes, Zeus, the claims of paternity, male control of the house with all that implies, and ultimately the goddess of Athens itself, Athene, the institutor of the trial. With the Erinyes are drawn up the claims of the mother, the devaluing of the ties of civic authority in favour of the ties of blood-kinship. Before the establishment of the trial and its procedures, however, the Erinyes sing the 'binding song'. This is their hymn to 'show forth the power and terror of our music' (308–9). It is a spell to bind Orestes by the power of words, the incantation of song, to the altar at which he has taken refuge. It is a song whose very constitution attests to the performative power of language, the religious force of words – which lies at the basis of curses, oaths, imprecations as well as prayers and blessing. With the powerful sense of composed structure we have already seen in the *Oresteia*'s narrative, before the new institution of legal definition, before the new civic power of speech to designate formally, the chorus sing a lengthy poem about their ancient powers of revenge, a spell which asserts the religious power of language.

Indeed, the very constitution of the trial depends on the rejection of the old procedure of simply taking oaths to determine the truth:

> Chorus: He is unwilling to give or to accept an oath!
> Athene: You wish to be called righteous rather than act right?
> Cho.: How so? Teach us. You are not poor of wit.
> Ath.: I say what is not right must not win by oaths.
> Cho.: Examine him yourself, then. Decide the case in a straight manner.

The normal procedure of oath-giving is for the swearer to claim under oath that an action was or was not committed. Here the admission of matricide is freely given and the criterion of judgement that is being claimed is of a different order: the case will be conducted in terms of motivation and clashing claims of authority, not in terms of committing a particular deed. Athene claims that the Erinyes wish merely to be called righteous, rather than to do right. She introduces a distinction between action and description which once again emphasizes the essential role of language in the debate and its work of definition. Indeed in this clash of authority and reasonings, the trial is to proceed to right action through the *saying of what is right*. The determination of Justice is an act of a legal discourse's definition. The trial constitutes a determination in language. That is the newly instituted legal power of language.

The means of the goddess's persuasion of the Erinyes here to accept the institution of the lawcourt is, interestingly, based on a shift of words, a sort of inherent pun or verbal play, that is hard to capture in translation. For the Erinyes in seeking Orestes' punishment (*dikē*) – by which they mean the reciprocal revenge of his immediate death – cannot but concede to Athene's offer of *dikē* (a trial), which is also her acceptance of their willingness to see her decide the case (*dikē*) or allot punishment (*dikē*) rightly. And the goddess appoints in full solemnity people who will judge (*dikastai*, the same term Electra had earlier used, the normal Greek for 'jurors'), citizens of Athens to perform the duties of the new institution. Thus constituted, the lawcourt proceeds towards its definition of the justice (*dikē*) of the case through the rhetorical opposition of the god of truth and the goddesses of punishment.

It is notable that the decision which is reached is far from the end of the conflicts of the play. The Erinyes turn in violent anger now to threaten Athens, the elders of which city have delivered the decision. The city before which the *Oresteia* was first acted is the final stake in the conflicts of the drama. But it is the goddess of Athens, Athene, who persuades the Erinyes to cease from their wrath and take a part in the institution of the city. With a mixture of threats, blandishments and promises, the goddess of wisdom wins them over. For the first time, the dramatized conflict of words does not involve a conflict of the sexes or a victory in the form of the destruction of one party. Athene makes it clear what is the agency of reconciliation in this exchange (970–5):

> ... I admire the eyes
> of Persuasion, who guided the speech of my mouth
> towards these, when they were reluctant and wild.
> Zeus, who guides men's speech in councils was too
> strong for them; and my ambition
> for good wins out in the whole issue.

The victory for good has come through the performative power of persuasive language and the force of Zeus as witnessed in the verbal exchanges of councils, linked to the aim of a good end. The triumph of the city's vindication, the triumph of the institutions of Justice and the rehabilitation of the Erinyes, is the triumph of the power of language.

The final scenes of the trilogy are once more demonstrative of the active force of language. After the chorus' binding-song and curses, now the scene shifts to their power of blessing. The Erinyes offer a series of glorious prayers and predictions for the future welfare of their adopted city, for the wealth of crops, children, livestock, soil. These blessings bring the successes they promote (968–70):

> Athene: It is my glory to hear how their generosities are fulfilled for my land

No sooner said, than fulfilled. In a trilogy which has turned so much on the fear and uncertainty, the dangers and misunderstandings, the aggression and powers of language, the final scenes turn to the restorative strength of the well-uttered, controlled prayer for goodness in the city.

For all that the *Oresteia* seems to end in the triumph of the established civic discourse, it is also the case that the play performed before the city it lauds has depicted with immense force the internal tensions and difficulties of that discourse, not only in the clash of sexual and social interests but also in its challenge to the very security of the formulation of civic language. The ability of humans to specify in language, to control the power of speech, to rely on the categorizations that form society's order, have been radically challenged in the view of communication put forward in this trilogy. The misunderstandings and deceits, manipulations and transgressions in and of language, that have made up the verbal exchanges of this play, challenge society's basis in the ordered exchange and agreed value in communication. Moreover, this under-mining cannot be finally resolved by the legal institutions of the city: in fact, the human jurors in the trial cannot specify a decision to determine the justice of the case before them, but rather it is the divine casting vote of Athene which achieves Orestes' acquittal. This is important to our sense of the ending of this trilogy not just because it points once more to the gaps and difficulties in human interpretation, not just because it shifts the final scenes of recon-ciliation to divine rather than human figures, but also because of the emphasis it places on Athene as agent of reconciliation. For Athene is an interesting figure in terms of the categorizations of social order in Athenian civic discourse. She is a female divinity, but as she says in her famous speech of support for Orestes, she is for the male with all her heart (736–8):

> There is no mother anywhere who gave me birth
> and but for marriage I am always for the male
> with all my heart, and strongly on my father's side.

Athene is a female who is a warrior; she rejects the female role in patriarchal society which is to be given and taken in marriage. She is a virgin. She has no mother. Unlike the rigid sexual difference in which the trilogy's confront-ations have been constructed, she is a female who is descended solely from the male, who supports the male, who acts like a male. Athene transgresses the boundaries of sexual definition. Like Clytemnestra in her usurpation of power, Athene cannot be fitted into the norms of social definition of gender. What is more, like Clytemnestra, Athene achieves her aim by the manipula-tion of language, by her persuasive rhetoric. In other words, the final reconciliation of divine and human forces in the city is achieved by a figure who transgresses the boundaries of definition and the definition of boundaries that make up the social order which the reconciliation is intended to achieve. Paradoxically enough, the realignment of norms of sexual relations in the city is achieved through a figure who breaks across those norms. The reassertion of the control and order of civic discourse is made by a figure who demonstrates the uncertain power of persuasive rhetoric. As Winnington-Ingram writes of Athene's decisive role 'we may fall into error if we attempt to answer this question without reference to Clytemnestra'.[33] The figure of Athene, much as Clytemnestra, stands apart from, as she is part of, civic discourse. The final reconciled triumph of civic language develops also a powerful sense of its transgressions. The *Oresteia*'s radical uncertainty with regard to the processes of communication, naming, categorization – the verbal basis of social order – continue through the movement from conflict to reconciliation.

The *Oresteia* dramatizes a concern with the processes of communication and exchange, with language and its social role. It depicts the possibilities of violence and transgression in the language which strives to order the world. It asserts the dangers and risks in the necessary human exchanges of language and sexual relations. As such, this trilogy offers a challenge not only to man's

[33] 1949, 144.

place in the city, but also to our latter-day attempts to read that challenge. As literary critics, we too are involved in the enterprise of ordering through language, interpretation, categorization; we too search for clarity and accuracy in the vocabulary of vision and control; we too are involved in the institutionalized determination of meaning. We too are forced to face the critique of this work. The *Oresteia* provides an important opening study for this book not only because its concerns with language, sexuality and the city will return again and again in the tragedies I shall discuss in the following chapters, but also because it is a work which demands that a reader question and requestion his or her role in the processes of communication, interpretation, meaning that are involved in reading. The *Oresteia* does not merely reflect these critical concerns but questions such attitudes to language. It is to this self-aware, self-questioning recognition of the active involvement of the reader in the processes of reading that I shall have cause to return also. For one of the major aims of this book is to reconsider tragedy's continuing ability to question man's place in language. The questioning instigated in and by the text of the *Oresteia* will resurface throughout this book's consideration of the tragedies of ancient Athens.

2 · THE LANGUAGE OF APPROPRIATION

> Were wisdom gauged alike of all and honour,
> no strife of warring words were known to men.
> But 'fairness', 'equal rights' – men know them not ...
> they name their names: no being they have as things.
>   EURIPIDES

In the first chapter, at several points I referred to the difficulties of the term *dikē* in the *Oresteia*. In this chapter, I intend to consider in more depth the notions surrounding this word and its cognates in the trilogy. This discussion is important for several reasons. First, after my investigation of the exchange of language with its focus on the process of interpretation and understanding, it is interesting to attempt to follow through the shifts and plays of meaning through which a word passes in the clashes of persuasive rhetoric and deceitful manipulation. I discussed language's role in the ordering of social relations and language as the means and matter of social transgression. How does a prime term of social order, *dikē*, relate to this discussion? Secondly, the concept of *dikē*, few would disagree, is a major concern in the *Oresteia*. This concern has formed the basis for many literary critics' readings of the trilogy. As well as investigating the various influential views put forward on this topic, it is important to see in what ways the focus on language changes our appreciation of this debate. This leads to my third reason: the different critics' attempts at interpreting the *Oresteia* in the light of this set of terms will offer an important insight into a major problem of reading Greek tragedy. For, as I argued in the concluding paragraphs of Chapter 1, the *Oresteia*'s tragic critique of the exchange of language as social process is highly relevant to the institutions and attitudes of literary criticism; and the history of the interpretation of the notion of *dikē* will offer an understanding of the way the play's problematic view of interpretation and comprehension is all too applicable to the reading of the play itself.

First, I want briefly to develop some of the connotations of the term *dikē* in a wider context, and explain why I call it a 'prime term of social order'. I have already mentioned *dikē*'s range of meaning from the abstract 'Justice', 'right', through 'retribution', 'punishment' to the particular legal senses of 'lawcourt', 'law-case', and while these terms clearly relate to the expression of social forces, a mere lexical analysis gives little feel for its powerful and extended range of usage. For *dikē* is one of the dominant terms in the public discourse of fifth-century Athens. The role of the lawcourts and the law (*nomos*) is regarded by the ancient writers (as well as modern historians) as essential to the development of the political system of democracy.[1] The general publishing and discussion of laws, the equality of citizens before the law, the citizens' part in the adjudication of cases, the citizens' duty to uphold the city's laws – the movement away from the authority of an individual ruler in the process of decision-making towards the idea of the sovereignty of the city and its laws – are major topics in the discussion of the growth of democracy and democratic ideology.[2] The full range of legal language draws on *dikē* and its cognates. *Dikē* is used for the institution of the lawcourt itself which is so important to the civic life of Athens, and it forms the connection between that institution and the widest sense of a world-picture, the 'natural justice' (to use our eighteenth-century term) from which man's legality draws its descent and authorization. The technical terms for prosecution, punishment and the procedures of court depend also on *dikē* and its cognates. Moreover, as one might expect, the rhetoric of the lawcourt relies heavily on general appeals to what is *dikē*, 'right', 'proper', 'legal', 'fair', and on the charged opposition of *dikē* to *hubris* which means both 'excess', 'transgression', 'insolence', and also, in legal terminology, 'assault'.[3]

The wider political rhetoric of the Assembly, the other major institution of public political life in Athens, also returns again and again to claims of *dikē* in the search for 'right action', or in the judgement and evaluation of people, behaviour, policies. In the sphere of religion, too, the language of *dikē* remains important not only as an expression of the ordered universe with the essential place of the divine in that order, but also as a moral criterion. And it is particularly evident in the specific role of the gods as the preservers and implementers of *dikē* in its sense of punishment and of justice.[4] Often, in plays like Euripides' *Hippolytus* or the *Oresteia* itself, tragedy develops through the sense of a possible disjunction between notions of punishment and notions of justice and the gods' involvement in the expression of that disjunction.

Indeed, the overlap and interrelations between religious, political, and legal aspects of public life that distinguish fifth-century Athenian citizens' involvement in their city's affairs are marked in the shared vocabulary and rhetoric of *dikē* and its cognates, which constitute an essential dynamic of Athenian discourse. The English word 'right' and its cognates 'to be right, righteous,

[1] Cf. e.g. Ostwald 1969; or Ehrenberg 1960, 20–4, 51–2, 71–4.
[2] Cf. e.g. Finley 1983, 134ff.
[3] See e.g. MacDowell 1976.   [4] For one view of this material, see Lloyd-Jones 1971.

rightful' offer an interesting counterpart to *dikē* in understanding the range of sense of a key term of evaluative and normative categorization in the various discourses of a complex society. It is a term regularly used in a similar range of legal, political and social issues. Human rights, the rights of man, the right to life, the right to work (etc.) have been calls to action in numerous causes of modern history. It is used in more delimited legal language – 'rightful owner', 'right of way' etc. – and although it does not necessarily have the connotation of 'court' or 'penalty', the verb 'to right' has the sense of redressing a wrong, as well as returning to balanced order, that is close to some of the implications of *dikē* and its cognates. It is used in moral discussion from the conversational to the philosophical, and in religious language 'righteous' (etc.) remains a relevant category in the judgement of people and action. It is a general term of moral approbation as well as marking correctness with regard to a specific question's answer. In politics, 'right' (as opposed to 'left') is used to designate a wide range of principles, beliefs and policies. It is this sort of complex interconnection of different areas of social relations, different connotations and attitudes, expressed through a shared vocabulary, that makes translation of a term like *dikē* (or 'right') so difficult. In the *Oresteia*, where legal, political, religious and moral discourses form a so closely intertwined network, the shared evaluative and normative vocabulary constitutes an essential articulation of the text.

The roots of this fifth- and fourth-century emphasis on *dikē* as a term essential to the definition and workings of social and moral order have been much discussed.[5] The place of Hesiod is of particular importance to this fifth-century discourse, and to Aeschylus in particular.[6] Both the *Theogony* and the *Works and Days* retained throughout the fifth century an immense influence as authoritative texts on religious and social matters. The *Works and Days* in particular is dominated by the rhetorical opposition of *dikē* and *hubris*, an emphasis quite different from the Homeric texts.[7] Hesiod, a small-holding farmer, has been wronged by his brother, Perses, and he offers advice, exhortation and mythic stories to persuade Perses to behave 'in a just way' rather than pursue the course of *hubris*. This leads to a didactic description of the right running of a farm which maintained its status as an authority throughout the fifth and fourth centuries. The combination of extended homily to his brother to act justly and advice on the year's management of the land according to the seasons and nature's signs shows the connections that are felt between a sense of natural order and a sense of justice or right in the social

[5] See e.g. Hirzel 1966; Lloyd 1966, Ch. 4; Lloyd-Jones 1971; Gagarin 1986 (for further references, see Lloyd-Jones 1971, 186 n. 23).
[6] See e.g. Solmsen 1949.   [7] See Vernant 1983, 3–72; Pucci 1977.

context of correct behaviour. Hesiod's moral imperative is constantly echoed in the argumentative, litigious world of fifth-century Athens. Indeed, as the Erinyes cede the authority of judgement to Athene in the *Eumenides* ('decide the case in a straight manner'), it is with an echo of Hesiod's famous injunction to Perses to let their case be settled with 'straight judgements', and not by 'gift-devouring kings'.[8] That Athene abrogates her individual authority in favour of a court of Athenian citizens marks the acceptance and trans-formation of the Hesiodic imperative in the fifth-century city.

The connections between the widest sense of *dikē* as a world order and the behaviour of individuals can be emphasized in a different way by regarding the presocratic philosophers. For *dikē* seems to play an increasingly important role in these early philosophical texts as a universal principle, as a cosmolo-gist's description of the natural order of things. It is in this light, for example, that critics have read Anaximander's fragment 'Destruction comes from the same source from which existence comes to them in accordance with their destiny: for they pay each other penalty (*dikē*) and retribution for their injustice (-*dik*-) according to the assessment of time.' Lloyd comments, for example, 'The alternative cycle of "justice" and "retribution" does not hang on the arbitrary whim of a despotic ruler: it is guaranteed by the rule of law.'[9] *Dikē* is an essential expression of 'self-regulating cosmological relationships, i.e. an idea of cosmological *order*'.[10] Both Kitto and Lloyd-Jones have emphasized the continuation of this sense of *dikē* in the texts of Sophocles in particular. For Sophocles, writes Lloyd-Jones '*dikē* means not only "justice" but the "order of the universe", and from the human point of view that order often seems to impose a natural rather than a moral law'.[11] One may argue with Lloyd-Jones' too easy separation of 'natural' and 'moral' as categori-zations with regard to *dikē*, but it is certainly the case that the connections articulated by the language of *dikē* between what is 'just', what is 'natural' and a sense of the order and fixedness of things is important not only in the philosophers' systems but also in tragedy's questioning of the system of thought from which it arises, its interrogation of the sense of what is right, proper, natural as well as man's rightful place in the order of things.

The importance to philosophers of this notion of *dikē* continues into the fourth century – Plato's dialogue the *Republic*, which discusses a full gamut of social relations, is conducted in terms of·the search for a '*just* city'. His enquiry into what makes up a perfect society in its structure of sexual, political, military, educational relations is an enquiry specifically into the 'justice'[12] of a

---

[8] Hesiod, *Works and Days* 35–9. Compare Hesiod, *Theogony* 81–93 for a picture of a just king who judges 'with straight judgements' (86).
[9] Lloyd 1966, 213.   [10] Ibid.   [11] 1971, 128.
[12] Plato uses the cognate term *dikaiosune*.

city's constitution. 'Justice' involves not merely legal order, but the right organization of all the parts and relations of the city. It is in this sense also that one can refer to *dikē* as 'a prime term of social order'. There is more at stake in the complex dynamics of *dikē* in the *Oresteia* than the specific judgement of Orestes' guilt or acquittal.

It has become a commonplace of the interpretation of the textual dynamics of *dikē* in the *Oresteia* to assert that the trilogy dramatizes a movement from the sense of *dikē* as retribution to the sense of *dikē* as legal justice. On this view, the play offers a sort of myth of origin of the institutions of law so important to the development of the city and its democracy. I want first to look briefly at this view of the play and I will base my description of this interpretive strategy on H.D.F. Kitto's eloquent and representative attitude.

The sense of revenge or retribution is built up throughout the *Agamemnon*. The Argive expedition, writes Kitto, is led by the sons of Atreus who are 'ministers of retribution (Dikē) to punish the crime of Paris. They were sent by Zeus. As some god, Apollo or Zeus or Pan, hears the cry of a vulture robbed of its young and sends an Erinys to avenge it, so has Zeus sent the two kings to avenge the wrong Paris did to Menelaus.'[13] The delay to this expedition is caused by Artemis: in anger at the wanton bloodshed before Troy (as symbolized by the eagles' killing of the pregnant hare), Artemis demands a price: the sacrifice of Iphigeneia. This will be important in Clytemnestra's reaction: 'In killing Agamemnon, she is consciously avenging her private wrongs, but since "the gods are not regardless of those that shed blood", she is also satisfying Artemis' anger and avenging the dead slain before Troy.'[14] Paris had committed wrong; he had kicked over the 'altar of Dikē'. The war to revenge the adultery is declared under the aegis of Dikē. 'Agamemnon has taken it for granted that a war for a wanton woman is a proper thing: it is his conception of Dikē. It is also Zeus' conception and Zeus is going to follow it by destroying the destroyer.'[15] Agamemnon cannot avoid shedding the blood of his daughter and of the rival armies except by ignoring the dictates of *dikē*. Thus by following the consequences of his own policy Agamemnon approaches his own tragic death. Kitto comments on this as follows: 'The obvious implication is that we have a conception of Dikē that cannot work even though it is the present will of Zeus ... The instinct for violent and bloody retribution dominates and unifies the whole play, and in the end it leads to a complete breakdown.'[16]

The odes on either side of the messenger scene develop the drama's 'architectural scale'.[17] The first ode 'sets up a proportional sum: the crime of

[13] 1961, 67.   [14] 1961, 69.   [15] 1961, 71.   [16] 1961, 72.   [17] 1961, 74.

Paris, the punishment of Paris:: the crime of Agamemnon:?'[18] The second restates that open equation with the messenger's added knowledge of the sacrilege of the Greek fleet and the storm that dispersed the returning ships. 'The sin of Paris: the destruction of Paris:: the sacrilege of the Greek host: the destruction of the Greek host:: the sin of Agamemnon:?'[19] The latter of these two odes indeed further raises the tension and foreboding with the fable of the lion-cub which grows to fulfil its murderous potential, a fable which is juxtaposed to the story of Helen's happy first arrival in Troy which led finally to the bloodshed and mourning of war. Kitto continues his analysis with a paraphrase of the chorus' general remarks (750–81), which seem to offer a significant conclusion: 'It is not prosperity that angers the gods but wickedness. Hubris provokes more hubris and then the day of reckoning comes at last. Dikē leads everything to the end appointed. *Enter* Agamemnon, *royally with a young woman*. Was ever dramatic entry more finely prepared?'[20]

The remaining scenes of the play act out the implications of this highly dramatic entrance. Agamemnon is slaughtered with Cassandra, but as the queen taunts the chorus with her victory, even she too begins to change. More and more, she takes on 'the aspect of a doomed criminal . . . the successful hunter who will herself be hunted'.[21] The murder is not a single act of regicide but an instance of a pattern. 'There is the law of Dikē – not "justice" but "requital" – that wrongs done must have their revenge, "the doer must pay"'.[22] Indeed, Aegisthus enters and with his first words praises the 'retribution-bringing day'. That adjective had been used for the pickaxe of Zeus which destroyed Troy, and Aegisthus offers a further version of events in terms of bloody retribution for bloody crime. The final recognition of this chain of transgression and transgressive retribution is, for Kitto, a major climax of the *Agamemnon*.

The *Choephoroi* opens with the next link of that chain. 'On Orestes falls the task of avenging the outrage done to his father. Here is nothing new, it was foreseen by Cassandra. The law of Dikē is eternal, the question is, how its demands are to be met. So far they have been met in the spirit of blind and guilty retribution; Orestes approaches the task very differently. For the first time we meet an avenger whose motives are pure.'[23] The question as to how *dikē*'s demands are to be met is instantiated for Kitto in the dialogue between Electra and the chorus which I quoted in Chapter 1, and specifically in her distinction between the 'one who brings retribution' – the adjective used by Aegisthus for the day of regicide and by the chorus for the weapon of Troy's destruction – and the 'one who judges', 'juryman'. The second term offers to

[18] 1961, 73. [19] 1961, 74. [20] 1961, 74. [21] 1961, 77. [22] 1961, 77.
[23] 1961, 78–9.

Kitto 'a glimmer of something less crude'.[24] Electra prays indeed 'to be more pure by far than my mother'. This is the different motive for the transgressive acts of murder.

The difference in the approach of Orestes remains for Kitto the basis of progression in the *Choephoroi*: 'we see the new avengers, very different in spirit from the old, but menaced by the same threats'.[25]

But as the murder is approached, the view of *dikē* from the *Agamemnon* emphatically returns. The sense of direct retribution, blow for blow, is restated. 'Only the kinsmen can set the family free. "Ares (Violence) will confront Ares; Dikē will confront Dikē." But if Dikē conflicts with Dikē (as presently Olympians conflict with Erinyes), the universe is chaotic, and Dikē cannot yet be "Justice".'[26]

The parallelism of Orestes' killing Clytemnestra as she had killed by deceit and guile makes manifest the reciprocal workings of Dikē, as indeed does the paradoxical sense of his transgressive righting of wrong: 'She threatens him with the pursuit of her Erinyes if he kills her: he can reply only that if he does not kill her, his father's Erinyes will pursue him. Nothing could more forcibly express the bankruptcy of the cosmic and social system of Justice which we have been contemplating hitherto.'[27] The bankruptcy of this notion of Dikē as retribution is finally manifested in the pure-motivated Orestes' confused exit, pursued by the agents of Dikē, the Erinyes. The progress from the *Agamemnon* seems brief and endangered. There is still chaos at the heart of the notion of *dikē* as it is instantiated in violent retribution.

In the *Eumenides* the action moves towards the institution of the lawcourt. This begins with the split between the Erinyes and the Olympians. In the first two plays, the Erinyes have been agents of the gods, but now ancient rights will be infringed 'because in no other way can order be imposed on chaos'.[28] The difference between the Olympians and the Erinyes is seen directly in the opposition of Apollo and the chorus. Apollo, says Kitto, dominates the first half of the *Eumenides*: 'There is indeed a radiance that plays around Apollo, there is purity, beauty, order.'[29] On the other hand, there is still not the means of reconciliation. 'Neither Apollo's extreme and decidedly unconvincing arguments about the primacy of the male nor the lofty disdain that he shows towards the older deities, crude though they are, allows us to feel we are on firm ground.'[30] (There may seem some difficulty in reconciling these last two quotations.) Apollo, however, completely passes from view after the trial; and the second half of the play is dominated rather by Athene, a different

[24] 1961, 79. [25] 1961, 82. [26] 1961, 84.
[27] 1961, 86. [28] 1961, 92. [29] 1961, 92. [30] 1961, 92.

representative of Zeus, one who 'takes a wider view than Apollo'.[31] She agrees with the Erinyes' claim that Fear must not be removed, that social order depends on the restriction of transgression, and that crimes like matricide may not go unpunished if the fabric of society is to be maintained. But, to Athene, the Erinyes remain as one-sided as Apollo in their total disregard for motive, circumstance and the claim of marriage as the keystone of society; it is the opposition of the Erinyes and Apollo that Athene transcends. What the goddess brings to the trial is 'tolerance, level judgement'.[32] She accepts the valid part of the Erinyes' case, but she tempers the argument with reason and mercy. 'These', says Kitto, 'are divine attributes in man ... The court of the Areopagus is a divine institution; a barrier against violence, anarchy, despotism.'[33] What the reconciliation of the final scenes of the trilogy indicates is that 'wrath, ... as the means of Dikē, gives place to Reason'.[34]

This movement represents also a change in the sphere of the divine. 'Zeus has moved forward from violence and confusion in which the Erinyes were his unquestioning agents, to arbitrary interference, which angered the Erinyes, and from that to reason and mercy.'[35] The triumph of Athene's persuasion is the triumph of Zeus and the triumph of the return to order from chaos. Dikē, as the expression of the bonds, order, maintenance of social relations, has become coextensive with the glories of the Athenian polis. This provides for the end of the play not simply 'undiluted optimism but ... conditional assurance: the Eumenides, ex-Erinyes, will give prosperity to a city that reveres Dikē; a city that does not expose itself to their wrath'.[36] It is, in the end, a combination of moral, religious, social exhortation and teaching that constitutes the message of the Oresteia, it is a protest 'against blind rage and violence, against both despotism and anarchy'.[37] It is to the humanist virtues of mercy, toleration, and justice that the Oresteia appeals.

This view of the narrative of the Oresteia has had many powerful advocates. Stanford sums up the force of the Oresteia thus: 'Dikē must evolve from the blood vendetta of the tribe to the social justice of our hopes.'[38] 'Our hopes' include the hopes of Kuhns ('There has been an evolution in heaven towards justice and right rule to serve as a pattern or "form" for a like history among men'[39]), Podlecki, Lesky and many others. The institution of criticism proclaims the institution of social justice. Aeschylus' masterpiece for these critics takes its place in a long line of political texts glorifying the city as much, the state as harmonic organization. The Oresteia reflects the ideals of these critics, who find in it an expression of 'our hopes'. When Kitto concludes 'the

[31] 1961, 92. [32] 1961, 94. [33] 1961, 94. [34] 1961, 94. [35] 1961, 94. [36] 1961, 95.
[37] 1961, 95. [38] 1975, 13. [39] 1962, 15.

problem of dikē is solved',[40] his optimism is shared by numerous readers of the *Oresteia*.

Before I turn to the extensive tradition of critical dissent from what has become a standard institutionalized view of the trilogy's development, I want to turn back and look at some of the key points in this analysis and consider the text in a little more detail than Kitto allows himself. What is the relation of the language of *dikē* in these scenes to this eloquently proposed transition from vendetta towards the institution of Justice and cosmic order?

Agamemnon's entrance is indeed one of the most finely prepared entrances in Greek drama. For Kitto, it was an entrance that had been developed as an open equation in terms of a pattern of reciprocal revenge. How will the sin of Agamemnon be requited? The last lines of the chorus before Agamemnon speaks draw attention to quite a different sense of *dikē*, however (807–9):

> Ask all men: you will learn in time
> which of your citizens have been just
> in the city's sway, which were reckless.

It is a commonplace from the *Odyssey* onwards to address a returning ruler with the warning that not all those who stayed at home have remained loyal and trustworthy. But here the chorus specifically refer to the running of the city according to the principles of justice. The adverb *dikaiōs* ('with, according to, *dikē*') seems to imply a far wider notion than Kitto's reading of the structure of the scene would suggest. 'Justice' seems to draw on the wide range of social attitudes I discussed in the opening of this chapter. Moreover, Agamemnon's first lines notably echo the chorus' term (810–16):

> To Argos first and to the gods within the land
> it is right (*dikē*) I give due greetings, they have worked with me
> to bring me home. They helped me on the vengeance (*dik-*) I have wrought
> on Priam's city. Not from the tongues of men the gods
> heard Justice (*dik-*) but in one unhesitating cast they laid
> their votes within the urn of blood . . .

The triple repetition of *dikē* and *dikaios* (the adjective formed from *dikē*), in three consecutive lines is strongly marked in the mouth of the returning king. In the first instance, *dikē* seems to imply a general standard of correct behaviour with regard to the thanks owed for the revenge wrought by the gods. In the second case, it seems to imply the sort of retribution Kitto has been describing. Agamemnon speaks of vengeance, the reciprocal act of revenge that he has performed. But in the third case, *dikē* (in the plural) implies 'cases', 'pleas'. Like the kings of old in Hesiod, the gods listen to *dikē*

---

[40] 1961, 95.

as it is discussed before them, and deliver judgement. The gods, however, unlike mortals, do not need to listen to words, to tongues, in this procedure. Above the doubts and uncertainties of language, all their votes without hesitation go into a single urn – the opposite of the tied human voting of the *Eumenides*. The phrase for 'unhesitating' itself punningly echoes the repetitions of *dik-* in the previous lines. The gods do not vote *dikhorropōs*. The expression which marks the certainty of the god's voting ironically echoes the triply repeated term whose very uncertainty is the cause of so much tension for the humans in the *Oresteia*. Although Agamemnon's entrance is prepared with some foreboding, the complex interplay of the senses of the word *dikē* are not readily subsumed to a single notion of retribution. It would seem that in order to maintain the clarity of his dramatic equation, Kitto, who quotes no lines from this 'finely prepared entrance', must repress the language of the scene.

This repression of the workings of the language of *dikē* can be traced throughout Kitto's analysis. A line which he quotes – as do many other critics – as an example of the untenable construction of the notion of *dikē* in the pattern of revenge, is 'Ares will confront Ares, Dikē will confront Dikē' (*Cho.* 461). Kitto comments 'if Dikē conflicts with Dikē ... the universe is chaotic and Dikē cannot yet be "Justice".' The next line in the text, however, which Kitto does not quote, reads 'O gods, be just in what you bring to pass' (*Cho.* 462). The gods are exhorted to bring things to pass 'in a just way' (*endikōs*), that is, an appeal is made to precisely the ordered, general standard of Justice, Right, that the previous line was quoted to show as utterly lacking.[41] The chaos of conflict is not the neatly ordered opposition of Right to Right, as Kitto maintains, so much as the juxtaposition of a line proclaiming the clash of *dikē* and *dikē* to a line maintaining a criterion of judgement for that clash which is constructed in the same vocabulary. It is not the absence of a sense of 'Justice' in the use of the term *dikē* so much as the excess of meaning produced by these juxtaposed uses of *dikē*, that marks the sense of a lack of order and consistency. Once more, Kitto's description of the untenable logic of revenge depends on a repression of an appeal to a seemingly different principle of *dikē*, here in the very next line.

The possible ambiguities of *dikē* are also essential to the understanding of the important scene that Kitto analyses at length, where Electra questions the chorus in order to find the right language to make a prayer at her father's tomb. Kitto's analysis rightly stresses the importance of the distinction Electra makes between the 'one who brings retribution' and the 'one who judges', both of which terms are formed from the root *dik-*. For Kitto, this

---

[41] It is noticeable that Lattimore attempts to reduce the difficulties of these lines by translating *-dik-* first as 'right' and then as 'justice'.

question offered 'a glimmer of something less crude', an expression of the possible higher motive in the avengers' actions, which he saw further instanced in Electra's prayer where she hopes to be 'more pure by far than my mother'. As we saw in Chapter I, however, Electra does not pray 'simply for one who will kill in return'. Rather, she adds the adverbial expression 'with *dikē*' to her prayer for the death of the usurper, and thus opens again the doubts concerning the precise nature of the matricide. She hopes the murder will be committed 'with *dikē*', 'in *dikē*', but the precise sense of *dikē* here remains uncertain. Lattimore's oversimplified translation 'as they deserve' precludes the implications that what Electra prays for is an act of revenge, as Kitto suggests, but also, importantly, that it is an act which is being claimed to be just and right. It is in the uncertainty of choice between these different semantic areas, or rather in the combination of suggestive connotations, that the uncertain status of the act of matricide is formed. In what sense can a daughter pray for matricide and determine it as *dikē*?

There is a further important qualification in Electra's prayer which I have not yet mentioned, that also depends on a claim for *dikē*. Her final appeal is as follows (478):

Let Earth and conquering justice and all the gods beside give aid.

The prayers to Earth and the gods are to be recalled in the *kommos* in particular. But I want here to focus on 'conquering Justice'. The word for 'Justice' is (of course) *dikē*, and once more Electra is hoping to claim *dikē* on her side. Instead of praying for a *dikephoros* 'one who brings retribution' or for a *dikastes* 'one who judges', she prays directly for the aid of *dikē*, which is the root of both of the terms of her earlier question. Again it seems uncertain precisely what sense of *dikē* is meant. But the qualification 'conquering' is also important. It could be translated more precisely as 'who brings victory'. It differs from the relevant term 'who brings retribution' only by its first letter: *nīkephoros* as opposed to *dikephoros*. Not only does Electra not pray for one 'who brings retribution' (as the chorus had implied was right) but also the language she uses seems to echo the very term she is markedly not using. Instead of praying for *dikephoros* she prays for *dikē nīkephoros*. The similarity in sound helps to emphasize the different implications of Electra's prayer. It is not enough for her to pray simply for 'one who brings retribution'.

This qualification is important, for the term 'victory' is essential for our understanding of *dikē*, and not only in this scene. For 'victory' was how Agamemnon described the queen's desire in the exchange of the carpet scene – 'Does such a victory mean so much to you?' (942) – and it was for the permanence of his victory that Agamemnon prayed at the conclusion of his

first speech in the play – 'My prize was victory; may it never fail again' (854) –
an ironic enough prayer as it is followed by his concession of, precisely,
'victory' to Clytemnestra in the subsequent dialogue. 'Victory' is indeed a
constantly repeated term throughout the conflicts of the trilogy and it is, as
Kitto notes (following Schadewaldt) 'something of a key word in the *Choephoroi*' in particular.[42] The *kommos* ends with a prayer for 'victory'. The
prayer to Zeus that I quoted in Chapter 1 ends with the same hope for 'victory'
(868). As Clytemnestra approaches the confrontation with her son, she
exclaims 'Let us see if we are to have victory or if victory's to be over us' (890).
'Victory' is a notion that links the armed strife and military imagery to the
other conflicts of the play.

It is, however, particularly the connections between 'victory' (*nikē*) and the
terms for right, revenge etc. (*dikē*) that concerns me here. The importance of
these connections becomes most evident in the aftermath of the trial of the
Eumenides. After Orestes' acquittal and speech of thanks, the chorus burst
into outraged song at their overthrow and threaten poisonous revenge. A
further conflict is threatened. Athene's reply is significant (794–6):

> Be persuaded by me not to take it badly in grief.
> For there has been no victory (*nīk-*) over you,
> but the trial (*dīk-*) was equal voting.

Athene uses the tied vote to argue that although Orestes has escaped
punishment there has been no defeat for the Erinyes. It has been an action of
dikē that has not led to a *nikē*. Unlike the narrative of retribution and revenge,
the trial, she claims, has not resulted in a victory and defeat that needs further
redressing in a further action of violent revenge. The pattern of reciprocated
violence is halted in part by the separation of the ideas of victory and defeat
from the notion of *dikē*. One can have *dikē* without *nikē*. Indeed, when the
reconciled Erinyes ask what they should bequeath to Athens in blessing,
Athene's general first remark is (903):

> Such things as have no traffic with evil victory (*nikē*)

The proverbial phrase 'evil victory' indicates 'a victory which involved the
victor in the disaster of dishonour'[43] – an expression which could describe the
various victories of the trilogy (Clytemnestra over Agamemnon, Orestes over
Clytemnestra etc.). The final blessings of the reconciled Erinyes will be
consonant only with a victory that escapes the dangerous connotations of
further strife, defeat and retribution which came with the close association of
dikē and *nikē* in the pursuit of revenge in the earlier conflicts of trilogy.

---

[42] 1956, 47.   [43] Thomson 1966, ad loc.

Electra's qualification of *dikē* by *nīkēphoros*, then, is especially significant. The way in which the term *dikēphoros* is echoed but significantly not repeated in *dikē nīkēphoros* marks the interconnections of the vocabulary of *dikē* and *nīkē* that are important to our understanding of how the language of *dikē* moves towards the reconciliation of the ending of the trilogy. *Dikē* must be comprehended through its relations to other words and images in the trilogy. Here in particular the connections of *dikē* and *nīkē* stress the uneasy relation between 'justice' and 'conflict' that constitutes an essential dynamic of the narrative of violent revenge. It is not simply 'a glimmer of something less crude' or a new 'purity of motive' that is expressed by Electra's questions and prayer. Rather, it is the continuing radical uncertainty about the nature of *dikē* even as it is appealed to. Once more, Kitto's particular selective reading maintains its clear, ordered pattern only by oversimplifying the language of the text.

There is one further scene in the *Choephoroi*, important to Kitto's analysis, that I wish to investigate briefly. After the matricide, as he stands over the bodies of his mother and her lover, Orestes calls on the Sun to be a witness to his actions. His speech, like Agamemnon's first lines, reverberates with the language of *dikē* (987–90):

> ... be a witness for me in my day of trial
> how it was in all right I achieved this death,
> my mother's: for of Aegisthus' death I take no count,
> he has his seducer's punishment, no more than law.

I have quoted Lattimore's translation for the build-up of untranslatable puns in these lines. The expression 'in my day of trial' is *en dikēi*, 'in *dikē*', 'in court', 'in the case'. Here *dikē*, particularly juxtaposed to the term 'witness', seems to stress a precise legal context – indeed , to look forward to the trial of the *Eumenides*. The word translated 'in all right' is *endikōs*, an adverb formed from *en* and *dikē*, and it is in the same metrical position as *en dikēi* in the previous line. It's as if the adverb could be seen as broken into its parts. But the adverb *endikōs* has the connotations of a general standard of justice, right, rather than the institution of the law court that was suggested by the phrase 'be a witness *en dikēi*'. The term for Aegisthus' punishment is *dikē* also. Juxtaposed to 'no more than the law', 'as the law has it', it certainly implies a legal context, but rather than the institution of justice, it suggests the outcome of the case, the penalty, retribution, suffered by a wrongdoer. As Orestes attempts to justify his matricide, it is the dubious relations of that action to the different semantic areas involved in the notion of *dikē* that are expressed in these multiplying echoes and shifts of sense.

As Orestes feels himself becoming less and less stable, he turns once more to justification in terms of *dikē* (1026–7):

> While I am still in my wits, I say publicly to my friends:
> I killed my mother not without some right . . .

The double negative of 'not without *dikē*' seems to emphasize Orestes' claim to right, but at the same time to mark the effort to repress the possibility that the matricide was an act committed 'without *dikē*'. But what could be a sufficient translation for *dikē* in this expression? It recalls all the senses of 'retribution', 'penalty' and 'justice' that have been at play, as well as the legal implications of the forthcoming trial.

What these two passages indicate is that for the reader or audience there is a double movement involved in the dynamics of *dikē* in this trilogy. On the one hand, different characters at different times appeal to *dikē* as a criterion, support, or reason for action. Clytemnestra, Agamemnon, Electra, Orestes, the Erinyes, Apollo, Athene and the various choruses, as we have seen, each claims *dikē* to be on his, her or their side. Each character appropriates *dikē* to his or her rhetoric. It is this sort of one-sided laying claim to evaluative and normative words that I term 'the rhetoric of appropriation'. It is not so much that the term cannot 'be justice', as Kitto puts it, when it is used in these conflicting ways, but that these shifts of sense and control of words are an essential element of tragic conflict. 'On the stage, the various heroes of the drama employ the same words in their debates but these words take on opposed meanings depending on who utters them.'[44] In this way, the exchange of words on stage dramatizes the points of conflict in a discourse, the blockages and barriers between humans attempting to communicate in the tragic world, divided against itself. This 'rhetoric of appropriation' goes through many twists in the course of the trilogy, leading sometimes to violent collisions (as between Apollo and the Erinyes), sometimes to unexpected reversals (as when Clytemnestra is turned into the object of Orestes' revenge by her own logic of *dikē*), sometimes to extreme changes of understanding (as when Athene instantiates the Erinyes' plea for *dikē* as the lawcourt for the city). Such dynamics are equally essential to the dramas of Sophocles and Euripides. On the other hand, the very multiplicity of use, the range of meaning that is so marked in passages like the lines I quoted from Orestes' plea to the Sun, stands in significant tension with such rhetorical appropriations of the charged moral and social vocabulary. As much as each character appropriates *dikē* to a particular case or argument, so the uncertainties surrounding the notion of *dikē* undermine the possible security of a delimited certain sense for the appropriated language. The reader's or audience's understanding is wider than each individual expression. The ever expandable context for each remark changes, deepens, extends its significance.

This double movement can be seen well in Orestes' two speeches. In the second, Orestes claims *dikē* for his action: 'I killed . . . not without *dikē*.' He asserts his justification for matricide through the term *dikē*. But the first speech's triple repetition of *dikē* and its cognates in a wide range of contexts and implications remains in a significant tension with the claim of Orestes. Can Orestes avoid suggesting the legal implications of murder, the possibility of his own punishment, the lawcourt to come? In other words, for the reader or spectator, even when a character utters a strong claim to have *dikē* on his or her side and seems to stress a particular implication of the term, the network of meanings in the text involves that claim in a series of further implications and connotations. 'In the language of the tragic writers there is a multiplicity of different levels . . . this allows the same word to belong to a number of different semantic fields depending on whether it is a part of religious, legal, political or common vocabulary or of a particular sector of one of these. This imparts a singular depth to the text and makes it possible for it to be read on a number of levels at the same time.'[45] Thus, as we saw to be the case in numerous expressions, the boundaries between respective domains of meaning remain opaque and cannot be clearly and rigidly delimited in the complex, reverberating repetitions and echoes of the text. It is both such depth of signification and the role of the clashing rhetorics of appropriation that are suppressed in a reading which supposes a secure and ordered transition from vendetta to law in the language of *dikē* in the *Oresteia*.

In the first chapter, we saw how the uncertainties and dangers of language produced fear, doubts, and many attempts for a sure control. Here we have seen how a key term of moral and social order is marked by its ambiguities, indeed, how the narrative of the play revolves around those ambiguities. As Vernant writes, 'The tragic message when understood, is precisely that there are zones of opacity and incommunicability in the words that men exchange'.[46] Moreover, the message of ambiguity is stressed in the very process of the dramatic exchange of language, as the different characters' rhetorical strategies appropriate the language of *dikē* to their own causes. This play dramatizes the 'strife of warring words'; and such a challenging critique of man's ability to know 'fairness', 'equal rights' as more than mere names is echoed throughout the course of Greek tragedy. Unlike Kitto, the writers of Greek tragedy do not seem to have believed that the problem of *dikē* was solved.

I have not yet looked in any detail at the trial itself, on which so many

---

[45] Ibid.   [46] Vernant and Vidal-Naquet 1981, 18.

interpretations of the trilogy turn, particularly for those critics who maintain that the transition to law is the civilizing message of the trilogy. It is to the trial and the ending of the play that I wish to turn for the final section of this chapter.

The dynamics of the rhetoric of appropriation and the shifting semantic fields of the evaluative vocabulary are especially important to an understanding of the establishment of the court. A key point for any analysis of the role of the legal institutions in the *Oresteia* is the relation between the stasimon on the subject of *dikē* sung by the Erinyes (*Eum.* 490–865), and Athene's echoing of their words in her speech where she establishes the court (681–710) – an echoing so close that at least one critic presumed Athene's words spurious.[47] The Erinyes stress the role of *dikē* as a social force: if there is no fear to protect the ties of society, either anarchy or despotism is the result. Without punishment, without the appeal to *dikē*, not even the wronged mother or outraged father would have any recourse. Respect for *dikē* is necessary, if violent transgressions are not to destroy the fabric of social order. This is applicable to Apollo's apparent countenancing of matricide as well as a general argument. The Erinyes see their role as protecting society by insisting on punishment for transgressions, and in particular for Orestes' sin.

Athene as she announces the establishment of the court also asks her citizens not to give way to anarchy or despotism – an especially relevant remark in the context of a democratic city festival – and not to cast fear utterly from the city. Rather, reverence and fear will prevent injustice and tampering with the laws. Why does Athene echo the Erinyes' words so closely before voting against them? To what extent does she accept their argument? What will be the relation of the Erinyes to the new legal institution? There are, of course, numerous answers to these questions. Here, I am going to look at two recent, influential approaches, Kitto's again and Lloyd-Jones'.

Kitto argues that Athene is granting the Erinyes a basic point, that 'the authority of a god can hardly be allowed to condone matricide'[48] but also that 'she recognizes too that the authority of the social order is logically prior'[49] to the Erinyes' 'instinctive punishment'. For the 'institutions of the ordered polis are the indispensable conditions of Justice'.[50] Indeed, 'no instinctive Justice can be successfully defended if society itself is in chaos'.[51] Thus for Kitto Athene reconciles the Erinyes to Zeus, and they become once more on the side of the Olympians after their opposition to Apollo, the Olympians' representative, in the trial: 'The daughters of Night have something to

[47] Dindorf deleted the lines.   [48] 1956, 64.   [49] 1956, 85.   [50] 1956, 85.
[51] 1956, 85.

contribute as well as the god of Light.'[52] The Erinyes have experienced a 'conversion from blind and bloodthirsty persecutors ... into awful defenders of that true Justice which is the only source of spiritual and material well-being'.[53]

For Kitto, then, Athene's repetition of the Erinyes' expressions of the place of *dikē* indicates the goddess' transcendent role in the advancement and progression of *dikē* towards 'that one true Justice' – a notion wider than the purely legal institution. The goddess agrees on an essential place for *dikē* in the restraint of wrongdoers and in the upholding of society, but surpasses the moral vision of the Erinyes by tempering their instinctive desire for instant punishment with mercy and humanity – as evinced by the lawcourt, where 'disputes are submitted to reasoned judgement, and ... punishment, when it is necessary, is inflicted not by the party who has been wronged, but by the impersonal hand of the judge'.[54] With Kitto, we remain on the road of progressive social justice towards 'moral and material well-being'.

Lloyd-Jones is concerned with elements of continuity in Greek ideas of justice from Homer to the end of the fifth century, and the *Oresteia* provides an interesting case for his argument for the conservatism of Greek moral attitudes. He rejects Kitto's approach out of hand: 'the cliché we have heard repeated all our lives that the *Eumenides* depicts the transformation from the vendetta to the rule of law, is utterly misleading'.[55] For him, the repetition of the Erinyes' words by Athene suggests not a progression but a straightforward analogy: 'we can hardly avoid concluding that an analogy between the Erinyes and the court of the Areopagus is being indicated; what the Erinyes, the helpers of justice, are in the universe, that the court of the Areopagus is in the Athenian constitution'.[56] Indeed, in the trilogy, he claims, there is no real change in the Erinyes' traditional functions, although, he concedes, their 'aspect' changes from curse to blessing and their power is exercised now through the courts. 'The new court of Justice ... is not to replace but to assist the Erinyes.'[57] Moreover, Lloyd-Jones is so unwilling to see any tension between the claims of the Erinyes and the claims of Athene, that when he turns to the fact (one of many problematic for his theory) that Athene votes against the Erinyes on the matter of Orestes' punishment and the Erinyes turn on her city in rage, he delivers one of the most bizarre of recent critical appraisals of the trial scene: 'when Athene gives her casting vote, she does so for a reason that has nothing to do with the issue that is being judged'.[58] In a telling phrase, Lloyd-Jones characterizes scholars who, like Kitto, have seen

[52] 1956, 64.   [53] 1956, 85.   [54] 1956, 85.   [55] 1971, 94.   [56] 1971, 93.
[57] 1971, 95.   [58] 1971, 92.

the Erinyes as losing part of their traditional function of inflicting punishment, as 'incautious in their liberalism'.[59] The fact that Kitto and others saw in the *Oresteia* a message of liberal humanist values, is for Lloyd-Jones itself a symptom of incautious liberalism.

It is not merely Lloyd-Jones' reduction of the terms of Athene's crucial speech to an irrelevancy nor his underplaying of the importance of the institutions of law to fifth-century ideology and practice that makes his reading insufficient. It is also his argument that Athene's repetition of the Erinyes' words should ('one can hardly avoid') indicate a particular sort of analogy. Because the goddess uses similar words, argues Lloyd-Jones, she must imply a similar thing. Yet it is precisely the shifting of the sense of *dikē* that has enabled Athene to establish the court in the face of the Erinyes. As they demanded *dikē* (justice as punishment), she offered *dikē* (justice as lawcourt). The Erinyes wanted, claimed the goddess, not to do *dikē* but to be called *dikaioi*. Now the court is to establish what is to be called *dikē* (in order to do *dikē*). The goddess's appropriation and manipulation of the chorus' language is essential to the establishing of the court and, through it, Orestes' acquittal, the escape from punishment which so outrages the Erinyes. The rhetoric of appropriation and the ambiguity of the terms in question make it far from certain that two characters' use of similar words can be simply and directly assumed to have a coextensive sense. When Athene and the Erinyes each appeal to *dikē*, it does not follow that the identical sense is implied. The conflict in the world of words that tragedy dramatizes cannot be so reduced.

But the vagaries of Lloyd-Jones' analysis do not mean we must simply follow Kitto's reading of the scene, and, indeed, Lloyd-Jones' description of critics like Kitto as 'incautious in their liberalism' indicates an interesting question about the more traditional interpretation of the trilogy. For although Kitto clearly recognizes that Athene cannot simply be repeating the Erinyes in agreement, if Orestes' acquittal and Athene's role in the ending of the play are taken into account, nevertheless it is certainly possible to question the end to which Kitto puts his recognition of Athene's rhetoric. For the emphasis on the closing scenes of the play, for Kitto, is on the wider *dikē* of the city and for him the play represents an expression of the harmonized organization of the state. When Kitto writes 'The problem of *dikē* is solved', the suggested solution of the problem is in the social order proclaimed by the rehabilitation of the Erinyes, a social order which is 'that one true justice' of 'our hopes'.

I have already shown in Chapter I some ways in which the triumphant civic discourse of these final scenes cannot fully repress a sense of its own insecurities. It was not merely that the human jurors could not reach a

[59] 1971, 93.

decision and had to rely on the goddess's vote, but also the very nature and attitude of the goddess that marked a certain continuing tension in the new social order. I argued that the role of Athene, the divine harmonizer, could not be understood apart from, in particular, Clytemnestra's role in the trilogy. Like Clytemnestra, Athene transgresses sexual norms, like Clytemnestra, the goddess in her search for the city's order uses manipulative language. The tension of the human jurors' tied decision is resolved by a divine figure who is a part of the human order of the city only in the way she stands apart from it. In the figure of Athene, the tensions in the opposition between the sexes and in the role of language in the city's order are displaced but not finally resolved. These are important qualifications to the sense of an ending as construed by Kitto. But there is a further more general point to be made about the way Greek tragedy is read that I want to approach by considering here in some detail a particular tradition of criticism that specifically questions the nature of the social order in terms of its confirmation of 'our hopes'.

In broad terms, this critical tradition can be said to begin with the Swiss jurist and historian J. J. Bachofen. His most influential work is *Das Mut- terrecht*, 'Mother-right', published in 1861. It is subtitled 'an investigation of the religious and judicial character of matriarchy in the ancient world' and in it Bachofen draws on extensive archaeological and mythological material to describe what he regarded as a universal pattern in the history of human society. It is a work of evolutionary anthropology of the sort that dominated much Victorian study.[60] The first period in this history he calls 'hetairism' which is distinguished for its 'unregulated sexual promiscuity'. This is followed by 'Amazonism', which is a 'universal phenomenon', where women rise up and slaughter men for their sins. For example, the Greek myth of the women of Lemnos (which is told in the *Choephoroi* 631–7) is described as 'an assault on woman's rights which provokes her resistance, which inspires self-defense followed by bloody vengeance'.[61] Amazonism, writes Bachofen, 'despite its savage degeneration signifies an appreciable rise in human culture'.[62] The third phase of this world history is the fully established 'Mutterrecht', the rule of the mother or female. In this period, women ruled 'whose unblemished beauty, whose chastity and high-mindedness . . . [whose] special aptitude for piety' inspired male heroes like Bellerephon to deeds of 'chivalry' and 'valour', by which men could 'combine bravery with voluntary recognition of the feminine power'.[63] This period, however, cedes finally and often in violent fashion to patriarchy, the present rule of men.

---

[60] See Coward 1983 for a survey of this material. For its influence on Victorian fiction, see Beer, 1983; Shuttleworth 1984.
[61] 1967, 104.   [62] 1967, 105.   [63] 1967, 84.

The *Oresteia*, for Bachofen, is a central text which charts this history. The *Eumenides* and in particular the trial scene represents the overthrow of the ancient rights of women in favour of the patriarchal state. Apollo's and Athene's arguments for the supremacy of the male are significant precisely for their evidence of the move away from 'das Mutterrecht'. Rather than fulfilling the social justice of 'our hopes' the *Oresteia* depicts the fall from the achieved perfection of the past.

This interpretation has been remarkably influential especially among Marxist and feminist writers. Engels, for example, called it 'brilliant', and the *Oresteia* plays an interesting role in *Origins of the Family, Private Property and the State*, a work which has influenced much subsequent writing on the family, property and the state, not only in Marxist circles. But Engels specifically rejects what he regards as Bachofen's mystical, indeed religious tendencies as ideologically biased. Engels does not believe that the overthrow of matriarchy was an event which was brought about by divinities in the heroic world of Greece. Rather, in the developing Marxist economic argument he maintains that the rise of patriarchy and the suppression of women occurred with the development of private property. There is an economic logic of change. 'As wealth increased it made the man's position in the family more important than the woman's.'[64] Women 'acquired an exchange value' as they became part of the economic system's growth. Among classicists, Thomson in particular has followed this interpretation. 'Aeschylus', he writes, 'perceived that the subjection of women was a necessary consequence of private property.'[65] But for Engels the causation of historical change is not simply economic. Indeed, the change in women's status that was brought about by the move towards regulated sexual mores was achieved by women for women. 'Hetairism', Bachofen's earliest period of unregulated sexual promiscuity, must have led to an increasingly oppressive sexual relation: women, he writes, 'constantly longed for the relief of the right of chastity', of 'becoming exempt from the ancient community of men and acquiring the right of surrendering to one man only'.[66] This development must have originated with women: 'this advance could not in any case have originated with the men, if only because it has never occurred to them even to this day to renounce the pleasures of actual group marriage'.[67] In place of Bachofen's religious mysticism, Engels originates change not only in economics but also in what he regards as the natural sexual behaviour of men and women – men to pursue women, women to long for stability and chastity.

Kate Millet focuses on precisely this element of what constitutes a fact of nature with regard to the sexes for Engels. She writes that Engels supposed

[64] 1972, 119.   [65] 1941, 288.   [66] 1972, 117.   [67] 1972, 117.

'with a naiveté characteristic of [his] era that women submitted willingly to the sexual and social subjection of pairing and then monogamous marriage because in fact women find sexuality burdensome ... one is tempted to see an absurdity in such a confident assumption that women dislike sex'.[68] Millet continues with the work of Masters and Johnson (and others) to set women's biological capability for sexual pleasure against Engels' attitudes which are affected by his cultural expectations. 'In fact', she writes, 'he is only being Victorian.'[69] This for Millet also leads to a reading of the *Oresteia*, in which Athene is constituted as something of the villain of the piece in her false consciousness: 'Athene born full-grown from the head of her father Zeus marches on, spoiling to betray her kind ... this sort of corroboration can be fatal.'[70] For Millet, the *Oresteia* ends with 'five pages of local chamber of commerce rhapsody' and 'until Ibsen's Nora slammed the door announcing the sexual revolution, this triumph [of patriarchy] went nearly uncontested'.[71]

In these readings based on Marxist and feminist ideas, the *Oresteia* remains a text of an evolutionary sort, but its evolution is not a progression towards the 'social justice' of 'our hopes'. For the readings of Engels and Thomson the *Oresteia* documents a move towards the legal authority of the state, but one can read in this movement the further signs of economic causation. Indeed, the *Oresteia*'s view of the growth of the state reflects the conflicts in the economic and social system in which the tragedy was produced. The end of the *Oresteia* is not so much the blossoming of 'our hopes' as the tale of the growth of a form of state authority with all the problems that can arise for a Marxist literary critic or historian. For Millet and subsequent writers on the women's movement the *Oresteia* occupies a privileged position as an early text of western culture documenting the logic and argumentation of the repression of the female in the state – a repression from which we have never yet escaped. So Simone de Beauvoir can write without hesitation 'The *Eumenides* represents the triumph of the patriarchate over the matriarchate. The tribunal of the gods declared Orestes to be the son of Agamemnon before he is the son of Clytemnestra – the ancient maternal authority and rights are dead, killed by the audacious revolt of the male.'[72]

But this is by no means the end of dissenting views of the end of the trilogy in terms of social justice and sexual opposition. Simon Pembroke, for example, whose work precedes the influential studies of Bamberger and Zeitlin, develops a subtle approach to the Greek discourse of sexuality.[73] For Pembroke, too, the *Oresteia* is an important test case. He argues that explicit

---

[68] 1971, 115–16.   [69] 1971, 116.   [70] 1971, 114.   [71] 1971, 115.
[72] 1972, 111 n. 9.
[73] Pembroke 1965; 1967; Zeitlin 1978. See below, Chapter 5.

statements on the relations between the sexes must be understood in relation to one another and in terms of a different culture's different construction of a picture of reality. For him, the many tales in Greek culture of matriarchy overthrown, or their stories of women being in charge in strange and foreign places, do not constitute a true version of a passage of history but an ideological expression of a state of affairs. These stories give 'an invented "historical" explanation of how this really was created'.[74] This idea has been well expressed in general form by Vernant, who writes 'For mythic thought, every genealogy is at one and the same time the expression of a structure.'[75] The story of a rejected matriarchy is the expression of the patriarchal structures of Athenian society. It is important to view the historicism of Bachofen, say, in the light of this understanding of the way in which the stories a culture tells of itself work. But, as we have already seen and will see throughout this book, the texts of tragedy do not simply reflect or repeat a general fifth-century discourse. How can we relate the necessary awareness of the way a discourse functions to the undercutting questions set in motion by the tragic dramas?

There are several answers to this question, and it is in the difficulty of determining this relation that the problem of discovering the author's own political attitudes from the text is made most clear. One answer is suggested by Anne Lebeck, who offers in her rejection of Millet in particular a further view of the end of the *Oresteia*. She finds it difficult to take the triumph of patriarchy with such fervour. 'There is an aura of tongue in cheek about this "divine" drama.'[76] She writes: 'In the trial both paradox and parody reach their height.'[77] 'The trial is a parody which does not present the Athenian law-court in a most attractive light.'[78] As to the triumph of patriarchy, she continues, 'weighing Cassandra and Clytemnestra against all the male figures of the trilogy one would scarcely conclude that Aeschylus believed in the moral superiority of the male'.[79] One must recognize, she claims, 'wit and humour' in the *Oresteia*. For Lebeck, Millet has not understood the tone of the text because she has as biased an ideological slant on the text as Engels. How else could she describe Cassandra's prophetic fervour as a state 'maddened by rape and enslavement'? For Lebeck, Aeschylus questions with a boldly ironic stance the dominant Athenian discourse. But this questioning progresses through wit and humour and parody rather than the unsettling manifestation of the paradoxes and uncertainties of human attitudes that might be a more expected characterization of the tragic drama.

[74] Bamberger 1975, 267.   [75] 1965, 16. My translation.   [76] 1971, 134.   [77] 1971, 134.
[78] 1971, 137.   [79] 1971, 136.

Now there are many arguments from many critics (including myself) which could be set against Lebeck's assertion of the levity of the conclusion of the *Oresteia*. The round of interpretations could be extended at greater and greater length, but this selection of readings is quite sufficient to make my point. For Bachofen, the *Oresteia* was a history of the fall from the earliest days of rule by women. Engels rejected Bachofen's mystical and religious conception of history because of its ideological bias, and developed an economic pattern of causation for the history of the relations of the sexes in the state. Millet rejects Engels' view of the history of the sexes as ideologically biased, before developing her view of the *Oresteia* as a text in the history of the repression of women. For Pembroke, Engels' work is 'not a contribution to knowledge' and the sort of reading that Millet or de Beauvoir offers can only misrepresent the workings of a mythic discourse in society. For Lebeck, too, it is through ideological bias that Millet utterly misreads the tone of the conclusion of the trilogy. Critic after critic in this series of interpretations rejects a previous reading for its ideological bias, which is seen as leading to a misrepresentation of the facts. In this way, Lloyd-Jones rejected Kitto and others as 'incautious in their liberalism' but Stanford claimed that the social justice he read in the trilogy represented 'our hopes'. Whether it is expressed as really Aeschylus' message or really the message of the play in a more general sense, each critical reading finds itself appropriated to further argument. And it would not be difficult to see the same process in my partial, selective juxtaposition of earlier writers' words. Can there be a reading of the *Oresteia*'s claims of social justice which does not implicate a reader's ideological bias and thus open itself to further appropriation? Is it possible to avoid self-involvement in approaching the questions of this tragedy? Can one discuss 'right', 'justice' in a neutral fashion? It would seem that the language of *dikē*, twisted and turned by the rhetoric of appropriation in the *Oresteia*, can be read only by a further act of appropriation – the critic's own rhetoric.

As much, then, as the different characters of the trilogy appropriate the language of *dikē*, so too the different critics, repeating the play's dynamics of conflict, appropriate the language of the *Oresteia* to arguments about social justice. The 'strife of warring words' has no neutrals. I have already quoted Vernant's remark that 'the tragic message . . . is precisely that there are zones of opacity and incommunicability in the words men exchange'. This message applies to the reading and understanding of the words of the tragedy itself. As Vernant continues, with a fine sense of the paradox of tragedy for the reader or spectator: 'the language becomes transparent and the tragic message gets across to him only provided he makes the discovery that words, values, men themselves are ambiguous, that the universe is one of conflict'.[80] The most unsettling recognition from the tragic texts is that the reader's or spectator's own convictions, attitudes and postures become implicated, questioned and undercut in what at first sight seem so clearly the disastrous conflicts of others. This applies both to an ancient Greek spectator watching the heroes of old tales and to the modern reader approaching the texts of an ancient culture. Tragedy's challenge is precisely to the sense of the secure and controlled expression of the order of things that for so many critics in their different ways has constituted the end of the *Oresteia*. The problem of *dikē* in this trilogy and its critical readings is not solved but endlessly restated.

[80] Vernant and Vidal-Naquet 1981, 18.

3 · THE CITY OF WORDS

The city is in nature prior to households and each of us individually.

ARISTOTLE

If we wish to understand the force and direction of Greek tragedy, it is impossible not to bring into consideration the city of Athens, which gave rise to the institution of the tragic festivals and which, as we saw in the previous chapter, can be regarded as offering specific conditioning to its dramas. I do not mean by this to take for granted any simple relation between a society and the texts produced in it, nor do I wish to add my name to the roll call of those who have seen in the order of the *polis* one of the greatest glories of Greece. Rather, in this chapter I intend to develop briefly some sense of the ideology of the *polis* and a view of its structure: naturally, I shall not be attempting a full description of its institutions or of its history, two topics to which many words have been dedicated,[1] nor am I attempting to define in full the term *polis*, a word whose transliteration covers a multitude of insufficient translations.[2] Rather, within the terms of this book I shall be attempting to investigate some ways in which the structure of civic ideology may relate to the dramatic festivals and the sorts of transgressions enacted in tragedy and comedy. For even if the relations between the social conditions of production and the texts themselves remain obscure and difficult, it does not follow that the texts can simply be read divorced from any sense or investigation of those conditions.

There can be little doubt as to the pervasive and multiform strength of the *polis* ideology in the fifth and fourth centuries. The sense of the primacy of the *polis* which is expressed in this chapter's epigraph with its apparently bizarre reversal of what might be regarded as the expected historical progression or social development, could be repeated in different ways from almost any fifth- or fourth-century Athenian writer: Plato's ideal Republic is a *polis*; Pindar's victory odes celebrate a victor through his *polis* and the *polis* through its victorious citizen; whatever the variety of ruling systems proposed or fought

---

[1] For good introductions, see Andrewes 1971; Davies 1978; Finley 1983; Austin and Vidal-Naquet 1972. For a solid description of the institutions, see Ehrenberg 1960.
[2] I myself have used 'city', 'state' and 'city-state' on occasion in this and other chapters. None quite captures the sense of *polis*.

for, whatever the variety of size or constitution of actual city-states, the *polis* is continually depicted as the very condition of possibility of any existence deserving the name of civilization. Aristotle's famous remark that 'man is a political animal' defines man as essentially involved in the life of a *polis*.

There are two major ways I wish to investigate the ideology of the *polis*. The first is through the sense of citizenship: what does it mean to be a *polites*, a citizen of a city – not merely in the sense of what obligations or what rights does citizenship confirm, but also what sense of the self is projected by the term 'citizen'? The second line of enquiry is through the sense of place: how do the generations of Athenian citizens organize, utilize, conceive the civic space? Both questions will have answers important to our notions of tragic drama. Let me begin with the sense of citizenship.

Citizenship implies belonging, being an insider. The question 'who is a citizen', however, cannot be answered in purely legal terms but requires a more complex range of criteria.[3] Certainly the Athenians were concerned with the legal aspect. On the one hand, descent constitutes the primary quali-fication. Being legitimately born into an Athenian family, being accepted by the wider social and kin group of the phratry and deme[3a], taking one's place as a member of the Assembly as a fully-fledged citizen offered a pattern of recognition for a male Athenian. 'Descent' as Davies remarks,[4] 'is built into the institutions of the state.' Indeed, the legal definition of citizenship that comes into being in the democracy under Pericles is 'being the child of two citizens'. But on the other hand both the very need at this time to find a re-specification of citizenship, especially when one considers the valuable privi-leges, economic and social, of being counted a citizen, and also the numerous law-cases concerned with individual examples of qualification, have prompted historians to see in their discussions of citizenship 'deep status anxiety on all sides'.[5] 'The rules generated obsessions, anxieties and insecurities.'[6] Indeed, the influx of foreigners into the leading city of the time, the increase in population and wealth – not necessarily in the hands of the traditionally wealthy – the growing complexities of a powerful empire, resulted in considerable tensions in the hierarchical separation of citizen and non-citizen according to a criterion of birth alone: 'The descent group criterion of citizenship ... was under pressure and attack from many sides.'[7]

If the legal boundaries between belonging and not belonging to the city are under some pressure, there are also considerable areas of possible tension within the system in a different way. I said that the legal requirement of citizenship was being born from two citizens. This translates the phrase *ex*

[3] Cf. Ehrenberg 1960, 39.   [3a] On inscription into the deme, see Whitehead 1986, esp. 258–60.
[4] 1977, 110.   [5] Davies 1977, 113.   [6] Davies 1977, 111.   [7] Davies 1977, 121.

amphoin aston, which uses a different expression for 'citizen' than the term
polites, a word from the same root as *polis* and the term normally translated as
'citizen'. This is because women are not called 'citizens', and the term *polites*
cannot be applied to both parents of a future citizen. The men (as a group) are
spoken of as 'Athenians', 'men of Athens' or 'citizens', but women *en masse*
are referred to as 'women of Attica'. Women do not have the name of citizen
nor are they named from the *polis*, Athens. Indeed, these 'women of Attica'
could not hold office in the *polis*, could not vote, could not possess or deal with
property,[8] and could take little part in the leisured life of the gymnasium and
market-place – all the tangible benefits which the citizen enjoyed. One should
say, then, more strictly that a citizen (*polites*) is to be regarded as the male child
of a citizen who is married to the daughter of another citizen. We will return to
the difficulties that arise from the position of the women in the civic ideal
shortly. It is enough here to note that the tension between the sexes that is
often an explicit feature of tragedy is not without parallel in the city's
projection of what it is to be a citizen. When Apollo in the *Oresteia* says that
only the father is a true parent, it must be seen in the light of a bias already
present in Athenian discourse.

Perhaps then, in these ideological terms a 'citizen of Athens' is to be
considered as the male who belongs, the male insider. It is, however, not only
women who provide a sense of the other by which this citizen defines himself.
Agamemnon in the *Oresteia*, for example, when faced by the tapestries and his
wife, has this to say (918–25):

> ... do not try in women's ways to make
> me delicate, nor as if I were some Asiatic
> bow down to earth and with wide mouth cry to me;
> nor cross my path with jealousy by strewing the ground
> with robes. Such state becomes the gods
> and none beside. I am a mortal, a man.

Here Agamemnon distinguishes himself first from woman: not for him is the
female way of delicacy with its associations of weakness and incapability. As
we have mentioned, in the fifth century the opposition of the sexes is a charged
polarity affecting many areas of language and the widening of cultural life.
Here the Greek war-lord dismisses the possibility of effeminacy. Secondly,
Agamemnon rejects the manner of 'some Asiatic'. The word translated by
'Asiatic' is more normally rendered less specifically as 'barbarian'. The
'barbarians' are all those who are not Greek: that is one of the widest
categorizations of Greek cultural thinking deeply embedded in the writing of

[8] Except to the value of a *medimnos* of barley; see Kuenen-Janssens 1941. On the legal rights of
women, see Schaps 1978.

numerous different authors, and within the polarization common to Greek cultural thinking many customs and habits which are the reverse of the male Athenian norm are widely predicated of barbarian behaviour, including rule by women, general effeminacy, and all manner of degenerate attitudes.[9] The victories over the barbarians such as the defeat of the Persians at the battle of Marathon provided the democratic city with a paradigmatic model of the superiority of the Greek male to which Athenian rhetoric loved to return.[10] The third distinction is perhaps the widest of all: Agamemnon is not to be likened to the gods. Man, as Detienne and Vernant have outlined,[11] is to be distinguished from the divine on the one hand and the bestial, uncivilized world of domestic and wild animals on the other. Man defines his place in the order of things between two poles of existence, supra-human godhead and sub-human animality. This tripartite systematization recurs in various formulations and various media: temple sculpture often depicts the battle of gods over the wild, uncivilized giants, or the human Lapiths fighting the bestial centaurs. Religious ceremonies, sacrifices and festivals have been interpreted as enforcing this system of categories throughout the pattern of daily life.[12] Poetic imagery and mythic tales often concern themselves with the maintenance of, or dangers to, such categorizations of man's place in the order of things. Even with such a general system of ideas, however, we must be careful not to assume that it coincides absolutely with modern, western definitions or ideals; as Finley has recently outlined, for example, slaves, that so often forgotten group in Greek history, are treated largely as property and rarely as possessing the range of human rights or qualities that modern liberal philosophy would often attempt to assign to all members of the human race.[13] Nor can one assume such categorization to be without difficulties or uncertainties for its users, however, pervasive it might at first glance seem. As we will see throughout this book, it is precisely the defining of such notions as 'man' that is put at risk in tragedy, which often focuses on the grey areas and boundaries of such a process of categorization or defining.

After these negative evaluations of Clytemnestra's request, Agamemnon offers his positive definition: he is a mortal male, a man. Through this positive and negative defining, then, in his exchange of words with his wife Agamemnon projects a sense of himself in broad categories that find echoes throughout

[9] In general, see Lloyd 1966; Pembroke 1967. See Hartog 1980 for an interesting analysis of this polarity of self and other in the historian Herodotus.
[10] Cf. e.g. Thuc. 1.73-4, and below, Chapter 5, for Jason's reaction to Medea in such terms.
[11] Especially 1979.
[12] On sacrifice, see e.g. Detienne and Vernant 1979; Girard 1977; Rudhardt and Reverdin 1981; Burkert 1983. On this theme in Sophocles, see Segal 1981; in Euripides, see Foley 1985.
[13] Finley 1980, and his bibliography there. For connections between women and slaves as categories, see Willetts 1959; Vidal-Naquet 1970.

fifth-century Athenian language. The male subject defines himself through a sense of the other: he distinguishes himself from the gods; the barbarians; the women. Finley conveniently provides a summing up:[14] 'Not all Athenians held the same views ... but the evidence is decisive that nearly all of them would have accepted as premises, one might say, axioms, that the good life was possible only in a *polis*, that the good man was more or less synonymous with the good citizen, that slaves, women and barbarians were inferior by nature and so excluded from all discussion.'

So far, of course, this description has been in the most general terms concerning itself primarily with the Athenian citizen's notion of being a man in the very widest sense: my aim has been not only to establish briefly a general idea of some basic terms of Athenian cultural thinking, but also to introduce the logic of polarized definition so common in the Greek organization of things.[15] The Athenian sense of being an Athenian, however, may be described with more specificity. I am going to approach this complex topic in two ways. First, through the notion of the citizen's relation to the democratic ideal, and secondly through the Athenian myth of autochthony ('autochthony' means 'being born from the soil which one inhabits'), a myth which will lead us towards the discussion of civic space in the second part of this chapter. First, then, the sense of being a citizen of a democracy.

Now the emergence of Athenian democracy was quite unlike that of its patron goddess, Athene: rather than springing forth fully armed, democracy developed slowly and with considerable wrangling, bitterness and blood-shed:[16] indeed, even when it had been established there remained consider-able tension between conservative and radical elements, between different power groups and individual leaders.[17] Moreover, from the middle of the fifth century on, there was a discussion of constitutional and political matters that was 'continuous, intense and *public*'.[18] Indeed, such was the possibility of violent change in the *polis* that the 'cycle of constitutions' became an obsession of generations of political analysts:[19] in city after city, political history is described as an oscillation between the ruling systems of oligarchy and democracy, with civil wars, killings, exiles and confiscations. And there were tyrants,[20] too (the technical name for an individual who rules a city, a dictator), the anathema of democracy. So, in the light of such instability of both constitutional establishment and political activity, the strength of the

---

[14] 1983, 125.   [15] The standard work remains Lloyd 1966.
[16] For a history of the development of democracy, see e.g. Forrest 1966. The Cleisthenic reforms were, of course, a major reorientation of the political system.
[17] For such tensions, see Davies 1978 Chapters 4 and 9.
[18] Finley 1983, 123. Aeschylus' *Supp.* and *Pers.* are early evidence for the debate.
[19] See Ryffel 1949 for this discussion.
[20] See Andrewes 1956 for a history of the tyrants.

ideology of allegiance and obligation to one's *polis* indicates perhaps a somewhat different attitude towards what we would regard as the central political questions of what gives legitimacy to a ruling system and what obligations a citizen is to honour. The citizen of the Athenian democracy was expected to take his part in civil affairs in an extensive way. Whatever the level of apathetic withdrawal, which is hard for us to estimate, and however much conservative writers despised the involvement of the less well-born in city business, there was a considerable measure of popular participation:[21] meetings of the Assembly were open to any and every citizen who cared to attend; there, all matters of state business were discussed and he had a direct vote on issues which were proposed and debated openly. There was also a council consisting of five hundred men over the age of thirty, which was selected by lot from all the citizens who allowed their names to be considered, but which had a compulsory geographical spread of members. The Council considered matters before they came to the Assembly and was charged to put the will of the Assembly into practice. The balance between executive Council and Assembly was essential. 'The far reaching independence of the Council remained restricted by the unquestionable authority of the popular assembly.'[22] Nearly all officials were selected by lot (not election), and office was tenable for one year only and was not renewable. The qualifications of an appointed official could under certain circumstances be challenged, and all officials had to present full accounts at the end of their period of office. Most court cases, too, in what was a highly litigious society were heard before bodies open to all citizens – the Assembly, the Council and the 'jurors', who were chosen by lot from a roster of 6,000 volunteers and paid for their services by the state.

The mention of 'compulsory geographical spread' in the selection of Council members points to a specific area of doubt in this picture of commitment to radical democracy. For, with the exception of certain war years when the pressure of invasion resulted in the countryside of Attica being abandoned for the protection of the city walls, many citizens lived in the outlying districts of Attica, from where the distances and difficulties of travel must have limited participation in city life both in its more institutional forms that I have been discussing and also in the more informal aspects. Particularly for the poorer farmer who did not necessarily have the slaves, managers or indeed land to produce surplus food or time, the rigours of agricultural life forty kilometres or more from the city must have limited the possibilities of regular attendance at the city throughout the year.[23]

[21] See Finley 1983, Chapter 4.   [22] Ehrenberg 1960, 64. See also Hansen 1987, *passim*.
[23] See Osborne 1985, Chapter 4. See also Hansen 1987, 14–19.

Nevertheless, my description of the institutions of the city implies considerable participation by an extended range of citizens in the running of the *polis*. Not only could such pressing matters as the declaration of war be discussed and voted on directly by the prospective soldiers, but also within a decade something between a quarter and a third of citizens could reasonably expect to have served on the Council, the executive body of government. With its lack of bureaucracy and hierarchy of office, and with its immediate involvement in the maintenance and application of law, this direct democracy is far removed from a modern western representational government. There were no structured political parties, no government in the sense of an appointed or elected group formally entrusted with special powers: direct, personal participation was a permanent necessity and was followed up often with personal action. When in Thucydides' history Pericles says of Athenian citizens 'all of us are fit to judge . . . each of us is willing to fight and to die' the democratic rallying cry of free participation for all sounds in opposition not only to the elitist, specialist theories of Plato, but also to the traditional standards of Homer's Odysseus, say, who 'whenever he found any man of the common people (*dēmos*) giving tongue . . . he rated him severely: "You there", he said, "sit still and wait for orders from your betters, you who are no warrior and a weakling counting for nothing in battle or debate"'.[24]

The emphasis on 'battle' as well as debate in that quotation from Homer, and on 'fighting and dying' in Thucydides is not merely due to the circumstances of war in which both sets of remarks are being delivered. For the military outlook is an essential part of the sense of being a citizen in a way that it is hard for us to appreciate. Not only was being a hoplite, the soldier of the *polis*, largely dependent on citizenship and to a certain degree on a financial qualification, not only was taking one's position in the hoplite rank or navy a central way of determining one's citizenship (in a way that I will discuss further in Chapter 6), but also, far from soldiering having a ceremonial or casual aspect, there were very few years and almost no years in succession without some military engagement. The patriotic rhetoric of fighting for one's country, women, and children, had a special significance for a true citizen militia when it was regularly fighting to prevent enslavement, death or the destruction of one's ancestral property – even, in the case of smaller cities, to prevent the total razing of the *polis*. Ancient Athens had no standing army: the vote given for war was a vote given to have oneself and one's sons risk life and limb. Indeed, the close connections of civil and military power and office can be appreciated in the fact that the ten positions of 'general', 'military commander' were usually filled by the most influential politically, who were

[24] *Il.* 2.200ff.

elected to the highest military command because of their political authority (rather than the other way round). When Pericles, who was elected 'general' for many years, says 'each of us is willing to fight and to die' he is pointing to the essential involvement of the democratic citizen in the military defence of the *polis*, and each citizen's necessary sense of himself as soldier.

The fact that Pericles was elected 'general' for many years – Thucydides himself calls his period of supremacy rule by the first man rather than democracy – points to a further specific area of doubt in the instantiation of the ideal of democracy. For Pericles comes from one of the great, traditionally wealthy families of Athens, as do many of the influential political figures we know of. Even such a demagogue as Cleon, who was described with great rancour and bitterness by Thucydides and parodied by Aristophanes as demonstrating the worst side of populism, came from the sort of background, which, if not of the highest order, produced many rich conservatives.[25] Interestingly, for our discussion of citizenship and belonging, many writers express their (conservative) dislike of such anti-aristocratic populist and popular figures 'in repeated but so far as we know quite false allegations that the demagogues were of foreign or bastard birth'.[26] Athenian pride in equality before the law and in equality in the political process does not conceal that some remained 'more equal than others'. Although one must not elide the important differences between oligarchies, democracies and tyrannies, expressed so strongly by the Greeks, there is a certain continuity of the holders of power throughout the fifth and fourth centuries in Athenian society. Despite recurring tensions between the rich and poor in Athenian civil struggles, it seems to be the same families, the same classes, who produced the dominant political figures of democracy, oligarchy and tyranny.

The democratic ideal and political practice of democracy, then, are structured to form in a citizen an essential allegiance and obligation to Athens. This ideological commitment to the *polis* can be seen even in what might be regarded as high treason: Alcibiades, the brilliant and mercurial general accused of plotting against the democratic state, defends his going over to Sparta (according to Thucydides) with these words:[27] 'as for love of *polis*, I do not feel it for the one that is wronging me but for the one in which I safely exercised my rights as a citizen. I do not accept that I am marching against my fatherland. On the contrary, I seek to recover a fatherland that has ceased to be mine. It is genuine love of *polis* not when one refuses to march against it, having lost it unjustly, but when through the ardour of one's desire one tries all means to recover it.' This may be, as has been suggested, the 'shabby

[25] Cf. Davies 1978, 112–28.   [26] Davies 1978, 113.   [27] Thuc. 6.92.

self-serving argument of a traitor',[28] but the reliance on the criterion of allegiance and obligation to the *polis*, while actually campaigning against it with its enemies, offers an excellent example of the rhetorical ease with which the ideology of unity and support for the *polis* can be reconciled with the political tensions and rivalries that racked Athens and the Greek world throughout the fifth and fourth centuries. Even in rebellion or other internal strife 'love of *polis*' and one's obligation to the city remain a paramount expression of one's position in the world.

The sense of involvement engendered in democratic Athens is far from merely institutional, however. Not only was Athenian society a face-to-face society,[29] small enough and intimate enough to foster that sense of involvement, but also it was a Mediterranean society, in which people congregated out of doors, on market days, on numerous religious or festive occasions, and all the time in the harbour and the town square. Here is Finley's description: 'Citizens were members of varied formal and informal groups – the family and the household, the neighbourhood and village, military and naval units, occupational groups (farmers at harvest time or urban crafts which tended to concentrate in particular streets), upper-class dining clubs, innumerable private cult-associations. All provided opportunities for news and gossip, for discussion and debate, for . . . political education'.[30]

Finley's description, which is primarily of the various forms of social interaction in a complex culture, offers us two important insights into the specific case of classical Athens. On the one hand, even Finley may be thought to fall into something of an idealized view of the equalities and educative power of ancient democracy, if he is simply linking upper-class dining societies, farmers at harvest, the family, as all providing opportunities for political education and discussion. For there are important differences in the informal as well as the formal distribution of power, knowledge, social control, which, as Finley himself argues elsewhere so eloquently, must not be elided if a description is to do justice to the complexities of Athenian society. On the other hand, it is certainly important to stress these multiple forums for discussion, political or otherwise, in Athenian democracy. For with such increased, direct participation in the process of decision-making in Athens, the boundaries between formal and informal political action are far from clear-cut. The sense of the involvement of a citizen in the life of a city goes far beyond the democratic institutions of power, and a description of the city cannot sensibly limit itself to a history or description of the formal institutions

[28] Finley 1983, 122.
[29] For important qualifications of this often over-used phrase, see Osborne 1985, Chapter 4.
[30] Finley 1983, 82.

of power. Indeed, it is this complexity of power relations and possible rivalries within such a polymorphous system that makes the political analysis of Athens so complex – or, for Plato and others, that makes its order so unwieldy and unstable.

It is precisely on this sense of democracy and democratic involvement that Pericles' funeral speech over the war-dead of Athens concentrates, especially to distinguish Athens from all other nations: 'Our system of government does not copy the institutions of our neighbours. It is more the case of our being a model to others than of imitating anyone else. Our constitution is called a democracy because power is in the hands not of a minority, but of a whole people.'[31] There is in Athens equality before the law, no-one is debarred from politics by poverty; those in authority are obeyed, and the laws, written and unwritten, are treated with the utmost respect. Everyone has and plays his part. This is the ideology Pericles is depicted as promoting on the state occasion of the funeral speech. It will be important to remember this sort of speech for a great civic event when we turn to another great *polis* institution, the drama festival.

So the sense of being a citizen, rather than depending on simply a legal or institutional definition, stems from an extensive series of cultural values and, to a certain degree, from an active participation in the running and discussion of the affairs of the city, from local gossip to fiscal policy and military planning. Most authors writing of the glories of Periclean Athens have in mind (as well as the art, literature and architecture) an open society of men, freely debating in an atmosphere where politics and political philosophy have not been separated and institutionalized, where discussion and action grant a sense of active individual participation.

In the light of my focus on the ideological projection of what it is to be an Athenian citizen – I am not forgetting, as we have seen, that like most ideological projections it works hard to assimilate its paradoxes and difficulties, and is sometimes far from the actual social circumstances – it is interesting to read one of the central myths of Athenian power relations, namely, the myths associated with autochthony, being born from the earth one inhabits. It is often through such myths that the process of reconciling or accommodating gaps and difficulties in a system of thought can be viewed, and indeed the myth of autochthony plays a fascinating role in Athenian self-definition and in its representation of itself with regard to other cities. In particular, this myth of autochthony relates both to Athenian claims to political hegemony (and hence its fifth-century empire) and also to the position of women in the civic ideal, to which I said earlier I would return.

[31] Thuc. 2.37.

Here we will confront a specific gap between ideological representation and social circumstances.

The myth itself offers in a series of related stories a complex language in which to describe the origin of the city. The first Athenian is Erichthonios, who was born of the earth itself, impregnated by the desire of Hephaestus for Athene. Descendants of Erichthonios, the Athenians claim themselves to be sons of the soil that they possess, not invaders or colonizers like other peoples, but genetically connected, as it were, to the land on which they live. The child Erichthonios is brought up by Athene, after whom he names the city Athens. Another story tells of Cecrops the first king and civilizer of Athens, who is the judge of a contest between Poseidon and Athene as to who should be the patron of the city. He judges Athene's gift of the olive more useful than Poseidon's gift of the horse; and names the city for the goddess, its future patron. From Cecrops comes the line of kings resulting in Theseus and the contemporary organization of Athens as a *polis*. There are many variations and additions to the myths that I have so barely told.[32] But the fecundity of the evidence is less important to my argument here than the work to which it is put. For the rhetorical uses of the implication of the autochthony myths indicate first the possible authorizing function of the myth within the secular political discourse of Athens – a use which Loraux finds the Cecrops legends in particular utilized. Herodotus, for example, has the Athenian envoy before the Persian invasion of Xerxes explicitly claim the right to command the whole Greek fleet because of their ancient autochthony: 'Are we not Athenians – the most ancient of all Greek people, the only nation never to have left the soil from which it sprang',[33] and the success of the campaign against the barbarians is later attested to have been because of Athenian autochthony in passages as widely different as Plato's *Menexenus* (245d) and Aristophanes' *Wasps* (1075ff.).[34] There are, of course, numerous strategies for justifying claims to hegemony or empire,[35] but here the specifically Athenian belief in a right to leadership or even conquest is reflected in their own myth of permanent possession of the land, their own sense of how their origins determine their unique citizenship. The city's myth works to make the claims of the right to rule seem natural and proper.

More important for my purposes here than the use of myths of autochthony in Athenian political rhetoric is the specific way that tales of autochthony may concern the position of women in a civic ideal, a theme with which Loraux associates in particular the tales of Erichthonios and the world of the Acropolis. For if the various tales of autochthony and the origins of Athens do

---

[32] For which, see Loraux 1981b to which my analysis is greatly indebted.   [33] Her. 7.161.
[34] See also Loraux 1981a, 151–2; 1981b, passim.   [35] See e.g. Davies 1978, 117–19.

indicate something of the Athenian self-projection, it is not by chance that the city which in practice relieved women of power, position, even the name of citizen, should in its mythic projection tell stories which either exclude women totally in even their function as child-producers, or, alternatively, in some versions of the myths told, establish the race of women not only as separate from men but also as a race whose control or overthrow is necessary for the progress of civilization. Indeed, one even reads of true Athenians being termed 'citizen-sons, legitimate by birth, of the fatherland',[36] as if the fatherland still reproduced itself as once it gave birth to the first Athenian. Yet the role of motherhood cannot be totally removed. Not only is the production of children a civic duty incumbent on women, but also the protection of this strict paternal line can be maintained only by the vigorous protection of the chastity of citizens' wives. The desire to maintain a certainty over who is the father recognizes woman as necessary at least in the need for her control. It is in this light that we may read the numerous myths which assert the dangers of female lawlessness or lust, culminating in that negation of all male values, the race of the Amazons, defeated finally by Theseus, king of the Athenians. So while civic language refuses women the name of citizen, the institutions of the city confine a woman to her maternity – and the myths project a notion of civilization without or despite the race of women. As Loraux writes, 'All the city's projections of power (*instances imaginaires*) agree to reduce . . . the place set out for women in the *polis*.'[37]

It may seem strange, then, that the patron divinity of Athens should be Athene, a goddess. But Athene, as has been extensively discussed, is a goddess who is no ordinary female.[38] She sprang fully armed from Zeus' head: not only is she armed and fights like a man, but also she has no connection at the moment of her birth with the process of normal female reproduction.[39] Moreover, Athene is a virgin who herself takes no part in the process of birth and sexual reproduction. The goddess herself has a place in the devaluation of women in the city, a place in the dominant male cultural thinking of the *polis*. The city bears the name of the goddess, as the goddess plays a key role in the network of myths through which the city finds itself.

The myths of autochthony, then, offer an interesting example of the way civic discourse develops through a range of strategies the complex sense of what it is to be an Athenian. Moreover, the ways that the myth interrelates ideas of sexual reproduction and sexual difference, ideas of land and origin, ideas of Greekness and barbarism, show how closely the topics I separated for

[36] Dem. *Epit.* 5.   [37] 1981b, 131.
[38] Loraux 1981b, especially Chapter 3; also Goldhill 1984a, 279–81.
[39] Zeus had swallowed Metis, who in some versions of the story was pregnant with Athene. See Detienne and Vernant 1978, especially Chapters 3–5.

the process of analysis in the earlier part of this chapter are intertwined. The strong sense of being an Athenian citizen with its obligations and duties, privileges and honours, is a complex system of ideological strategies, a complex self-projection, that goes far beyond mere patriotism. It is to this sense of being an Athenian citizen that tragedy returns, as we will see, with its specific rhetoric of questioning.

The sense of place and belonging attested by the implications of autochthony in the idea of citizenship can be seen in many other ways in Athenian culture and it is this sense of place and belonging that I wish now to investigate in the second part of this discussion of the *polis* and its structuring. Rather than to the distribution of property and public, state monuments, I wish first to turn to another essential factor in our understanding of Athenian society, the domestic space of the *oikos*. *Oikos* is a term, like *polis*, that defies translation. It implies the physical house, the idea of home, the household members (both alive and dead, slave and free); it indicates farm-land as well as dwellings, crops as well as chattels. The ideal of the *oikos* is not only a good and harmonious or rich life for its present members but a permanent continuing existence. The continuity of the *oikos* is often stressed both in the sense of children to provide generational continuity and in the sense of thrift and careful management to maintain economic continuity.[40] Inheritance is a prime concern of the *oikos*, which displays a clear link with our earlier discussion of the role of rigid, certain patrilineal descent in Athenian culture overall. Marriage can be seen as the necessary means of procuring continuity for the *oikos* rather than a matter of personal feelings or romantic attachment. The woman is to bear a son to inherit the father's property. The maintenance of the *oikos* is a traditional virtue that remained a powerful force throughout Greek culture. The idea of permanence that we saw in the myth of autochthony is most strongly asserted in the relation of a citizen to his *oikos*: one might lose one's family home through economic, military or some unforeseen disaster, but the modern ideas of moving home, property dealing, or going home for Christmas are simply inexpressible in terms of the values and ideals of the *oikos*.[41]

The *oikos*, then, is the private life of the public citizen we have considered so far. Unlike the competitive, egalitarian, argumentative world of the Assembly,

---

[40] Cf. Glotz 1904 passim; Lacey 1968, especially Chapters 5 and 6; Jones 1962, especially 82ff.
[41] Even in the fourth century, no property market developed as it did in Rome. The alienability of land is much discussed by scholars, sometimes as if it were strictly impossible. For a balanced argument against too simple a view, see Finley 1968. Despite an ideal of continuous ownership through patrilineal inheritance, 'the *polis* world', he writes, 'saw the emergence not only of new kinds and new aims of alienation and of increasing frequency, but also of new restrictions' (1968, 32).

market-place, lawcourt, gymnasium, and unlike the institutionalized civil religious festivals, the *oikos* is the closed space. Its relationships are primarily hierarchical and dependent on the head of the *oikos*, the father; citizens undertaking public position took an oath to fulfil their civic responsibilities and to disregard private interest. Both the architectural and social norms made entrance into or exit from another man's *oikos* difficult (except on such special occasions as dinner parties – *symposia* – at which wives were simply not present). Indeed, the inside of the *oikos*, the closed-off space, is the area associated not just with family life, but with the women in particular – as much as the worlds of Assembly and gymnasium were the province of the men. This is not to say, as we will see in Chapter 5, that women of all ages and classes simply were not seen outside, or did not go outside, but as much as the ideology of the city served to devalue women in general, even in the necessary role of childbirth, so the connection between the inside and the female, the outside and the male is regularly asserted as natural and proper.

Nor is it by chance that for all our variety of views of Athenian public life, we have but a few glimpses of this private home life of the Athenian *oikos*.[42] Indeed, rather than demonstrating any sustained interest in the private life of the *oikos per se*, most of these insights are passed through the distorting public language of the lawcourts or didactic literature, where the view of home-life is expressed to defend or expound a particular argument or a particular client's character. As Humphreys puts it: 'The law-court becomes . . . a theatre for the dramatization of an ideological view of the *oikos*'[43] rather than a transparent view of the Athenians at home.

This far from entirely physical topography of inside and outside can be seen in several areas of Athenian cultural attitudes. It is highly relevant, of course, to the dangers that are supposed to arise when women come out of the enclosed world of the house or when strangers come in – dangers particularly to sexual honour, a notion which, as we have seen, is closely connected to ideas of property, inheritance and citizenship. We shall return to the notion of women 'coming out' in more detail in Chapter 5. It can be seen secondly in the determination of the special nature of women's participation in the city life, particularly in the large, all-female, religious festivals such as the Thesmo-phoria. Although these festivals seem to have been connected with fertility and offer at first sight an interesting example contrary to the pervasive devaluation of women in an image rather of the female as protector and nourisher of life-giving forces, they are none the less occasions consciously

---

[42] Often quoted are Socrates' dismissal of his wife to be with his friends at the moment of his death, and certain law cases (e.g. *de Neaira*) which revolve around family life. For the special nature of this evidence, see Humphreys 1983, Chapters 1 and 2.

[43] 1983, 9.

marked as sacred, different, abnormal time.[44] The festivals carefully segregate the women, and surround their behaviour and actions with the prescriptions and restrictions of rite. The controlled and delimited nature of these cere-monies has often been seen as enforcing the normal pattern of restrictions in everyday life – like so many of religion's temporary freedoms. Rather than offering the liberty to move outside the house into civic life, the female religious processions, precisely because they are special, can be seen as specially controlled events that support the ordering of a woman's place under more normal circumstances 'on the inside'.

The third area in which I want to look at this sense of inside and outside offers us another insight into the way a sense of place relates to various forms of representation of the self in Athenian culture. This area is the specific pairing of the divinities Hermes and Hestia in the art and thought of Athens, so well analysed by J. P. Vernant.[45] Outside each house in Athens stood a statue that consisted generally of a head on a quadrangular pillar and a large, erect phallus. The figure was known as a Herm and represented the god, Hermes. Hermes is often described by commentators rather vaguely as the messenger of the gods but his function in the mythic system is far wider and more complex. For Hermes was also, for example, the god of merchants and thieves, of tricky communication, and the passage from life to death. Indeed, as Kahn has brilliantly shown, Hermes figures in numerous forms of transition and exchange.[46] Hermes is the figure who marks transition and exchange, whether it be the transition of a soul from life to death (he is portrayed on tombs), or the exchange and transition of money between people (hence he is patron of merchants and thieves), or the communicational exchange of words (when silence fell in a conversation, the Athenians said that Hermes was passing; Hermes is a witness to oaths). Hermes travels always in the middle, marking the boundary to be crossed. 'Nothing about him is settled, stable, permanent or restricted or definite. He represents in space and in the human world movement and flow, mutation and transition, contact between foreign elements.'[47] Hermes marks the liminal processes of crossing. *Limen* in Latin means 'doorway' and the statue of the Herm stands by the door to mark the transition from inside to outside, from the public to the private.

Hestia, on the other hand, is the goddess of the hearth (the word *hestia* means 'hearth'). She resides, it goes without saying, in the house. More than that, however, she, the hearth, is the centre of the house: 'sealed in the

---

[44] See Detienne 1979 for a good description of the Thesmophoria in this light. The sacrificial rite, he writes (194), takes place 'in circumstances so particular that they function as a re-emphasis of the marginality of the space of women in the city'.

[45] 1983, Chapter 5, where many examples of this pairing are linked.   [46] 1978, passim.

[47] Vernant 1983, 129.

ground, the circular hearth denotes the navel which ties the home to the earth. It is the symbol and pledge of fixity, immutability and permanence.'[48] If Hermes is constantly on the move, Hestia is permanently fixed, centred. Interestingly, Hestia, like Athene, is also a virgin goddess, who occupies the central place in the house, according to Homer, precisely 'instead of marriage'.[49] This idea can be seen to relate particularly to the role of women in Athenian religious representation and cultural thinking, in a way which furthers our sense of the connection of the inside and the female in the conception of the space of the *oikos*. For if there is one instance where the orientation of the man towards the exterior and the woman towards the interior is reversed, it is in the institution of marriage, where the woman offers the mobile social element. It is the daughter who leaves her household and hearth to become another household's wife and mother, while the man remains tied to his *oikos*. The image of Hestia offers, however, a permanent feminine aspect, while her virginity and refusal of marriage set her apart from the movement of the strange outside woman into the house. 'As she bestows on the house the centre that sets it in space, so Hestia ensures to the domestic group its continued existence in time. It is through Hestia that the family line is perpetuated and remains constant, as though in each new generation the legitimate offspring of the household were born direct "from the hearth".'[50] It is as though Hestia is a way of projecting the indefinite prolongation of the paternal line without the difficulties of introducing the strange woman from another household. 'Hestia thus incarnates ... the tendency of the *oikos* towards self-isolation, withdrawal, as though the ideal for the family should be complete self-sufficiency'[51] – not only economic self-sufficiency, but a self-sufficiency that can bypass the need for the outside woman for the sexual process of reproduction. In this light, the permanence of the virgin Hestia is connected specifically with the desire for the stable continuity of the *oikos* under its male rule, and the undervaluing of women in patrilineal inheritance.

But Hestia does not show quite so simple an aspect, as Vernant makes clear. She also demonstrates the other side of the representation of the female in Athenian thought, that we have seen so often denied or ignored, despite its evident and important role in some religious festivals and ceremonies, namely, the female as the protector and preserver of fertility and abundance. For in order to fulfil her role of ensuring permanence in time, the virgin Hestia is also strangely depicted as if she were a mother, the potential giver of life, like the earth herself, in which Hestia is rooted. Indeed, the image of the female as the source of life, nourishing the fruitfulness of the *oikos* and its land, begins to

[48] Vernant 1983, 128.   [49] Hom. *Hym to Aph.* 29–30.   [50] Vernant 1983, 133.
[51] Vernant 1983, 134.

take shape at the centre of the household.[52] So, in this guise, Hestia is associated with the accumulation of precious objects and food in the household – the opposite of Hermes' association with circulation and exchange – as, indeed, the normal separation of labour in the household associates the male with work outside the home and the woman, the 'good wife', with the collection, arrangement, preservation of the fruits of that toil. Hestia, depending on circumstances, as Vernant has stressed, is 'able to justify either one of these two contradictory images'[53] of woman as nourisher of fruitfulness like mother-earth, and of woman as excluded from the necessary process of generational continuity in the idea of the male as sole agent of procreation. In this double aspect of Hestia, we find once more the uneasy status of women in the civic ideal. The dual image of the goddess at the centre of the house marks the uncertain balance of the projection of the patrilineal, patriarchal autochthony and the projection of the idea of maternal fruitfulness and fecundity. Once again, our discussion of the representation of space leads us back to the representation of the self with which it is intertwined.

Even in this brief analysis of the representation of the couple Hestia and Hermes, we can see now how these figures help to structure the way in which the Athenians conceptualize space and, moreover, the sense of one's place in society with which such thinking is connected. The polarities of the interior and exterior, the static and the mobile, the open and the enclosed, organize the sense of the domestic institution of the *oikos* within the *polis*, even the idea of sexual difference. The Herm that stood by the door, on the tomb, at the crossroads, the hearth to which the man returned each night are the physical marks of the conceptual divisions of public and private, male and female, in the ordering of the *polis* and *oikos*.

There is, then, a strong sense of the separation of public and private, which is important to our idea of how the Athenians thought of themselves as citizens of their *polis*. But it is also in the areas of overlap between *oikos* and *polis*, public and private, that tensions may be seen developing that bear closely on the institution of tragedy. For the ideology of the *oikos* that I have described often fits uneasily with the ideology of the *polis*: the public and private, which should, according to the ideologies in question, be kept separate or at any rate which should constitute a hierarchical continuity of obligations without clash of interests, often seem to be at odds with one another in various ways. For example, the demands made by the democratic city on its citizens in time of war could be seen as working against the interest of the landowning farmer. The fact that the city offered to pay all its soldiers a flat rate in an egalitarian way implied one man's work was the equivalent of another's – but the farmer's

[52] See Vernant 1983, 133ff. for a further discussion of this.   [53] 1983, 145.

work could not be delayed, especially at harvest time, and prolonged campaigns were especially undesirable. Even the very duty of fighting could be depicted also as the sacrifice of the *oikos'* children for the city – a possible source of conflict of interest. Economics, however, (unlike today) were so .much regarded as the province of the *oikos* that 'economic interests were seen as essentially private, egotistic forces opposed to rational policy-making in which only the good of the city as a political entity should be considered'.[54] Throughout the *polis* world, connections between families and kin served to undermine the egalitarian structure of the democratic political system. The very strength of the *polis* ideology, the force with which it is asserted particularly on public occasions, may well attest in itself to the force of the more traditional ties of the household and family. Plato's attempt in the *Republic* totally to suppress the family as an emotional and social unit may have struck most Athenians as outrageous or ridiculous, but it draws on, and attempts to remove, a specific tension in the civic ideology and practice of his native Athens by attempting to ensure for his projected city the total dependence and allegiance of the citizen.

I have considered so far the self-projection of the city through a civic discourse, in particular through the polarized oppositions – and overlap – of public and private, inside and outside, male and female, to discover some sense of how the Athenians developed a notion of citizenship and idea of a citizen's place in the order of things. Before turning to the tragic festival in particular, I wish to stress the connections between two parts of my argument. The first is this: in writing of 'discourse', of 'ideology', I have been focusing not on a strictly physical description of the *polis* (though we have touched on the topics of space, land-holding, the house); nor on the political structure or history of the city in the sense of its institutions of authority, its military or governmental history (though we have discussed the importance of the public realm and the areas of citizen participation). Nor have I investigated the calendar and structure of religious involvement (though certainly the gods and myths and ceremonies have featured in my description); nor have I dealt with the daily life of Athenian inhabitants (although the strength of *oikos* ties has been described). Instead of these sorts of histories or descriptions of the *polis*, examples of which I have included in the bibliographical notes to this chapter, I have concentrated on what Vernant would call the 'structure of social thought', of what Foucault would term 'discursive practice' – the way one's place in the order of things is thought about and organized conceptually. This is because it is through its relations to such norms that tragedy develops its

---

[54] Humphreys 1983, 11. See her Chapter 1 passim for more evidence of a clash of public and private interests in Athens.

particular sense of transgression and its specific attitudes of questioning. Indeed, in the next two chapters, I shall be concerned in particular with two topics in tragedy I have discussed in part in this chapter: relations and relationships in the city, and ideas of sexual difference. The second part of my argument that I wish to recall here is the extraordinary prevalence of the spoken word in Athenian society: not only were the political and legal arenas dominated by speech – and to a certain degree the political and legal arenas dominated city life – but also the private life particularly of Athenian males seems to have revolved a great deal around the exchange of spoken word. We have already mentioned the constant informal exchange of gossip and more serious ideas in the market-place or gymnasium that seems to have formed an important part of Athenian male leisure; also a regular event at citizens' dinner parties seems to have been speech competitions on a particular topic – the best-known example being Plato's dialogue the *Symposium*, where the subject is 'love'; a great part of education, particularly for the upper classes and especially towards the end of the period we are considering consisted in a training in rhetoric and making speeches.[55] Linguistic philosophy starts to be discussed.[56] The spoken word plays an extended and important role that would be hard to underestimate in fifth-century Athens (which is not to ignore the ideological importance of the construction of the many public monuments in the fifth-century *polis*). As much as the civic ideology we have been considering is formed in and through what can be called (in the widest sense) the language of the city, so the exchange of language plays a vital and extended role in the workings of the city. The sense of the city, its order and organization, its boundaries and structure, is formed in language, a language which dominates the various arenas and practices of city life. The city as such is constituted in the media of language. Fifth-century Athens is truly the city of words.

The dramatic festival of the city or Great Dionysia was one of the great occasions in the Athenian year. All business was abandoned; the lawcourts closed and for five or possibly six days the city was given over to the Dionysia.[57] This was the major dramatic festival in the year, and Athens was thronged with visitors as well as the citizen body, who could spend a large portion of the day in the theatre watching the dramas produced. This was a city festival in every sense: the playwrights were chosen and paid by the state, prominent individuals regarded it an honour to fund a chorus and competed to provide the most lavish display. The judges were elected by a complicated

[55] See e.g. Marrou 1956; Kennedy 1963; and below Chapter 6.
[56] Guthrie 1962–81, Vol. III, especially 176ff.; Kerferd 1981, 68–78; Graeser 1977; and see below, Chapter 9.
[57] Pickard-Cambridge 1968, 63–7. Allen 1938.

system of lots, as befitted the democracy, and the competition for prizes, as befitted Athenian society, was fiercely conducted, and attended to. The audience consisted of a vast number[58] of Athenians and foreigners, who, if the anecdotes passed down about them are true, could be a passionate, intense, and quickly moved or dissatisfied audience.[59] A play about the historical event of the Persian sack of Miletus, an act the Athenians failed to prevent, so moved the audience that the author, Phrynichus, was fined and the play banned. There are tales of actors being booed and whistled off stage for mis-pronunciations, or other misdemeanours. The frequency with which notorious lines of tragedy are quoted elsewhere in comedy or prose writings indicates something of the instant effect of the shocking or scandalous on the Athenian audience – as do the tales of prosecution, riot or miscarriages that have been passed down as examples of audience reaction.[60]

The festival itself consisted also of processions and sacrifices of some considerable seriousness, and much eating, drinking and party-holding of perhaps less seriousness: 'For the Athenians the great Dionysia was an occasion to stop work, drink a lot of wine, eat some meat, and witness or participate in the various ceremonials, processions and priestly doings which are part of such holidays the world over.'[61] The festival, unlike theatre today, involved the majority of the city – even some women and children, notwith-standing the disbelief of 'pious' Victorian scholars, seem to have attended the tragedies and comedies.[62]

The festival was truly a civic occasion, then. This could not be more strongly emphasized than by the ceremonies that during the period of Athenian supremacy took place after the opening sacrifice and before the performances. Before the tragedies began, first the names of the citizens on whom the special honour of a crown had been bestowed for civic duties were read out before the whole audience. To be so proclaimed before such a vast gathering of citizens was a considerable honour. Then the tribute collected from the dependent states of the Athenian empire was divided into 'talents' – a large weight of bullion – and solemnly deposited in the orchestra of the theatre. Before the city and its guests, the importance of Athens as an international force was displayed. Third, the orphans whose fathers had been killed in battle and who had been educated by the state and had now reached

---

[58] Taplin 1977, 10 suggests 15,000; Pickard-Cambridge 1968, 263, suggests 14,000–17,000. Haigh's figure of 20,000 may be too large.

[59] See Haigh 1907, 343–8; Pickard-Cambridge 1968, 272ff.

[60] See Pickard-Cambridge 1968, 272ff. for anecdotes of audience reaction.

[61] Taplin 1978. 162. For a critique of Taplin and a fuller discussion of the festival, see Goldhill 1987.

[62] The evidence is varied and disputed. See Haigh 1907, 324–9; Pickard-Cambridge 1968, 263–5. Ribald comedies were deemed unsuitable for Athenian ladies by Victorian gentlemen. See Haigh 1907, 325 n. 2, for examples.

the age of manhood paraded on stage in full hoplite armour. A herald made a speech, proclaiming what the state had done for the boys and announcing that they were now discharged from direct state control and were to adopt the status and obligations of ordinary citizens.[63] This ceremony draws on many themes of the civic ideology I have been outlining in this chapter. It marks the military aspect of the idea of citizenship, the past willingness of citizens to die for their city, and the future military involvement of those now of age to join the ranks; it marks the *polis* as educator and nourisher, as if it were the parents of the individual, in the place of the fathers fallen in battle; it marks the idea of the obligations of the individual to the city, specifically in return for upbringing and education – again as if the city were one's parents; it marks the sense of a citizen being recognized by the city as a citizen – publicly being shown to take on the role of citizen as adult, male, hoplite, and to adopt the obligations associated with such a role. More than anything perhaps, this ceremony demonstrates the public display of the civic ideology here before the city and its guests. Before the dramas, the great festival of the city puts on stage an assertion and display of the strength of the democracy and its civic ideology.

It may seem somewhat surprising after that introduction to consider the nature of the plays that follow. Even in the *Oresteia*, a play often taken to support wholeheartedly a civic ideology, we have already seen the undercutting of the security of communication (here in the city of words) and the questioning of the ideal of Justice (here in the city so proud of its legal innovations as well as its overall democratic justice). We will go on to see throughout this book how a whole series of notions which are important to the city and the development of civic ideology are put through a profound questioning in the dramatic texts. After the opening ceremony with its display of civic power, tragedy explores the problems inherent in the civic ideology. It depicts a crisis of belief not only in people who hold power but also in the very system and relations by which the hierarchies of power obtain. It is not just the power of a dictator that is questioned in Sophocles' *Oedipus Tyrannus*, but also the qualities of pride, ambition, the search for knowledge, certainty, control – characteristics not irrelevant to the fifth-century rationalist ideals. It is not only the qualities of a hero that are questioned in Sophocles' *Ajax* but also the petty wranglings of the contemporary arguments that follow the hero's death.

Indeed, the institution of tragedy seems to flourish precisely over the period in which the democratic city comes into being. As the city itself lives through the tensions of a changing society, tensions between public and private life,

[63] See Stroud 1971 for recent archaeological evidence on this ceremony.

between the old, traditional ways and the new requirements of the new political order, the tragedies produced in the city seem to draw on the vocabulary, issues, and power struggles of that developing civic language. Tragedy's moment, tragedy's force, is in the articulation of the struggles of the city's discourse.

The festival of the Great Dionysia, then, whatever its origins, has a special role in democratic Athens. Before the citizen body, the city's discourse was treated to the radical critique of tragedy, its divisions and tensions were explored. After the tragedies, the satyr play offered the immediate explosive gratification of buffoonery and ribaldry which led to the afternoon's comedy. There, too, in humour the city approached itself through transgression. In the fantastic plots of political and sexual reversal, in the *parabasis* where the comic poet stepped out of line to address his fellow citizens, in the lampooning of political figures, in the free play of obscenity and aggression, we see how the special circumstances of Dionysus' festival offer licence to escape the normal restrictions and delimitations of the ordered social life of the city. In comedy, you can do precisely what is normally not allowed. Although both comedy and tragedy involve Dionysiac freedom, comedy seems to flaunt the rules with more final safety than tragedy. Rather than the tragic conclusions of disso-lution and death, error and disorder, its reversals and overturnings lead more to the other Dionysiac world of eating, drinking and liberated sexuality – pleasures attained, desires fulfilled.

But the two faces of Dionysus form the one festival: the tensions and ambiguities that tragedy and comedy differently set in motion, the tensions and ambiguities that arise in the transition from tragedy to comedy, all fall under the aegis of the one god, the divinity of illusion and change, paradox and ambiguity, release and transgression. Unlike the displays of civic rhetoric we have seen in such set pieces as Pericles' funeral speech over the citizens fallen in war, the Great Dionysia, Dionysus' festival for the city, offers a full range of Dionysiac transgression from the intellectually and emotionally powerful and dangerous tragedy, through ironic and subtle questioning, to the obscene, scatological uproarious comedy. The drama festival offers not just the powers and profundity of a great literature but also the extraordinary process of the developing city putting its own developing language and structures of thought at risk under the sway of the smiling and dangerous Dionysus.

4 · RELATIONS AND RELATIONSHIPS

> If I had the choice between betraying my country and betraying my friend I
> hope I should have the courage to betray my country.
>
> E. M. FORSTER

In the last two chapters I have considered first how a series of terms concerned
with civic order and relations within the city is placed at risk in the tragic
arena, and secondly, in more general terms, how the city itself constitutes a
specific ideology as well as a specific social organization. Now in this chapter I
am going to investigate a particularly important system of ideas concerned
with relations between people in the city and family, a system which is
especially difficult for the modern reader to determine, namely, the notions
constituting and surrounding the adjectives *philos* and *ekhthros*. I have left
these terms untranslated as yet because part of the problem for the modern
reader is the extensive semantic range of these and related terms, not just in
the way that words in different languages are rarely coextensive in connotation, but also in the way that the force and direction of usage in this case are
so varied. In much the same manner as one can say in English 'Shoshana loves
ice-cream' and 'Juliet loves Romeo' to imply with the same word quite a
different force and direction of emotion, so *philos* is a common term of address
between the characters of a Platonic dialogue, where it is often translated 'my
dear fellow' and the like, but at the same time *philos* is also used in the *Oresteia*
to indicate the emotional relationship between Clytemnestra and her adul-
terer, Aegisthus, which Orestes despises and puts as a cause of her necessary
death when he cries 'Die then, and sleep beside him, since he is the man you
love (*philein*) / and he who you should have loved (*philein*) got only your hate'
(*Cho.* 906–7).

As is clear from the above, one dictionary definition of the verb *philein* is
'love', apparently in the sexual or psychological sense that 'love' may be used
today. Indeed, since the normal Homeric Greek for sexual intercourse is
philoteti migenai 'to mix together in love' (*philotes*, a noun formed from *philos*)
and *philema* (another noun formed from *philos*) means 'kiss', it is clear that
this sexual sense is woven into the semantic range of the term. But to suggest
that as a form of address *philos*, 'my dear chap', is somehow a weakened form

of the heady expressions of love (as one might with the sentence 'Shoshana loves ice-cream') would be seriously to distort the sense of the term *philos*. It might be more apposite to compare the meaning in a Victorian context of a sentence such as 'a daughter should love her father', where the connotations of 'duty', 'propriety', and 'devotion' with a backing of religious conviction come closer to many uses of the term *philos* and its opposite *ekhthros*. For as we will see, the values of these terms of sentiment cannot be separated from a range of social concepts and there is no English word or institution which can express the range of relationships implied.

To begin an investigation of these terms, I shall first have to go back to Homer (as so often in any study of Greek literature) and in this case I shall be following the guidance of the brilliant French scholar of linguistics E. Benveniste.[1] He begins by noting that in Homer all the vocabulary of moral terminology is strongly permeated with a force that is not personal but *relational*. What we often take as psychological or ethical vocabulary indicates rather a series of relations between the individual and the members of his group. This can be interestingly seen in the close connection made in Homer between the adjectives *philos* and *aidoios*, which often occur as a linked doublet in Homeric diction, as do the corresponding verbs *philein* and *aideisthai* and nouns *philotes* and *aidos*. Now the noun *aidos* is normally translated 'respect', 'shame', or 'reverence', and it is used particularly with regard to the proper attitudes to take towards members of one's own family or group. When a member of the group is in some way threatened or attacked by another member, it is *aidos*, 'shame', which may be appealed to both to prevent the outrage, and, if the outrage has taken place, to rally the other members of the group to assert its collective morality in revenge. In the wider context of the community at large *aidos* expresses a notion of the suitable maintenance and expression of the hierarchical bonds of association: 'Within a much larger community, *aidos* defines the sentiment felt by superiors towards their inferiors (regard, pity, mercy, sympathy in misfortunes etc.) as well as honour, loyalty, collective propriety, the prohibition of certain acts, of certain modes of behaviour – and it develops finally to the several senses of "modesty" and "shame".'[2]

The close connection between *philos* and this notion of respect, reverence helps to gloss in particular the relational aspect of the term *philos*: 'Relatives, "in-laws", servants, friends, all those who are linked by reciprocal duties of *aidos* are called *philoi*.'[3] *Philos* is used to indicate people linked by a bond of

---

[1] 1973. Some of Benveniste's conclusions were anticipated by Adkins 1963.
[2] Benveniste 1973, 278.
[3] Ibid.

'respect' in the community and here clearly implies a wider notion than one purely of sentiment.

The term *xenos* can help in a similar way to show how *philos* is concerned with reciprocal relations in society. *Xenia*, the bond between a *xenos* and a *xenos*, is an extremely important notion in Greek society of all periods. *Xenos* means both 'guest' and 'host' (a problem of translation in English, though less so in French where *hôte* has a similar sense); *xenia* is the regulated tie of 'guest-friendship' between stranger and householder. This is not just a question of polite rules between people, but an essential functioning of ancient society. The condition of a man in a foreign country or city, away from his friends and own family, was one of considerable risk. For 'human beings have no rights *qua* human beings in Homer, only in virtue of some definite relationship'.[4] The man away from his *oikos*, without rights, was without all protection and without any means of livelihood. The appeal to *xenia* was his only manner of proceeding, and a tie of *xenia* was passed on between families throughout generations. In a famous scene in the *Iliad*, two warriors, Glaucus and Diomedes, are about to fight when through the proud exchange of names and titles they discover that they have an inherited bond of *xenia* from their grandparents and thus instead of exchanging blows they exchange armour on the battlefield as a reassertion of that bond – an exchange that becomes legendary for its foolishness on Glaucus' part, since his armour was gold and Diomedes' was bronze and worth far less. But their tie of *xenia* proves stronger on the battlefield than their military opposition in war.

The exchange of gifts between *xenos* and *xenos* is the visible instantiation of the ties of reciprocity, and the collecting of such gifts is one of the distinguishing marks of the Homeric world, particularly as viewed through the travels of Odysseus in the *Odyssey*. Indeed, the theme of the treatment of guests[5] is played through many variations in that epic from the Cyclops' ironic offer to Odysseus that for a guest-gift he should be eaten last, to Odysseus' appearance as a disguised guest in his own house. The treatment of a *xenos* functions as a criterion between the different societies Odysseus visits, as his own playing of various guest roles goes toward the development of his character.

There are many close verbal links between *philos* and *xenos* and between the verbs *philein* and *xenizein*. Indeed, *philein*, which we have been translating as 'love', 'feel affection for', 'be friendly to', often has to be translated as 'play the role of host', 'give proper treatment to a guest'.[6] So Benveniste writes 'the notion of *philos* expresses the behaviour incumbent on a member of the

---

[4] Adkins 1963, 33.   [5] Cf. Stewart 1976, passim.
[6] Cf. e.g. *Il.* 3.207, 6.15; *Od.* 8.208, 4.29.

community towards a *xenos*, the "guest-stranger" '.[7] Indeed, Benveniste has argued further that this relation of reciprocity between a *xenos* and *xenos* is the basic institutional foundation of the notion of *philos*. So, to be 'loved' of the gods is to be shown the regards and favours due to a *philos*, and we see the reciprocity of a military truce called a *philotes* (*Il.* 3.94) and accompanied with solemn exchange of vows and sacrifices. So the 'kiss' (*philema*) is a kiss first of recognition, greeting and acceptance. The notion of *philos* goes far beyond the sentiment of love or friendship. Indeed, as Adkins writes,[8] *philos* 'need not be accompanied by any friendly feelings at all'.

Philos, then, in these links with *aidos* and *xenos*, marks the close links between the head of the household and strangers as well as the members of the extended family itself. The mutual relationship entails a certain form of affection or at any rate a certain form of 'affectionate action' which is obligatory between two *philoi*, and thus there may grow an emotional colouring to the term *philos* through which a sense of feeling may develop beyond the bounds of the institution. The appellation *philos* is applied by the master of the house to all relations living in his *oikos*, and it is especially applied to his wife, who has been brought in as a stranger, as an object of exchange. Indeed, *philos* is one of the commonest adjectives applied in the Homeric poems to words for 'spouse', but 'dear', its usual translation, scarcely renders its connotations. The young girl who is given by her father to the young husband is a sign and means of a relation of reciprocity between households, and is a newcomer to her husband's household and family. As such, the term *philos* marks not only the tie of affection between husband and wife, but also the bonds and agreements of a social interaction.

Philos, then, may be summed up from these usages as a way of marking a person's position in society by his relationships.[9] The appellation or categorization *philos* is used to mark not just affection but overridingly a series of complex obligations, duties and claims. Although in fourth-century Greek, say, it may develop towards a more general notion of friendship or love that Dover describes as the 'affection strong or weak which can be felt for a sexual partner, a child, an old man, a friend or colleague',[10] in Homer it seems to have this wealth of connotations and expressiveness, and in fifth-century Athens, as we will see, it is a term closely involved with the development of a civic discourse, precisely because of the shifting of a person's sense of position in society and the shifting of relationships in the development of the fifth-century *polis*.[11] Rather than translating *philos* differently in the many

---

[7] Benveniste 1973, 288.   [8] 1963, 36. See also Hands 1968, 26–48, especially 33.
[9] Benveniste also argues conclusively against the common translation of 'one's own' for some uses of *philos* in Homer. See especially 275ff.
[10] 1974, 212.   [11] See Connor 1971, 3–136.

places that it will be referred to in the following discussion, I shall transliterate it in order to maintain some sense of this 'complex network of associations, some with institutions of hospitality, other with usages of the home, still others with emotional behaviour'.[12]

An *ekhthros*, as I have said, is the opposite of a *philos* – an 'enemy'. As much as *philos* implies positive ties and obligations, *ekhthros* implies equally binding requirements to be disobliging. This relationship may perhaps seem difficult for a 'modern mind' to conceive. Dover remarks 'while few of us nowadays can expect that no-one will ever deliberately do us harm, few of us expect to be involved for long in a relationship deserving the name of enmity, and a man who spoke of "my enemies" could fairly be suspected of paranoia'[13] – and that from a man well versed in academic politics! In Athens, however, *ekhthros* indicates a personal enemy (rather than an enemy in war), and such hatred is taken very much for granted as a fact of life. Like a bond of *philos*, enmity can be inherited through the generations, and long-standing feuds with accompanying provocation and retaliation can be discerned in many of the speeches from surviving law-cases. Indeed, such enmity was not only rarely disguised but also brazenly flaunted. Athene herself expresses to Odysseus in Sophocles' *Ajax* a far from strange or unpleasant sentiment when she says 'But to laugh at your enemies (*ekhthros*), what sweeter laughter can there be than that?' (79). *Philos* and *ekhthros*, then, are key terms for expressing in Greek the conjunctions and disjunctions of social intercourse, the interplay of relationships between people.

Now one of the main reasons why *philos* may be thought to retain a good deal of its force as a word involving a series of connotations concerning obligations is the fact that it is constantly used as a term in moral discussions or judgements. Aristotle in a famous and lengthy section of his *Nicomachean Ethics* attempts a definition of the word,[14] and in Plato's *Republic* the search for the just city starts as a matter of course from discussion and criticism of the position that justice is to be conceived of as doing good to one's *philos* and bad to one's *ekhthros*. For unlike any Judaeo-Christian notion of loving one's neighbour or turning the other cheek, perhaps the most basic and generally agreed position with regard to correct behaviour in the ancient world was 'to love one's friend and to hate one's enemy', that is, *philein philous ekhthairein ekhthrous*. The principle is seen throughout the range of Greek writing and is certainly not limited either to philosophical debate or to popular morality. Indeed, it is often an assumed common point in verbal exchanges in the tragedies I am considering in this book. For example, as Electra is preparing to offer prayer at the tomb of Agamemnon in the *Choephoroi*, she is concerned

[12] Benveniste 1973, 288.   [13] 1974, 181.   [14] Books 8 and 9 (1155a3ff.).

as to whether it is pious to pray for revenge (122). The chorus reply 'How could it not be pious to repay your *ekhthros* with evil?' (123). The chorus' assumption of the morality of 'do good to your *philos*, do bad to your *ekhthros*' offers for them a simple and direct justification of the prayer for revenge. At the same time, however, such a justification fails to take into account the fact that Clytemnestra is Electra's mother and thus must be treated as a *philos* by her daughter. Much of the build-up towards the matricide is concerned with the necessary redefinition of Clytemnestra as a possible *ekhthros* and impossible *philos*. For it is in strife within the family that the possible tensions in the traditional moral position are most clearly seen. At what point can members of one's own family cease to be *philos*?

At the extremely dramatic moment of tension before the matricide, Orestes asks 'Pylades, what am I to do? Am I to feel shame (*aidos*) to kill my mother?'. Is it possible not to feel *aidos* for one's mother and thus not treat her as a *philos*? Pylades answers with the only lines he speaks, which, as Kitto comments, come 'with the effect of a thunderclap':[15] 'What then becomes thereafter of the oracles declared by Apollo at Delphi? What of trusted oaths? Count all hateful (*ekhthros*) rather than the gods.' In answer to Orestes' question about *aidos*, Pylades offers a hierarchy of the relations of *philos* and *ekhthros*: the gods have priority. It is better to treat all, including your mother, as *ekhthros* rather than the gods. The tie of *philos* between mother and child is to be overcome. Thus the agents of matricide authorize themselves or are authorized by the divine. It is in the following speech, Orestes' acceptance of Pylades' pronouncement, that we read the lines that I have already quoted in this chapter, though now the insufficiency of the translation 'love' will be clear: 'Die then, and sleep beside him since he is the man you love (*philein*) / and he whom you should have loved (*philein*) got only your hate' (906–7). Following Pylades' authorization of the matricide in terms of *philos* and *ekhthros*, Orestes stresses the corruption of the ties of *philos* that his mother's adultery constitutes, her corruption of her social position and obligations as a wife – as he himself is forced to transgress that tie of *philos* between mother and son in order to rectify her transgression. Such are the paradoxical reversals of the tragic text of the *Oresteia* as the language of kinship attempts to deal with the family at war with itself.

It is interesting in this light to recall the recognition scene which follows Electra's prayer for revenge. Recognition plays an extremely important function in society and language. The systems of categorization of kinship, morality, social exchange depend on recognition not just in the epistemological sense that recognition is an inherent part of any process of categorization,

[15] 1961, 86.

but also in the more normative sense that a father recognizes a child as his own, or a state recognizes some institution's authority: recognition is also a process of legitimizing. It is not, then, by chance that in the tragic texts which so often revolve around uncertainty as to the legitimacy of particular relationships or obligations in the sphere of family relations and civic duties we see so many 'recognition scenes'. For these scenes – regarded by Aristotle as one of the two most powerful types of scene in tragic plots (*Poet.* 1450a32–4) – dramatize not just the moment of a sentimental rediscovery of a family member, but also the reaffirmation of the legitimacy or obligations of a particular tie. As much as the tragic texts seem so often to challenge the position of an individual in society, so the 'recognition scene' in different ways in different plays reasserts a relationship between people. Recognition is always of a *philos*, of a tie between *philos* and *philos*. As Clytemnestra must be redefined as an *ekhthros* through Electra's prayer and the following scenes of the *Choephoroi*, so we see the significance of the recognition scene between Electra and Orestes as reasserting a particular family tie between the children, set against the doubts and uncertainties surrounding their relationships with their parents. And as we have seen in Chapter 2, these family struggles lead towards the trial before the city's elders and the institutions of civic justice. *Philos* and *philia*, the bond between a *philos* and *philos*, as they mark relations of reciprocity and respect in the family and city, are constantly in play with the wider markings of the discourse of power and authority in society.

The texts of Sophocles often revolve around tensions in the morality of 'do good to your *philos* and do bad to your *ekhthros*', as indeed they regularly focus on conflicting claims of obligation in terms of *philos* and *ekhthros*. The *Ajax*, for example, opens with the situation of the hero Ajax having turned against the Greek army for whom he was previously a tower of strength, because they voted the honour of the prize of the arms of Achilles to Odysseus in preference to himself. With the sword of his erstwhile enemy, Hector, he has gone on the rampage, only to be tricked of his plan to kill the commanders of the Greek army by Athene, who has distorted his sense of sight. Ajax's consort, Tecmessa, explains the situation to the chorus of men from Ajax's ships, and she exhorts them to try and help their lord if they can; for he may listen to *philoi* (330). But as Ajax comes back to his wits, he decides his only recourse to preserve his honour and self-esteem is suicide. His reasoning is worth noting (457–69):

> And now Ajax – what is to be done now?
> I am hated (*ekhth-*) by the gods, that's plain, the Greek camp detests me.
> Troy and the ground I stand upon detest (*ekhth-*) me.
> Shall I go, then, from this place where the ships ride,

> desert the Atreidae, and cross the Aegean to my home?
> But when I'm there
> what countenance can I show to my father, Telamon? . . .
> . . . Shall I rush against the walls of Troy . . .
> join with them all in single combat, do
> some notable exploit and find my death in it?
> But that might give some comfort to the sons of Atreus . . .

He sees his position as being an *ekhthros* to all. Athene's prevention of the success of his plan of murder marks clearly his position with regard to the divine; his plan itself was a sign of his hatred of the Greeks who had dishonoured him, and now that his plan has been made clear, he is himself matched with reciprocated enmity; and the Trojans against whom he has been fighting are in no way to be termed *philos*. Ajax, as well as being deprived of honour, has been deprived of the relationships of support and sustenance by which his position of honour in society was determined. He cannot even kill himself by killing Trojans lest it should in some way help his *ekhthroi*, the Atreidae – do good to your friends, but always harm your enemies.

Tecmessa in the moving speech which follows not only marks the total dependence of the family and community on the head of the household, but also shows the interrelations of terms of the dependence. For she appeals to her man to 'revere (*aidos*) your father . . . and revere (*aidos*) your mother'. The restraint she urges in the appeal to *aidos* also stresses the force of the mutual relations of *philia* between members of the household and particularly between the head of the household and his *oikos*. It is such ties that Ajax rejects.

In the famous 'deception' scene, Ajax appears to have relented, as in a speech constructed around a series of highly ambiguous statements he reflects on the changeability of things in a way quite alien to his previously obdurate attitude. The concluding section of this reflection concerns precisely the limits of the rigid opposition of *philos* and *ekhthros* (678–82):

> . . . Have I not learnt this,
> only so much to hate (*ekhth-*) my enemy (*ekhthros*)
> as though he might again become my friend (*phil-*),
> and so much good to wish to do my friend (*philos*),
> as knowing he may not always stay so.

These lines echo Odysseus' earlier unwillingness to laugh at his *ekhthros* (121–6), and look forward, as we will see, to the final scenes of the play where the correct attitude towards an enemy is what is at stake. Despite (or perhaps because of) this insight into the changeability of things, Ajax is next seen on stage alone and about to kill himself. It is extremely rare in our extant tragedies for a chorus to leave the stage in the course of a play, and this is the only occasion that I know of in our corpus of plays in which a mortal blow is struck on stage. For all the bloody and murderous stories of Greek myth that make up the stuff of Attic drama, in tragedy violence is verbal. The solitude of Ajax, as he turns his sword inward on himself, matches his desertion of the external ties of *aidos* and *philia*, as he has been rejected by the enmity of his surroundings. The self-destruction of Ajax is the concluding act of the stripping of the relations by which his self was defined.

The final scenes of the play are concerned with the treatment of Ajax's corpse. The body of an *ekhthros* may be tossed aside unburied for the dogs and birds to eat, whereas proper burial is the due care of *philoi*. Time and again in the *Iliad* the Greeks and Trojans fight over a corpse, and the final scenes of that epic are Priam's mission to recover from Achilles the mutilated corpse of his son, Hector, and bury it. Teucer, Ajax's brother, is the defender of his *philos* in the face of the Greek leaders. First, Menelaus, outraged that Ajax has turned out to be a worse enemy (*ekhth-*) than the Trojans (1054–5), exchanges violent words with Teucer, and then Agamemnon with an authoritarian argument demands obedience to his supreme command. Into this deadlocked debate Odysseus, who was previously Ajax's worst enemy, injects his own brand of rhetoric. Appealing all the while to his bond of *philia* with Agamemnon (e.g. 1327–8, 1351, 1353), he sets a series of moral qualities above the rigidity of opposition of *philos* and *ekhthros*. For him Ajax was 'good' (1345), 'noble' (1355), 'great' (1357) and these qualities outweigh his enmity. Finally, Agamemnon agrees (1371) out of respect for his *philos*, Odysseus, to let happen precisely what he said he would not let happen – namely, to allow the body to be buried. But he leaves it in no doubt how he regards Ajax (1372–3):

> But as for him, whether on earth or in the underworld
> he will be nonetheless the most hated (*ekhth-*) to me

Agamemnon will not accept any shifting in the way he terms Ajax but none the less changes his attitude to him. He no longer must do harm to even this most *ekhthros* man. The interchange between Agamemnon and Odysseus, then, not only marks Odysseus' undercutting of the rigid determination of the opposition of *philos* and *ekhthros*, but also introduces an uncertainty into the rigid application of the moral position of 'Do harm to your *ekhthros* and good to your *philos*.' And this argument takes place between two men professing the greatest *philia* for one another as a basis for their exchange of views!

The final irony of this play remains, however. Odysseus, professing his change of attitude towards Ajax, requests to be allowed to help with the burial as a *philos*. But Teucer, while recognizing Odysseus as an unexpected and necessary benefactor, will not allow his assistance in the rite. For it may not be wanted by the dead man. Teucer will not accept on Ajax's behalf the shifting of *philia*, even though he calls Odysseus a good and noble man – the very terms by which Odysseus avoided the rigidity of determination of *philos* and *ekhthros* and procured the permission for burial. Odysseus replies with touching simplicity 'Well, I wanted to . . . But if it isn't *philos* to you for me to do this, I'll go, respecting your decision' (1400–1). *Philos* is here normally translated 'pleasing', 'dear', but after the debate concerning the implications of precisely *philos* and *ekhthros* and considering its use as a criterion for permission to take part in the burial rites (cf. 1413–14), it sounds an ironic echo of the doubts and changeability of its sense, particularly in juxtaposition to Teucer's refusal of Odysseus' offer of *philia*. The apparent simplicity of *philos* here ironically recalls the complexities of its meanings and implications in the play. The close of the play rather than reconciling all the strands and oppositions of *philos* and *ekhthros* ends in ironic juxtaposition and a recollection of the fracturing and dislocation of any traditional certainty as to the sense and force of the terms.

I have attempted to show, then, in these very broad outlines how a concern for the sense of *philos* and *ekhthros* is an essential dynamic of the *Ajax*. For the remainder of this chapter, I intend to look in more detail at these terms in the *Antigone*, which will offer us a further insight into the specific fifth-century nature of the workings of tragedy and the importance of *philos* and *ekhthros* as terms defining the individual's role in society.

Since Hegel's reading of the play, it has been difficult not to consider the text of the *Antigone* in terms of dialectic and opposition. Even critics who have added important qualifications to Hegel's interpretation have felt, like Reinhardt, that conflict in this play 'emerges finally as a kind of "dialectic" in spite of everything'.[16] The arguments between Creon and Antigone have been seen as struggles of right against right, idea against idea, individual against society, family against state, feminine against masculine, divine law against secular order, or, to give Reinhardt's formulation, 'on the one side, we have what is to our way of thinking a very diverse collection – family, cult, love for one's brother, divine command, youthfulness and unselfishness to the point of self-sacrifice; and on the other side, imperiousness, the maxims of the state, the morality of the *polis*, pettiness, rigidity, narrowness of heart, the blindness of age, insistence on the letter of the law to the point of breaking a divine commandment'.[17] As we will see, many of the terms of Reinhardt's descrip-

---

[16] 1979, 66.
[17] 1979, 65. See Rosivach 1979; Hogan 1972 for extended treatments of the world of Creon and the world of Antigone. See also Knox 1964, 76–90; Musurillo 1967, 37–60.

tion will need some modification, but already the juxtaposition of, say, 'unselfishness to the point of self-sacrifice' and the 'blindness of age' could itself be set in opposition to another juxtaposition of 'the self-destructiveness of youthful excess' and 'the wisdom of age overturned by fate and circumstance' which is how some other critics have characterized the clash of Antigone and Creon. It is difficult, in other words, to read the *Antigone* without making not only moral judgements but the sort of one-sided moral judgements that the play itself seems to want to mark as leading to tragedy. Indeed, as one could see from D. A. Hester's catalogue[18] of many such judgements with their proposers and opposers, to write a history of the interpretations of the *Antigone* would itself rapidly approach the questions of dialectic and opposition, authority and challenge![19]

The tendency of critical judgements to mirror the distorted and distorting idealisms of the play is given an extra twist for twentieth-century readers by the story of Anouilh's version of *Antigone*. This apparently subversive work was given permission to be performed in Paris during the German occupation of the Second World War, since Creon's appeals to law and order were thought sufficiently appealing by the authorities. Where politics and literature are so intertwined it becomes difficult to read without implicating oneself in the dialectic. It is always interesting to see for which readers Antigone is a noble idealist, a defender of individual liberties, a misguided, hysterical woman, an instrument of fate . . .

In choosing to approach the complexities of this play's debates through the notions of *philos* and *ekhthros*, which may seem at first sight a somewhat narrow opening to such poetry, I am aware that there is an apparent claim to approach the play through a Greek conceptual system rather than nineteenth-century metaphysics. It is true that I hope to avoid talking in terms of the clash of Will and Will or Idea and Idea, words which seem today to have less purchase on the fifth century B.C. But this is not to say that through such an approach a homogeneous, univocal response of the Original Audience can be reached or postulated. As much as critics of the past centuries cannot but be implicated in the dialectic of the play's dislocations and tensions, so it would appear that the postulation of a uniform body, The Audience, with a univocal response cannot but mirror Creon's and Antigone's and Haemon's assertions of the support of the whole city in their actions. Can the appeal to what The Audience (The City, The People) must have felt or believed be more than a gesture of appropriation to support a critical view? Why should a critic want to

[18] 1971, passim. He notes that while it was normal to leave a traitor's body unburied, the body would normally be left beyond the boundaries of one's own territory to avoid pollution. The tensions of the play are emphasized by having Polyneices' body left on the land of the city.
[19] For one form of such a history, see now Steiner 1984.

assume that Athenian society of the fifth century was so lacking in internal tensions, so without differences, so without the interplay of social forces that faced with a play which depicts a complex challenge to the order of things it would react, unlike so many critics since, with common accord and recognition? Is it inevitable that Sophocles' questioning of human certainty, authority, and knowledge should merely give rise to critics' assertions of certainty, authority, knowledge?

It is, then, more to determine the terms in which judgement might have been made than to decide on the judgement or judgements reached that I approach the play through the language of *philos* and *ekhthros*. As we saw in the *Ajax*, while *philos* and *ekhthros* may imply a moral imperative, the force, direction and application of that imperative may be far from fixed or certain.

The opening speech of Antigone immediately marks her concern with *philos* and *ekhthros*. Her address to Ismene in the first line strongly emphasizes the family connection. She uses a strengthened form of the word for sister, 'very sister', 'sister with the same mother and father', and an adjective implying both this joint link and also a common bond of interest through kinship. The translation of Jebb 'Ismene, my sister, mine own dear sister' captures the stress more than Wyckoff's 'my sister, my Ismene'. Antigone concludes her emotional questions to Ismene with 'Or don't you know that the foes' (*ekhthros*) trouble comes upon our friends (*philos*)' (9–10). Creon's proclamation is expressed by Antigone precisely in terms of its treatment of *philos* and *ekhthros*.

Ismene's response is interesting. Picking up Antigone's use of *philos*, she says first that she has had no news of their *philoi*, since the loss of their two brothers, Polyneices and Eteocles, who killed each other in combat the day before. This would appear to imply the tie of blood linking the four children of Oedipus as *philoi*, the claim which Antigone will go on to make regularly. But Ismene continues 'And since the Argive army went away this very night, I have no further news of fortune or disaster for myself.' The Argive army refers to the force led by Polyneices which was besieging the city. Her reference to the opposing military forces after her mention of her brother implies the wider political scenario of enemies and allies in which the family of Oedipus is involved. She widens the possible connotations of Antigone's 'news about *philoi*' away from the family alone.

As the argument between the two sisters proceeds, this juxtaposition of family ties and city politics is developed. Ismene's first reaction to Antigone's plan is the surprised question (44):

Do you actually mean to bury him, when the city's forbidden it?

To which Antigone replies (45–6):

> My brother and yours, though you wish he were not.
> I shall never be found to be his traitor.

The term 'traitor', so often applied in the circumstances of the city in war is used in relation to what is hers and Ismene's, their brother. This tie Antigone opposes to the authority of the city. Ismene adds to her argument the dictates of the commander, their uncle, Creon (47):

> Ah! Too bold! When Creon has forbidden it?

But Antigone again places what is her own above the word of the king (48):

> It is not for him to keep me from my own.

In my discussion of the Homeric sense of *philos*, I argued that *philos* was used to express the relations of the individual with regard to the society of the *oikos*, or between *oikos* and *oikos*, or between man and god. These relations were closely involved with the notion of the individual Homeric hero, the household head, and with the establishment of the self-reliant *oikos* as the socio-economic unit *par excellence* of the Homeric world. It is in this sense of self-reliance that Antigone can appeal to what is hers and to a freedom to ignore a centralized, democratic or autocratic authority. As Achilles in the *Iliad* is at liberty simply to down arms and refuse to fight, or as Telemachus when he calls the council of Ithaca at the beginning of the *Odyssey*, is convening for only the first time in nearly twenty years this conglomeration of family heads, so Antigone asserts her dependence on her own, her own relationships, her own power, her own authority. It is not simply – though to a good degree – a question of kin and family, so much as a question of the individual, the self, in society. For what Ismene places against Antigone's basis of action in a long speech of persuasion (49–68) is the self-destructive inwardness of their particular family, the dependence of women on the authority of men, and the need to obey those in authority – a network of relations beyond the simple definition of 'one's own' which suggests quite a different positioning for the sisters. For Ismene, to be a woman in the city is to be set in a range of dependent relationships.

As we will see, this is the first of a series of challenges to Antigone's self-reliance. For in democratic Athens, an essential demand of the ideology of city life is the mutual interdependence of *citizens*. I emphasize 'citizens' because with that term comes a host of assumptions and qualifications lacking in the Homeric poems. As we saw in the previous chapter, and will see again from a different perspective in Chapter 6, the individual man is related to other men in the city in ways quite alien to any Homeric ethos:[20] fighting together in the hoplite citizen army, voting together in policy and legal matters, taking part in community religious expressions, having communal social ties which cross simple family groupings. So Pericles is made to say in Thucydides: 'we do not say that a man who takes no interest in the affairs of the city is a man who minds his own business, we say that he has no business here at all' (2.40). Being a part of the city requires taking part in a wide range of corporate activities and obligations.

Antigone, however, in her self-reliance speaks and behaves more like a Homeric hero. Moreover, the duty of care for the body of a dead relative is duty especially for female kin throughout the Greek world. For this reason in particular, Lefkowitz writes 'Sophocles' audience would have seen Antigone's action as courageous, laudable, but risky . . . and certainly within the bounds of acceptable female behaviour.'[21] Lefkowitz, like Antigone, has to repress the fact that Polyneices is an enemy of the city – and what the status of enemy implies in and for the city. Indeed Ismene, although she will come to admire her sister and claim a part in her deed, challenges Antigone's attitudes and plan from precisely such a different social perspective which includes a recognition of the obligations of civic life and the dependent status of women. Because Antigone rejects what constitutes the position of a woman in the city, Hester, for example, suggests that a straightforward approval of Antigone must be excluded from an ancient audience's reaction,[22] and MacKay can write 'The question at issue between Creon and Antigone is not what constitutes piety but what constitutes citizenship.'[23] In the paradoxical tensions of this play where a brother can be enemy, where the heroic past and contemporary world clash, the various attempts to find a univocal audience reaction or univocal reading seem merely to repeat one strand of the text. How can such over-simplifications of both Audience Response and the problems of reading to do justice to the complexities of this drama?

Indeed, Antigone in her reply to Ismene's argument seems to mark the strangeness of her attitude with a ready acceptance of death[24] and an oxymoronic recognition of her 'holy crime' (72–4):

> . . . For me, the doer, death is best.
> Friend (*philos*) shall I lie with him, yes, friend (*philos*) with friend,
> when I have dared the crime of piety.

---

[20] See Forrest 1966, Davies 1978 for the rise of this sense of life in the city and its precedents in the Homeric world.
[21] 1983, 52.   [22] 1971, 22–3.   [23] 1962, 166.
[24] Daube 1972, 9 writes of Antigone's attitude: 'I would not have allowed her to drive me though I am fond of lifts.'

'Friend' is quite clearly insufficient here as a translation. Antigone is claiming an obligatory and joint relationship with her brother. It is as kin to Polyneices and in performing the duty of kin, particularly female kin, by completing the burial that Antigone is to be determined *philos*. Significantly, Ismene also rejects the dishonour to her brother but further says 'But to act against the citizens. I cannot.' For her, the authority of the citizen body cannot be outweighed by their ties to a brother. So Antigone retorts (80–1):

> That's your protection. Now I go to pile
> the burial mound for him, my dearest (most *philos*) brother.

The relationship with her brother is for Antigone the most *philos*, the bond of *philia* which cannot be passed over.

The last exchange of this scene stresses these conflicting claims of *philia* around which their debate has turned. Ismene has doubted once more that there is any point in Antigone's aim. Antigone retorts (93–4):

> If that's your saying, I shall hate (*ekhth-*) you first
> and next the dead will hate (*ekhth-*) you in all justice . . .

It is as if Antigone is implying that even to disagree with her attitude towards a *philos* is to make one an *ekhthros* (even though Ismene is a sister as much as Polyneices is a brother). The tendency towards binary opposition, always easy in Greek thought and syntax,[25] is especially marked in this polarizing language of *philos* and *ekhthros*. Ismene responds (98–9):

> Go, since you want to. But know this: you go
> senseless indeed, but loved (*philos*) by those who love you (*philos*).

Once again, the insufficiency of the translator's rendering of *philos* is patent. The emphatic last phrase of this scene is 'to those who are *philos* you are rightly, properly *philos*'. That is, Antigone is in a proper sense fulfilling her obligations of *philia* to those who are her *philoi*. Ismene, after Antigone's threat of enmity even of the dead, and her own refusal to help, and despite her belief that Antigone is 'senseless', asserts ironically enough that Antigone is in a strict sense (*orthos* is used of the correct application or the correct meaning of the word)[26] behaving as a *philos* should. She is not merely asserting her affection for her sister, but indicating something of Antigone's basis for action. The juxtaposition of 'senseless' and 'correctly *philos*' echoes the oxymoronic paradox of Antigone's 'holy crime'. From the opening scene,

---

[25] Cf. Lloyd 1966, passim.
[26] It is a key term in contemporary philosophical and linguistic debate. See e.g. Guthrie 1962–81, Vol. III, 204ff., and below, Chapter 9.

Antigone's actions are constituted in an uncertain blend of transgression and exaltation.

Creon's first speech, marking his assumption of office after the turmoils of war and announcing his decision concerning the burial of the bodies of Eteocles and Polyneices, further emphasizes the relations of *philos* and *ekhthros* in a civic context. I quote here a lengthy and important section from the middle of his address where he is both justifying his decision concerning the burials and explaining the basis of the authority he has assumed (182–91):

> And he who counts another greater friend (*philos*)
> than his own fatherland, I put him nowhere.
> So I – may Zeus all-seeing always know it –
> could not keep silence as disaster crept
> upon the town, destroying hope of safety.
> Nor could I count the enemy of the land
> friend (*philos*) to myself, not I who know so well
> that she it is who saves us, sailing straight,
> and only so can we have friends (*philos*) at all.
> With such good laws shall I enlarge our state (*polis*).

For statesman Creon, the man who could rate any relation of *philia* higher than the individual's duty to his own fatherland is to be discounted. He has no part in Creon's view of things. That is why Creon himself has taken up the duties of authority. It is not choice but necessity that involves him in the affairs of the city. Indeed, such is the strength of the ties of a man to his city that no personal relationship could be considered which might stand in some way in conflict with the fulfilment of civic obligations. The rejection of the possibility of an enemy of the land being counted as a *philos* is a thinly veiled remark towards the treatment of his nephew Polyneices. As a nephew, Polyneices should be regarded as a *philos* to Creon. As an enemy to the city, Polyneices has forfeited his claim on Creon's sense of duty. Such, once more, is the polarizing force of the vocabulary of *philos* and *ekhthros*. Indeed, for Creon the correct establishment of the state is the very condition of possibility of having *philoi* at all. Unlike Homer and unlike Antigone, for Creon it is the *polis* and not the *oikos* which offers the institutional basis of *philia*. The word for 'straight' in line 190 is once more *orthos*. As Ismene had suggested that Antigone was 'in a straight sense' *philos* to her *philoi*, so Creon places the possibility of the definition of *philos* dependent on the 'straight sailing' of the ship of state. It is the correct use of the term *philos* which is being set at stake. Time and again, it is to this notion of 'straightness', 'correctness' that Creon will refer.

Creon sums up his position in the phrase 'with such good laws ... ' The published and debated laws of the city are one of the most important ways that the culture of the city defines itself as civilized culture. A city cannot exist as a city without laws. Plato's last massive work of political philosophy, for example, is the *Laws*, a programme for the institution of a just state in the form of a series of laws, and the law-givers of each state were held in great renown. The sophists, however, as we will further see in Chapter 9, partly in reaction to the strength of this ideology, initiated an extremely influential debate concerning the relation of these established cultural laws to an inherent natural system, a debate which reflects in many ways the modern anthropological discussions of 'nature' and 'culture' and also the sociological concerns of 'environment' and 'inherited', 'genetic' causation. Many of their arguments strove to assert the arbitrariness of man-made laws, and the belief that such laws were repressive of the natural impulses of man. Partly for this reason, the sophists are often depicted as the dangerous enemies of the city, and Socrates was executed as such. But despite arguments such as the sophist Antiphon's that there is no need to follow the laws if there are no witnesses and punishment can be escaped, the belief in the establishment of laws as a fundamental sign of the development of society and the belief in obedience to the laws as a necessary part of the social contract are not simply the conservative argument of the powers that be, and for all the political strife and violence that dominates the histories of the Greek cities, there is surprisingly little evidence of the modern contention that an 'unjust law' should be disobeyed (as opposed to the many mutual accusations of 'injustice' between factions). Indeed, although that prime example of civic disobedience, Socrates, is made to say in his *Apology* that he would follow god rather than the court if they were to ban him from philosophizing, nevertheless in the *Crito*, a dialogue whose dramatic time and setting are the prison on the eve of his day of execution, Socrates elaborately defends his decision not to flee from prison on the grounds that the laws must be obeyed, as they are the parents, the nurturers and educators of the individual, that the laws are the contractual agreement which holds the city together.[27] Although he allows for the possibility of 'persuasion' as an alternative to 'obedience', 'disobedience' as such seems firmly rejected. By such an argument, Socrates rejects Crito's appeal, which, like Tecmessa's to Ajax, begged him not to desert his children and satisfy his enemies' desires to be victorious over him.

Creon's faith in the maintenance of law, then, does not in itself define him as an especially hard-line authoritarian or dogmatist, but very much as a man of the *polis*, a citizen. Indeed, when he first hears of the burial, he finds it hard to believe that anyone, least of all the gods, should want to do a good turn to a

[27] On this argument, and for further bibliography on breaking the law, see Woozley 1979, 28–61. See also now Kraut 1984, and Allen 1980.

man who 'came to burn their pillared temples and their wealth, even their land, and break their laws' (285–8). The citizen who could not imagine someone putting any obligation before his duty to the city, the man of law, rejects Polyneices, the aggressor against the city, the man who came to scatter the laws.

In the choral ode which follows this scene, the famous 'ode to man', the double-edged praise of man's endeavours in the progress of civilization[28] ends fittingly with that apogee of civilization, the *polis* (368–75):

> When he honours the laws of the land and the gods' sworn right
> high indeed is his city; but cityless the man
> who dares to dwell with dishonour. Not by my fire,
> never to share my thoughts, who does these things.

The upholding of the laws and the justice of the gods constitutes the man 'with high city'. The phrase translated 'gods' sworn right' is a very dense expression. Jebb suggests an expansive gloss: 'Justice, which men swear to observe, taking oaths by the gods'. This gloss need not conflict with the translation's emphasis on 'the justice from the gods'. For it was a commonly made assertion that civic justice was god-given or at least divinely inspired,[29] and that there should be no possible disjunction between the laws of the land and the unwritten laws of the gods. This link of the laws of the land and the gods' *dikē* looks forward, then, to the next scene where Antigone sets the laws of the gods *in opposition to* the laws of the land. It is through the terms of the chorus' praise of the city that the arguments of the following scene will progress.

The opposite of being 'with high city' is to be 'without a city', 'cityless'. Heidegger attempts a full translation in his inimitable style: 'without city and place, lonely, strange and alien . . . at the same time without statute and limit, without structure and order'.[30] To be without a city is to lack 'the historical place, the there *in* which, *out* of which and *for* which history happens'.[31] The immediate juxtaposition of 'high in his city' and 'without a city' in terms of the ability to uphold the ordering of the laws and justice stands, then, as the immediate and significant prelude to the entrance of Antigone, the law-breaker: it is not just the law that is at stake, but what the laws imply in and for the city.

The question which prompts one of the most famous and discussed speeches in western literature is precisely 'And still you dared to overstep these laws?', and Antigone's justification of her transgression opposes the 'unwritten and sure precepts (*nomima*) of the gods' to the pronouncements of

---

[28] See Segal 1964 for an analysis of this ode.
[29] See Guthrie 1962–81, Vol. III, 117–31 for examples.
[30] 1959, 152.   [31] Ibid.

the ruler of the city, his *nomoi*,[32] and the meting of punishment (*dikē*) in human society (458–9) to the punishment of the divine (459–60). Antigone draws on traditional ideas of a common bond of agreed universal principle, a divine law assumed to include respect for the dead of one's family; but her arguments also echo and contrast with the contemporary sophistic debates which question exactly the terms of law, nature, unwritten law, state authority.[33] The very appeal to 'unwritten laws' by Aristotle's time at least seems to have been a common rhetoricians' gesture when the written law did not support a case,[34] much as the 'spirit of the law' is sometimes appealed to in our society. Antigone's authorization by a traditional and eternal law takes on a different light in comparison with Creon's contemporary arguments about law and order, as her 'heroic' behaviour contrasted with Ismene's reasons for restraint. For Antigone, it is as if Creon and the law he has passed are to be disobeyed because the treatment of a traitor and enemy is at odds with the divine law concerning the family, as if there were no problem in the definition of *philia* with regard to family members when the family wars with itself and with the city. For her, it is the fact that Polyneices comes from her mother (467–8) that justifies her action, and so she defines her action later as honouring 'the children of my mother's womb' (511), and giving 'my own brother funeral' (503). 'My own brother' is the masculine form of the word she applied to Ismene in her opening address, 'brother with the same two parents'. So Polyneices is 'Full brother, on both sides, my parents' child' (513). As Segal writes, 'the tie through blood alone, through the womb, Antigone makes the basis of her *philia*'.[35]

Creon's opposition to what he terms Antigone's hubris in breaking the law, as in his opening speech, comes down to his 'politicisation of burial'.[36] Polyneices is distinguished from Eteocles as a political enemy and treated as such. Creon's rejection of Antigone's appeal to *philia* relies on his appeal to the establishment of the law, as indeed the constitution of the city itself depends on the extension of ties of *philia* beyond the family or clan groupings, as well as on the laws. As before, the interplay of *philos* and *ekhthros* here implicates the

---

[32] On the difference between 'precepts' (*nomima*) and 'law' (*nomos*), see Ostwald, 1973.

[33] There is, for example, an interesting parallel to Antigone's argument in Xen. *Mem.* 4.4.14ff., where Socrates and the sophist Hippias debate the subject of the unwritten laws. Socrates suggests that the transgressors of man-made laws may escape punishment, but never those of divine law. Antiphon the sophist also argued about the advantages of breaking the law if one can escape notice (cf. e.g. fr. 44). Plato seems to be referring to these ideas when in his arguments in favour of doing justice he considers the extreme positions of a man who does injustice but is held in high esteem and the man who acts justly but is wrongly punished and reviled (*Rep.* 2, 357a1ff.).

[34] See Arist. *Rhetoric*, especially Ch. 13, which is interestingly analysed by Guthrie 1962–81, Vol. III, 124–5.

[35] 1981, 85.   [36] Benardete's phrase.

claims of the institutions of law and the city. As much as the terms *philos* and *ekhthros* serve to place a man in society through his relationships, so they are interwoven with the terms of power and the hierarchical orderings of society. So Antigone is rejected by Creon not only as a transgressor of the law, but as a 'slave' (479), and as 'woman' (484–5). His exclusive allegiance to the city (as opposed to the house or family or blood-ties) is the allegiance also to the privileged autonomy of the male ruler. And so *philos* and *ekhthros* are defined by him in terms of that exclusive allegiance. Such exclusivity demands rigid determination of opposites. Polyneices as an enemy of the state remains an *ekhthros* and cannot be predicated with the opposite term (522):

> Never the enemy *(ekhthros)*, even in death, a friend *(philos)*

To which with fine rhetoric, Antigone replies (523):

> I am not of a nature to share in hatred *(ekhth-)* but to share in love *(phil-)*

This is an interesting line which has provoked much argument. It has been called on the one hand 'her finest moment',[37] and on the other hand reviled as an obvious rhetorical exaggeration on the grounds that she was quick enough to threaten Ismene as an *ekhthros* when it suited (93–4) and will reject her sister as not a true *philos* twenty lines further on (543). That both verbs 'share in hatred' and 'share in love' occur nowhere else in extant Greek literature also makes it hard to judge the force of the line. Is the expression an attack on Creon's polarising vocabulary – as if one could determine *philos* without *ekhthros*? Or is it to mark Antigone's excessive reliance on the bond of *philia* much as Creon's exclusive allegiance to the city attempts to ignore totally the ties of family and blood? Creon's reply is equally rhetorical (524–5):

> Then go down there, if you must love *(phil-)*, and love *(phil-)*
> the dead. No woman rules me while I live.

Her appeal to *philia* is turned to scorn which ironically echoes her own ready acceptance to lie in the tomb *philos* with her *philos*. His last gibe once more stresses the sexual and political connotations of the debate. As a man, he rejects the woman in terms of government, rule. As Ismene has warned, it is against her position as the weaker, the politically subordinate that Antigone acts.

Interestingly, that is the last direct conversation between Creon and Antigone in this scene;[38] the chorus spot Ismene approaching and the rest of

[37] Kells 1963, 51.
[38] Some editors have distributed the lines differently from the manuscripts here and given more lines to Antigone, because Creon appears to address her at 573. There can be little certainty, unfortunately, and I have followed the unanimous manuscript reading as does the translation from which I have been quoting.

the action is played around Ismene's and Antigone's further argument, and finally Creon's and Ismene's exchange. The juxtaposition of Creon's rigid separation of *philos* and *ekhthros* on political grounds and Antigone's rhetorical claim to share only in *philia* is left to stand.

The two characters' positions, however, are seen in juxtaposition to each other with regard to Ismene. Although at no point is there a three-way conversation, the subtleties and variations made available through the third actor are evident. For Creon immediately accuses Ismene in extremely aggressive terms (531–5) and when Ismene claims part responsibility she is rejected as forcefully by Antigone, who can find no affection for a *philos* who is a *philos* only in words (543). Antigone's willingness to die is repeated (555, 559–60) and Creon's devaluation of 'affection' even in his own household comes to the fore in his final argument with Ismene, where it is made clear that in condemning Antigone he is condemning his own son's fiancée. Even in this hostile silence towards one another, the opposition of Creon and Antigone continues in their respective arguments with Ismene.

The scene with Haemon and Creon is fascinating in light of these oppositions. It opens with Creon first appealing to his son's allegiance of *philia* (634):

> ... are we friends (*philos*) whatever I may do?

For himself at least, Creon seems happy to claim the permanent family obligations whose validity he denied for Antigone and Polyneices. This relation, however, is not so much reciprocal as hierarchical: the son is expected to follow his father in all respects, especially those of personal relationships (641–7):

> It is for this men pray they may beget
> households of dutiful, obedient sons,
> who share alike in punishing enemies (*ekhthros*)
> and give due honour to their father's friends (*philoi*).
> Whoever breeds a child that will not help
> what has he sown but trouble for himself
> and for his enemies (*ekhthros*) laughter full and free?

Creon here draws on the full expression of a conventional morality: we have seen the common links between father and son as members of the *oikos* explicitly in terms of the inheritance of ties of *philia* and *xenia* already in our discussion of these terms in Homer. So, too, Creon draws on the wisdom of 'doing good to your friends and bad to your enemies'. These two precepts are readily adapted to his logic of hierarchical obedience. His argument is extended to the selection of a wife, the woman brought in from the outside to be the young man's consort (649–52):

... well you know
how cold the thing he takes into his arms
who has a wicked woman for his wife.
What deeper wounding than a friend (*philos*) no friend?

These lines find echoes in, for example, Hesiod's didactic poem the *Works and Days*, which warns about the wrong sort of woman to take as a wife, and Hesiod was held in a position of considerable authority throughout the ancient world as a poet and moralist. Moreover, as we saw earlier, *philos* is a term implying the obligations and duties of the social interaction of marriage which Creon suggests would be subverted by a 'wicked woman'. However, the general statement that to take a *philos* who is somehow bad or evil will lead to disaster also recalls Antigone's passionate appeal to 'share in *philia*' and Creon's rejection of such rhetoric. Set within the specific interplays of this work, as well as the inherited morality of earlier writers, Creon's general statements are also marked by the doubts and echoes of the earlier arguments, as now the man who claimed the rigid determination of *ekhthros* in political terms manipulates the language of family ties towards the necessity of obedience.

Creon's concern for the order of the household is explicitly linked to his concern for the ordering of the *polis* (659–663):

If I allow disorder in my home,
I'd surely have to license it abroad.
A man who deals in fairness with his own,
he can make manifest justice in the state (*polis*).

The word for 'one's own' is *oikeioisin*, the people, affairs and business of the *oikos*. The model of family obedience is the model for the hierarchies of the state: as he is father in his house, so he is father to the city, invested with the word of authority. The reverse of such order is disobedience and anarchy, which 'ruins cities ... and tears down our homes' (673–4). In both spheres, the same structure of authority, the same threat of collapse obtains. As a further point of agreement between the two areas of action, Creon concludes with his unwillingness to be beaten by a woman. The hierarchy is a male, civic order.

Particularly after the clashes of the previous scene, the assumed continuity of family and state seems precisely to ignore the possible conflicts of interest which motivated the earlier arguments. Indeed, Haemon's reply focuses not on the requirement of subordinates to obey, but on that of leaders to yield and show flexibility. The possibility of the rigid application of one man's assumed wisdom which seems to be the conclusion of Creon's hierarchical model, is precisely what his son questions. Creon seems to depend on his own individual judgement as much as Antigone (705–9):

> Then, do not have one mind, and one alone
> that only your opinion can be right.
> Whoever thinks that he alone is wise,
> his eloquence, his mind above the rest,
> come the unfolding, shows his emptiness.

The term for 'right' is once more *orthos*. The correct use of language, the correct running of the state, the correct attitude of the individual are linked in the search for demand for this quality of being *orthos*.

The reasoned positions of father and son in the vitriolic exchange that follows are quickly distorted. The respect for authority which Creon espoused turns towards the tyrant's principle of ignoring the people and relying solely on his own judgement. His wariness of female disobedience in particular tends towards more explicitly misogynistic bandying of the term 'woman' and finally the degradation of the insult 'woman's slave' (756). Haemon's argument in favour of yielding and flexibility itself bends towards rigidity under the pressure of the exchange, and with a threat that his father will never see him again, he rushes from the stage. With their mutual accusations of corruption of mind, or madness (754–5), the earlier reasoned debate about authority and flexibility has itself reached a point of exclusion and opposition in the same terms. Creon's assumption of an easy continuity of authority in the family and state has not only been set at odds with itself by the arguments within the family and by the conflicting claims of family ties and civic obligations, but has also been forced to an extreme position of tyrannical autocracy. Like Antigone, in relying on himself and his own, Creon the defender of the city puts the constitution of the city at risk.

The choral ode which follows this scene adds a further colouring not only to the previous action but also to the opposition of *philos* and *ekhthros*. For it sings briefly but with seductive beauty of the power of Eros and Aphrodite. The significance of Eros for the preceding scene is explicitly marked at the beginning of the second verse of the ode (791–4):

> You twist the minds of even the just. Wrong they pursue and are ruined.
> You made this quarrel of kindred before us now.

The word for 'kindred', *sunhaimon* (which means 'with shared blood'), puns on the name of the king's son, Haemon, stressing again the tension in Creon's family and not just in the ordering of the city, as the words 'minds' and 'just' recall the terms of their family quarrel. Although Haemon never mentioned it as motivation, the chorus take for granted that the force behind his argument and exit was desire, desire for the bride he has been denied by his father. This explanation does not only stress the insistence of the role of irrational and indeterminate forces that was lacking in Creon's rationalist arguments and notably missing from the picture of civilization offered in the ode to man,[39] but also importantly qualifies the sense of both Eros and *philos*. For unlike Ismene's protestations against Antigone's punishment, Haemon, who begins by speaking for the city, and then speaks for the gods, 'ends by cherishing Antigone unto death'.[40] The force of Eros underlying Haemon's actions (in the chorus' view) qualifies and extends our sense of *philia* both by distinguishing Ismene's restraint and by emphasizing the strength – and strangeness – of Antigone's passion to do good to her *philos*, her dead brother. *Philia* and Eros overlap in certain areas but remain importantly distinct: as much as *philia* stresses the normally affectionate relationship between husband and wife or lovers in terms of the reciprocal obligations linked to the development of the house, the city and an individual's relations to social order, so Eros marks that relationship as one of a possible irrational and overwhelming force, a principle that threatens the principles of law and order. And indeed the 'playful goddess with whom none can fight', a paradoxical mixture of sport and lethal battle, will indeed lead to destruction in this play.

The verses to Eros also colour in an important way the funeral procession of Antigone, her mourning song, into which the ode develops. For as Antigone marches her lonely journey to the cave of her interment, she refers to herself repeatedly as the 'Bride of Hades'. Like Persephone, the bride of Hades in myth, Antigone goes down into the 'underground bridal chamber' of the cave (891–4), but unlike Persephone, Antigone cannot and will not return to give earth fruitfulness and growth. Creon in giving Antigone as a bride not to his son but to Hades allows her to live out the etymology of her name, which is 'instead of' or 'opposed to generation'.

Antigone's earlier willingness to die takes on a different force here. For although she has constantly depicted herself as supporting the ties of the family, of blood, of the same womb, as bride of death it is Antigone herself who denies for the *oikos* the possibility of its own continuation. Instead of her marriage constituting a bridge between the generations and aiming at the generational continuity of children, her marriage inters her as a virgin, sterile and unproductive. Her marriage to death, which recalls her regularly expressed desire to die,[41] tragically inverts the functioning of marriage in the

---

[39] As Kitto 1961, and especially Winnington-Ingram 1980, 91ff., have pointed out.
[40] Benardete 1975b, 44.
[41] Interestingly, when the Hippocratic Corpus talks of the 'hysterical' diseases of young unmarried girls, for whom marriage and pregnancy are a suggested cure, one symptom mentioned is 'desire (*eran*, to experience *eros*) for death' (*peri parth.*). King 1983, 114 translates this passage as 'take death for a lover'.

oikos. Unlike Persephone, whose story seems to offer an aetiological tale for the recurrence of the seasons and the perpetuation of fertility, Antigone, 'anti-generation', calls herself the lone remnant, the 'last of your royal line' (941).

As Oedipus and Jocasta stand to confuse the normal process of generational continuity in incest and patricide, so their daughter, acting, she claims, for the family's sake, is led to the death which destroys the family. Antigone, as Ismene had warned at the beginning of the play (48–60), has taken her place in the family history of self-mutilation and self-destruction. So the chorus say to Antigone in a telling phrase, not translated adequately by Wyckoff: 'but mistress of your own fate, alone among mortals you will descend in life to the house of Death' (821–3). The word I have translated with Jebb as 'mistress of your own fate' and which Wyckoff translates 'of your own motion you go', is *autonomos*. The construction of the term is simple: *auto-* indicates 'self' and *nomos* means 'law', a term which we have already discussed at some length. Antigone is 'under her own law', 'self-willed'. As she put herself above the law, it is on her own, by her own law, she is going to die. The girl who wanted to protect *philia* dies, as she cries repeatedly, without a *philos* to mourn for her. Antigone has completed the self-destructive, inward-turned fate of the incestuous family of Oedipus.

Teiresias has often been regarded as offering a divine authorization for Antigone, and he certainly does require Polyneices' burial in the name of the gods. But he does not mention Antigone at all and his words of reproach to Creon have also been seen as applicable to Antigone: 'Self-will incurs the charge of folly' (1027, Jebb). Nor does the seer in his prediction after he has been reviled by the king make any mention of the girl. He addresses himself rather to Creon's stubbornness and self-will. It is interesting in this light to read the lines in which Creon does finally relent, which seem a good example of Sophoclean irony. In his very change of heart, Creon foreshadows Antigone's death: 'I've come to fear it's best to hold the laws of old tradition to the end of life.' Creon's fear will be realized in Antigone holding to her principles precisely 'to the end of life'. But there is a further irony lost in Wyckoff's translation. Her phrase 'the laws of old tradition' would more accurately be translated 'the established laws', 'the laws as set up'. In this moment of yielding Creon cannot but echo his earlier argument. Unlike Teiresias, or the chorus, or Antigone, Creon does not speak of 'the gods' or 'tradition', but still of the need to obey the instituted laws. Creon's yielding, then, does not simply vindicate Antigone and question his earlier support of the law (here before the city in one of its dramatic festivals), but seems to stress again the terms of the earlier arguments, the questions as to what constitutes the established law, should obedience be absolute, can the laws be adequate to conflicts of interest. As much as Creon's earlier use of apparently traditional wisdom, set within the context of the argument, belied its own 'good sense', so here Creon's retreat from his autarchical position ironically echoes his earlier defence of autarchy. As so often in Sophocles, the apparently simple statement – made apparently easier by insensitive translation – does not reflect in a simple way a traditional position.

Creon himself must march the same path to the cave. The messenger's tale of what happens there completes the imagery of the bride of death. Haemon is discovered in the tomb hugging Antigone, who has hanged herself. He wordlessly rejects his father, aims to strike but fails to kill and turns his sword upon himself: the patricidal, self-mutilating curse of Oedipus haunts this play. And the *Liebestod* is consummated (1237–41):

> While he was conscious, he embraced the maiden
> holding her gently. Last, he gasped out blood,
> red blood on her white cheek.
> Corpse on a corpse he lies. He found his marriage.
> Its celebration in the halls of Hades.

Creon's own son and heir, the continuation of his family, has been destroyed through Creon's attempt to maintain the order of the city and the hierarchy of the home. Significantly, this tale of the messenger is told to Eurydice, Creon's wife, the dear (*philos*) mistress of his household. Wordlessly, she leaves the stage. And in the course of the king's first lament for his son there comes the messenger with the news that she too has killed herself inside. The disaster is both in and for Creon's house: 'His home instead of being a locus of civilized values and the place that transmits new life from generation to generation, becomes like the house of Antigone and Oedipus, a place of death and savagery, a cavern-like "harbour of Hades".'[42] Creon has been stripped of the people of his family, as he had tried to suppress Antigone's claims of family ties, and now he himself can only wish for death and obscurity.

So Creon accepting his responsibility for their deaths and his own ignorance is led away. As he sought throughout the play for the *orthos*, the 'straight and true', so his final line marks the distortion of that desire (1345–6):

> My life is warped beyond cure, my fate has struck me down.

The desire for the accurate and upright has led to the warping of tragedy.

The critical view which has gained some of the authority of a tradition, namely, that Creon argues from and supports the ties and obligations of city

[42] Segal 1981, 187.

life, rejecting irrationality and what he can't fit into his male hierarchical structure, while Antigone argues from and supports the ties and obligations of family life, rejecting the laws and ordinances of the city in favour of the female *oikos*, needs some considerable qualification. The tragic text resists the stability of such oppositions.

Creon adapts the vocabulary of generation and the household to the order of the city in a single hierarchical model (which itself marks the impossible separation of the vocabularies of civic and household organization), but this systematization is split and challenged by the disasters in his own complex household. The city's opinions and order remain something of an uncertain murmuring in the background as Creon's house threatens to imitate its terrifying and chaotic double, the house of Oedipus, as Creon tumbles from his certain position as ruler, father, figure of knowledge. So his wife silently exits, like Jocasta, to kill herself. And the repetition of words indicating self-driven, self-performed actions joins the two houses in parallel self-destructive movements. As much as Creon attempts to support the city through the repression of the family, it is through his family that his whole life becomes warped. Teiresias, rather than simply vindicating Antigone, seems to warn against extremes, even of order. Indeed, the very household which Antigone claims and is claimed to support is also the source and transmission of the curse which she consummates in death. Her backward-looking support is for the house of the dead, the ancestors whom she places above the possibilities of procreation, marriage, and a future home, a future of the home – the logic of 'anti-generation'. Antigone seems to support 'civilized values', but she also seems to destroy them in the rejection of the *oikos*'s essential aim of continuity. As in the first scene, where we saw the uncertain blend of transgression and exaltation in Antigone's actions, so as the play progresses the paradoxical nature of her attitude to *philia* increases. As much as Creon's apparently traditional and rational support of obedience and order develops towards the tyrannical egoism of continual self-assertion, so Antigone's devotion to the house gives rise to death and destruction rather than the continuity of birth and generation. This, too, is a disturbing context in which to read her statement that she is of a nature to share in loving not in hate.

Within these distorted and distorting idealisms neither the city nor the household can be maintained as the locus of order, value or principle. As Creon's and Antigone's views of *philia* seem divided against each other, each seems divided against itself in the very strength of its formulation. Such divisions in the language of personal relationships and obligations constitute this play's tragic view of the terms *philos* and *ekhthros* and the positioning of the individual that they develop. The possibility of the secure positioning of the individual within the conflicting claims of *polis* and *oikos* ideology is what this tragedy seems to put at risk. The *Antigone* works through the logic of the conventional moralities of the terms to the point of destruction. The secure conclusion of an Hegelian synthesis or *Aufhebung* at the end of this 'labour of the negative' seems notably absent. The questioning of the morality and obligations surrounding the terms of relations and relationships remains unresolved.

In the light of such questioning, is there not some need to qualify what might be meant by the epithet 'conservative' as traditionally applied to Sophocles? What sort of reading of *Antigone* can lead a critic to assert of Sophocles 'In his plays the ideas expressed are conventional and conservative and we are not invited to reject them'?[43] For it would seem rather that it is precisely through the limitations and contradictions of the conventional and conservative morality surrounding the terms of *philos* and *ekhthros* in juxtaposition to the values of the city that the tragedy of *Antigone* develops. After the complex interplays and dislocations of the moral language of relations we have read in this play, it seems to me difficult to see in what terms it would be possible to assert that Sophocles simply reflects a conventional or conservative attitude. As we have seen before and will see again in the course of this book, it is only for conservative and conventional critics that the texts of tragedy have lost their power to question and challenge.

[43] Hester 1971, 46.

5 · SEXUALITY AND DIFFERENCE

A woman is a sometime thing.
GERSHWIN

Time and again the line of argument in my discussion has approached the question of sexuality, and has been forced to restrain itself. In the *Oresteia*, I argued, the relations between the sexes are an essential dynamic of the trilogy and any discussion of language, politics, imagery in that work is forced always to reconsider its siting in a sexual discourse. I attempted to show further that in any description of how the Greek city might try to delimit itself the polarized realms of a male world and female world were an essential, if difficult, marking of that not entirely physical topography. With regard to those primary words of human relations in the family and city, *philos* and *ekhthros*, the sexual was explicitly interwoven in the semantic range – and dislocations – of such terms. In this chapter, I wish to focus on this topic of sexuality, which is so important to Greek tragedy, and after I have looked at some of the complex problems involved in approaching this subject, I shall be considering in particular Euripides' *Hippolytus*.

In Homer's *Odyssey*, which I will have cause to discuss in more detail in the next chapter, there is a continuing focus on the relations between the sexes.[1] In his journeys, Odysseus passes through a series of liaisons with various females, divine and mortal, which reflect (in a fractured manner) the relation between Penelope and himself towards which he is travelling. Part of the extended process of homecoming is this constant redefining of the male and female positioning in the home. Indeed, whereas Virgil's Aeneas sees in the underworld above all a procession of the future military and political heroes of Rome, Odysseus sees a procession of the famous women of the past – starting from his own mother. In both narratives, the journey to the underworld offers a sense of an insight into the truth of the epic.

Hesiod, too, in perhaps a more directly didactic manner, concerns himself with the role of women in the *oikos*. In his *Works and Days*, not only is there an extensive discussion of the sort of woman to marry, but this is also linked to a mythic narrative which places the origin of human woes in the hands of the

[1] See Goldhill 1984a, Foley 1978.

over-curious first woman, Pandora.[2] In the iambic poet Semonides' most famous extant work, various sorts of women are humorously described in terms of a bestiary, which combines an epic cataloguing with iambic derogatory malice.[3]

There is, in other words, a continuing and varied emphasis on sexual difference in the works of the Greek literary tradition, an emphasis that has prompted some critics in recent years to talk of a continuity of Greek misogyny.[4] The way in which the extant fifth-century tragedies return again and again explicitly to a conflict of the sexes, as the comedies of the period frequently play with the possibility of sexual role reversal, has prompted an extensive discussion of the role of women in Greek theatre and society.[5] It is, of course, not by chance that this debate has flourished in the last twenty years – a period which coincides with the rise of the women's movement and the very widest discussion of the role of women in society. The debate goes back, however, as I mentioned in Chapter 2, at least as far as the influential work of Bachofen, which has fuelled many modern Marxist and feminist polemics.[6] And among classicists challenged by the dissenting voices of Gomme and Kitto, and, most recently, Gould, there has also been considerable argument about the description and evaluation of women's lot in classical Greece.[7]

I write 'description and evaluation' but this 'and', rather than linking two self-evident terms, is precisely the locus of the most fervent discussion. For Kitto, the problem of the relation between description and evaluation is one of the irreducibly alien status of Greek culture for us: 'As far as Greece is concerned, the most Hellenic of us is a foreigner, and we all of us know how wide of the mark even an intelligent foreigner's estimate can be ... The foreigner so easily misses the significant thing.'[8] This difficulty is compounded by the textual nature of the evidence that has been brought to bear in the debate. With the exception of some archaeological remains and some pictures (which few would regard as evidence which does not involve similar problems of interpretation) scholars have used the written remains of fifth-century Athens to build up their picture of 'the accepted view ... that the Athenian woman lived in an almost Oriental seclusion, regarded with indifference, even

---

[2] On Hesiod and the sexes see Arthur 1973; 1981; 1983; Bergren 1983.
[3] For an interesting study of Semonides and women, see Loraux 1981b, 75–117.
[4] This sense of continuity has been challenged in different ways by Arthur 1973; Goldhill 1984a.
[5] A good general introduction to the material is Gould 1980. Several collections of essays have recently been published: Foley 1982b; Cameron and Kuhrt 1983; *Arethusa* 6 (1973), and *Arethusa* 11 (1978) (now republished under the editorship of J. Peradotto and J. Sullivan). These contain extensive bibliographies.
[6] For a survey of the Bachofen heritage, see Coward 1983.
[7] Gomme 1925; Kitto 1951; Gould 1980.
[8] Kitto 1951, 223.

contempt'.[9] This 'accepted view' has, for example, made much of Pericles' famous dictum that woman's 'greatest glory is to be least talked about by males, either for praise or for blame'.[10] This is said to be 'typical of the disdain Athenians felt for women'. Kitto retorts 'But suppose Gladstone had said "I do not care to hear a lady's name bandied about in general talk whether for praise or dispraise", would that imply disdain or an old-fashioned deference and courtesy?'[11] A good rhetorical question, for sure, but a rhetoric which today might well get a different answer from the one Kitto may have expected – particularly if the question were asked of recent feminist scholars of Victorian England. Being 'alien' is not limited to the fifth century B.C.

What do we make of that dictum of Pericles, then, which was after all written by Thucydides? It occurs in that most famous of Thucydides' set pieces, the funeral speech which was delivered over the first Athenian dead of the war that would finally break Athenian power. The funeral speech over the city's war-dead in the special cemetery for those fallen in battle was an institution that formed a constituent part of the civic discourse of Athens.[12] In this institutionalized speech, the city glorified itself through the burial of the members of the citizen army who fought and died for it. The force of Pericles' speech in Thucydides' narrative, however, is more than that of good political rhetoric. Towards the beginning of the narrative of that fateful war, the first casualties of the city still at the height of its power bring forth from the figure who gave his name to the golden years of Athenian supremacy a statement that is to sum up the nature of Thucydides' own city. This is a speech from Pericles on the glories of Periclean Athens. But as much as it serves to express the view of an era, it also looks forward to the destruction of that era in the history to follow. Periclean Athens is constituted as a zenith by the downfall which follows. Not only is the special ideological nature of the funeral speech marked, but also its siting in the artfully composed narrative of glory and disaster suggests one should be careful before accepting it as the transparent representation of 'Athenian Thought'. Perhaps Kitto should have asked 'But what if Disraeli wrote a piece about the collapse of the British Empire in which Gladstone gave a speech in which he said . . .?'

Moreover, Thucydides himself writes programmatically about such speeches in his history: 'I have found it difficult to remember the precise words used in the speeches which I listened to myself and my various informants have experienced the same difficuilty; so my method has been, while keeping as closely as possible to the general sense of the words used, to

[9] Kitto 1951, 219.   [10] Thuc. 2.46.   [11] Kitto 1951, 224.
[12] See Loraux 1981a, passim.

make the speakers say what, in my opinion, was called for by each situation.'[13] As Finley comments 'There is no way to get round the incompatibility of the two parts of that statement. If all speakers said what, in Thucydides' opinion, the situation called for, the remark becomes meaningless. But if they did not always say what was called for, then, insofar as Thucydides attributed such sentiments to them, he could not have been keeping as closely as possible to the general sense of the words used.'[14] So with Pericles' funeral speech are we reading the gist of what Pericles said or what Thucydides thought the situation required?

The layers and lies of such rhetoric are often repressed or ignored by the simple selection of such a piece of writing as a portion of bounded 'evidence' for Greek Thought. Not only is the 'description' of such a remark forced to become involved in the ins and outs of voice and discourse in that speech in that narrative of that war (involved, that is, in 'evaluation'), but also the selection of such a dictum to serve as 'description' of Greek culture out of its context marks in its very selectivity a degree of evaluation – the far from innocent naivety of the argument which simply selects a series of remarks from Greek literature as a transparent illustration ('anthology', 'reader') of Greek Thought.

From this example, we can begin to see the problems involved in approaching the textual evidence. Even when we take a remark from a historical text, a work which proclaims its own truth value, if we try to put it in its context, we find that such a remark no longer seems as clear and simple and offering ready access to truth as its common use in arguments on the status of women would suggest. Moreover, Thucydides' text is, of course, not a text in a vacuum: we can extend the context further by considering other relevant texts to help us build up the picture. Indeed, the more one attempts to take into account the contexts of explicit remarks on the relations of the sexes, the more the texts for consideration multiply and the problems of relating all these different texts to a stable entity 'Greek Thought' increase. As Just[15] has pointed out, the very variety of types of evidence, which includes texts of history, philosophy, medicine, myth, law, makes it less surprising that a uniform or consistent view of the sexes has been difficult to formulate. Indeed, even such constants as the fact that all the surviving fifth-century texts are written by men[16] introduce a particular bias which disorients a simple link between the written evidence and a view of the whole society, with regard to how sexual difference is conceived. As Gould writes, it is 'naive and misleadingly, even grossly, over

---

[13] Thuc. 1.22.   [14] Finley 1972, 26. See also Sainte-Croix 1972, 7–16, and appendix III.
[15] Just 1975. See also Pomeroy 1977a, 141.
[16] Female writers did exist, however. See Pomeroy 1977b; Lloyd 1983, 60.

simple . . . to proceed as though there were some single and univocal scale of values on which it would be possible to place "women" as evaluated by "men".'[17]

These problems of evaluating and describing a heterogeneous body of texts in relation to the society that produced them have been treated in different ways with varying subtlety and force. One of the most stimulating approaches to Greek Thought and the body of Greek texts in recent years has come from Jean-Pierre Vernant and those influenced by him and his colleagues in Paris.[18] Drawing on a wide range of material from different genres of texts in the ancient world and from comparative anthropological work, Vernant and others have developed a sophisticated series of readings of Greek culture. For Vernant, the problem of reading the relations of the sexes in ancient Athens is a question of 'discourse'. Rather than considering each statement as a transparent illustration of thought, Vernant attempts to read the systematic relations between the more or less explicit statements on sexual difference. Like Foucault, he approaches the question of determining the conditions of possibility that give rise to these expressions, that is, the verbal, social, mental organizations implied by and constituted in the system of statements that the texts offer. Being alien to a culture meant for Kitto a dangerous increase in the possibility of a reader's misinterpretation or misrepresentation of what the culture itself believed. Vernant, however, rather than repressing his necessarily alien status, insists on the possible advantages of such a position. Like many anthropologists, rather than taking a culture's explicit agreement or recognition as the criterion of judgement for his analyses, Vernant stresses that the outsider's view can investigate the tacit knowledge of a society; it can illuminate the blind-spots of a culture's ideas by investigating what is taken for granted or assumed. Indeed, Bourdieu, the highly influential theoretical anthropologist, has argued that a stable society continues on its course precisely by *not recognizing* the arbitrary limits and organization of its own system of beliefs, which it determines as 'natural' and 'proper'. For Bourdieu, the establishment of what is thought 'natural' in each culture depends on such 'misrecognition' – which is how he terms the working of the unquestioned organization of ideas inherent in a culture's attitudes and assumptions. Despite the evident risk of the arbitrary imposition of the observer's own categories (which is part of Kitto's fear), the anthropologist involved in the investigation of such 'misrecognition' cannot expect to maintain the recognition or express agreement of the observed culture as the criterion of judgement

[17] 1980, 39.
[18] I include Detienne, Kahn, Loraux, Vidal-Naquet. See also the essays published in his honour in *Arethusa* 16, 1983.

for his analyses. Rather than relying, like Kitto, on what a society determines as 'the significant thing', the anthropologically based critique looks also at the unrecognized system of ideas and organization of attitudes giving rise to the express statements of significance. In times of flux in a society, however – such as fifth-century Athens – the stability of the agreed 'nature' of things is no longer assured. There develops a recognition of the process of 'misrecognition', a realization which marks and emphasizes the tensions in a system of thought. What was taken for granted and assumed 'natural' is placed under question, replaced with a different series or organization of beliefs. It was indeed precisely through the consideration of the relation between what constituted the 'natural' and the 'conventional', 'arbitrary' and 'proper', that the sophists proved such a threat to the traditional pattern of ideas in fifth-century Athens. An investigation of what is thought 'natural' will also question the boundaries and area of the sexual, a topic which always attracts statements about what is 'natural' and 'proper' – a topic, too, which many recent writers have shown to rely all too often on an unrecognized system of ideas.[19] Thus in my investigation in this chapter of the markings of a discourse of sexuality in fifth-century Athens it will also prove necessary to attempt to take into account the complex relations of explicit statement, tacit knowledge, and a culture's possible questioning of its own ideas. For a discourse is not necessarily a stable system, as the work of the anthropological critiques outlined above may help us appreciate.

Although it will be through a study of such a discourse of sexuality and its interrelations with the various languages of the city (e.g. economic, spatial, linguistic . . .) that I shall first approach the *Hippolytus*, this is not to suggest that the anthropologically based ideas of Vernant and his associates provide a grid into which specific tragedies can be slotted for explanation. Although tragedy has provided an important body of material for such studies, and there have been some literary readings based on such material,[20] there is still an important methodological tension between the generalizing attitude of anthropological studies of Greek culture and the difficulties of reading specific literary texts. For not only do the projects of such anthropological critiques in general not aim at literary explication or consider its problems, but also literary language, particularly in the public festival of tragedy with its transgressions, paradoxes, archaisms has an oblique relation to the formulation of such a discourse, contesting as it constructs, challenging as it develops. Not only does the make-up of a non-stable society with its interplay of tacit

---

[19] Two examples: on 'natural' and changing ideas of the family, see Stone 1977; on childhood, see Ariès 1962.

[20] See e.g. Vernant and Vidal-Naquet 1981; Loraux 1981b, 197–253; and the contributors to *Arethusa* 16, 1983. Zeitlin 1978; 1982a; 1982b are especially useful.

knowledge, explicit statement, and self-questioning create difficulties with regard to formulating a general view of a subject like sexuality, but also the specific genre of tragedy with its disruptive questioning highlights these tensions and differences in a normative discourse rather than offering any harmonized view of the workings of society's attitudes. As we will see, it is not a safe assumption that the texts of Greek tragedy simply and directly 'reflect' a Greek view of sexuality. As I shall be outlining the features of a sexual discourse in my reading of the *Hippolytus*, so I shall be investigating the fractures of that discourse in the tragic text, the challenge in tragedy to the stability of a discourse of sexuality.

There have been a series of readings of Greek tragedy that consider this difficult notion of the way the texts 'reflect' society, often specifically with regard to the status of women. Indeed, tragedy has often proved a central subject for many arguments on the role of women in Athens. There is a clear and specific reason for this. The tension in the debate is this: whereas much explicit ideology particularly from prose works, as we saw in Chapter 3, indicates a specific linking of the women with the inside, with the house, and with a denial of public life and language, nevertheless tragedy flaunts its heroines on stage in the public eye, boldly speaking out. This tension between repression and outspokenness has been resolved by critics in various ways with regard to fifth-century attitudes. For Kitto, Attic tragedy is a major argument against the extreme view of the repression of women: 'it is hard to believe that the dramatists never, even by accident, portrayed the stunted creatures among whom (we are to suppose) they actually lived, and got these vivid people out of books – from Homer'.[21] For Slater on the other hand, who offer a psychopathological view of the Greek male through his literature, tragedy is the expression of the social pathology of Athens. A combination of 'sex antagonism, maternal ambivalence, gynephobia and masculine narcissism'[22] gives rise to tragedy as a sort of fearful expiation of the double feelings of men towards women. Women, repressed in life by men, find a voice through men in the institution of tragedy. The tension is, for Slater, a tension in Athenian life between the rejection or repression of women and the guilty projection of their power in the special worlds of myth and literature. Shaw, however, has coined the phrase 'the female intruder' for the role of women on stage. He argues that in drama women step out of the enclosed world of the *oikos* whose values they represent, not as a psychopathological projection, but as a dramatized response to the failure of the male to respect the interests of the household in his own sphere of action, the *polis*. The woman's action does represent an upsetting reversal of the norms of behaviour. But, Shaw argues,

[21] 1951, 228.   [22] 1968, 410.

the dramas close with a compromise, explicit or implicit, between male and female, *oikos* and *polis*, which blocks the assertion either of a pure masculinity or a pure femininity. He sees therefore the battle of the sexes in Attic theatre as 'dramatising the points of conflict between the *oikos* and the state'[23] and he regards the artist as seeking to 'chart the limits and shortcomings of the civic virtues'.[24]

His excessively schematic reading fails to take account of the fact that the struggles that dominate so much of tragedy are often intrafamilial; also, as Helene Foley has pointed out, while useful in pointing to the 'intrusive female', his analysis 'fails to recognize sufficiently that a dialectical opposition puts both poles (male and female, *oikos* and *polis*) into a relation in which each defines the other'.[25] For the city's male is also the ruler of the *oikos* – the one who enters and leaves, who gives in marriage, who controls the finances and property. And the woman is not only the guardian of the house but also of state fertility, particularly through the exclusively female state religious festivals. As the producer of the citizen army, she donates her son, the hoplite, to the army and the state, much as the man can offer the tax of *leitourgia*.[26] Attic drama plays out the recognition of the tension between, on the one hand, the assumed continuity of *oikos* and *polis* as institutions of power and, on the other hand, the conflicts of interest between *oikos* and *polis*, which seems to set them in opposition to each other; but, as we saw in the *Antigone*, there is no simple opposition of 'household' and 'state'.

Nor is it easy to accept Shaw's postulated final compromise of opposites. While many have seen the end of the *Oresteia* as glorification of a civic harmony (and many have seen the opposite), when one considers the end of such plays as *Bacchae, Antigone* or *Medea*, where dissolution, aggression, and disappointment seem to stress the shattering tragic oppositions, the construction of any final reconciliation seems placed in question.

There is a further specific problem of interpretation which these critics have not articulated adequately. Unlike the historian's work, tragedies do not claim to represent a true history of contemporary society, but rather they are fictional depictions of a series of ancient stories most often set in cities other than Athens. The question is not simply how to discuss the representation of sexual difference in the texts of a society but also how to evaluate and describe the range of differences and similarities between a society and its fictionalized portrait of the past. How are we to determine to what degree and in what ways these women of archaic tales in modern plays are to be thought of as different

---

[23] 1975, 266.   [24] Ibid.   [25] 1982a, 21.
[26] *Leitourgia* was a contribution to the state, a sort of personal sponsorship of, say, a warship or the costs of a tragic festival. See Loraux 1981c for the parallel between *leitourgia* and children.

from fifth-century society, or as commenting on that society, or as offering parallels to society? As we saw with Antigone's heroic stance, the archaism of Greek tragedy introduces a series of tensions and paradoxes which resist a simple, univocal reading. So, although the challenge of women in Attic drama may be thought to remain a challenge to the dominant orderings of patriarchal society, it is not a challenge that can be reduced to the sort of all-embracing formula that Shaw and others have proposed. The disruptive interplay of civic and familial discourses in which the specific roles of women play an essential part, and the archaism of tales of other times, other places (for which the prominence of women may have a variety of significances) challenge the possible simplicity of any relation of 'reflection' assumed between tragedy and society. As we will see in *Hippolytus*, far from any 'final compromise' the crisis of transgression and the dissolution of order threaten precisely the security of the discourse of sexuality.

I hope I have outlined, then, some of the problems involved in attempting to read a discourse of sexuality in Greek tragedy – problems all too often ignored by critics keen to understand Athenian society through its drama. In the light of this discussion, Euripides offers an especially interesting set of texts for study. Reviled by Aristophanes and others in both antiquity and modern days as a misogynist, hailed by many more recent writers as a feminist, Euripides brings to the fore many of the difficulties of description and evaluation that I have been discussing. Many of his plays revolve around a specifically sexual tension. In the *Bacchae*, which I shall discuss in Chapters 10 and 11, the doubt and suspicion of the young Pentheus towards the women in the city – and the feminine in Dionysus – form an essential dynamic of the tragic tensions and reversals of the play. In the *Women of Troy (Troiades)*, the heroic focus of the *Iliad* shifts to the fate of a city's women in the disasters that war brings: the concentration on women as the object of men's sexual and military aggression helps to develop the harshness of this play. Medea in *Medea*, a fine example of the heroic woman taking control of her affairs with a force and determination which seems at odds with much of the ideology of contemporary prose writing on women, delivers a famous speech which brings up many of the problems I have been discussing (230–51):

> Of all things that are living and can form a judgement
> we women are the most unfortunate creatures.
> Firstly, with an excess of wealth it is required
> for us to buy a husband and take for our bodies
> a master; for not to take one is even worse.
> And now the question is serious whether we take
> a good or bad one; for there is no easy escape
> for a woman, nor can she say no to her marriage.

She arrives among new modes of behaviour and manners,
and needs prophetic power, unless she has learned at home,
how best to manage him who shares the bed with her.
And if we work out all this well and carefully,
and the husband lives with us and lightly bears his yoke,
then life is enviable. If not, I'd rather die.
A man, when he's tired of the company in his home,
goes out of the house and puts an end to his boredom
and turns to a friend or companion of his own age.
But we are forced to keep our eyes on one alone.
What they say of us is that we have a peaceful time
living at home, while they do the fighting in war.
How wrong they are! I would very much rather stand
three times in the front of battle than bear one child.

On the one hand, although this speech clearly echoes (from a woman's viewpoint) the didactic narrative of Hesiod, say, about the right sort of woman to choose or Semonides' humorous view of the different types of women, it also draws on what Vernant and others have outlined as a specific fifth-century set of attitudes towards sexual relations particularly with regard to marriage: the idea of the difficulties for a woman in a strange house needing new knowledge to deal with the strange alteration in position from daughter to wife would find an echo in a piece as different, say, as Xenophon's didactic prose work the *Oikonomikos* ('Household management'), where he describes precisely the problems from the husband's point of view of educating and overseeing a new wife. The emphases on marriage as an exchange parallel to a financial transaction, on the husband as master with the freedom to leave the confines of the house to spend his time with his friends or associates in the city, are, as we will see, important ways of describing the relations between male and female in the household. In particular, the opposition Medea draws between warfare, the male prerogative of standing in the battle-line, and childbirth, the necessary risk to female life, can be seen drawing on a whole system of interlocking ideas in fifth-century ideology that I shall be outlining later in this chapter. Medea's opposition of warfare and childbirth is not just bravado rhetoric but a remark which draws its force from the common oppositions of Athenian attitudes. It is important, then, to see how this speech draws on such ideology. And in complaining of the state of women in this system of ideas – the very adoption of the female's standpoint marks a certain reversal of traditional ideas – Medea has been taken as espousing a feminist cause, and (of course?) as representing Euripides' own views on the matter.

On the other hand, Medea exhibits all the signs of 'otherness' of which I have written. She is a woman from ancient myth, in a foreign city.[26a]

[26a] On the foreign city in tragedy, see Zeitlin 1986; Vidal-Naquet 1985.

Throughout the play, Jason remarks on her being a barbarian and capable of things no Greek woman would attempt (cf. e.g. 536ff., 1330ff.). It will be in Athens that Medea is promised by King Aegeus that she will find sanctuary. She is related to the gods, a sorceress, a semi-divine figure who appears in a divine chariot for her final exit – an apotheosis which some have felt to be unsuited to her crimes. The woman, indeed, who makes this speech of female helplessness kills her rival and her children to hurt her husband, the male yoke she complains of here. 'I'd rather die', she says, but it is killing that she will adopt as plan of action. Indeed, as she speaks to the chorus, she goes on to mark her difference even from them (252–8):

> Yet what applies to me does not apply to you.
> You have a country. Your family home is here.
> You enjoy life and the company of your friends.
> But I am deserted, a refugee, thought nothing of
> by my husband – something won in a foreign land.
> I have no mother or brother, nor any relation
> with whom I can take refuge in this sea of woe.

Rather than the strange loneliness of married life, that Medea earlier decribed, these women enjoy themselves with the company of friends. Medea is the female outsider as much as she is the female intruder. Medea's speech with its various slants on 'the lot of women' cannot, then, be taken as a transparent expression of Euripides' or a Greek view of the status or position of women, although it seems to draw on what have been considered to be specifically fifth-century Athenian attitudes. The ideas of a woman's plight may seem clear and traditional enough – but they are not only ironized by Medea's murderous actions of power and trickery against her husband, and her escape by divine chariot: they are also delivered in the complex context of a tragic festival by a character depicted as an ancient barbarian sorceress, as someone 'other' to the chorus and to the audience. The description and evaluation of Medea, like Antigone, remains involved in a complexity of relations which challenges the possibility of univocal response. The insights that Medea and the *Medea* offer into a sexual discourse, then, cannot be separated from the complex problems of interpretation and reading that I have been outlining in this chapter.

Hippolytus provides a good focus for this discussion of a discourse of sexuality, as it is a play which explicitly revolves around relations of the sexes and attitudes to the sexual – and it is to *Hippolytus* that I wish to turn for the remainder of this chapter.[27]

---

[27] While writing this book, I have had the good fortune to see and discuss several drafts of Froma Zeitlin's article on *Hippolytus* which will be published by the time my book is out (Zeitlin 1985). My debt to her is large; her article offers the best extended reading of the play I know.

The dramatic scenario which Aphrodite announces in the prologue to *Hippolytus* – Hippolytus' rejection of sexuality and Phaedra's divinely inspired passion for her stepson – is played out in the opening scenes of the drama in a way which marks the structuring force of the relations of the *oikos* in the discourse of sexuality. For Hippolytus' rejection of the goddess Aphrodite cannot be separated from the idea of the male role in the *oikos*. His self-enforced virginity has none of the Christian overtones of self-denial, chastity and control:[28] the need for sexuality is also the need for procreation, the often expressed desire for the continuity of the *oikos* through children. While virginity[29] was generally regarded as a virtue for girls before they married, the aim of successful child production is of paramount concern to the household. Although 'sexual desire', *eros*, is often portrayed as a dangerous, mastering force over the mind and actions of men, which Plato for one regarded as a disruption to the philosophical life that had to be controlled,[30] such exhortations to self-control do not involve a monk-like total avoidance of sexual life as part of an ideal. Indeed, permanent virginity or even prolonged abstinence from sexual activity was regarded by the writers of the Hippocratic corpus as unhealthy; frequently, protracted virginity is regarded as the cause for various, often 'hysterical', symptoms in girls, which marriage and procreation could cure.[31] For men in fifth-century Athens, prostitutes and slaves offered further regular opportunities for sexual activity, apparently quite without moral or social stigma.[32] Periods of abstinence from sexual activity for religious reasons are required for women in certain cases and for men far less commonly;[33] and some cases of abstinence for medical reasons, or, at any rate, cases describing the detrimental effects of sexual activity are recorded;[34] and, as Onians mentions, there is a common belief in the weakening effects of sexual intercourse, the 'drying' which follows from loss of vital fluid.[35] But despite these hesitations, the interest in continence and chastity which the later medical writers of the Roman and Christian eras maintain[36] seems not to have been a similar concern of the writers of the

---

[28] For the development of the valuing of virginity in the ancient world, see Rousselle 1983.
[29] For virginity in general, see Gernet 1981, 23–4; Lloyd 1983, 58–111, especially 84; King 1983; Sissa 1984.
[30] For examples, see Dover 1973, 61–5, and especially 70; Dover 1974, 208–9.
[31] For examples, see Lloyd 1983, 84 n. 102.
[32] There was a stigma attached to becoming a prostitute – one was liable to lose citizen rights. But this does not apply to the use of prostitutes. On the dangers of extravagant expenditure on prostitutes, see Dover 1974, 179–80.
[33] See Fehrle 1910 for examples, especially 28–35. Virginity is a common requirement for certain priestesses, usually for a short-term office. It is almost unheard-of for priests, see Fehrle 1910, 75ff. See now Parker 1983, 74–103 and 301.
[34] For examples, see Lloyd 1983, 84 n. 103.   [35] Onians 1951, especially 109 n. 103.
[36] For one view of this, see Rousselle 1983; but see also Lloyd 1983, 168ff.

Hippocratic corpus, and through a great variety of texts in the fifth century the notions of the self which are developed link ideas of self-control to a narrative of sexual development and procreation within the *oikos*, rather than any ideal of total abstinence. Hippolytus' total rejection of sexuality sounds, then, already a note of disruption.

With this strange rejection of sexuality and the goddess Aphrodite, Hippolytus dedicates himself to Artemis and the hunt, and Hippolytus' first entrance is with his hunting companions, praying to the virgin goddess, Artemis.

This entrance is also to be seen within the terms of Hippolytus' rejection of sexuality. For hunting is not merely a sport or a means of getting food. It has a particular and important functioning in the ideological representation of the development of a person, which has been a topic of much recent analysis. 'Hunting', writes Vidal-Naquet, 'has a wide range of representational meanings.'[37] In the first place, 'it is a social activity which is differentiated according to the various stages of a man's life'.[38] Thus one can distinguish between the *initiatory hunt*, the first hunt of the young man who wishes to join the adult male sphere of action, and the *hunt of the hoplite*, the heroic hunt of the men, leaving the city together to confront wild animals. In the hunt of the young initiand, cunning, trickery and individuality stand as a reversal of the values of the heroic hoplite hunt, where the men in a group face a direct and straight challenge. So through the first hunt, first kill, the youth aspires to join the world of men in an activity rigidly male – and, as is characteristic of initiation practices, a period of reversal precedes the actual incorporation into the body of the men. Indeed, the hunt performs a primary function, argues Vidal-Naquet, in the self-definition of man in his world: he leaves the city, marking its boundaries, to face the wild animal, and brings the conquered animal back to the city to be cooked. So, for Vidal-Naquet, 'hunting is an expression of the transition between nature and culture'.[39]

Hunting places man in a relation to the wild, then, in much the same way as sacrifice, the other way of obtaining meat to consume, places man in a relation to the divine. Both express man's sense of himself through a relation with something other than himself. Indeed, the sacrifice, with its links with agriculture and the city's order, forms a complement and contrast to the hunt. With the killing of a domestic animal, sanctified by corn and wine, the products of man's labour, the sacrifices of the city and the household serve to express man's differentiation from the divine and the bestial in the systematiz-

[37] 1981c, 151. See also Vidal-Naquet 1968; 1974. The relevant articles have been collected and revised in Vidal-Naquet 1981a. For the connections of hunting and sexual development, see Schnapp 1984.
[38] 1981c, 151.   [39] 1981c, 151.

ation of things, much as the hunt with its slaughter of the wild animal places man in relation to the wild, uncultivated world of nature. So, it is interesting to note that in the *Oresteia* and the *Philoctetes*, for example, two plays very much involved with young men coming of age, there is a regular return to the imagery of hunting and sacrifice, particularly in the corrupt form of illicit sacrifice and human hunting,[40] which forms a complex system of ideas essential to the reversals and transgressions of those plays, and essential to the representation of the placing of man in his world. In the *Bacchae*, too, where the young ruler Pentheus attempts to control and order his surroundings with authority, it is in a wild parody of a hunt, a pursuit of a human prey by the city's women, half-dressed and armed with natural weapons or with merely their bare hands rather than man-made spears, that the destruction of the young man is completed.

War has an important part in this system also, not only in its similar cultural determination of the functioning of violence in society, but also in the way it helps to specify and organize the placing of a man in society. The aim of the Athenian male, the *telos* of his life, is, as Vernant has influentially argued,[41] to take his place as a citizen in the hoplite rank ready for war. This is also a point of rigid delimitation of sexual role: the man is the one who is recognized as a full citizen, the man is the one to take his place in the citizen army. War, like hunting and sacrifice, is not just the outbreak of violence, but constitutes a group of concepts which functions as a means of ordering and distinguishing differences and relations in society. Hunting, sacrifice, war form an interrelated system of ideas through which man finds his place in the order of things.

Hippolytus' denial of his sexuality and dedication to hunting, then, places him in a specifically distorted role. The hunt, in the interlocking system of ideas I have been outlining, should mark a part of Hippolytus' role as male entering a position and status in society. But his desire to remain apart from society in his refusal of sexual relations and continual worship of Artemis through the chase perverts this functioning of the hunt: it marks his desire to remain outside society, on the edge, away from his role in the *oikos*. Hippolytus' rejection of Aphrodite, then, is not just a desire for chastity or purity, but also a subverting of his passage to manhood. His entrance on stage from the wilds of the countryside with the youths of his own age to spurn the worship of Aphrodite marks how Hippolytus resists the narrative pattern of the development of his role in society, the distortion of the positioning of the self. As he himself says 'May I turn the post at life's end (*telos*) as I began' (87).

---

[40] See Vidal-Naquet's two essays in Vernant and Vidal-Naquet 1981; also Zeitlin 1965; Foley 1985.
[41] See Vernant 1980, 19–70.

He hopes to finish in the same place, manner, as he started; he hopes to avoid the passage, the stages of a man's life.

After Hippolytus' exit to fodder his horses, the focus shifts to the female world, as the chorus of women enter to tell of Phaedra's sickness. The queen's illness is keeping her inside on a sick-couch with her head hidden under her robes, fasting herself to death. They suggest various possible sources for these strange symptoms. First, divine possession, or sickness as a punishment for a ritual offence – though the real divine cause is notably not mentioned. Second, ironically enough, her husband's supposed infidelity. Third, bad news that has weighed upon her spirit. These suggested causes lead to a general statement of the condition of women's misery (161–9):

> Unhappy is the compound of woman's nature;
> the torturing misery of helplessness,
> the helplessness of childbirth and its madness
> are linked to it for ever.
> My body too has felt this thrill of pain,
> and I called on Artemis, Queen of the Bow;
> she has my reverence always
> as she goes in the company of gods.

The phrase 'unhappy compound' translates the Greek words *dustropos harmonia* which imply 'troublesome (hard to turn, badly turned) harmony, balance of parts'. This is a suggestive phrase, which in this play's focus on the balance and organization of the self seems almost programmatic for the dislocations and struggles to come. Nor do 'is . . . the nature' and 'linked to' capture the strong sexual hints of the Greek verbs *philei* and *sunoikein*. *Philos* and related words, as we have seen, are often explicitly sexual terms, and *sunoikein*, translated 'linked to', is the normal Greek for to 'share an *oikos*', 'live together', often in a sexual sense. This vocabulary looks towards the specific helplessness of the woman's lot, which is to risk life and pain in childbirth. As the *telos* of a man's life is found in the hoplite rank and war, so for woman the aim and final point is marriage and the procreation of children. 'Marriage is to the girl what war is to the boy.'[42] The word for 'woman' and 'wife' in Greek is the same (*gune*). In Greek, being a 'woman' – that is, changing one's status from young girl, unmarried female, virgin (*parthenos, kore, numphe*) – cannot be easily separated from, indeed implies, being given and taken in marriage for the procreation of children. And indeed the vocabulary of childbirth and war is often constructed in similar terms, particularly in Euripides,[43] as we have already seen in the *Medea*: Medea's opposition of childbirth and fighting, like this juxtaposition of childbirth and

[42] Vernant 1980, 23.   [43] See Loraux 1981c.

the returning hunt, is not just the opposition of actions involving risk to life but the opposition of concepts defining the essential difference of male and female roles. As hunting can mark a transitional moment in the young male's gradation to the status of man (*aner*), so marriage and child-production mark the point of passage from girlhood to womanhood for the female.

The final address to Artemis in these lines is interesting. If it appeared at first sight from the opening scene that the opposition of Aphrodite and Artemis was clear-cut (sexual life-creator versus virgin huntress), the connection of Artemis with childbirth confuses any such polarization in terms of a life involved with sex and one unsullied by it. For Artemis, the virgin huntress, is also the goddess who presided over childbirth.[44] Nor is childbirth the only moment of a woman's life over which Artemis exerted influence. As has been much discussed in the scholarly literature of late, the festival of Artemis at Brauron seems to have been an important part of the conception of the stages of a woman's life in Athens.[45] Harpocration tells us that girls 'had to become bears before marriage in honour of Artemis at Mounychia or Artemis at Brauron'.[46] Little is known for sure about the details of this ritual. It seems to have consisted of a procession from Athens (the women leaving the city, crossing its boundaries) and a stay at the shrine of Artemis at Brauron for a period of seclusion preceding and preparing for marriage. The myths told concerning this ritual 'involve an original killing of a bear by some boys, the retribution for which was at first a human sacrifice and later this ritual of substitution was performed by the girl-bears'.[47] Vidal-Naquet, noting the initiatory quality of this myth, offers this analysis: 'In exchange for the very advance of culture implied by the killing of wild animals, an advance for which the men are responsible, the girls are obliged before marriage – indeed, before puberty – to undergo a period of ritual "wildness".'[48] It would seem that at moments of transition in the passage of a woman's life, her explicit connections with Artemis, the goddess of the wild, in a similar way to hunting for the man, mark that transition in terms of a relation of culture to wildness, in terms of the city's self-determination through its sense of an other.

The female's connection with the natural world in the basic biological function of childbirth shows how in certain ideological formations the woman tends towards occupying an uneasy, liminal position in the Greek city. She

---

[44] See King 1983, for connections between women and Artemis in terms of flow of blood.
[45] See Lloyd-Jones 1983 for a survey of the recent material.
[46] The small size of the shrine building suggests the rite could not have involved all Athenian girls of a certain age every year. See Lloyd-Jones 1983, 93.
[47] Vidal-Naquet 1981d, 179.
[48] 1981d, 179. Osborne 1985, 162–6 notes that the bear, which walks on hind legs and has some other human characteristics, is possibly more difficult to classify than the simple determination 'wild'.

seems not quite a full member of the city as a cultural ideal (despite her necessary role), nor yet a creature of the outside, the wild. Indeed, throughout a great variety of texts[49] in a series of hierarchical oppositions we see, associated with the female, darkness as opposed to light, left as opposed to right, odd as opposed to even, and, as in the stanza I am still glossing, irrationality as opposed to rationality, that prime civic virtue – disorder as opposed to order. Through these oppositions, the female is conceptualized in a devalued position, with a tendency towards exclusion. The Dionysiac women of the *Bacchae*, scarcely dressed in the skins of wild animals, ripping apart animals or even humans with their bare hands, can be seen as a specific tragic distortion of this already devalued positioning of the female – a transgression into an extreme wild state. In a different way, the women in the assembly of Aristophanes' *Ecclesiazusae* constitute a comic reversal in the opposite direction, as women usurp the male civic roles.

Her biological, religious and cult connections with fertility and childbirth mark woman as necessary and as separate from man. But in that all too often hierarchical separation, as she is ideologically at any rate kept 'on the inside', so at moments of transition or transgression she tends towards the extremes of the uncertain realms beyond the boundaries and order of the city. It is not merely her entrance into the outside world of the state that marks woman's intrusive, transgressive movement – she is, indeed, a *dustropos harmonia*, a balance-of-parts that is troublesome!

It is worth stressing here again, however, that the inside and the outside, as I argued in Chapter 3, are not to be thought of as a strictly and entirely physical topography. The fact that this chorus of young noble ladies go to fetch water immediately marks a tension in the rigidity of the opposition of inside and outside, if the inside is thought of as an 'Oriental seclusion' of the house itself – unless this chorus' freedom stresses the difference between contemporary fifth-century culture and the archaic world of the tragic story. Despite scholars' disagreements about the precise limits and licence of movement outside the house for women of different classes[50] or backgrounds, the regular association of women with the inside and the dangers associated with women when they go outside are extremely important to the normative discourse of sexuality. Whatever the realities of fifth-century Athens – and there is a variety of evidence suggesting that women, especially those of poorer backgrounds, were more involved with work outside the house[51] – the requirement to keep women 'on the inside' is often and forcefully stated. Medea, like Orestes reproaching Clytemnestra in the *Oresteia* (*Cho.* 919–21),

[49] See Lloyd 1966.   [50] See Gould 1980 for the discussions, especially 47–51.
[51] See Gould 1980, 47–51 for examples. Also Jameson 1977.

recalls a commonplace of Athenian writing when she asserts men's claims to toil on the outside while women sit at home.

The entrance of Phaedra and the nurse indeed explicitly marks the movement outside – as so often in Attic drama[52] (179–82):

> I have brought out the couch on which you tossed
> in fever – here clear of the house.
> Your every word has been to bring you out,
> but when you're here, you hurry in again.

Indeed, Phaedra responds by trying to remove the covering from her head and then (208–11) by expressing her desire for a pastoral escape beyond the house and city 'beneath the poplars in the tufted meadow'. The 'uncut meadow', the virgin field untouched by man, was the place from where Hippolytus brought his offering to Artemis in his opening iambic lines (73–4). Phaedra follows her far from respectable requests with the even more outrageous appeal to go hunting in the hills (215–21):

> Bring me to the mountains! I *will* go to the mountains,
> among the pine trees where the huntsmen's pack
> trails spotted stags and hangs upon their heels.
> God how I long to set the hounds on shouting!
> And poise the Thessalian javelin, drawing it back –
> here where my fair hair hangs above the ear –
> I would hold in my hand a spear with a steel point.

Phaedra's sickness is seen in her transgressive desire for the outside, the male world of hunting in which Hippolytus roams. Indeed, she addresses Artemis (228–31) not as the chorus had in the goddess's connection with childbirth and women but as the huntress and horse-tamer. This address not only marks her transgressive desire, but also recalls in this juxtaposition of the male and female involvements in the conceptualization of Artemis how one-sided a view of Artemis Hippolytus himself worships. 'It is precisely because of the complexity of divinities like Aphrodite, Artemis, and Poseidon ... and the conflicting drives they instil in men that this simple view is doomed.'[53] In this light, it is interesting that the chorus sing of Diktynna (145) as one of the possible causes of Phaedra's malaise. Diktynna is a Cretan goddess (suitably enough for Phaedra, whose Cretan origin is emphasized later in the play), who is regarded later in the play and elsewhere[54] as the equivalent of Artemis especially in her relation to wild animals. Their mention

[52] Gould 1980, 40 notes well that women's freedom on the stage is not as absolute as it is sometimes made out to be.
[53] Segal 1965, 140.
[54] See 1130. Also *I.T.* 126ff.; Ar. fr. 1359. See Barrett ad loc. for further discussion.

of this goddess not only brings Artemis to the fore as a goddess of the wild, as Barrett suggests, but also implies a variation of cult and name in the worship of Artemis, as well as the variety of implications for both sexes in the portrayal of this divine figure.

Phaedra's appeal to go hunting in the wild makes the nurse cry: 'This is sheer madness that prompts such whirling, frenzied, senseless words' (231). In her sickness, Phaedra's desire for the outside world of the hunt is seen as a corruption of her rationality. With her transgressive move outside comes the tendency to excess – totally to abandon her female role, leave the city like a Bacchant, rush out to hunt in the hills. Such is the corruption of woman's mental processes, her 'madness'. Such is the corruption that follows from the unhinging of female desires. Her outburst is not just 'a hysterical expression of her desire for Hippolytus',[55] but is intertwined with the process of self-definition which is at risk in this play. Wildness, madness, female desire – dangers that society must define and control.

The movements inside and outside in the *Hippolytus* are closely interwoven with the interplay of speech and silence. After Phaedra is brought out into the open, it will be an attempt to make her bring her hidden desire into the open by speaking out that will dominate the next scene. The nurse will slip into the recesses of the house to speak of the queen's passion to Hippolytus, who in the famous third scene rushes from the house threatening to tell all. This drives Phaedra back into the house where she will kill herself – but not before leaving a letter, which, brought into the open, causes Theseus to accuse Hippolytus. The boy's silence in the face of the accusation of rape leads him to being driven off-stage, out of the country. And his death will be caused by Theseus having spoken out. If her confession of desire seems to set Phaedra's tragedy in motion, so Hippolytus' silence seems to hasten his. 'The choice between speech and silence', writes Knox in his classic article, 'is the situation which places the four principal characters in significant relationship. The poet has made the alternation and combinations of choice so complicated – Phaedra chooses first silence, then speech, the nurse speech, then silence, then speech, then silence, Hippolytus speech, then silence, the chorus silence and Theseus speech – that the resultant pattern seems to represent the exhaustion of the possibilities of human will.'[56] Indeed, the apparent fulfilment of Aphrodite's plan through the ins and outs of this patterning suggests the uncertain basis, even the futility, of the continually expressed concern for the outcome of action and the logic of moral choice. Moreover, as we shall see, this game of speech and silence also points towards the problematic role of language itself

[55] Knox 1952, 6.   [56] Knox 1952, 5–6.

in the flow of events. Uncertainty as to which words to use, and whether to use words at all, is an essential dynamic of this tragic text.

The scene between the nurse and Phaedra revolves, first, around the attempt to get Phaedra to name her malaise. For the nurse, as Knox notes, 'there is no problem which cannot be resolved by speech'[57] (295–9):

> But if your troubles may be told to men,
> speak, that a doctor may pronounce upon it.
> So, not a word! Oh, why will you not speak!
> There is no remedy in silence, child!

When, however, after the fencing of hesitation, questioning and manipulation, the secret is out, the nurse has at first no retort, words fail her, and she can only leave the stage, bewailing the lot of her house so cursed by Aphrodite. This leaves Phaedra, unburdened of her silence, to explain her position to the chorus. In a speech famous for its obscurities as much as its nobility, Phaedra expounds her processes of thought. Eros, that external force, has struck. Her first notion was to fight with silence: 'for the tongue is not to be trusted' (395). The doubleness and uncertainty of language is to be combated by a grim silence. Secondly, she planned to overcome this corruption in her attitude (*anoia*, 'madness') by a strong determination to display *sophrosune*, that is, the quality which saves (*sozo*) the mind (*phren*) – self-control, orderly, social, controlled attitudes. *Sophrosune* and related words, as we will see later in this chapter and in Chapter 7, are a prime group of terms of moral valuing – and appropriation – in Attic drama. Thirdly, she resolves finally to die.

Phaedra's reasoning here reflects well that what might be expected of an upper-class Athenian woman. She evinces a self-marked misogyny ('I know I am a woman, object of hate to all'), and this misogyny is juxtaposed to the need for the control of women's dangerous desires in enforced monogamous chastity ('Destitution light upon the wife who plays the tempter and strains her loyalty to her husband's bed by dalliance with strangers'). The fear of uncertain paternity is also a fear of confused property status in inheritance and thus the collapse of the economic order and continuity of the *oikos*. The desire for the continuity of the *oikos* through stable, male inheritance combines with the belief in woman's uncontrollable (hysterical, irrational) sexuality to justify a belief in the rigid maintenance of the strict control of women sexually and socially. With women controlled on the inside, the dangers of the corruption of the paternal order are reduced. Women are given (exchanged) in marriage by men, and their alienability and inviolability are essential to the functioning of the maintenance of the boundaries and social organization of property, of what is owned, one's own. Adultery threatens precisely the bonds and links of

[57] Knox 1952, 7.

society, not just a relationship between man and wife.[58] The woman's chastity is essential to the continuity of the *oikos* as social and economic unit through the production of legitimate children to inherit the family property and continue the paternal line.

It is interesting in this light that Hippolytus is a bastard. He was the offspring of Theseus and Hippolyta, the queen of the Amazons, who had been defeated by Theseus. The Amazons, the warlike race of women who fight and hunt, notably confuse the characteristic boundaries defining the difference between male and female roles. Moreover, they alternate between a virginal rejection of sexual relations with men, and a promiscuity necessary to propagate their race. For them, the bonds and bounds of marriage and society have no place – or rather, these females stand as a permanent transgression of the city's constitution. Theseus' defeat of these women is as much a part of Athenian self-projection as the Lapiths' defeat of the half-beast, half-man centaurs – another fight to protect the inviolability of marriage.[59] Both Theseus' and the Lapiths' victorious battles against the forces of wild anarchy and the corruption of sexual roles were popular subjects for state-financed temple sculptures: like modern political murals, the triumph of the forces of good marks the self-glorification of the state and its ideology. The Amazons and the centaurs are part of the postulation of a negated form of life by which the city determined its own boundaries. They 'affirm the normative values of the male, city-dwelling, hoplite, agriculturally supported warrior by enacting the non-viability of the opposite'.[60]

The bastard Hippolytus (a 'natural child') stands on the edge of these normative values, then, not only in his rejection of sexuality but also in the transgressive sexual act by which he was engendered. As bastard stepson, his role in the family is far from secure.[60a] Phaedra, too, has a dubious sexual background. Her mother was Pasiphae, who through divine displeasure was driven into a passion for a bull, by which she gave birth to the Minotaur. As much as the expected model of generational continuity postulates a moral order and regulation, so in this situation there is a history of transgressive desire and disorder. Well might Phaedra say 'It makes the stoutest man a slave, if in his soul he knows his parents' shame' (424–5). The sins of the father . . .

The nurse returns to dispute with her mistress: 'Second thoughts are somehow better.' Her arguments in juxtaposition to the morality of Phaedra

---

[58] See Tanner 1980 – an excellent study.
[59] The centaurs attacked the Lapiths during the marriage of the king, to carry off the bride. See du Bois 1984.
[60] Segal 1981, 30–1. See also du Bois 1984; Tyrrell 1984.
[60a] On bastards, see Vernant 1980, 50–1; Hansen 1985, 73–6.

draw on all the manipulative powers of sophistic rhetoric, and in contrast to her previous despairing lack of an answer to her mistress, now the nurse finds the situation 'not beyond thought or reason' (*logos*). It is through the deceptive qualities of *logos* that the nurse proceeds to combine the vocabulary and mythic images of traditional morality and religion in order to suggest the ignoring of both – to the point that she can argue that since the gods are divine and unconquerable, it is hubris to attempt to fight the god Eros. Not giving in to her passion is to be seen as an arrogant act against the power and authority of the gods.

She concludes: 'men would take long to hunt devices out, if we women did not find them first'. The ambivalent valuing of the ability to use the manipulative rhetoric and devices to get one's way – an ability which is one of Odysseus' most notable characteristics – is here aligned with the female, and specifically female speech. Indeed, the seductive vagaries of communication, as well as deviousness in action, are often construed as female qualities in the hierarchy of values – as we saw with Clytemnestra in the *Oresteia*. As much as this Athenian discourse attempts to place woman on the margins, so she is conceived of as using forms of language and action which manipulate the boundaries and margins of proper behaviour. And it will be a deceptive device of a woman, the letter of Phaedra, on which the plot will turn.

Despite her initial horror at the nurse's argument, Phaedra finds that her notion of 'good name' is being systematically undercut by the appeal to the 'real need' to save Phaedra's life by some action – an argument which is itself a neat reversal of Phaedra's opposition of 'fair-seeming words' and the reality of morality. The nurse offers a *pharmakon* for the queen's sickness in her speech. The hoped-for cure, which will turn out to be a poison, marks the irony in this ambiguous term, which can imply both a good medicine and a harmful drug. Indeed, the nurse markedly side-steps the queen's request that she say nothing to Hippolytus, and it is with some foreboding – Phaedra's and the audience's – that the nurse is seen to leave the stage. It is at this point of tension and uncertainty in the narrative that the chorus sing the famous ode on the destructive force of Eros.

At a juncture, then, between the establishment of the cause of Phaedra's sickness and the downfall into disaster through the nurse's revelation and its results, the chorus significantly reflect on the murderous results of Eros' influence. It is interesting that unlike, for example, Aeschylus' ode on Eros in the *Choephoroi*, it is not the transgressive desires of women that are placed at the centre of the collapse of human relationships. Rather, the externalized force of Eros is depicted as attacking human beings, and in the mythological examples of Iole and Semele it is women who suffer destruction, abasement, and misery through the warlike aggression of males under the sway of Eros. Are these examples to be taken as programmatic for the Aphrodite-inspired actions to come, the rash aggressiveness of both Hippolytus and Theseus?

The baneful influence of passion and its results are all too quickly in evidence. Hippolytus rushes out of the house, claiming his purity tainted by the words he has heard. He extends his outrage into a lengthy diatribe against the whole female sex, in terms which relate closely to the discourse of sexuality I have been discussing. He wants to remove the necessity of women completely; to replace the exchange of marriage as a means of producing children with the exchange of money for children in a temple. He objects in particular to the woman who is clever (that is, who demonstrates the deceitful wiles of the seducing corrupter). And for Hippolytus the cause of this corruption of the clever is lust, Aphrodite's weapon (642–4):

> ... Lust breeds mischief
> in the clever ones. The limits of their minds
> deny the stupid lecherous delights.

It is only stupidity which prevents all women from following the path of the clever. Hippolytus, moreover, rejects the very possibility of communication for women, for whom language is means and matter of transgression (646–7):

> ... give them as companions voiceless beasts,
> dumb ... but with teeth, that they might not converse.

It is to the company of wild beasts that the hunter Hippolytus, who cannot have his fill of hating women (664), would reduce the female sex.

This diatribe, then, like Medea's speech on the race of women, may be read in terms of the discourse I have been outlining. Woman as necessary producer of legitimate children, but whose lusts challenge the status of the house and property, which must be maintained through the rigidity of certain mono-gamy; woman as dangerous both in her attributes of cultured life (language and communication in her mouth become deception and seduction) and in her tendency towards the wild world beyond the boundaries and order of the city. But this speech also marks the difficulty of reading particularly an explicitly misogynist statement in such a dramatic text as a transparent means to either Euripides' or a Greek audience's view. Is Hippolytus' total rejection of womankind to be seen as part of the tendency to excess in his attitude? Does it mark an unlikely corruption and distortion of the civic valuation of women? And if this diatribe is such a distortion, is it in order to point towards the danger of such excess inherent in a more normal Athenian male standpoint? Or is it in order to justify the status quo by putting forward an obviously distorted extremism which can safely be rejected by an appeal to the norms of everyday reality? Or is this speech designed to question that status quo by a *reductio ad absurdum* of such a male standpoint? How is it to be seen in relation to the searching struggle of Phaedra to maintain her honour? Or in terms of the nurse's sophistic manipulation? Or the chorus' supportive uncertainty? Despite Euripides' misogynist reputation in antiquity, it is difficult to separate this speech out from the dialectic of the drama as a privileged insight into 'male attitudes' (the poet's or the audience's).

It will, however, be a female communication and trick which will finally compel Hippolytus to defend himself against a charge of rape before his enraged father, Theseus. And it will be the word of the father, with the full weight of his own father, Poseidon, which will not only banish Hippolytus from his paternal home, but also send him to his doom, torn by his own horses.

Although many critics, especially in our post-Freudian age, have been quick to see the bull from the sea in terms of the discourse of sexuality so important to this play, the reversals and distortions of this tragic disaster also reflect the wider markings of the system of human relations in the language of the city. For this curse from the father which kills the son (the denial of the possibility of generational continuity) sets in motion that domesticated animal of agriculture, the bull, the father of the herd, whose sacrifice is normally the most important and the most circumscribed with controls and regulations. And this monstrous aggressor is sent against the hunter and his team, with the result that the team turns and destroys its master, the hunter. And his body is brought in by his companions, as it were, their own prey – a scene which mirrors[61] Hippolytus' first entrance in a tragically different light. The inversions and transgressions of order that we have seen throughout this drama, the distortions of man's and woman's positioning of the self in society and in language in terms of sexual difference, are reflected in these oxymoronic images of the *tauron, agrion teras* (1214), the 'bull from the wild, a monster': the dangerous animal which must be domesticated for agriculture is here wild (and as such a 'monster', 'prodigy'); the hunter is hunted; and destroyed by the very beasts with which he normally proves himself the hunter and master – his own team. It is not only the illicit passion of Phaedra's mother that is recalled by the prodigy of the bull from the sea, but the interlocking series of images of the play by which sexual roles have been expressed.

So through a discourse of sexuality and its interrelations with the other languages of the city I have approached a reading of this play which focuses

[61] Cf. Taplin 1978, 134–5, who regards Hippolytus' exit in exile also as a 'mirror scene' of his first entrance.

explicitly on the role of man and woman, sexual desire, sexual fulfilment. We have seen how the hunter Hippolytus' linkings with Artemis relocate his notion of himself as a (young) man: his rejection of sexuality is involved with a dislocation of this role in the *oikos* (which may reflect his status as 'natural child'), as his particular form of hunting-life seems to fit uneasily into the city's model of its own organization. Phaedra, whose divinely inspired passion for her stepson stands to corrupt her role as chaste protector of the economic, sexual, spatial boundaries of the household as social unit, fights to maintain her values in the face of the dual onslaught of the attacks of Eros on the one hand and the sophistic rhetoric of the nurse on the other; but, in reaction to Hippolytus' savage denunciation of the whole race of women, she resolves both to die and to avenge herself on his lack of understanding. The divine Aphrodite's resolve to punish the excess of one man sets in relief the doubts and inversions, the misreadings and errors, the over-determination of cause and motivation that characterize the human interrelations of this tragedy. Each character distorts or is distorted by his or her relation to his or her sexual role. Indeed, it would seem that the possibility of anything but a *dustropos harmonia* for mortals in this play is evinced only in absence and lack. The misogyny of Hippolytus is not merely a sign of his inverted or distorted attitudes but also a symptom of a specifically tragic *Weltanschauung*.

There is, however, as always, another twist and turn to the process of interpretation that interrupts the passage of that argument, and returns us to the problems of reading a discourse of sexuality with which I opened this chapter.

The *Hippolytus* is unique among extant tragedies in that what we possess is a second version by the same writer. The first *Hippolytus* has not survived except in a few fragments and in some reports of its lack of success. In this first version, it would seem that Phaedra made an explicit attempt on stage to seduce her stepson, who fled covering his head in shame – an act which gives the play its title *Hippolytus Kaluptomenos* ('Hippolytus veiling himself'). About the remainder of the play little is known for certain, but the character of Phaedra was singled out as especially shameless and outrageous, and the play seems to have caused a general outrage. It was the second *Hippolytus*, with a virtuous Phaedra, which won first prize.

Now there are specific echoes of the first play in the second, discernible even from the few fragments we possess. Phaedra's covering and uncovering of her head in the opening scene, as with the bringing out and taking back inside of her bed, seems to suggest even in Phaedra's struggle for morality Hippolytus' earlier moral outrage at the direct sexual approach. So, too, Hippolytus' final covering of his head (1458) as he dies on stage pathetically recalls the earlier bold rejection of Eros: the result of the upright Phaedra's action is the same, finally, as her immoral predecessor. On a specifically textual level, the few lines of the first play which survive find interesting repetitions and differences in our *Hippolytus*. Fragment 430 (Nauck), for example, claims Eros as the best teacher for boldness (*tolma*) and daring (*thrasos*) when faced with a hopeless situation. The word for 'boldness', *tolma*, indicates often a spirit of transgression, the impulse to evil, as well as the power of endurance. In this fragment, it is normally assumed, Phaedra prepares herself to approach Hippolytus. In the second *Hippolytus*, the nurse, that teacher of the ways of Eros in Phaedra's hopeless situation, attempts to educate Phaedra through a notable ambiguity: *tolma d' erosa*, she exhorts, which means both 'endure your passion', 'bear your love', and also 'be bold, daring in your love'. The nurse as manipulator of language towards evil adopts the language of the earlier Phaedra to persuade her moral mistress. So, indeed, Theseus cries at Hippolytus (937) in direct echo of the first Phaedra's line 'Where will daring impudence find limits?', 'Where will there be an end to *tolma* and *thrasos*?' His accusation of Hippolytus, ironically enough, marks the continuation of the outrageous language of the first Phaedra's steps towards seduction at this turning-point of the moral Phaedra's revenge.

Such specific interplays can be multiplied, but it is a wider intertextual irony that I wish to follow. I have already discussed the focus in this work on language as language. Specifically, I looked at the way that the exchanges of speech and silence in contrast with the explicit divine planning marked the imbroglio of mortals' attempts to control communication and choice. And it is to this focus on language, with regard to the use of the vocabulary of moral, sexual control that I wish to return.

In Chapters 1 and 2, I discussed the self-reflexive concern with language as language and the rhetoric of appropriation which twists language into a power struggle over meaning rather than a transparent medium of communication. Now in *Hippolytus*, 'Euripides is keenly aware of the ambiguous, "protean", quality of moral terms which most strongly guide our conduct ... His attention to the shifting meaning of words like *semnos* and *sophron* is obvious.'[62] Indeed, the terms of purity and self-control in relation both to a person's conception of herself/himself and to the nature of moral action (inasmuch as these can be separated) set in play not only the various tensions between humans (as in the opening scene between Hippolytus and the servant) but also the motivations of divine reasoning. Aphrodite in her prologue, for example, expresses her disapproval of those who *phronousin eis hemas mega*, 'have a great, proud disposition of mind towards me'. This is

[62] Segal 1970, 278.

picked up by the servant, after Hippolytus rejects his appeal to show some honour (*time* 107) to Aphrodite (as she had declared, 'honoured (*timomenoi*) by mortals the gods rejoice' 8). He prays to Aphrodite, rejecting the young men whose 'disposition of mind is thus' (*phronountas houtos*). So Phaedra describes her attempt to reach a safe disposition of mind in similar terms (376, 378, 390, 412 repeat words of the root *phren*, 'mind'). And the nurse's rhetoric against the queen, her second thoughts (*phrontides*), echoes Aphrodite herself as she warns against 'having a great, proud disposition of mind' (445) against the goddess. Hippolytus' final words in his diatribe against women exhort the need for women 'to be chaste', as Grene translates. But the verb is *sophronein* (from which, the noun *sophrosune*, and adjective *sophron*). The etymology of the term *sophronein* is *sos phren*: 'safe, sound, mind'; and it means something closer to 'sound attitudes', 'self-control', 'due observance of limits' than 'physical chastity'.

Phaedra's last line ironically echoes that final outburst of her stepson. I quote again from Grene's translation: 'he will have his share in this my mortal sickness and learn of chastity in moderation'. The strange phrase 'chastity in moderation' is another attempt to render the same word in the same metrical position, *sophronein*. She returns precisely his threat of a future learning of this quality.

The choral ode which follows describes the locus of the tragedy firmly as in the *phren*, 'mind' (765, 775, translated by Grene 'spirit' and 'heart'). Moreover, the debate between Theseus and Hippolytus which follows opens with an exchange again explicitly in terms of *phren* (919–22):

> Theseus: ... One thing you never hunt for – a way to teach fools wisdom.
> Hippolytus: Clever indeed would be the teacher able to compel the stupid to be wise.

The term for wisdom (920) is *phronein*, which I translated earlier as 'to be of a particular disposition of mind'. Hippolytus' answer picks up but specifies further Theseus' bitterly ironic language. 'The stupid' is *tous me phronountas*, those who do not *phronein*. And the term for 'to be wise' is *eu phronein* – not merely *phronein* but qualified by the adverb *eu*, 'well': 'It would be a wise teacher who could teach those who can't think to think well.'

From this beginning, the vitriolic argument between son and father continually harps on the mutual accusation of and concern for the other's state of mind. *Phren* and related words are repeated 926, 930, 983 (where they are not translated explicitly by Grene) and 936, 969. Indeed, Hippolytus' claim in his own defence is that no man is 'more *sophron*' than himself (995). The translation 'chaste' here continues to blur the issue: for it is the general word for soundness of mind, or observance of the boundaries and order of things that

Hippolytus has appropriated for his regime, rather than a direct expression of chastity or virginity (which scarcely allows of degrees). Bound by his oath, Hippolytus cannot speak out the truth – but in his tortured attempt to indicate something of his dilemma, it is precisely his language of *sophronein* that divides against itself. In the following lines, 'virtuous' translates *sophron* (1034–5):

> Virtuous she was in deed, although not virtuous:
> I that have virtue used it to my ruin.

The vocabulary of *sophronein* at this point seems to display a disjunctive and corrupting force rather than its normal association of moral virtue and a positive value as a criterion of action.

From this all too brief analysis, it will, I hope, be clear that the correct attitude of mind and observance of bounds and limits in terms of the vocabulary of *sophronein* and *phronein* is an extremely important part of the discourse of sexuality and the self in this drama. The notion of a 'correct' form of *sophronein* is postulated only through its absence from the system of different and competing claims. As an object of appropriation and dislocation, the moral terminology serves to undermine the prospect of a unified didactic message in this play (unless, perhaps, if such a message concerns the disjunctions of moral language). Indeed, in the final scene as Artemis apparently explicates and expounds the truth to the characters on stage, she disconcertingly calls Hippolytus *sophron* (1402). If there is one character in the play whose notion of *sophronein* has been at risk from the opening of the play, it is Hippolytus. It is surprising to have it authorized by the divinity at the moment of his demise. The security and harmony that some have felt from the divine framing and from the final reconciliation of father and son in this play does not extend to any neat bounding or limitation of the moral vocabulary. How are we to read Artemis' claim that Hippolytus showed himself *sophron* and Aphrodite hated him for it? The open-ended language resists any comforting harmonization. Rather than simply developing the nobility of Phaedra, the readoption of the vocabulary of the observance of proper limits brings its own ironies and uncertainties.

Phaedra herself in famous lines (338ff.) also discusses the ambivalence of another key term, *aidos*. Now I do not intend to look at the various arguments as to what she might mean by this ambivalence,[63] but I do want to consider the vocabulary by which she expresses her sense of the doubling of language. I use my own translation (385–7):

---

[63] Cf. Barrett ad loc.; Segal 1970; Avery 1968; Willink 1968, who discuss these lines.

... There are two sorts of *aidos*; the one is not evil,
the other a burden on the *oikos*. If the right measure were clear,
then there would not be two things having the same letters.

The ambiguity in moral language is expressed as the ambiguity in the signifying form of the letters: one set of letters for two ideas. This is what hinders the clarity of the 'right measure', of 'hitting the target'.

The nurse in her speech to the queen recalls old written texts[64] (451) in which Zeus' love for Semele is depicted. This example is used as an argument for the need to give way to love, which cannot be conquered. It seems significant that in the following choral ode, the chorus recall that same story (555–64) to indicate the murderous, destructive force of passion – immediately before the cries of the outraged Hippolytus are heard. It would seem that the nurse's appeal to written evidence is doubled into doubt by its juxtaposition to the chorus' reading of the myth.

The letter of Phaedra is the prime example of the possibility of misinterpretation of the written word (both in its composition and its reading). The letter 'cries aloud' (877), it has 'a song' (880), it is a 'sure accusation' (1057–8). This is opposed to Hippolytus' appeal to the house to bear him witness (1074), which Theseus dismisses scathingly as a 'clever appeal to witnesses without a voice' (1076). The assumed certainty of the written word leads Theseus to utter the irreversible curse, the spoken word which bears no retraction. And it will be the very uncertainty, the very doubleness of letters as a signifying medium, which will lead him to wish back his curse in vain.

In these terms, it is interesting that the most famous line of this play, which reputedly caused a scandal for the Athenian audience, asserts the possibility of a complete disjunction between words and thoughts, moral choices, intellectual decisions – and so the impossibility of sure reading: 'my tongue has sworn but my mind (*phren*) is unsworn'. That Hippolytus does not speak out but obeys his oath to his own death, does not totally repress the fearful spectre of a language, a religious invocation, totally divorced from intention, clarity, truth. At one pole, stands Theseus' curse, performative language with no slippage, no error, but the total fulfilment of intention in expression (though his intention becomes seen as misplaced); at the other pole, the possibility of a complete disjunction between words and what they might be read to signify. It is not surprising that Phaedra regards the tongue as not to be trusted (395).

Now the device of Phaedra's letter 'must be private to this one play'.[65] How, then, does that piece of writing relate to the rewriting of the *Hippolytus*,

---

[64] *Graphai* can mean either paintings or writings. Barrett, following Dodds, regards writings as the only possible meaning here.
[65] Barrett 1964, 38.

the second writing (reading) of the myth? The second play, which wins first prize with its reconstruction of its heroine in terms of the traditional morality of a 'good woman', does not simply 'correct the impropriety so objectionable in the first play'.[66] For not only does it place at risk specifically the vocabulary of moral restraint that it seems to have readopted (as we saw with *sophronein*), but also it challenges and disrupts the positioning of such morality both by its juxtaposition to the cynicism of sophistic rhetoric, and by the disturbing portrayal of the divine world (that authorization of the traditional moral tenets). Moreover, the notion of 'second thoughts being wiser' is put in the mouth of the sophistic nurse to justify her lengthy challenge to traditional morality, as the need for rereading Phaedra's letter, the nurse's written stories, the letters of the words of moral language, all suggest the uncertainty of the process of textual interpretation. Misreading is an essential dynamic of the *Hippolytus*.

Between this emphasis on misreading and the shifting of misleading language, the security of the interpreter of Euripides' play is undermined. Where does he stand in the twisting, ironic inversions of language and reading that constantly assert his tendency to error? In other words, rather than offering a simple rectification of the first play's representation of corrupt femininity, the second *Hippolytus* through the very act of *rewriting* restresses the divisions and divisiveness of language and discourse, that undermine the accurate and fixed determination of sexual, social, intellectual boundaries and order. The interplay between the two *Hippolytuses*, rather than stabilizing the moral vocabulary, can only re-emphasize its instabilities. Rewriting, rereading cannot but mark the problems of *difference* in repetition. Division and divisiveness are constantly being stressed in the relation between the two plays, even as the latter is accepted as rectifying the first. And the introduction of the letter of Phaedra into the second play, the text within the text, written to deceive, read and reread, itself suggests that the dangers of slippage in the process of communication stem from the possible inversions of a text's message.

It is, then, not so much 'morality', but the difference between 'morality' and 'immorality' as classifications that seems to be set at risk in this play. Could it be that Euripides' drama questions the Athenians' judgement, which nevertheless went on to give him first prize second time round, but reviled the first play for its flaunting of morality?

The sense in which these ironic inversions of Euripides' play undermine the definition of morality and immorality in relation to each other must affect our reading of the sexual discourse of the *Hippolytus*. As much as it seems

[66] This phrase is translated from the play's hypothesis (II, 6–7).

necessary to approach the play through a sense of the Athenians' different system of ideas that constitutes the way the relations between the sexes are formulated, so the play itself seems to be challenging the possibility of the definition or delimitation of that system. The language of the play does not simply reflect a discourse of sexuality but challenges, ironizes, undermines the safe use of the language of that discourse, particularly in the way that the play contests the security of the processes of classification, reading, interpretation, by which distinctions, decisions, regulations are determined. A sexual discourse cannot provide the grid, the framework, into which this play can be fitted, and controlled, and ordered. Rather than offering an explanatory model, as some Freudian or anthropological readings have asserted, the language and logic of sexual difference reinscribe the divisions and divisiveness of meaning within the tragic text.

There is, then, a constant tension in the dialectic of the play between explicit statement, tacit knowledge, and the questioning that the tragic text instigates. This tension or interplay between the necessity of a reading which takes into account a specific cultural discourse of sexuality and the necessity of a reading which is alive to Euripides' decentring, vertiginous ironies, requires a constant reinterpretation, a constant turning back on oneself, one's self. The final fixing of meaning with regard to the moral, social languages of sexuality is subverted in Euripides' tragic text. One cannot hope to avoid rereading the rewritten . . .

6 · TEXT AND TRADITION

> Trailing clouds of glory ...
> WORDSWORTH

'Reading a poem', writes Geoffrey Hartman, 'is like walking on silence – on volcanic silence. We feel the historical ground; the buried life of words.'[1] This sense of uncertain depth, uncertain soundings, is nowhere more evident than in Greek tragedy's relation to the tradition of earlier writings. Although a relatively small proportion of the stories of the three major tragedians appear to have been drawn directly from the Homeric poems, and although the poetic language of tragedy does not reflect constant and close dependence on Homeric usage (as do some other genres),[2] it is none the less impossible to understand Greek tragedy without a consideration of the way Homer and Hesiod resound and echo through these texts at a variety of levels and in a variety of important ways. I have already mentioned in Chapters 4 and 5 the complex dialectic between past and present that is enacted by the plays performed before the city but set in the heroic past,[3] and in Chapter 1 I discussed the specific democratic rewriting of the Hesiodic injunction not to give crooked judgement in the *Oresteia*'s depiction of the establishment of the lawcourt. In this chapter, I intend to discuss in as much detail as space permits the relations of the texts of Greek tragedy to the tradition in and against which they are written and must be read. Aeschylus is said to have claimed his works were 'slices from the banquets of Homer'[4] (though whether this means left-overs or choice pieces is less than clear) and, 'Sophocles might have taken for himself the Aeschylean claim.'[5] Euripides, too, is impossible to understand without some sense of the heroic tradition and the place of Homer in more than a literary context. It is on the varying attitudes to and uses of the past, and on the literary tradition, particularly of Homer, in and against which the plays of the tragic corpus are formed, that this chapter will focus.

[1] 1970, 342–3.
[2] Gould 1983, 32–3 makes this point, but rather overstates his case. On lyric poetry, see Harvey 1957; on Hellenistic poetry see e.g. Giangrande 1970; and now Bulloch 1985; Hopkinson 1984.
[3] A partial exception is Aeschylus' *Persae*. It is still set in a foreign place, and 'mythologized' to a degree; see Winnington-Ingram 1983, 1–16. Phrynichus' *Sack of Miletus*, about which little is known, is assumed to have treated a modern subject.
[4] Athen. 8.347e.   [5] Knox 1964, 52.

My subject is itself deeply involved with the past and with the traditions of scholarship: as we will see, not only is the study of Homer the basis of ancient Greek scholarship and education, but also the specific question of the relation of tragedy and Homer is, of course, traditional. Recent literary scholarship has outlined the insufficiency of the commonest earlier ways of approaching this topic. Most Victorian editions and translations of Greek plays – and modern works which take these Victorian approaches as a model – suffice themselves by outlining differences in 'plots' between a play and its epic version and offer little attempt at explanation or analysis of why such changes should be formulated or what dramatic point may be understood by them. So, too, although specific Homeric echoes are duly noted, little attempt is made beyond the noting itself to explain or analyse why a specific passage or passages of Homer should be brought to the fore at a particular point. More recently, however, Knox[6] and Winnington-Ingram[7] have written important analyses of the Sophoclean hero in terms of a relation between the heroic past and democratic, contemporary, social norms; and Vernant's notion of the 'tragic moment' revolves around a tension between heroic, traditional norms and a new spirit of legal, civic values in a society in flux.[8] Each of these critics will be important to the following chapter. But although the texts of tragedy are often used in the history of intellectual thought in the Greek world, or in the history of particular ideas or moral terminology, there have been surprisingly few major investigations in more literary terms of the relations between tragedy and earlier Greek writing.[9]

This lack of study of the role of tradition in the process of writing and reading tragedy is in marked contrast to literary studies outside the field of Greek tragedy. It is not by chance that this chapter's epigraph is from a Romantic author. For it is the Romantic poets' dependence on and dislocation from the literary past, and the subsequent modernist writers' reaction against the Romantic and other authors, that have provided a subject for an extended tradition of subtle and influential scholarship. From Eliot and Leavis with their different determinations of the dictates of tradition to the more recent work of Bloom, Hartman, Kristeva, the relations between different texts, between texts and tradition, have been analysed in a variety of ways that have greatly developed what can be understood by 'influence' or 'echo' or 'reference'. I hope that some of these critics' different approaches also will help in making clear the interconnections of the texts of tragedy and earlier writings.

Throughout the fifth century, Homer maintained his value as 'the best and

[6] 1964, especially 5off.   [7] 1980, especially 15 ff., 6off.
[8] Vernant and Vidal-Naquet 1981, 1–5.
[9] See e.g. Solmsen 1949, which I have not found especially useful.

most divine of poets', as Plato put it.[10] This judgement, however, is not just a commonplace of ancient aesthetics. For the value of Homer is not merely in terms of his poetic merits, or rather the value of poetry in ancient Athenian society is quite different from its determination in modern culture. For poetry is regarded and used as a most important didactic medium. Both in the education of children and in the wider dissemination of ideas, policies, attitudes, poetry plays a major social role in Athenian culture. At the simplest level, the study of the Muses – poetry, singing, dancing – is linked to gymnastics as the dual basis of children's education. Poetry provided the texts used for study, and Homer in particular appears to have constituted a major area of traditional teaching. A fragment of Aristophanes' earliest comedy *Daitales*, for example, depicts a teacher's lesson, with a boy being questioned on the meaning of archaic Homeric vocabulary;[11] and poetry and music are discussed as a necessary basis of education even in such radical programmes as Plato's *Republic* and *Laws*, where the general view is summed up in the expression 'lack of training in singing, dancing and poetry is synonymous with lack of education'.[12] Even if in Aristophanic comedy, which may be predisposed to seeing 'discipline' as something of the past and disappearing, we are given an impression that such training appears conservative and old-fashioned compared with the new methods of teaching practised by the sophists,[13] there is none the less a large degree of continuity throughout the fifth and fourth century in the important place of music, dancing, poetry and in particular Homer in early education.[14]

Recent studies have tried to chart the historical development of the importance of poetry and singing in Greek culture.[15] In particular, choric training and performance for young people, especially adolescents, appear to have played in the sixth century an interesting educational role in a wider social sense – as with so many institutions connected to the times of puberty and adolescence. The training of groups of young people for choric performance, rather than simply being an occasion to teach singing and dancing, seems to have been part of a general educational process in which the poet and his poetry constitute a way of transmitting the cultural heritage of the society. The poet plays a special role as the one who 'preserves and transmits the whole

---

[10] *Ion* 530b9–10.
[11] Fr 222 K. For pictures of such study, see Beck 1975, especially of the Berlin School Cup (14–15).
[12] *Achoreutos apaideutos* (*Laws* 654a). Of course, Plato goes on to distinguish between the relative values of good and bad poetry and music.
[13] See especially *Clouds* 961ff. On the sophists, see below, Chapter 9.
[14] See Marrou 1956, 41ff. Papyri finds also confirm the continuing predominance of Homer in education.
[15] Calame 1977; Detienne 1967; Svenbro 1976.

system of ethical values and the collection of mythology on which the coherence of the life of the community is based'.[16] In this sense, the poet is the 'educator *par excellence*'[17] – a 'master of truth'.[18] It is in the light of this important educational role that we must read both the often expressed dangers of the possible deceptive qualities of poetic utterance,[19] and also the poets' claims to be divinely inspired and to be capable of perpetuating a memory through poetic utterance. There is a certain power in poetic language. When the poets of the fifth century and later claim to be 'educators of the citizens' it is in part a claim to be aligned with this tradition of the divinely inspired teacher of myth and value through song.

Throughout the fifth and fourth centuries, then, the study and practice of poetry remained with gymnastics an essential part of children's education.[20] But the didactic force of poetry stretches beyond the schooling of the young. Influential philosophers such as Parmenides and Xenophanes wrote in verse, and so too did great reformers and political leaders such as Solon, or such didacticists as Theognis. When poets claim in ancient Athens to be the educators of the city it is also a claim to be aligned with such figures as Solon, whose political, social, moral reforms established him as one of the great law-givers for the democratic state.[21] This notion of poetry not as esoteric art or mere entertainment, but as a medium for important, general and true utterance to the city is also highly relevant to the institution of the tragic festival as a civic occasion.

Homer, too, the 'best and most divine' of these poets, was performed or recited publicly. Professional singers, known as 'rhapsodes' ('song-stitchers'), who often travelled around the country, recited and held regular competitions in reciting. The Panathenaic festival, which as its name suggests was another celebration in which the whole city of Athens was involved held a competition for the recitation of Homer (as well as races in armour and a torch-lit procession). A rhapsode was expected here to pick up his recitation from where the previous singer had finished – presumably to know the whole of Homer off by heart.[22] There are indeed stories of young men being required to memorize all of Homer in order to develop 'character',[23] although it is pointed out in Xenophon's story that the rhapsodes who learn all of Homer remain the stupidest bunch! A more developed view of the rhapsode and his art is seen in

---

[16] Calame 1977, 399.   [17] Calame 1977, 399.   [18] Detienne's phrase.
[19] As Detienne 1967, 72ff., emphasizes. See also Pucci 1977.
[20] See Marrou 1956, 46ff.
[21] On Solon and democratic ideology, see Mossé 1979; Fuks 1953, 84–101; and particularly with regard to the law against neutrality in city affairs, see David 1984; Manville 1980.
[22] See Xen. *Sym.* 3.5–6; Plat. *Hipp.* 228b; Diog. Laer. 1.57.
[23] Xen. *Sym.* 3.6 (for example) where the same person now claims to listen to a Homer recital every day.

Plato's short and witty dialogue, the *Ion*, where Socrates with customary irony argues with a leading rhapsode, Ion. Ion is forced to confess that the wide knowledge he claims to come from a deep study of Homer – his educator – is insufficient when compared with any expert's understanding. Finally, the rhapsode seems compelled to choose between being called inspired or a liar and he happily chooses the former. The rhapsode gives up the assertion that poetry has educated him in all fields, and Plato will go on in the *Republic* to press the claims of philosophy over poetry for the title of 'master of truth' – indeed, to ban the poets from his city. The length and vigour of Plato's opposition to poetry finds its cause at least partly in the continuing high status of the poet and poetry with regard to truth and teaching in the social world of Athens in the fifth and fourth centuries.

The Homeric texts, then, were essential not only to the actual procedure of teaching but also to the fabric of Athenian social attitudes and understanding as a privileged source of and authority for knowledge, behaviour, ethics. Homer is regularly quoted in support of arguments (as to a lesser degree are other poets), the characters of Homeric tales offer models of behaviour,[24] the variety of subject and tone of the Homeric texts allows almost any situation to be related back to Homer. It is with some justification that Homer has been termed the Greek Bible. 'He was "the poet" . . . who had produced images of human experience that were true and right and timeless, in a variety of modes, and with a mastery and sophistication that were for Aeschylus, Sophocles and Euripides their education.'[25]

The criticism of Homer, however, also begins early. Xenophanes was a rhapsode of high reputation who travelled throughout the Greek-speaking world at the turn of the sixth century.[26] He sang his own verses, in which he attacked Homer and Hesiod because 'they had imputed to the gods all that is shame and blame for men . . . unlawful things; stealing, adultery, deceiving each other'.[27] Xenophanes wrote in hexameters, as did Homer, and his language demonstrates an extensive debt to Homeric diction and style. But his rejection of Homeric anthropomorphism on moral grounds offers a first example of what becomes on the one hand an extended tradition of Homeric scholarship and on the other the rejection of poetic views of the divine.

His questioning of Homer as a source of knowledge was immediately opposed by Theagenes of Rhegium, who was said to be the founder of allegorical interpretation of such scenes as the battle of the gods, and also the founder of grammatical and philological study of the Homeric texts.[28] The

[24] Cf. Plat. *Hipp. Min.* 365b.   [25] Gould 1983, 45.
[26] Pfeiffer 1968, 8, suggests 565 as a birth date.
[27] DK 21B11–12.   [28] Cf. Pfeiffer 1968, 11–12. See also Clarke 1981, 60–105.

sophists in the fifth century develop both this linguistic study of ancient poetry,[29] and also the questioning of the value of more traditional theological ideas.[30] When Hippolytus in Euripides' *Hippolytus* addresses the gods with 'You should be wiser than mortals, being divine', there seems to be an echo of this tradition of uncertainty expressed about the nature and depiction of gods in Homer.

Stesichorus, one of the most influential lyric poets, offers a further view of the ins and outs of Homeric authority and the poetic voice of truth. According to Plato, Stesichorus wrote a poem about Helen as the cause of the Trojan war and for this 'slander' was blinded.[31] He recognized the cause of his blindness and wrote a recantation, a palinode, which began 'That story is not true; you did not go in the well-benched ships nor did you reach the towers of Troy.' It was, according to this new version, a phantom, an *eidolon*, a mere image, that the Greek heroes in their ignorance struggled over, while Helen herself went to Egypt. Whatever the truth of Plato's biographical anecdote, the fragment of Stesichorus' poem further justifies the remark of the Suda,[32] that Stesichorus introduced new versions of Homeric and Hesiodic stories. The palinode, with all its doubleness of literary rewriting – and focused on the idea of a battle over an 'image', a 'representation' – is difficult to reconcile simply with the bardic claim of certain inspiration, a difficulty which points to the complexity of the developing ideas of poetic voice in Greek literary tradition. It is not only the questioning tragic poets or sceptical philosophers whose writing takes a stance against the texts of the past. With the authority of tradition comes an extensive range of challenge and innovation.

Now although the Homeric texts are thus already in the sixth century both invested with the force of greatest authority and challenged by poets and philosophers in this position of authority, the fifth-century democratic society of Athens offers a very particular sort of barrier against the straightforward assimilation of the traditional views of the heroic tales, despite the continuing evaluations of Homer as the 'best and most divine of poets'. In Chapter 3, I attempted to describe some sense of what it meant to be a citizen of Athens in the latter part of the fifth century. In particular, I stressed the special sense of community, of belonging, of taking part in social and political processes. Equality before the law, the importance of the institutions of the courts and assembly, the role of the army in the city's defence, made the possession of citizenship a defining quality of a male in society. When we turn to Homer or Hesiod, however, the differences are readily appreciable. The common mass of citizens are ignored or despised by the individualistic heroes. The right to

---

[29] Cf. Kerferd 1981, 68ff.   [30] Cf. Kerferd 1981, 163ff.   [31] *Phaedr.* 243a.
[32] 193, 17–18. The Suda is a reference work of a much later date (A.D. c. 1000).

speak in assembly is the prerogative of the leaders, and at the beginning of the *Odyssey* the assembly in Ithaca has not even been convened in the nineteen years of Odysseus' absence. Before turning to consider the tragic plays with regard to the Homeric poems, I want to look at two specific areas of difference in social outlook between the fifth-century democratic ideal and the ideals of the Homeric poems, both of which are highly relevant to the reading of tragedy and have recently been discussed at length by scholars.

The first specific area of difference is the contrasting ideals of military involvement – at first sight perhaps a rather unusual topic. But as I argued in Chapter 3, the sense of being a citizen in democratic Athens and being a soldier were linked in an essential way. As Davies writes, 'Fighting ... involved so high a proportion of the free adult male population ... and was so embedded in the exemplary exploits of myth and history from the *Iliad* through the labours of Heracles to the heroes of Marathon and Salamis and Plataea, that it provided a common ideal of manly action and the framework for a substantial portion of the moral code.'[33] The common ideal of a fifth-century democratic hoplite, however, is in several ways quite different from its Homeric counterpart. In Homer, the hero is all. The individual warrior, around whom smaller and weaker supporters cluster, dominates the battlefield and the language of warfare. In the *Iliad*, Achilles' decision to withdraw from battle causes a reversal of Greek fortunes. They are driven right back to their ships. When Achilles is persuaded by the death of Patroclus to return to the fighting, his individual rampage brings carnage to the Trojan forces and ends with his single combat with and victory over Hector. In Homer's war poetry, victim after victim is named, the manner and perpetrator of death recounted; hero clashes with hero, exchanges names and boasts, and fights for the personal honour of a personal victory. Even Hector, the 'bulwark of the city', offers the explanation to his wife that he is fighting for his and his father's honour and fame. Because he is the best of the Trojans he would be ashamed not to fight, even though he knows the struggle may be doomed. Achilles refuses to fight because of a slight to the respect that he feels his fame and honour demand. Moreover, when he returns to battle, it is despite the fact that he knows from his divine mother that he will certainly die young and not leave Troy. Achilles' famous choice of eternal personal fame and a short life instead of a long and stable existence without fame involves a tragic self-destructiveness that is essential to the description of the 'best of the Achaeans' in the narrative of the *Iliad*. Achilles is the only hero who fights with the certain knowledge of his own death in battle. There is a hierarchy of heroes at

[33] 1978, 31. See also Ehrenberg 1960, 8off.; Vernant 1968, passim.

Troy according to their valour and respect: the heroes fight to increase that status. Achilles, the best of the Achaeans, is the man who takes the desire for personal glory to the extreme of sacrificing his own possible future life for the future life of his reputation. The individual's sense of self in terms of fighting and of fame is always at play and at stake in the *Iliad*.

The different requirements of the fifth-century warrior are marked. As with the Homeric warrior, for sure, there is a continuing ideal of strength, refusal to flee and victory. But such requirements of individual prowess are quite differently organized. For the hoplite fights in a closed phalanx. The phalanx was a tightly packed brigade trained for set-piece, close-formation fighting on level ground. Rather than relying on individual strength or improvisation, the phalanx depended on collective, prepared capabilities. Not only was each man's right, spear-carrying, arm defended by the shield of the man next to him, but also the success of any engagement depended on the ability of the line to hold together. Once broken into individuals a phalanx was easily routed by an unbroken phalanx. So, too, rowers in a trireme succeed or fail as a unit. The values of a warrior are necessarily tied to a sense of collective endeavour.

Indeed, in the funeral speech for the war dead, an institution I have already mentioned, the names of the dead were not even announced and the burial rites constituted a communal civic event. This ceremony neatly marks the difference of fifth-century military ideology and its involvement in a wider civic system of thought. Unlike Homer's heroes who fought for the perpetuation of their names, for their individual status and honour, the fifth-century hoplite fights in a necessarily joint enterprise of the city. He fights for the city and is buried as an honoured but unindividuated member of the class of civic hero. The sense of the self is subsumed to the continuity of the city.

So, then, while the vocabulary and ethics of warfare may seem at first sight to offer a certain continuity between the Homeric and fifth-century worlds – bravery, excellence, morale remain the terms in which military behaviour is evaluated and described – none the less there is a radical shift in the direction in which these values are channelled and in the way in which these values are understood to relate to an ideal of military involvement.

This shift from individualistic heroism to collective endeavour is marked in the second major area of difference that I wish briefly to investigate, namely the shift in focus in moral vocabulary and interests. In previous chapters, I have often discussed *dikē* and *sophronein* and their cognates as basic but ambiguous expressions of the relations between people or of evaluating behaviour in the tragic texts. It is noticeable that neither of these sets of terms is especially common in Homeric vocabulary, though both do occur.[34] This is not merely because of a shift in the type of extant evidence: rather tragedy's retelling of stories from Homer specifically recasts their narratives in the light of fifth-century concerns. In *Ajax*, Ajax's behaviour, as we will see in Chapter 7, is evaluated in terms of *sophronein* in a quite different way from the Homeric poems; the norms of behaviour are challenged by Ajax's actions and this is expressed through the value of *sophronein*, the value of self-control, yielding and balance that seem so alien to the extreme self-aggrandizing fervour of Ajax. As we will see, the play seems to focus on Ajax's inability to fit into social norms, his inability to subsume his self to the hierarchy and order of the world of the army. What I wish to stress here is that this tension between the hero and the surrounding society is constructed through the language of a primarily fifth-century ethical interest – and one which reflects the democratic ideology of commitment and involvement in the social life of the city. The ideology of city life, which is so important to the determination of the sense of self through military action, also radically affects the sense of ethical norms. There develops with regard to a certain sort of attitude to living in the democratic city a new emphasis on the value of such terms as *sophronein*. We will see in the course of this chapter that this shift between Homeric and fifth-century worlds is articulated in different and complex ways in tragedy. For it is too simple, indeed, untrue, to assume that Homer does not know or value 'quiet' or 'co-operative' virtues[35] or that the Homeric depiction of the search for individual expression through personal fame and reputation is not seen throughout Greek culture.[36] But tragedy's rewriting of ancient tales develops a specific fifth-century self-awareness and questioning of its relation to Homeric values. If tragedy expresses 'a torn consciousness, an awareness of the contradictions that divide a man against himself'[37] then the tearing of fifth-century man from his whole-hearted affiliation to the texts and values of the past is a violence germane to the tragic festivals.

Indeed, Vernant regards the opposition of the collective values of a citizen body and the individual expression of the hero, the actor, as an essential element in the formal structure of tragedy. The chorus, he argues, offers an 'anonymous and collective being whose role is to express through its fears, hopes, and judgements, the feelings of the spectators who make up the civic community'.[38] The actor provides, however, 'the individualized figure whose actions form the centre of the drama and who is seen as a hero from another

---

[34] On *dike*, see Havelock 1978, and *contra* Lloyd-Jones 1971. On *sophronein* see North 1966, 1ff. See also Winnington-Ingram 1980, 69–70.
[35] Adkins' terms.   [36] See e.g. Dover 1974, 226ff.
[37] Vernant and Vidal-Naquet 1981, 2–3.
[38] 1981, 2.

age, always more or less alien to the ordinary condition of a citizen'.[39] As we will see especially in Chapter 11, this generalization needs qualification; but it does point towards the way in which the articulation of relations between individual and community, hero and city, remains a major concern of the tragic texts and performance.

I want to begin by considering how the narrative of a tale told at length in Homer is picked up, altered and developed in a specifically fifth-century way, and I intend first to look at the *Oresteia*. It is a commonplace of criticism to compare the three tragedians' different versions of the Orestes narrative, but the importance of the relations between in particular the *Oresteia* and the *Odyssey* have in general been under-discussed.[40] This is particularly surprising when one considers that the story of an *Oresteia* is told nine times in the first twelve books of the *Odyssey* and referred back to later on several occasions. As has been often noted, one major reason for this telling and retelling of Orestes' story in the *Odyssey* is to hold up Orestes' execution of revenge as an exemplary model to Telemachus, Odysseus' son, beset and threatened as he is by Penelope's suitors. The interrelation of these parallel stories, however, functions in a more complex way than as a simple exhortatory paradigm. On the one hand, certain parallels are clear: both young men are threatened in their position as heir to a patrimony. Both are threatened moreover by a sexual challenge – in the one case the usurpation of Aegisthus through seduction and murder, in the other, the fear of Penelope giving in to one of her riotous suitors, whose sexual licence is commented on more than once and who plot to kill Telemachus. On the other hand, there is a considerable difference between the situations of Telemachus and Orestes. For Orestes, the directives of correct behaviour are depicted as quite straightforward. He has lost his position to a male usurper and the male usurper must be punished by revenge. Zeus in the opening scene of the *Odyssey* points out how Aegisthus had only himself to blame for his death because he ignored the explicit commands of the gods, and Athene praises Orestes' actions as the exemplary behaviour of youth. Matricide is not mentioned and the moral uncertainty around the idea of matricide is never considered: indeed not only does Aegisthus organize and perform the regicide – the queen merely offers the support of feminine guile and untrustworthiness – but also the death of Clytemnestra, that prime moment of Aeschylean tragedy, is never described in any of the versions of the story told in the *Odyssey*. There is one mention of the joint funeral of Aegisthus and Clytemnestra, but even this completely veils what happened to Clytemnestra: 'In the eighth year god-like Orestes came back from Athens and killed the murderer,

[39] 1981, 2.   [40] See, however, Goldhill 1984a, 183ff.; Gould 1983, 32–4.

guileful Aegisthus, who had killed his famous father. And when he had killed him, he invited the Argives to a funeral feast for his hated mother and the coward Aegisthus.'[41] The change from the masculine singular object of revenge 'when he had killed *him*' to the double funeral leaves a marked gap in the narrative of revenge.

This gap is not merely an attempt to offer a 'clean' picture of Orestes as a moral exemplum for Telemachus. It is also important for the understanding of the nature of the parallels between Telemachus and Orestes. For it is significant for Telemachus that both his parents are alive. Telemachus cannot be left, like Orestes, in sole and glorious control of the *oikos*. What is the position of Telemachus in the household when Odysseus returns? What is the relation of this son to his mother and father? How should he act in the uncertainty of his role that his father's absence has produced? The certainty of Orestes' position is in marked contrast to the hesitations surrounding Telemachus.

The similarities and differences between Telemachus and Orestes are highly relevant for the sexual discourse of the *Odyssey*. For as much as Odysseus travels towards his relationship with Penelope, Telemachus too is depicted as approaching manhood and a redefinition of his role in the *oikos* with regard to his parents. Indeed, the structure of the narrative of the *Odyssey*, where Odysseus tells most of his wanderings in a retrospective story at the palace in Phaeacia, sets parallel at the beginning of the work the journey of the young man Telemachus to find out about his father and the final stretch of Odysseus' return to Ithaca. The son and the father have parallel reintegrations into the household.

Many recent studies have focused on this sense of reintegration that is central to the process of Odysseus' return home, his *nostos*.[42] The societies and races through which Odysseus and Telemachus travel offer fractured and distorted images of different aspects of the household in Ithaca, thrown into disorder by the absence of the king and the behaviour of the suitors. As the narrative of revenge progresses, Odysseus is depicted as gradually building up or being reinitiated into the series of relationships by which his role in the *oikos* is defined.

The sexual relations in the *oikos* are essential to the sense of what an *oikos* means; in Chapters 3 and 5 I discussed how the needs of the *oikos* in terms of continuity of generations are linked to the control of sexual behaviour. The correct nature of the sexual relations between man and woman, and the problem of generational continuity are an essential structuring of the narrative of homecoming in the *Odyssey*. Odysseus rejects various females with whom

[41] *Od.* 3.307–10.   [42] Segal 1962b; 1967; Vidal-Naquet 1981b; Goldhill 1984a, 183ff.

he has sexual relations, in terms of the norms to which he wishes to return. With Calypso, Odysseus stays seven years but has no children and lives in no *oikos* but a cave. He explicitly compares Penelope to the goddess, and despite his wife's inferior looks and talents he opts to return home rather than accept the immortality proffered him. In the world of Calypso, Odysseus is without society. It is the point from which he has to return. Similarly, Circe, who has so often been taken as an allegory of lust, keeps Odysseus for a year, but is rejected finally by the memory of home and his responsibilities as household head. With Nausicaa, Odysseus is offered a home, an *oikos*, a place in society, by her father if he will stay. But it is to his '*fatherland*' that Odysseus desires to return – the *oikos* has a past as well as a future which is essential to its determination.

In the household of Odysseus, the suitors offer a threat to the home in many ways: they are destroying its economic and social stability. But as suitors it is specifically in their sexual role that they constitute a danger. As many critics have noted, the suitors indeed are constructed as a parallel to Aegisthus. Like Aegisthus, they hope to seduce the queen and overthrow the continuous line of inheritance in the *oikos*, as well as steal another man's wife. In the process of righting the household, not only are the suitors killed but also the maidservants who slept with them. Female sexual licence within the house leads to chaos and is punished with a grim death, vividly described.[43] The righting of the household includes the ordering of the sexual roles.

It is interesting to investigate the scene of the competition of the bow by which Odysseus wins back Penelope; and it is Telemachus' role in the competition for his mother that I want to turn to now. The competition is explicitly set up in terms of comparing the present suitors with Odysseus. Indeed, the suitors are afraid not of losing the chance of marrying Penelope but of proving themselves lesser men than Odysseus in the eyes of others – the external evaluation of 'honour' that I have mentioned as being central to the Homeric ethos. Telemachus takes part in this competition and offers an interesting explanation of why he is competing, since it can scarcely be to win his mother as a bride! His explanation is, however, notably ambiguous in syntax and sense.[44] Either, as Rieu, for example, translates, he explains himself thus: 'If I string the bow and shoot an arrow through the axes my mother can say goodbye to this house and go off with another man, for all I care, leaving me here satisfied that at last I am equal to handling my father's formidable toys.' In this reading Telemachus will have his mother leave the *oikos* since he will have proved himself man enough to take control as head of the household. But the sentence can equally well be read as Merry, for

---

[43] *Od.* 22.461ff.   [44] *Od.* 21.113–17.

example, takes it: 'but should I string the bow ... my lady mother need not then, to my deep sorrow, leave this house, going her way with some other lord, as long as I remain behind, man enough even now to win these splendid prizes of my sire'. In this reading, the son's ability to perform as well as his father will keep his mother in the home and prevent her going to another man as wife. There is for the son here a certain ambiguity of expression concerning the rejection or possession of his mother, which may seem only fitting as he approaches the competition for the 'prize of his father', while he knows his father to be present and watching.

Indeed, Telemachus' attempt on the bow is in a significant way both an assertion of his manhood and an act of submission to his father. He goes to the threshold, and 'three times he made it quiver in his efforts to bend it but every time he gave the struggle up, though not the hope that he might still succeed in drawing in the string and shooting through the iron marks. And the fourth time he put such pressure on the bow that he would have strung it, if Odysseus had not put an end to his attempts with a shake of the head'. Telemachus, standing on the threshold, would have proved himself the equal of his father, would have asserted himself as capable of taking the dominant role in the home, but he cedes to his father's 'No'; he accepts his father's authority even as he proves himself on the threshold of maturity.

Orestes moved through the just destruction of the older generation whose sexual misdemeanours required punishment to the possession of the *oikos*. Telemachus helps right the *oikos* through the destruction of the threat of sexual and social transgression in the form of the suitors. But Telemachus is also characterized as approaching the potency and authority of manhood. The narrative of the *Odyssey* depicts the possible integration of the newly potent and powerful son into the order of the household through the continued acceptance of the authority of the father – and through the father's own rejuvenation and continuing strength. Sons must take over from fathers – that is what is meant by 'generational continuity', but the transition is not a matter of course. The *Odyssey* depicts in the parallel narratives of Orestes and Telemachus two different views of that process of transition. The model of Orestes for Telemachus signifies in its differences as well as in its apparently exemplary similarities. The *Odyssey* is largely concerned with what it means to be a human being in society; its subject is expressed in the first word of the epic as 'the man'. But 'the man' is constituted in part through his relations with his son in the *oikos* and its concerns for generational continuity. Odysseus' return to the *oikos* and Telemachus' growth to manhood are parallel factors in the understanding of the necessarily temporal existence of the *oikos*.

When we turn to the *Oresteia* certain differences in the narrative are immediate and vivid. The regicide is planned, dominated and performed by Clytemnestra. The focus of Orestes' revenge is in a similar way on Clytemnestra and the uncertainties of matricide. Aegisthus is summarily despatched. The pursuit of Orestes by the Erinyes and the trial are not mentioned in Homer. What is the nature and force of these differences in narrative? Why is the fifth-century story markedly different from its predecessors?

Let me first define a little more closely the extent of the differences from and echoes of Homer that the *Oresteia* sets in play. A scholiast comments on the beginning of the trilogy that this watchman is one of Agamemnon's men.[45] This is not just a scholiast's dull enthusiasm for stating the obvious. For in the *Odyssey* it is described how Aegisthus sets up a watchman who warns him of the approach of Agamemnon, and allows time to prepare the plot. When the watchman of the *Agamemnon* announces that it is a woman's command that has set him to watch, and when he expresses his faithful hope to see his king return safely, there is already a strong shift in emphasis. Not only is Clytemnestra singled out as the danger to the *oikos* from a member of the *oikos*, but also the sexual determinants of the change in narrative from Homer are marked.

This shift in sexual emphasis is developed in an important way throughout the *Oresteia*. I have already noted the recurrence of sexual imagery and the expression of conflict in sexual terms in the trilogy. The narrative itself, however, is significantly turned from the Homeric sexual discourse. In Homer, Orestes kills Aegisthus in a male struggle for supremacy in the *oikos*. The woman, who may be seduced or remain chaste, is a figure who is corrupted by the agent of disorder in the house or who preserves the order of the household. In the world of his travels with its various dangers of disorder and reversal, Odysseus is in different ways threatened by, subservient to or dependent on powerful females – Calypso, Circe, Nausicaa, Arete, Scylla etc. In the series of male–female relations, the female is figured as a possible wielder of power, force, control; Odysseus' return is a return to his proper position in the house as man and ruler. But neither Clytemnestra nor Penelope in Homer, in terms of the power struggles in the social life of the *oikos*, aims at or achieves rule or authority. As Telemachus, the young male, reaffirms, 'Authority/power (*kratos*) is the man's in the house.'

The chorus of the *Agamemnon* greet Clytemnestra's first entrance with 'I have come in reverence, Clytemnestra, of your power (*kratos*).' Moreover, the strange use of *kratos* with regard to a woman is immediately explained in sexual terms, 'for when the male is gone and the throne void, it is right (*dikē*)

[45] The Medicean scholiast on 5. It must be noted that we have lost Stesichorus' *Oresteia*, which is an important intermediate version between Homer and Aeschylus.

to honour a ruler's wife'. Clytemnestra's transgression is to seek permanent power in the house, to overthrow the sexual hierarchy in the *oikos*.

Indeed, the narrative of the *Oresteia*, as critics have noted, constructs a whole series of male–female oppositions.[46] Agamemnon is forced to become a daughter-slayer in order to avenge his brother. Artemis, a goddess, demands the sacrifice, as Zeus, a male god, demands the revenge. Clytemnestra avenges her daughter by killing her husband. As we saw, the struggle of words in the carpet scene was also expressed in directly sexual terminology. Orestes returns home to avenge his father by killing his mother. It is this focus on matricide which marks the maximum divergence from the Homeric narrative, and is essential to the construction of the oppositions of male and female. Orestes is pursued by the female Erinyes and protected by the male Apollo, and in their clash in court the arguments are set up explicitly in terms of a sexual hierarchy. Is the man or the woman to be valued more highly? Which is the true parent, male or female? Athene's reasons for voting for Orestes also depend on her sense of how she was engendered and what this means about herself. As we saw in Chapter 2, the ending of the trilogy is often seen precisely in terms of a reconciliation of the sexes in the city as well as the integration of the Erinyes.

This narrative of sexual opposition affects the characterization of Aegisthus and Electra. Aegisthus, the dominant figure in Homer, is depicted as incapable of asserting himself. The chorus and Orestes indeed refer to him as 'woman' and despise him openly. As much as Clytemnestra dominates the stage in her power and transgressive fervour, so Aegisthus is reduced in scale and force to a subordinate, marginal position. Electra passes from view early in the *Choephori* also, so that the focus remains undiminished on the son's and mother's conflict. She is sent inside the house (the woman's position), but not before she has recognized Orestes. In lines that echo Andromache's famous appeal to Hector (*Il.* 6.429–30), Electra asserts that Orestes is to be called her mother and father now. Electra recognizes Orestes as the authority under which she will live in the righted *oikos*. She desires nothing more than to return to the position of the daughter in the male-dominated *oikos*.

The narrative of sexual opposition is also closely linked to what I have called a 'civic discourse'. For at each moment of opposition and tension the female tends to the support of a position or arguments that are based on the values of the *oikos* and the ties of blood to the point of the rejection of the ties of society, whereas the male tends to support a wider outlook of the relations between *oikos* in society to the exclusion of the claims of family and blood. Thus

---

[46] See especially Zeitlin 1978; Goldhill 1984a; and above, Chapter 2.

Agamemnon sacrifices his own daughter, 'treasure of the household', in order to enable the Panhellenic expedition to depart. He rejects his duties as a father to maintain his position in society as king and leader of the international expedition to avenge a transgression of the social ties of guest-friendship and marriage. Clytemnestra rejects the social ties of marriage not only in killing her husband but also in choosing her own object of sexual desire apart from the institution of matrimony. Orestes rejects that apparently most 'natural' of blood-ties, between mother and son, in order to regain his patrimony, and to set straight the disorder of the *oikos*. As the narrative moves into the wider sphere of the law-case before the city-elders, Apollo, the god of state religion, the great civilizer from Delphi, supports Orestes, whereas the Erinyes are depicted as unnatural, monstrous females, who seem prepared to ignore any claim of society in the pursuit of those who have killed their own kin, their own blood.

As we saw in Chapter 2, the final scenes of the trilogy move beyond the confines of male–female opposition. The city itself is at stake after the trial before its jury of citizens, and Orestes passes from view. The final reconciliation is of the Erinyes into the order of the city, and the final procession is something of a self-proclaimed triumph of the city. What we can now see is not only that this triumph of civic progression is an essential part of the trilogy's movement, a genealogical tale of the city's structure, but also that this movement is being constructed throughout the trilogy in the language of sexual opposition. For the terms of the conclusion are developed from the charged language of the series of male–female oppositions that have constituted the conflicts of the trilogy. The ending is not merely patriotism or an episode loosely stitched to the outside of the Orestes story, but a conclusion that progresses from the narrative's constantly developing dynamics of misogyny.

The radical changes to the Odyssean narrative of Orestes, then, are essential to the sense of the development of a civic language. The focus on Clytemnestra which enforces the polarities of male–female conflict is as relevant to an understanding of the direction of the narrative as is the mutual acceptance of the city and the Erinyes, the standing back of Orestes and Apollo from the final scenes and, indeed, the hymn of blessing and praise with which the work ends. The *Oresteia* constructs a different idea of what it is to be a human in society, or rather a citizen in a city, and a different idea of transgression. The *Odyssey* was largely concerned with sexual relations in the *oikos* to define the *oikos*. In the *Oresteia*, the *oikos* is shown to be essentially linked to the *polis*. The internal ties of the *oikos* are now to be understood through their interrelations with the wider society of the *polis*.

The *Oresteia*, then, a play before the city, cannot be understood without a recognition of how it transforms the narrative of the *Odyssey*. It is not merely a change in plot but a rewriting of the sense of what it means to be a citizen, of what it might mean to use the Orestes story as an exemplary tale in moral, social, political terms. This type of transformation of the language and the structure of a narrative and the way it affects a sense of the self in society has been called by Kristeva 'intertextuality', a term which since it was coined has often been applied in a looser way to any form of influence.[47] What the relations of the *Oresteia* and the *Odyssey* show is that tragedy is both rooted in and split from epic: the *Oresteia* articulates a specific fifth-century awareness of its own textual tradition and innovation. The *Oresteia* is written through Homer but throughout declares its generation in the discourse of the fifth-century *polis*.

For Kristeva, the 'unsettling, questioning process' of 'intertextuality' is associated particularly with periods of 'abrupt change, renewal or revolution in society' and with an uncertainty in the 'social framework with which a person identifies himself'. This 'unsettling, questioning process' is seen vividly in the tragic texts most deeply concerned with evaluative questions of right and wrong in which the interplay of the strata of more traditional and more innovative values testifies acutely to the way Athenian society of the fifth century was experiencing radical shifts and tensions in its systems of belief. With regard to the network of relations between individual and community which I discussed earlier in Chapter 3, and with regard in particular to the notion of a Homeric, heroic sense of the individual and a fifth-century sense of community involvement, the texts of Sophocles offer particular interest, and much excellent recent criticism has focused on the idea of a Sophoclean Hero. Now heroes were an object of worship in fifth-century Athens and even in the democratic city's order the presence of heroes may be seen to provide a sense of continuity with the past, a way of conceptualizing the links between the world of epic and the contemporary city. Sacrifices were offered at the site (real or supposed) of their burial; and heroes, a class which could include not only the heroes of epic but also founders of cities, local earth spirits, healing powers etc., were a source of strength and prosperity when properly appeased and a source of danger when neglected: 'The hero cult is more than any other apotropaic; it is designed to appease the mighty dead who are by no means slow to wrath.'[48] It is the heroes' abnormal powers which make them a factor

---

[47] Kristeva's own definition is in the technical language of structural linguistics: she glosses it as 'the transposition of one or more systems of signs into another, accompanied by a new articulation of the enunciative and denotative position'. Roudiez 1980 offers a useful introduction to this and other ideas of Kristeva.

[48] Nilsson 1925, 194.

in Greek religious experience. According to the life of Sophocles,[49] the poet was a priest in a hero cult, and he established a shrine for a different hero and was himself after his death worshipped as a hero by his fellow citizens. These stories point at least to a special connection believed to exist between Sophocles and the heroes in the religious life of the city. Indeed, each of Sophocles' surviving plays is dominated by a figure or figures who attempt to live out a pattern of heroic belief in the face of extended opposition. We have already seen how Antigone follows a course of self-determined, self-motivated opposition to the ruler of the city, that leads to disaster. I have also discussed and will investigate in the next chapter how Ajax's behaviour depends on a view of his self in society. Indeed, Knox has argued that this heroic outlook is an essential part of Sophoclean technique or vision: 'Sophocles pits against the limitations on human stature great individuals who refuse to accept those limitations.'[50] The appeal to yield and give way is made to all the Sophoclean heroes but 'the hero refuses to yield';[51] indeed, 'it is no easy task to urge surrender on the hero, in fact it is difficult to tell him anything at all; he will not listen'.[52] Moreover, 'the attempt to sway or hinder them provokes their anger; they are all angry heroes'.[53] 'To the rest of the world the hero's angry stubborn temper seems "thoughtless", ill-counselled.'[54] The hero remains unchanged and the hope that time will teach the hero remains unfulfilled: 'time and its imperative of change are ... precisely what the Sophoclean hero defies'.[55] Such character traits alienate the hero further and further from his surroundings: alone, disrespected 'the hero turns his back on life itself and wishes, passionately, for death'.[56] This strange and awesome figure is, Knox argues, the dominant character of Sophoclean drama: 'Immovable once his decision is taken, deaf to appeals and persuasion, to reproof and threat, unterrified by physical violence, even by the ultimate violence of death itself, more stubborn as his violation increases until he has no-one to speak to but the unfeeling landscape, bitter at the disrespect and mockery the world levels at what it regards as failure, the hero prays for revenge and curses his enemies as he welcomes death that is the predictable end of his intransigence.'[57]

How does this Sophoclean hero relate to the Homeric model, however? How is a figure like Ajax, who plays a major role in Homeric epic, represented in fifth-century tragedy? Knox writes as follows: 'Ajax is presented to us in this play as the last of the heroes. His death is the death of the old Homeric (and especially Achillean) individual ethos which had for centuries of aristo-

---

[49] On the value of ancient biography as sources in general, see Lefkowitz 1981. In this case, some corroborating evidence has come to light from inscriptions. See *I.G.* II/III² 1252 and 1253.
[50] 1964, 6.   [51] 1964, 17.   [52] 1964, 18.   [53] 1964, 21.   [54] 1964, 21.
[55] 1964, 27.   [56] 1964, 34.   [57] 1964, 44.

cratic rule served as the dominant ideal of man's nobility and action but which by the fifth century had been successfully challenged and largely superseded.'[58] For Knox, the extraordinary wealth of Homeric reminiscence in the *Ajax* is precisely to draw attention to the Homeric nature of the credo according to which Ajax lives and dies. The final scenes of the play represent the new ethos of *sophronein* in the mouth of Odysseus and, as such, the play overall traces the disjunction between more modern ideals and the Homeric ethos which still provided a source and sense of greatness in Athenian society.

Winnington-Ingram, although he largely follows the terms of Knox's description of the hero,[59] has tellingly criticized this view of the relation between Sophocles' and Homer's Ajax.[60] He agrees that Sophocles clearly draws on Homer not only for a model of Ajax himself but also in the way that Ajax's violent reaction to a loss of honour recalls Achilles' own withdrawal from his commitment to the Greek army. But he also develops the differences between the Homeric and Sophoclean hero. In particular, Winnington-Ingram recalls that Ajax's explicit rejection of help from the gods seems to strike a strongly discordant note: 'Ajax – and Ajax alone, the Sophoclean Ajax, feels that it would derogate from his prestige to accept help from a god . . . Ajax rejects . . . that sense of dependence upon the gods by which the pride of a Homeric hero is normally mitigated.'[61] The Homeric code's emphasis on individual prowess and on the external signs of honour and respect was 'a hard code for men living dangerously in competition, but it contained mitigations of its own hardness'.[62] Where Ajax goes beyond the normal sense of this ethos is in his ignoring of those mitigations. 'At every point we see Ajax – the Sophoclean Ajax – rejecting anything which might mitigate his fierce concentration upon the pursuit, maintenance and restoration of his prestige.'[63] Ajax rejects the appeals of Tecmessa and his other supporters. In the *Iliad*, Achilles too explicitly rejects similar appeals even from the dying Hector.[64] In his wrath he mutilates Hector's corpse and refuses to return it for burial. But in the final, moving scenes of the epic, Priam, Hector's father, visits the murderer of his son, and as both finally break down in tears, Achilles agrees to return the body of his enemy. Achilles finally yields. Ajax in Sophocles' play rejects even that sense of final mitigation in his unforgiving, cursing suicide. Ajax offers an extreme representation of a heroic code, 'he carries the implications of the heroic code to the extreme possible point, as no-one in Homer . . . ever did'.[65] The Sophoclean hero does not simply reflect a Homeric model but offers a specific depiction, distorted in its extremism.

[58] 1961, 20f.   [59] 1980, 304ff.   [60] See now the fine study of Easterling 1984.
[61] 1980, 18.   [62] 1980, 18–19.   [63] 1980, 19.   [64] Cf. *Il.* 22.337–60.
[65] Winnington-Ingram 1980, 19.

The other figures of the Greek army are interesting to look at in the light of this extremism in the representation of Ajax. Menelaus and Agamemnon are two of the leading figures in the *Iliad* and the *Odyssey*. They are the kings who lead the expedition to Troy. In Sophocles' play, however, they are represented in a quite different manner. Menelaus is the first to demand that Ajax should not be buried, but he delivers this judgement in a lengthy speech which in its excursus into political theory moves right out of the heroic context. Menelaus argues like Creon in *Antigone* that the army, like a city, must have its hierarchies and order. As a ruler, he expects to be obeyed, and fear is a necessary restraint of transgression. Teucer's reply rejects Menelaus' claim to supreme command by asserting that Ajax came to Troy in command of his own troops and not as subordinate to anyone – the self-reliance that we have already seen in the representation of Ajax. Teucer responds with such force that even the chorus of Ajax's sailors are taken aback: 'I cannot approve such bold speech in misfortune', they say. The argument which began with some claim to principle quickly turns to personal insult and wrangling. As Winnington-Ingram writes, 'Teucer's reply incites Menelaus to vulgarity where before he had been ungenerous and hubristic.'[66] Menelaus even brings up the old quarrel between the bowman and the hoplite, as he insults Teucer, the archer, for not being a 'real warrior'. Winnington-Ingram surprisingly calls this remark 'staggeringly irrelevant to the tragic issue'.[67] But the argument of these final scenes turns precisely on the evaluation of a human in terms of his military conduct, and the evocation of this value judgement of Menelaus marks not only the slip in argument from the discussion of Ajax to the trivia of personal insult, but also the distance between the complexity of evaluating the figure of Ajax and the simplistic prejudices that Menelaus and later Agamemnon will bring to bear on the issue. As much as Ajax in his extremism seems to bring to the fore the contradictions inherent in the network of attitudes that inform the Homeric ethos, so Menelaus' characterization offers a specifically slanted depiction of an aristocratic claim to superiority. Menelaus, the heroic figure of epic, can here merely repeat in an oversimplified form the terms of a contemporary political debate about order in the belief that his remarks justify both his claims to authority and his decision not to bury Ajax. Rather than instantiating the Homeric values of military prowess and the aggressive desire for personal honour and fame, Menelaus in his trite fifth-century argumentation shows how the aristocratic heritage can easily pass into the snobbery and foolishness of his simplistic evaluation of Ajax. It is precisely in the distance between the Menelaus of Homer and this Menelaus' arguments that our sense of the personae of this

[66] 1980, 64.   [67] 1980, 64.

scene is developed. Both in his argumentation and his characterization, this fifth-century Menelaus is written through his Homeric counterpart.

Agamemnon proves markedly similar to his brother. In the *Iliad*, it is his arrogant demand to repossess Achilles' war-prize that sets Achilles' wrath in motion, and more than once the great king is shown as lacking the authority and sense that his status demands. But these characteristics are developed in the *Ajax* in a specific new manner. Like Menelaus, he too argues for his authority through a claim of innate superiority and the need for the rule of the right people – a category of 'blood' and intelligence – from whom Teucer and Ajax are excluded. Ajax's strength, moreover, is dismissed as useless if separate from the control of the army and its generals. Teucer flings back the taunt of his low birth by raking up the criminal progenitors of the Atreids, and points out that Ajax was the one to fight bravely when Agamemnon himself was least willing. As with the breakdown of Menelaus' and Teucer's argument, this dialogue is turned immediately to mutual accusations of similar violence and oversimplification. For Agamemnon, Ajax was a 'hulking ox'; 'broad shoulders' are no guide to a man's value. For Teucer, Ajax was the military hero whose broad shoulders rescued Agamemnon and the Greeks. How is Ajax to be thought of? As the critics are involved in the evaluation of Ajax, so the final scenes of the play dramatize the process of evaluating the hero in the series of clashing oversimplifications.

Odysseus, whose controlled rhetoric finds a way through this impasse, picks up each of the criteria used so naively by Teucer and the Atreids. He determines Ajax the best of the Greeks after Achilles – though it had been the vote that Odysseus should have the arms of Achilles in preference to Ajax that had enraged the hero. He judges Ajax as 'good' and 'strong', and moreover as 'noble' – with the associations of fine breeding that Agamemnon and Teucer had been wrangling over as Odysseus entered. We saw, too, in Chapter 4, how Odysseus manipulates the language of obligation and evaluation: the terms for 'good' and 'noble' in Odysseus' language are interrelated with the terms for 'friend' and 'enemy' to transcend or untie the polarized aggressions of Teucer and the Greek kings. Now in Homer, among his other qualities, Odysseus is the statesman *par excellence*. Athene says to him (*Od.* 13.297f.), 'You are by far the best of all mortals in the business of counsel and speaking', and indeed his speeches when, for example, he is forced to confront the young girl Nausicaa when he is washed up naked on the beach at Phaeacia, are often described as masterpieces of tact and carefully controlled manipulative rhetoric. In the *Iliad*, Odysseus is the man who can control the mass of soldiery by his force of language and the Greeks often rely on his advice and rhetoric. His performance in public meetings is memorably described by the

Trojan, Antenor (*Il.* 3.216–21): 'But whenever Odysseus of the many wiles rose to speak, he used to stand stock still and look down, his eyes fixed on the ground and he didn't move the sceptre back and forth but held it stiffly like an ignorant fellow. You'd have said he was sullen and dense. But when he uttered his great voice from his chest and those words like wintry snow-storms, then there was no other mortal who could vie with Odysseus.' It would seem to be this side of the Homeric characterization that is foremost in the Sophoclean Odysseus. But at the same time, this Sophoclean Odysseus is far from an *heroic* figure, especially in contrast with Ajax. In the opening scene, Odysseus is far from willing to be confronted with his enemy, and in his awareness and manipulation of the shifting of moral values, and his general pity and humanism that has led him to be associated with the values of *sophronein*, this Odysseus also seems a figure adapted to and by the fifth-century enlightenment.

There is another side to Odysseus in Homer, however, which is also paramount for his characterization. Athene also says of her favourite (*Od.* 13.293ff.) 'And so my stubborn friend, Odysseus the arch-deceiver with his craving for intrigue, does not propose even in his own country to drop his sharp practices and the lying tales that he loves from the bottom of his heart.' Odysseus of the many wiles is a man most adept not only in the statesmanlike arts of rhetoric but also at lying, cheating, deceiving – his grandfather Autolycus was the most notable thief and liar of his generation. This side of Odysseus is also brought to the fore in Greek tragedy, particularly in Euripides' plays,[68] where Odysseus often appears as a paradigm of the unscrupulous politician, the pragmatic manipulator of truth to gain advantage or profit. In Sophocles also in his *Philoctetes*, Odysseus is depicted as a glib, unethical, unheroic opportunist.[69] These two different Sophoclean representations of the hero of the *Odyssey*, as well as pointing to the difficulties in the assumption that there is any single straightforward model for the transformation of the Homeric world to the fifth century, must also colour the nature of the characterization of Odysseus in the *Ajax*. For it is the subordination of the tricky, deceptive side of Odysseus' rhetoric to his view of the moral hesitation which comes from the mutability of things that marks the specific rewriting of the most developed figure of epic in Sophocles' tragedy. Odysseus' recognition of the relativism or shifting of moral and personal relations is not only set in contrast to the stubborn unchangeability of Ajax and to the naive 'certainties' of Teucer and the Atreids, but also must be seen in terms of the heroic persona, the master of shifting disguises, of which he necessarily is the heir.

[68] Cf. e.g. *Hecuba, Troades.*   [69] Cf. Segal 1981, Chapters 9 and 10 and his bibliography there.

Agamemnon yields to Odysseus while professing undying hate for Ajax; Teucer cannot accept Odysseus' help in the funeral, while calling him 'best' and 'noble' (1399). The ending of the play, as we have seen, is far from a conclusion of express moral certainty. The tension between on the one hand the great poetry, epic stature and sheer awesomeness of Ajax and on the other hand the small-minded bigotries and squabblings of Teucer, Agamemnon and Menelaus as they argue between themselves and with Odysseus about the evaluation of Ajax, leads to a growing sense of paradox concerning the position of Ajax. It is almost as if in this continual retrospective definition of Ajax, the hero, despite his untenable position, grows in stature in comparison with the men who follow him and argue about him. The paradox draws on the nature of the hero in Greek religious thought. For the hero by virtue of his very superhuman greatness becomes at best an ambiguous model, and often is positively dangerous to ordinary society.[70] 'He is no guide to life in the real city man has made or in the ideal city he dreams of.'[71] The hero is an outsider in his greatness and it is this greatness which highlights the limitations of human norms. It is perhaps the sense of the impossibility of containing this sort of greatness within the norm of human life, indeed the sense of (self-) destructiveness of such greatness, that gives rise to the feelings of loss that so many readers have expressed at the end of this Sophoclean drama.

The *Ajax*, then, develops a complex questioning of the processes of moral and personal evaluation through its interrelations with the Homeric texts. Ajax's extreme and obsessive attitudes of heroic self-esteem lead to his untenable position in society and ultimately to his self-destruction. But there is in Ajax a certain greatness compared in particular with Menelaus and Agamemnon, whose fifth-century argumentation serves to mark the disjunction between a Homeric grandeur and their more contemporary aristocratic or authoritarian stances. But Teucer's passionate support of Ajax is capable only of matching their aggressive oversimplifications with his own. Odysseus, the statesman *and* trickster of epic, uses the uncertainties of moral evaluation to make possible Ajax's burial. The heroic associations that come with the presentation of epic characters are a necessary part of the dynamics of Sophoclean representation of the stories of the past. Each of the characterizations in this play, each of the arguments and positions adopted, is developed through a sense of the heroic past. But although few critics today support, as once was fashionable, the notion of 'a "Homeric" Sophocles, turning away in disgust from a degenerate world to enjoy the congenial

[70] Cf. Knox 1964, 54–8. Crotty 1982 has interesting observations on this aspect of heroism in Pindar.
[71] Knox 1964, 57.

company of heroes',[72] it is also too simple to characterize Sophocles as totally rejecting Homeric values or the world of the past. Odysseus draws both on his Homeric characteristics and on a more contemporary concern for *sophronein* to deliver a positive value judgement of Ajax, the hero whose extremism led to his suicide. Odysseus can assert the value of Ajax in the face of the opposition of Menelaus and Agamemnon, whose naive categorizations of Ajax seem quite insufficient. If the self-assertion of the heroic Ajax is questioned but touched with glory, so too the authoritarian, social arguments of the Atreids mark both the impossibility of Ajax's position and the limited small-mindedness of those who follow him. The problem of the evaluation of humans and humans' conduct in a social setting is developed through the complex network of strands and strains of Homeric and contemporary values, associations, distortions. It is this interpenetration of ideas, this dialectic whereby the values and characterization of the heroic past and contemporary world clash with, undermine, illuminate each other that makes the moral and social evaluations of Sophoclean drama so complex. The concern with right action and moral judgement in Sophocles' drama is developed through the inter-relations of the tragic and Homeric texts. The 'unsettling, questioning process' of this 'intertextuality', then, informs Sophoclean tragedy. Sophocles may be read for and/or against but never without Homer.

Euripides is the tragedian most often associated with the force of innova-tion. His willingness to make major alterations in the received versions of myths, his reliance on sophistic methods of argumentation, his apparent anti-war plays, are all major factors in his complex attitude to tradition and modernity. In Chapter 9, I shall be considering in more detail the relations between the sophists and particularly Euripides' tragedies. To conclude this chapter I wish briefly to look at two aspects of Euripides' texts with regard to the Homeric poems, which will give a further insight, I hope, into the way tragedy is developed in terms of tradition and modernity.

One of the recurring concerns of Euripidean tragedy is for the applicability and shifting of terms of moral and social evaluation – as we saw in Chapter 5 with regard to *sophronein* and the norms of a sexual discourse. With regard to tradition and modernity, however, Euripides' focus on the vocabulary of 'nobility' is of especial interest. For 'nobility' and 'noble' in Greek (*eugeneia/ eugenes*) express both a criterion of birth – the words' etymology is 'well-born' – and at the same time a criterion of behaviour and action (as, say, with 'gentleman' in Victorian England). At a certain level of traditionalist assump-tion it is implied that there is no disjunction between the criterion of birth and

---

[72] Winnington-Ingram 1980, 307. Easterling 1984, 8, writes rather of the 'paradox of an author's distinctive originality finding expression through his reading of another's work'.

morality, as it is often implied in an aristocratic regime that there is no disjunction between birth and authority, the right to rule. Already in the sixth century, with a moralist like Theognis, who appears to have detested any shift of wealth and power from its traditional aristocratic manipulators, it is possible to see a tension between the polarized dichotomies of rich and poor, noble and ignoble, and social upheaval or mobility. Indeed the rise of democracy is depicted by both ancient and modern historians in terms of a shift of power away from its traditional holders. Yet this polarized vocabulary of 'the poor', 'the noble', 'the best', 'the few', 'the fortunate', 'the farmers' is not just a rhetoric of conservative polemicists and certainly does not pass out of use in democratic society. Indeed, even Aristotle's *Politics*, which sets up 'middle-class' as an ideal between such polarizations, also recognizes that such a 'middle section' is largely a projection rather than a social fact. 'The middle-class is in most states generally small; and the result is that as soon as one or other of the two main classes, the owners of property and the masses, gains the advantage, it oversteps the mean, and drawing the constitution in its own direction, it institutes as the case may be either a democracy or an oligarchy.'[73] The system of polarized expressions in which morality, wealth and status interpenetrate remains an organizing principle of Greek social language.

In Euripides, a challenge to the secure establishment of such evaluative terminology is constructed through a dependence on a literary tradition as much as on the conventions of popular belief. In the *Electra*, which I will discuss in more detail in Chapters 9 and 10, Electra has been married off to a poor farmer on the outskirts of Argos. This extraordinary change of dramatic scenario is explained in the farmer's prologue. Electra had been wooed by many of the 'first men' of Greece, but Aegisthus was afraid that if a child was born from one of these 'best men', such offspring would try to avenge Agamemnon. Aegisthus is dissuaded from simply killing Electra and has given her instead to the farmer as a wife. The farmer is a true-born Mycenean, as he explains, but however shining his heritage, his lack of wealth has resulted in the destruction of his 'nobility' (*eugeneia*) – the traditional connection of wealth and noble status. But none the less, because he regards himself as 'not worthy by birth' he has not consummated his marriage with this child of 'wealthy men'. When Orestes, in disguise, is told of this fact by Electra, his reaction is 'extraordinary! You've described a noble man and one to be well-treated' – a remark which is followed by Electra explaining that her marriage to this man was in fact to guarantee weak offspring. Even the farmer himself comments on the connections between his poor birth and his not

[73] *Pol.* 1295b23ff.

ignoble character: 'For even if I was born poor, I will not be shown ignoble/ill-born with regard to my character at least' (362–3).

Orestes' response to meeting the farmer is a long speech on the uncertainty of estimating a man's worth, which questions in a highly rhetorical fashion the traditional means of judgement (birth, wealth, strength) in favour of a recognition of a nobility of character, or disposition, or behaviour, which transcends the normal categorizations. This speech, ironically enough, may be thought to reflect somewhat badly on its deliverer: for throughout the play the weakness of Orestes is emphasized, not least in his failure to match up to his sister's expectations. He arrives in Argos prepared for retreat, he has little idea of how to plan or put into operation his revenge, he finally commits the murders in a shameful way, and is not allowed to remain in Argos to give the citizens a funeral feast and take up his role of king as in Homer but is sent to Athens by the Dioscuri, leaving others to pick up the pieces (1267ff.). Being the son of a noble father is indeed no guarantee of nobility.

Thus Orestes accepts the hospitality of the poor farmer with an interesting expression which has proved difficult for commentators to gloss in a sure way.[74] 'But since he is worthy, the present and the not present son of Agamemnon, for whose sake we have come, let us accept the hospitality of this house' (391–3). Orestes is still in disguise, and it is possible to read the lines as referring simply to 'the man who is present' (i.e. the speaker, Orestes' representative) and 'Orestes himself who is not there' both of whom are 'worthy' of the hospitality offered. The sentence, however, is also commonly read as referring with a particular *double entendre* to 'the son of Agamemnon whom you think is absent but who is really present'. But this strange double expression of the presence and non-presence of the worthy son of Agamemnon also points towards the wider thematic concerns of the play. I do not mean merely the difficulties of consistently predicating the key adjective 'worthy' of the character performing the acts Orestes does in the manner he does – many readers have been prepared to see the absence of worth in the son of Agamemnon presented on stage. But the idea of the present and absent Orestes also points to the way in which the depiction of this Orestes and his 'worthiness' depends on its literary antecedents for its force. For Homer, Orestes could be lauded as a moral exemplum. Aeschylus developed a tragic sense of division in Orestes' action, but vindication for the matricide was offered in Athene's reasons for voting. In Euripides, even the divine support for Orestes' action is undercut as the Dioscuri in famous and shocking lines accuse the wise Apollo of delivering not wise oracles (1245–6). As I will argue in Chapter 10, Euripides' *Electra* is a text written with a continual awareness of

[74] Cf. Denniston's discussion ad loc. (Denniston 1939).

its literary place in a literary tradition, and the representation of Orestes depends in part on its bold reversal of his predecessors.

The choral ode which follows Orestes' acceptance of the humble hospitality develops this sense of a tradition and Euripides' modernity through a pointed juxtaposition. For after the rag-dressed Electra has berated her husband for his self-proclaimed frugal nobility, and after Orestes' all too modern reflections on nobility, the chorus turn to sing about the Trojan war and in particular the shield of Achilles. In the *Iliad*, when Achilles decides to return to battle and to his certain fate, his mother, the goddess Thetis, has Hephaestus make new armour for her son, and the shield is described in some two hundred lines. It is a complex description of a work of art within the poem.[75] The many scenes that make up the shield depict aspects of the world and human society – the ordered world of peace and agriculture as well as war – which are the alternatives Achilles has rejected for his immortal reputation. Instead of a gorgon or other monstrous blazon, he carries on his weapon of war a depiction of the life he has chosen not to live. The 'best of the Achaeans' carries a shield which responds to his greatness. This passage of Homer is echoed time and again in Greek and later literature. Euripides' version of the work of art within a work of art marks the differences from Homer not just in the matter of detail, length and metre, although each of these is markedly removed from the Homeric model. Rather the action of Euripides' play, with its pragmatic marriage of convenience, its dubious scheming, moral ambivalence and uncertainty of character is juxtaposed to the echoes of the glories of the heroic wars, where the beautiful nymphs of the sea bring a marvellous weapon of war to the unanimously agreed best of the Achaeans, and this juxtaposition seems constructed precisely in order to mark the disjunction between Euripides' version of the story of Orestes and the versions of the myth told in Homer and Aeschylus. Homer's is an absent world by which the worth of the present is being evaluated. Homer and the epic tradition provide another vision of events the evocation of which highlights the lack of consonance between the past and present, between tradition and modernity. This ode seems to look back to a lost world, a lost system of values and ideas, another literary world. The work of art within the work of art, with its marked echo of and difference from the Homeric poems, stresses the other view, the modernity of Euripides' literary construct.[76] Tragedy, as I have argued in this chapter, often and in different ways stresses its move away from the heroic tradition. Euripides, more even than Sophocles and Aeschylus, seems to constitute, or to try to constitute, this move as a

---

[75] See du Bois 1982 on the role of the shield description.
[76] On this ode, see O'Brien 1964; Walsh 1977; King 1980.

radical disjunction. The old stories, the old values, the old characters have a place only as absent former standards. Between the present and the absent Orestes there is indeed a marked hiatus. 'The artist uses every device at his disposal to convey a sense of historical discontinuity with its attendant ambivalence that marks it both as emancipation from tradition and as a disinheritance and loss.'[77]

The second and final aspect of Euripidean drama I wish briefly to consider follows on from the way in which Homer, though constantly present as a literary antecedent, provides a sense of otherness, a sense of the excluded. This second aspect bears on the interrelation of military behaviour and an idea of the self with which I opened this discussion of Homer and tragedy. For an essential strand of Euripides' reputation for the twentieth century at least concerns his plays on the aftermath of the Trojan war, which are often aligned as tragic counterparts to Aristophanes' anti-war sentiments. The *Troades*, despite many literary critics' damning appraisals, has been one of the most commonly produced of Euripides' dramas.

Now pity, respect and fear are evoked in Homer as reactions to specific acts of martial brutality or to the fate of a soldier facing death, or a wife facing rape or enslavement. But none the less, as I have argued, the Homeric ethos consists in part, as does fifth-century civic ideology, in the development of a sense of what it is to be a man through the language and practices of military involvement. Euripides, however, challenges the security of this involvement in several ways that are well demonstrated by the *Hecuba* and *Troades*. In marked reversal of the focus of epic literature, both plays concentrate on the suffering of women. Both plays represent the time after the sack of Troy and before the Greeks depart – which offers a particular emphasis on suffering, maltreatment and the arguments that support such behaviour rather than the actions of heroism that distinguish the battlefield. Moreover, the suffering of the female protagonists is conceived as the direct outcome of the actions of men, whose motivations, arguments and responsibilities are represented in various unpleasant and ignoble guises. It may be that much misery is brought to the Greeks in the *Iliad* by Achilles' and Agamemnon's row, but they remain the best and most royal of the Argives. Hecuba, in *Hecuba*, aims to avenge her son, who has been murdered as a guest by his guardian out of financial greed, but at the same time she cannot prevent the sacrifice of her daughter by the Greeks – a violent, barbaric act to placate the ghost of Achilles, which is put into operation by a sly and unpleasant Odysseus, using his rhetoric to side-step all claims on his gratitude and respect from the queen who once saved his life. The effects of the changes in power and position that come from the success

[77] Zeitlin 1980, 51.

and defeat of war distort the action and attitudes into a litany of suffering and excuses that bear on the victors and victims. Indeed, in the *Troades* Cassandra, the prophetess of truth, argues, in an extraordinary example of sophistic rhetoric, that the victory of the Greeks is no victory, because they deserted their homes for ten years and destroyed the possibilities of their fatherland's life (379ff.):

> All went wrong at home,
> as the widows persisted and barren couples
> raised and nursed the children of others,
> no survivor left to tend the tombs . . .
> For such success as this congratulate the Greeks.

Moreover she prophesies that her marriage to Agamemnon will bring him destruction, and that the hated Odysseus will be forced to wander many years yet – so that he will often wish to have suffered the fate of the defeated. In contradistinction to the victors, the Trojans died nobly in defence of their country – an especial honour – and she herself is bringing destruction on those she hates most. It is in this spirit that she opens her speech with a bold and unexpected note of triumph: 'O mother, star my hair with flowers of victory.'

The unsettling effect of this argument, which is aimed precisely at an uncontested norm of military language – the benefits of victory and horrors of defeat – is doubled in force by being placed in the mouth of the prophetess of truth, who according to tradition is not understood or believed. If the blatant rhetorical flair of her paradoxical-sounding argument brings a sense of disbelief or uncertainty to a reader or audience, it can only leave the reader or audience in the position of those who disbelieve the truth of Cassandra – which usually leads to disaster. Euripides manipulates the scenario of the seer of disbelieved truth in a markedly different way from Aeschylus, to challenge the security of the normal categorizations of military language. The value of victory is questioned by setting it against the cost of a foreign war. To many in the city of Athens, great imperialist power, this voice of truth must indeed have seemed eminently unbelievable.

Euripides challenges, then, the direct linkage of fifth-century militarism to Homeric heroism not only by shifting the focus away from the arguments and deeds of the battlefield to their final outcome, not only by depicting his heroes as devoid of the grandeur of heroic values, but also by questioning the constant applicability of the charged language of warfare to the conditions it produces. Euripides uses the stories of the Trojan war to mark a disjunction in the lineage of Greek military values.

Each of the three major playwrights, then, is grounded in a tradition through, against and in which the texts of tragedy are written. The history and associations with which each proper name and so much tragic vocabulary resound create a remarkable depth and fragmentation in the voice of the poet. I talked in Chapter 2 of the different levels of reading required to take account of the clashing rhetorics of appropriation in tragic conflict. The gaps and linkages between the tragic texts and their traditions form a network of intertextualities which must be considered in the reading of fifth-century drama. The plays are rooted in and sundered from the past. The dialectic of text and tradition, however, cannot be reduced to just a question of 'background' or 'influence', for it constitutes an active questioning and discussion of the influence and background of the past on the contemporary world, an activity of rewriting. In the social upheavals of fifth-century Athens, the rewriting of the past plays a major role in the city of the present.

7 · MIND AND MADNESS

As if a man were author of himself.
SHAKESPEARE

In Chapters 4 and 5, I considered how the tragic texts reflected and disputed the ways in which an individual was placed in society, first in terms of family relations and civic ties as expressed through the vocabulary of *philos* and *ekhthros* and secondly in terms of the differences between the sexes. These two chapters were placed between a more general examination of the implications for the tragic texts of the contemporary ideology and structures of the city, and, in Chapter 6, an enquiry into the ways in which the Homeric poems provide an important textual background to the workings of Attic drama. In this chapter, I intend to follow this extensive discussion of what might be called the 'notion of the self' with an investigation of the related and important topics of 'character' and 'mind' which have been brought to the fore in recent critical exchanges not only in classical studies, where the tragic texts have long been the objects of a vigorous debate[1] concerning the term 'character', but also in modern researches in the philosophy of language, particularly in theories of reading and criticism, where the usefulness and implications for the reading of fiction of the term 'character' and the notions of the 'self', the 'subject' have been the focus of considerable interest.[2]

The tragic texts have often been regarded as constituting a specific and important historical moment in the development of a notion of character. Bruno Snell's influential studies, for example, attempt to place tragedy as a turning-point between Homer and later ideas of the self. 'There is in Homer', he writes, 'no genuine reflexion, no dialogue of the soul with itself.'[3] This lack of internalization he links with an idea of the self, particularly the sense of a physical self, which seems to have no sense of unity: there is, Snell notes, no word for body in Homer, only words for parts of the body or corpse. This attitude to an individual changes in the Archaic period between Homer and

---

[1] I have found of especial interest Winnington-Ingram 1980, 5–56; Easterling 1973; 1977; Garton 1957; Gellie 1963; Gould 1978; Jones 1962. See now Pelling 1988. See also Simon 1978.
[2] See on 'character' e.g. Bayley 1974; Cixoux 1974; on the 'self' and the 'subject' see for introductions and bibliography e.g. Coward and Ellis 1977; Silverman 1983.
[3] 1953, 19.

the fifth century, and in the lyric poetry of that period one can see a development of a notion of individuality and personality, which Snell argues, is quite different from the Homeric *Weltanschauung*. In Aeschylean tragedy 'personal decision is a central theme'[4] and by the time Euripides is writing 'knowledge of man and knowledge of the self become the chief tasks of reflection'.[5] For Snell, then, tragedy offers a specific indication of a rise of a new sense of mind and character, a move towards a developed, unified notion of the self. Snell's analysis has been echoed in numerous other works. E. R. Dodds in an equally influential study (1951) sought to mark Greek tragedy as the reflection of a move from a 'shame culture' to a 'guilt culture'. The emphasis on decision and doubt that characterizes much of the dramatic action of these plays, mirrors a general cultural process of internalization, a change in the very attitude to a person's value and status in society. Rather than the external marks of favour, success, responsibility that characterize the Homeric hero's desire for 'honour' and 'fame', in tragedy, Dodds argues, we see the beginnings of an internal valuation of internal qualities with the concomitant possibilities of 'guilt' and 'purity of mind' – the move from 'shame culture' to 'guilt culture'.

Both these scholars' books have come under attack for the nature of the oppositions they suggest and for their sense of a clear, consistent development. Elements of what might be called 'guilt culture' or 'internal life' have been read in Homer and there is a clear continuation of public, external evaluation throughout Greek writing and social life, with the result that the value of Dodds' characterization 'guilt culture' has been seriously undermined. So too some critics have been unwilling to predicate of the fountainhead of western literature an idea of the fragmentary, non-unified self.

Despite such criticisms of excessively rigid oppositions and oversimplified sense of development between ages, the historical moment of Greek tragedy has remained one regularly discussed in terms of a specific point of evolution or change. Vernant, for example, depicts the subject of tragedy precisely as man locked in a conflict constituted by the oppositions of 'legal and political thought on the one hand and the mythical and heroic traditions on the other'.[6] Drama depicts 'man actually living out this debate, forced to make a decisive choice, to orientate his activity in a universe of ambiguous values where nothing is ever stable or equivocal'.[7] But, Vernant argues, the tragic turning-point does not merely reflect such a division at the heart of social experience, but also affects the notion of man itself. For tragic action, he writes, has two aspects: 'it involves on the one hand reflection, weighing up the pros and cons, foreseeing as accurately as possible the means and the ends; on the other, placing one's stake on what is unknown and incomprehensible, risking oneself

[4] 1953, 105.   [5] 1953, 111.   [6] Vernant and Vidal-Naquet 1981, 4.   [7] 1981, 4.

on a terrain which remains impenetrable, entering a game with supernatural forces . . . '[8] The tragic character cannot escape this dialectic of determinism; and striving for personal expression and control, indeed, seems constituted by this interplay of personal responsibility and external compulsion. Tragedy, for Vernant, depicts a conflict within man himself.

These critics' analyses attempt to offer some idea of the specific historical moment of Attic tragedy in terms of a development of a sense of 'character', 'mind', and in my own chapters on the city and Homer, as well as on the individual's relations and relationships in the city and family, I have attempted to weave some of these more anthropologically based insights into my own discussion of the complexities of the institution of the tragic festivals. There is, however, also an extended tradition of a differently based criticism, which has treated character from a more distinctly literary perspective. In this century, many of the post-Romantic influences which are so important to Bradley, say, in Shakespearean criticism, have resulted in similar tendencies in the approach to Greek tragedy. Although it is rarer today to see full-length 'character-studies' of the personae of Greek plays, and editions rarely feel the néed to begin with potted psycho-histories of each character ('The union in Electra of tenderness and strength can be felt throughout . . .'), nevertheless critical judgements based on a view of character continue to be made and argued about. A notable example is the carpet scene of the *Oresteia*, where the two most distinguished modern editions in an attempt to explain why Agamemnon steps on the tapestries suggest diametrically opposed causes: that it is because he is too much of a gentleman to refuse his wife's request (Fraenkel), or because he is arrogant, vain and all too pleased to commit an outrage of this sort (Denniston–Page). With the lack of any explicit motivation, each line of Agamemnon has been taken to prove a view of his personality – and many readings of lines in this scene, as elsewhere in tragedy, are dismissed on the grounds that they are 'out of character'.

Opposition to such academic debates has been varied. Tycho von Wilamowitz (son of the great Victorian scholar Ulrich von Wilamowitz, whose studies often contain such character assessments) took the stance that Sophocles, far from having any interest in any consistency of dramatic character, deliberately manipulated audience expectation by bold variety so that each scene could be played for maximum dramatic effect. Any attempt at harmonizing characters is bound to fail and misrepresents both the author's intention and the audience's desire or focus of attention. Howald, who follows this line, suggests that an audience neither wishes nor is able to refer backward or forward in the experience of the individual moment. These extreme measures, which have

---

[8] 1981, 20.

found their apologists in each subsequent generation,[9] may seem through such a repression of the texts' emphases on states of mind (as well as of any sense of narrative or the constitution of meaning in difference) to be as distorted a view as the position they oppose. Nevertheless they sound an important note of caution against the easy assumption of the attitudes to personality founded on the novel and psychological studies. J. Jones, for example, who is often taken as supporting this view of 'no character', develops an important series of comments on Aristotle and characterization which are applicable (and applied well by him) to various tragedies. In particular, he denies that Aristotle entertained the later Aristotelians' concept of the 'tragic hero' and questions the supposed interest in the 'flaws' of such a character. He recalls that one of the main arguments of the *Poetics* is that tragedy is an imitation not of human beings but of action and life. In the carpet scene of the *Oresteia*, for example, Jones intelligently discusses the role of the *oikos* and particularly the desire for economic continuity in the determination of the sense of the act of treading on the tapestries, and this emphasis on action as opposed to character or supposed motive is followed through in different ways with the texts of Sophocles and Euripides. For Jones, the complement on stage of this intellectual argument is the mask, which, he says, resists the possibility of inwardness. 'Its being is exhausted in its features.'[10] Indeed, Jones and others have constituted something of a new orthodoxy for whom, in a stronger articulation of the younger Wilamowitz's views, 'the revelation of psychology is only incidental to a scene's primary dramatic purpose'.[11]

Against this new orthodoxy, however, some scholars have recently attempted to reclaim the 'intelligibility' in 'human terms' of the characters of Greek drama, which is not just a restatement of a Bradleian position. P. E. Easterling has suggested that we can still 'believe in' the people of these plays. She agrees that it is necessary for us to be 'wary of our natural preoccupation with idiosyncrasy and to distrust the modern view of what constitutes an "interesting character"',[12] but notes that there are 'words and actions which are susceptible to varying shades of interpretation'[13] and that 'behaviour that can be variously explained has great dramatic potential'.[14] Uncertainty or ambiguity about motives does not imply a lack of motives or lack of interest in character, but a realistic representation of the overdetermination of life. Lack of explicit discussion of motivation need not imply no interest in internal life. The qualitative differences between Sophocles and modern dramatists in characterization, she concludes, are often overstressed, and the fact that, for

---

[9] Dawe 1963, and Lloyd-Jones 1972 have in different ways defended Tychoism; for a critique of Dawe, see Goldhill 1984a, 70–2.
[10] 1962, 45. For a rejection of Jones on the mask, see Vickers 1973, 54–6.
[11] Taplin 1977, 312.   [12] 1977, 123.   [13] 1977, 126.   [14] 1977, 126.

example, 'the Greeks are interested in individuals as part of a community much more than in the individual's unique experience, a difference of attitude which is sometimes hard for us to share or appreciate'[15] does not mean that characters do not matter, but rather that we must realign our sense of what characters are.

This realignment has been developed further by John Gould, who has both restressed the role of language and discourse – a 'world of metaphor' – in the development of character in fiction and further questioned the common ground of 'human intelligibility', if this expression is taken to mean a sort of naive realism, the representation of the actual way actual people behave: 'Poetry is a complex thing: it resembles and it does not resemble our experience.'[16] Arguments that stem either from the belief that characters in fiction simply are or should be the same as 'real-life people', or, for that matter, from the assumption that 'real-life people' is a simple, self-evident construction, are, Gould suggests, a rather naive misprision of the complexity of reading poetic fiction, particularly a poetic fiction whose characters are drawn largely from an archaic world of epic stories and myth. Gould concludes with some hesitations that a notion of character cannot be dispensed with, even if a 'character' cannot be quite detached from the play's 'world', from the 'pervasive metaphorical colouring of the whole language of the play'.[17]

One of the most important points of discussion, especially when considering this realignment of a sense of character, is that there is no word in fifth-century Greek which means 'character' as it seems most often used in literary criticism. Although a famous passage in the Life of Sophocles is often translated 'he creates a character out of a mere half-line or a single expression' (21), and, according to Plutarch, Sophocles described his own mature style as 'the best and most expressive of character' (*de prof. in virt.* 7), the translation, as so often, misrepresents the Greek. The term translated by 'character' is *ethos* and, while it certainly implies a set of attitudes or a particular disposition, there is an important difference between *ethos* and the common sense of 'character'. For *ethos*, as Jones says, 'is without the ambition of inclusiveness'.[18] *Ethos* does not attempt, as 'character' often does in modern usage, to express a whole personality or the make-up of a psyche. Aristotle, for example, writes '*ethos* in tragedy is that which reveals a moral choice' (*Poet.* 50b 7–8) and for him tragedy can be 'without "characters"' – which need not imply some modernist attempt at abstract drama.

I intend here to reconsider John Gould's uncertainty as to the interplay of character and the play's discourse, and at the same time investigate the nature of the opposition of orthodoxies I have been outlining, in two ways. First, to

[15] 1977, 129.   [16] 1978, 62.   [17] 1978, 60.   [18] 1962, 32.

continue the theoretical overview now from a position outside mainstream classical studies, I intend to offer a further general perspective on character through the writings of Roland Barthes and others. Secondly, I intend to look at two plays of Sophocles, *Antigone* again, and, in far greater depth, *Ajax*, to see how this multiplicity of views on character relates to the texts themselves. For I have not been drawing up the battle-lines of criticism in this way in order simply to stake out my position in the academic debate, and certainly not in order to propose another conclusive argument on a topic in which the plurality of stands and authorities is so evident. Rather, it is important to have rehearsed, however briefly, these critical stances partly because it remains a complex and important area of discussion where modern readers' expectations are so often surprised and frustrated by the ancient texts, and partly because I hope my analysis of the plays, rather than following one of these views at the expense of all others, will help to show something of the conditions that give rise to such a plurality of attitudes. For as much as we have seen the tragic texts placing the language of relations in the city, say, at odds with itself, marked by conflicting rhetorics of appropriation; as much as we saw the language of personal exchanges fractured by divisions and divisiveness, and as much as the position of the interpreter in these tragic tensions and oppositions was implicated and undermined in its security, so the language of personality will be seen to be woven in warring claims and accusations, doubts and misplaced certainties. Disorder and transgression cannot be excised from the language of mind in these tragedies.

Barthes' work *S/Z* is a lengthy and brilliant analysis of a Balzac short story, *Sarrasine*, and his concern with characterization is naturally enough focused on problems bearing on the novelistic techniques of a prose quite different from the public poetry of Greek tragedy. Nevertheless, his insights into the interplay of language and character seem particularly apposite with regard to the critical debate I have outlined above. Barthes begins from the opposition of 'character' and 'discourse'. If on the one hand we have a realistic view of character, then we seek for motive in any surprising gap or apparent inconsistency in the text. Why does Oedipus, for example, in *Oedipus Tyrannus* not hear Teiresias' first pronouncement of who he is? Is it because he is too impassioned, angry, arrogant, foolish etc. to hear the truth about himself? If on the other hand we have a realistic view of discourse we will say that Oedipus must not hear the truth for the play's narrative to continue, for the dialectic of ignorance and knowledge, chance and control, to be developed, for the dramatic representation of that dialectic. But Barthes does not allow this opposition of views simply to stand. 'Now these two views, although derived from different likelihoods and in principle independent (even opposed) support each other: a common sentence is produced which unexpectedly contains elements of various languages.'[19] Oedipus is 'impassioned' because the discourse must not end; the discourse can continue because Oedipus talks without listening to the truth. 'Both circuits are necessarily undecidable. Good narrative writing is of this very undecidability.'[20] For Barthes, then, the critical opposition of 'character' and 'discourse' collapses into itself with a recognition of the plural functioning of literary language. It is from a critical point of view just as wrong totally to suppress character as it is to take a character off the page and turn him into a full psychological personality endowed with possible motives, emotions, a subconscious. '*The character and the discourse are each other's accomplices*: the discourse creates in the character its own accomplice: a form of theurgical detachment by which, mythically, God has given himself a subject, man a helpmate etc., whose relative independence once they have been created, allows for *playing*.'[21] Indeed, we will see particularly in the *Ajax* how the vocabulary of terms of mind and approaches to personal relationships is set in motion by the different personae of the drama, how the characters' discourses and the discourse of character interplay in the plurality of voices.

These initial comments on 'character' and the way critics have sought to determine the role of 'character' in these tragic texts will be developed and clarified in various directions through the analyses to follow. It will be as well here, however, to offer a summing-up of the argument so far. The emphasis on 'character' in the tragic texts seems quite different from, say, a Victorian novelist's perspective. The public, masked persona does not suggest a similar focus on idiosyncrasies of personality, and criticism whose aim or method of explication is based on inclusive modern notions of 'character' as a person's whole personality seems to ignore the tensions both in the notion of the self, and between 'character' and 'discourse' in these plays. Indeed, there does not seem to be any notion in fifth-century Greek that quite reflects the inclusive idea of 'character'. Whatever is meant by 'character' with regard to Attic drama, it must have different boundaries and alignment. But these necessary cautions do not mean that there is in Greek drama no interest in any internal life of its personae. As we will see, there is a considerable focus on the words which express such an internal existence, attitudes of mind, disposition. It becomes therefore a question now of reconsidering the structuring of such a discourse of mind within the text and the exchanges of dramatic personae, to investigate that realignment. How do these plays represent a sense of internal attitudes and states of mind?

Now when I looked in some detail at the oppositions of the *Antigone* in

[19] 1975, 178.   [20] 1975, 178.   [21] 1975, 178.

Chapter 4, at certain points we approached this question of 'mind'. At the end of the prologue, for example, as Antigone first leaves to complete the burial, Ismene sends her off with the words (98–9):

> Go since you want to. But know this: you go
> senseless indeed, but loved (*philos*) by those who love (*philos*) you.

As we saw, the paradoxical implications of Antigone's action are stressed in the way the term 'senseless', 'mindless', marks the corruption of a process of thought, even if it is through an excessive desire for a sort of piety. This emphasis on 'disposition' continues in Creon's first speech, where the political implications of 'correct mental attitudes' are made clear. He describes the citizens' reverence for the royal power of Laius – the authority he is assuming – as 'steadfast attitudes' (169). The word 'attitude' is picked up seven lines later in his remark which many have seen as ironically programmatic for Creon's own tragic attitudes to power (175–7):

> You cannot learn of any man the soul,
> the mind, and the intent until he shows
> his practice of the government and the law.

These lines would seem to place at stake in this tragedy precisely Creon's attitude of mind as ruler. So he concludes this first statement of his position with the same word for attitude of mind: 'Such is my mind' (207). For him, the person who is 'well-minded' (209) towards the city will be honoured. In the same way as Antigone's attitude was defined by Ismene in terms of *nous*, 'mind', so now Creon defines his politically based value system through the same terms of 'mind' in relation to the city.

So when Antigone is 'captured in folly' (382) as the perpetrator of acts against the laws of the city, and defends her conduct by her famous appeal to the principles of the gods, Creon's reaction to the speech of defence is again in terms of 'attitudes of mind' (472–9):

> But know that over-stubborn attitudes
> are most often humbled . . .
> Slave to his neighbour, who can think of pride?

The phrase for 'pride' is *mega phronein*, 'think big', the term we discussed in the *Hippolytus* where we also saw a debate over terms of mind and attitude prominently at work particularly with regard to sexual behaviour. It picks up the term for attitude (*phronema*) in a way which will be particularly important in the scene between Creon and Haemon.[22] For *phronein* in its range of senses moves from 'to be of a particular disposition of mind', to 'to think' and 'to be

---

[22] On *phronein* in the *Antigone*, see Kirkwood 1958, 233–9.

wise'. The wisdom of a course of action implies a disposition, a mood. Antigone indeed picks up Creon's reaction to her conduct as an attitude of mind by marking her disjunction from Ismene in terms of such a reaction to a quality of *phronein* (557):

> Some will have thought you wiser (*phronein*), some will not.

Creon responds to this argument of the sisters, by calling them both 'senseless' (561–2):

> One of these girls has shown her lack of sense
> just now. The other had it from her birth.

As Ismene had termed Antigone 'senseless' before, now Creon applies the same word to both sisters in their joint opposition to him. Ismene retorts (563–4):

> Yes, lord. When people fall in deep distress
> their native sense departs, and will not stay.

The bad fortune which Creon had claimed to be caused by such a disposition of mind is set by Ismene rather as the *source* of the lack of 'sound sense'.[23] The testing of the ruler's state of mind here proceeds through the conflict of his determination of the 'senselessness' of his opposition and their claim to a higher or at any rate different attitude.

The chorus' reaction to this scene is to sing of the disasters of the house of Oedipus, and they place the cause of the present troubles in the blood-stained aggression of the gods of the underworld and in 'senselessness of speech and a frenzy of minds' (603). The conflicts of the previous exchanges are depicted in terms of an interrelated corruption of the rational powers of language and the processes of thought. In the 'Ode on Man', the chorus had extolled (354–5):

> Language and wind-swift attitudes of mind (*phronema*)
> and all the moods that form the legal state.

Their bold enthusiasm for the qualities of speech and thought that lead to the establishment of the order of the city has turned in the space of one scene to despair at their corruption in the house of Oedipus. They conclude their stanzas with a recollection of a well-known saying that 'at some time evil seems good to the man whose mind god leads to disaster' (622–4). The disaster of the tragedies of the generations of Labdacids are summed up as god leading 'minds' towards recklessness. This is an important prelude to the interchange

---

[23] North 1966, 100–16, has argued for the importance to Thucydides of the idea that attitudes are distorted by disastrous events.

of Haemon and Creon which again questions the 'soul, mind, intent' of the man in power.

Creon in the course of his argument for the need of the hierarchical structures of law and order asks Haemon not to allow his mind to be distorted through desire for a woman (648–9), and the chorus conclude that the king has spoken wisely (*phron-*). But it is precisely Creon's position as 'thinker' that Haemon challenges. He opens his reply with the statement that the possession of a good mind is the greatest of the gods' gifts, and he soon turns to his father's character (705–9):

> Then do not have one set of attitudes (*ethos*) and one alone
> that only your opinion can be right.
> Whoever thinks that he alone is wise (*phronein*),
> his eloquence, his mind above the rest,
> come the unfolding, shows his emptiness.

Haemon's denial of self-reliance in terms of the triplet of 'wisdom, tongue and soul' seems a variation of Creon's earlier notion that a man's 'soul, mind, intent' are not tested until seen under the pressures of power, a variation which marks not only the continuing sense of the trial of Creon's attitudes in office, but also specifically the tendency towards the depiction of tyranny, excess, aggression in terms of a specific disposition of mind.

But Creon reviles his son's *ethos*, too ('O accursed character' 746) and the debate degenerates, as we saw in Chapter 4, to mutual accusations of lack of sense (754–5):

> Creon: You will regret this lesson (*phren-*), with your empty mind (*phren*).
> Haemon: If you weren't father, I should say you were not thinking
> (*phronein*) straight.

The triple use of words of the same root in the conflict of father and son over the source of order and rule emphasizes that it is not simply 'behaviour', 'action' that is at stake in the oppositions of the play but also 'attitudes of mind' in a social and political as well as psychological sense.[24]

The Hymn to Eros also marks the power of an irrational force expressly on the minds of men (791–2) – a god leading man's mind to disaster, as the chorus had threatened earlier (623–4), which seems now applicable to Haemon as much as to his father. And the exchange between Creon and Teiresias following Antigone's procession to the cave further stresses the role of a mental attitude in the downfall of the king. For Teiresias noticeably places the cause of the city's present sickness in the mind of Creon: 'The city is sick from your mind/attitude (*phren-*)' (1015), and the seer goes on to exhort him to

[24] For *sophronein* as a charged term in contemporary politics, see North 1966, 85–149.

'think (*phron-*) on these things' (1023). The seer adds his strictures to the testing of the ruler's mind. But the recurring tension in the vocabulary of mind is further emphasized in the stichomythia that follows Creon's denunciation of the seer. Teiresias says (1050) that good counsel is the best of possessions, and Creon retorts 'And not being wise (*phronein*) does the most harm' (1051). Creon ironically enough repeats the conventional wisdom on the need for wisdom, as if he were accepting Teiresias' injunctions to show good sense and to look to his mind. Indeed, Creon recognizes and rejects Teiresias' move against his authority in terms of an attitude of mind (1063):

> Know you will not trade upon my mind (*phren-*)

Teiresias had called Creon's mind the source of the city's troubles, but it is the position of that mind, intention, disposition that Creon will not allow to be questioned.

Teiresias departs the stage and his final ringing words forcefully echo this vocabulary of attitude of mind (1087–90):

> Boy, take me home now. Let him spend his rage
> on younger men and learn to keep a calmer tongue,
> and better mind than now he does.

Once more we hear an echo of Creon's willingness to have his soul, mind, intention tested in and by the position of power he has adopted, now at the turning-point of his failure in such a test.

It is a terror in his mind that Creon confesses to, as soon as Teiresias has left (1095), and he accepts the chorus' warning of what happens to those of 'evil disposition (*phron-*)' (1104). For the first time he gives up his position of self-assertion, and asks and accepts the opinion of another. But the disasters spreading from his attitude of mind have already been put in motion and cannot now be halted by Creon's rush to the cave of Antigone's punishment.

The chorus' final words in the tragedy are interesting in the light of our discussion (1347–53):

> Our happiness depends
> on wisdom (*phronein*) all the way.
> The gods must have their due.
> Great words by men of pride
> bring great blows in return.
> So wisdom (*phronein*) comes to the old.

On the one hand, there could be considerable force in these sentiments. The desire for wisdom, or a particular attitude, is rightly expressed as the flower of happiness, and reverence for the gods is certainly part of such wisdom. The excessive language and attitudes of the main characters, their violent arguments, have led to the great disasters of death and ruin. Both Antigone's passion for her particular type of family support and Creon's equally strong belief in the structure and order of the city have been characterized in terms of excessive language, proud argument, and, in particular, an excessive 'pattern of thought'. In this play of opposites it is left to the chorus alone at the end to make such a conclusive generalization: 'He closes with a moral on the lips of the chorus which tells the audience what to think.'[25] On the other hand, one could say with Coleman, for example, that 'they are singularly unhelpful. For there is not a single proposition here that anyone in the play would have dissented from.'[26] Indeed, we have seen Creon and Haemon express precisely such comments on the need for the good qualities of *phronein* in mutually exclusive ways. The conflicting acts of appropriation towards the language of mind through which Creon construed 'good sense', 'wisdom' within the hierarchical structures of social ordering and through which Antigone could justify disobedience and her desire to bury her brother at any cost, set at risk the status sometimes assumed for such simple gnomic utterances of the chorus. Rather than standing above the action, the chorus, like the critic, speaks from a position neither above nor below, neither comfortably inside nor beyond the periphery of this rhetoric of appropriation. These concluding remarks seem to stand as a final comment of the surviving citizens of the play to the citizen body of the audience, yet how can their statements avoid duplicating the interplay of languages of mind and attitude that I have been tracing? How can the chorus' language be securely hypostatized as offering any authoritative or authorial comment?

In *Antigone*, as we have seen in this rapid summary, a vocabulary of mind is closely linked with the oppositions of the discourse. Creon's and Antigone's tendency to excess is marked by characterizations in terms of attitude – 'senseless', 'mindless' and the like – but they are characterizations which clash with each other as the vocabulary of attitudes of mind is passed through the rhetoric of appropriation which dominates the conflicts of this play. The play's concern with conflicting ties and relationships in the city and the family is also seen with words of attitude and 'mind': rather than an interest, say, in an idiosyncratic character in and for itself, there is a focus on attitudes in regard to such relationships, attitudes towards other people, other ideas. The notions of 'wisdom', the quality of *phronein*, are not absolutes but set within specific systematizations of ideas which resist and contest the boundaries of the

[25] Bowra 1944, 66.   [26] 1972, 26.

individual self in society. The language of mind and attitude, which one might think to be a prime way of developing a sense of character, is constantly implicated in the wider markings of social discourse. It would seem that the interest in states of mind in *Antigone* is best seen as illuminating the conflicting language of mental attitudes involved in the specific orderings and transgressions of social life. There seems to be neither a stable vocabulary of mind, nor a stable polarization of mind and action.

Such an interest in order and transgression with regard to 'mind' is indeed a recurring theme of Greek tragedy. In the *Oresteia*, to take a single example from one play, the central ode from the *Choephoroi* on the transgressive passions of women focuses in its opening stanzas on desires precisely in terms of their relation to 'mind', 'attitudes' and in terms of their effect on the orderings of social life. So we have seen in *Hippolytus* the intertwinings of the language of 'mind', 'pride', 'self-control' and the discourse of sexuality towards a tragic conclusion. In both these plays, as in *Antigone*, it would seem that the opposition between 'plot' and 'character', 'action' and 'psychology' – an opposition which was so important to the critical discussions with which I began this chapter – tends to be unable to maintain itself as a rigid polarization. The correlation of the apparent lack of interest in 'idiosyncratic character' in and for itself seems to be that, rather than any total repression of 'character', 'action' – both in the sense of social behaviour and in the sense of a specific action – is continually being implicated in the vocabulary of 'mind', as, indeed, the vocabulary of mind in particularly its relational aspect cannot be easily separated from modes of behaviour and action. The interrelations of the vocabulary of an internal life of mind and the vocabulary of action resist the easy separation into the binary opposition of 'plot' and 'character', 'psychology' and 'action'.

The focus on transgression in and through particular states of mind is especially important in Sophocles. Not only has the state of mind associated with being a 'hero' long been recognized as a major theme of the Sophoclean corpus,[27] but also the sicknesses of Philoctetes in *Philoctetes* and Heracles in *Trachiniae* show in some depth the disastrous effects of a grievous physical state on a character. Ajax, too, holds a privileged position in our discussion as an extremely important example not only of Sophocles' interest in peculiarly excessive states of mind but also in particular of the interest (shared by the three major tragedians) in the depiction of the mad on stage, and it is to *Ajax* now for the remainder of this chapter that I wish to turn.

The interest in Ajax's 'mind' or 'character' has led to one of the most

---

[27] See especially Knox 1964; Kirkwood 1958.

extensive recent debates in classical studies.[28] This debate has tended to concentrate on the 'deception speech', the famous and beautiful lines of Ajax which lead the chorus and Tecmessa to think that their lord has given up his intention to suicide. The debate of earlier critics as to whether Ajax has changed his mind or not has hardened into a general opinion that his intention to commit suicide does not waver, and the resultant discussion has concentrated on why Ajax should be concerned to deceive his nearest and dearest, or whether indeed he is so concerned. We will see later how closely this speech is woven into the discourse of the play, which maintains a remarkable focus on the state of Ajax's mind and his intentions, and how these attempts to read Ajax's internal attitudes are mirrored by the chorus' attempt to understand their lord.

The opening scene revolves around Athene's display of Ajax in his maddened state to his enemy, Odysseus. In the works of Homer, as Dodds has emphasized, the responsibility for mental states or psychological change is often placed explicitly in the external compulsion or control of the divinities. In the opening argument of the *Iliad*, for example, where Agamemnon steals Achilles' concubine, his war-prize, it is Athene who is said to restrain Achilles' first reaction, which is to kill the leader of the Greeks for his outrageous behaviour. In the same way, when Agamemnon finally apologizes for his actions, he says that Zeus, Moira and the Erinyes must have stolen his wits (*Il.* 19.87). The disasters of mortal life, the errors and successes of planning, man's emotional impulses, are not expressed as coming from a psyche but as entering the psyche from divine forces outside. So in *Ajax* the cause of Ajax's delusion is explicitly claimed to be Athene. This mechanism of external causation would appear to stand against any system of psychology or character-drawing. But as we will see there is no simple adoption of any archaism on Sophocles' part. Indeed, the rest of the play goes towards building up a picture of Ajax's excessive state of mind in such a way as to limit Athene's intervention to the specific ocular delusion which leads Ajax to kill the sheep rather than the Greek leaders. As Vernant depicted tragic man situated between his internal decisions, personal responsibility, and 'a game with supernatural forces', so the responsibility of Athene, the external control of Ajax's mind, is set in tension with the extensive vocabulary of internal decision-making, which may be thought to lead towards the problems of reading Ajax's intentions in the deception speech, for example, where the focus on the internal workings of Ajax's mind, his intentions and attitudes, seems most strong. Sophocles but rarely introduces divine figures on stage in

[28] See e.g. Hester 1971; Knox 1961; Moore 1977; Sicherl 1977; Simpson 1969; Taplin 1978, 127–31.

his plays. The appearance of Herakles at the end of the *Philoctetes* to resolve the unmediated opposition of forces with the voice of finality is the only other example in our extant corpus of a divinity on stage, and Heracles is perhaps a supreme hero rather than a god. This is, of course, quite different from both Euripides and Aeschylus, though if we were to possess more plays it might be necessary to alter such a general view. It would seem that *Ajax* sets in tension the most obvious and direct influence of a divinity on human affairs with some of the most involved writing on introspection in the Sophoclean corpus: the tension between the internal and external in the make-up of man, already present in Homer, is forcibly dramatized in this play. The sense of the boundaries of a personality in terms of responsibility for personal action is always being questioned in the overdeterminism of divine causation of psychological and physical action.

The opening scene of the play presents us with the sight of the mad Ajax. There can be no doubt that all the characters regard him as beyond the bounds of any normal personality. Athene describes him as mad (59, 81) and as sick (59, 66) and taunts Odysseus with his fear to see the madman. Odysseus retorts that he wouldn't feel fear for a man 'in his wits' (*phronein* 82). But critics have long argued about the ways in which Ajax might be said to be mad. The problem is twofold, and bears closely on the question of character. First, Athene describes her intervention only as 'throwing hard-to-bear notions on his eyes, notions of a wild joy' (51–2). We will have to discuss, then, the interrelations of madness and sight. Secondly, as we will see, there is a continuing series of descriptions of Ajax's mind which seem difficult to reconcile into a single picture of previous sanity, temporary insanity, and later recovery, with the result that critics have even argued for positions as polarized as 'Ajax is mad throughout the play' and 'Ajax is never mad in any strict sense at any point in the play'.[29] In particular, these descriptions of Ajax's mental state raise not only the problem of the understanding of Ajax's internal character, but also the questioning of the relation between the act of slaughter and the attitudes of mind associated with it. As we saw in *Antigone*, it is not simply a question of mental attitudes but of attitudes in relation to action that is at stake. First, let us consider the interrelations of sight and madness.

The first scene plays in an extraordinary way on the sense of sight. Athene opens with a sight of Odysseus (1–3):

> Odysseus, I have always seen and marked you
> stalking to pounce upon your enemies.
> And now I see you . . .

---

[29] For such extreme views, see Vandvik 1942; Adams 1955. Most critics rightly eschew such oversimplified views.

But in contrast with the divine sight, Odysseus says he cannot see Athene.[30] He hears a disembodied voice (14–16):

> Voice of Athene, dearest utterance
> of all the gods to me – I cannot see you,
> and yet how clearly I catch your words in my mind.

This immediately sets up a problem of staging. Is Athene visible to the audience or not? Most critics assume that she is, and assume that she is regarded by the audience by convention as invisible to Odysseus.[31] A few critics have argued that she remains invisible to all throughout the scene, and speaks from off-stage,[32] which involves fewer problems of interpretation of the visual dynamics at any rate. For when Ajax comes on, there is no indication of any special circumstances (as there was with Odysseus' greeting of the goddess). Ajax merely says 'Hail Athene, daughter of Zeus. Hail and welcome. How well you have stood by me' (91–2). Does the audience assume Ajax to see Athene? On stage too is still Odysseus, but he is invisible to Ajax (83–5):

> Athene: He will stand near you and yet not see you.
> Odysseus: How is that possible if he sees with the same eyes still?
> Ath.: I can darken even the most brilliant vision.

So the spectators can see Ajax failing to see Odysseus, a divine distortion of his vision in madness, but they also see Odysseus failing to see Athene. Tecmessa moreover describes this scene as follows (301–3):

> At length he darted out the door and spoke
> wild, rending words, directed toward some phantom
> exulting with a harsh laugh . . .

What does she think she saw? A phantom, a shadow . . . Or does she mean a phantom of his mind? In the half-light of dawn, with Athene's tricky distortion of sight, things are not what they seem. The unparalleled stagecraft of this scene through such a manipulation of the convention of visibility and invisibility on stage develops the characters' oblique relations in terms of the easily distorted faculty of vision, the sense of sight. Even the selection of a particular staging for a particular production cannot finally remove the ambiguities and uncertainties of vision expressed in this opening section.

---

[30] Some (Taplin 1978, 40 n. 12; Ferguson 1970) have seen an ambiguity here, either because the word 'unseen' in later Greek at least can mean 'stared at', 'evident', or because of a belief that Athene is only temporarily invisible to Odysseus. Although this belief does not easily match with the syntax and emphasis on voice (see Jebb ad loc.), it is precisely on the ambiguity between seen and unseen in this scene that I will be focusing.

[31] Jebb argues strongly for this. Taplin believes she is visible to all including Odysseus.

[32] Kitto 1961 and Gellie 1972 argue strongly for this.

When Ajax returns into his tent, however, Athene again addresses Odysseus (118–20):

> Do you see Odysseus how great the gods' power is?
> Who was more full of insight than this man,
> or abler, do you think, to act with judgement?

But Odysseus replies (121–6):

> None that I know of. Yet I pity
> his wretchedness though he is my enemy,
> for the terrible yoke of disaster that is on him.
> I look to his state, yet also to my own.
> For I see the true nature of all of us that live.
> We are dim shapes, no more, and weightless shadows.

The word for 'I know' (*oida*) is etymologically the perfect tense of a word 'to see'.[33] Odysseus '*looks to*' his own position, and as Athene had asked '*Do you see?*' the power of the gods, he replies '*For I see*' the frailty of man – the *shadows* of existence. This exchange between man and goddess marks the close connection in Greek of words of sight and words of knowledge. As in English, one 'looks at' an argument, 'sees' a point, has an 'insight', and hopes for 'clarity'. As much as this opening scene in the theatre – and the word 'theatre' means the place for seeing – plays on the conventions of selective invisibility, so the play's movement towards knowledge is developed in the same vocabulary of vision. The intellectual insight of Odysseus cannot be separated simply from the visual blindness of Ajax. Indeed, the interpenetration of words of sight and knowledge provides a degree of continuity throughout the play joining the various characters both in their search for certainty as clarity, for knowledge as insight, and in their narrowness of vision, their partial views. This opening scene's emphasis on vision in its physical and intellectual senses provides an important link between mental states, physical symptoms and action not just with regard to the problematic definition of Ajax's madness.

The role of sight in the definition of Ajax's character and madness cannot, then, be separated from the wider implications of his state of mind, his intellectual make-up, or from the discourse of knowledge and insight, so important to the play and its criticism. The physical and mental imply each other in the shared vocabulary of perception and conception. The attempt to localize Athene's intervention in Ajax's character to his faculty of vision leads us again to a discussion of state of mind. There is no easy separation of characters, actions, responsibilities in the language and discourse of the play.

---

[33] For further plays on 'knowing' and 'seeing', see below, Chapter 8.

The chorus and Tecmessa agree on Ajax's madness, his sickness. The chorus wonder which god it could have been (171–82) to have driven him onto the flocks: 'for never, son of Telamon, would you so far have strayed to fall upon the flocks' (183–5). Indeed, Tecmessa calls his fits 'madness': 'madness has seized our noble Ajax' (216), but now she informs the sailors that he has returned to sanity, he is 'in his wits' (*phronimos* 259), and she goes on to describe his return to health. As the chorus reflect on this, the cries of Ajax are heard from within. But the chorus immediately show themselves uncertain as to his state of mind, just as they were as to the cause of his aberration (337–8):

> Either he is still mad or else can't bear
> the company his madness made around him.

Their doubts seem cleared to their satisfaction as he speaks his first recognizable words[34] – though their trust in the straightforwardness of Ajax's language by the end of the play may seem misplaced (344):

> No, he seems to be sane (*phronein*). Open the door . . .

Ajax is displayed among the signs of his madness to the chorus, as he had been by the goddess to Odysseus. Their reaction is in terms of the mind of their lord (355):

> Insanity (*a-phron-*) stands here revealed indeed.

As Ajax rails at his misfortune, they exhort him to yield and show sense (*phronein* 371). In this interchange of Ajax's impassioned lyrics and the chorus' iambics, the chorus' concern for Ajax's present and past state of sanity, and Ajax's own recognition of his mental and visual aberration place considerable emphasis on the uncertain questioning of the boundaries of normality with regard to Ajax's state of mind and behaviour. The return towards sanity weaves uncertainty around the precise boundary between madness and reason.

In the scene that follows we see an important development of this view of a character's relation to the bounds of normality. First, Ajax links his mental and visual errors together but shows no sign of regret for his original plan for murder (447–9):

> . . . if my eyes and mind had not leapt whirling
> wide from my aim, those two would never again
> cheat anyone with their awards and ballots.

---

[34] In the twentieth century, language is most often regarded as the locus of mental disorder (see McCabe 1981; Forrester 1980). This does not appear to be so in the ancient world, where visual disorder seems most often the sign of mental aberration. See Padel (forthcoming).

But he too recognizes Athene as the cause behind this whirling of mind and eye (450–2):

> But, instead, the fierce-eyed overpowering
> daughter of Zeus, just then as I was readying
> my hand and plot against them, set me sprawling
> distraught and frenzied ...

As much as the interest appeared to be focused on Ajax's state of mind in his own recognition of his insanity, the psychological causation is now placed outside the character as if he were not responsible for his actions, or as if his actions had little relation to the autonomy of his mind. The uncertainty as to the state of Ajax's mind is reflected in the overdetermination of suggested causalities.

We have already seen in my earlier discussion of the *Ajax* how the exchange between Ajax and Tecmessa and the chorus places Ajax in his social role as the great hero, head of the family, a central focus for the life of his extended family and his group of dependants and how Ajax rejects such a role. We have seen, too, how this claim to honour, his attitude towards himself, outweighs his ties to the community of which he is such an important part. Indeed, in the general discussion with which I opened this chapter, I have already marked as one of the major differences in the boundaries of personality the sense of the definition of an individual through his social role and relationships (as opposed to the idiosyncrasies of a character). But there is something more here. For throughout this scene, as has been long recognized and discussed with some subtlety,[35] there is a series of echoes and references back to Homer, to a similar scene between a hero and his woman and child, namely, the famous passage in the *Iliad* (6.390ff.), where Andromache attempts to persuade Hector not to fight. While the echoes of this Homeric passage indicate a certain similarity of situation, particularly in terms of the dependence of women on their military protectors, it is primarily the differences that create a significant tension in the exchange. On the simplest level, Hector's fight is to protect his house and family, and he runs the risk of self-sacrifice in their defence, Ajax's threatened action is to kill himself, knowing it will be a rejection of his family and home. But it is also in terms of heroic attitudes that the difference can be seen. Ajax's self-motivated action towards self-destruction shows the difference of his attitude to his community, it shows a certain tension in heroic self-assertion within a community reliant on reciprocal relations for its functioning. As we have seen, heroic values stand at a certain oblique angle to an ideology of the city and the workings of drama, but Ajax

[35] Adams 1955; Brown 1965–6; Kirkwood 1965 discuss this.

seems to take the individualism of the hero to an extreme of solitude and self-reliance in his rejection of the very ties for which Hector, the greatest hero of the Trojans, fought. 'Ajax ... is not just the typical Homeric, the Achillean, hero but rather one who carries the heroic code to the extreme possible point'[36] – an extreme point which shows the inherent strain of a reliance on self in a community of relations. This scene shows Ajax's different attitude to family also. When Hector's child was frightened by the waving plume of his father's helmet, Hector took off his helmet, laughing, and put it on the ground before saying farewell to the boy. Ajax asserts that his son will not be afraid of the blood and slaughter if the boy's nature is truly an extension of his father. Indeed, he wants his boy to be the same in all respects except fortune as himself (550–1), and to live by the same 'hard laws' as his father (548). The word translated 'hard' is the term used for 'raw' meat, for 'wild', 'uncivilized' values. It creates something of an oxymoron with *nomoi*, 'laws', 'custom'. 'Rawness', interestingly, was also the word applied to Antigone and Oedipus in *Antigone* (471–2)[37] to express the like wild nature of father and daughter. In the *Iliad*, Achilles in his supreme moment of frenzy desires to eat Hector's flesh 'raw'. It is a word associated with the world of beasts or with attitudes at odds with the norms of human behaviour in society. It is the anti-social 'raw laws' of his total self-reliance that Ajax wishes to propagate through his son in this moment of self-justification.

Ajax's reflections on his child's childhood also show an interesting attitude to states of mind. The great warrior asserts that to know nothing, not to *phronein* in any way, is best. For the man of action whose mind has indeed led to his present misery, the thoughtlessness of childhood may seem attractive. But it was precisely through the negation of *phronein* that Ajax's madness was expressed, as not showing the quality of *phronein* was the lack of sense, the excess, shown by Creon in *Antigone*. As Ajax reflects on a world free from mind troubles, he cannot but echo the distortion of sense that led to his position.[38]

Tecmessa with increasing fervour attempts to dissuade Ajax from his intent, and his final emphatic lines focus on states of mind and character once more (594–5):

> ... You have a foolish thought (*phronein*)
> if you think at this late date to school my nature (*ethos*).

It has been Ajax's 'nature', 'character', 'disposition' in this scene that has been expressed (as it was introduced with the concentration on his return to

[36] Winnington-Ingram 1980, 19.   [37] See Segal 1981, 191.
[38] Interestingly, Tecmessa speaks of being 'too mindful' of grief (942). Ajax's *meden phronein* may be echoed in her *agan phronein*.

his right wits), and the repetition of words of thought recalls the clash of intentions and attitudes throughout. But once more, as there has been an emphasis on internal life, and on attitudes in relation to a person's actions, so the simple drawing of the boundaries of personalities has been questioned. If it has seemed impossible to separate a character out from the language of the play as a psychological entity, so the attitude of Ajax is in part definable here through the relation of the text to the text of Homer. The reliance of tragic plots largely on the materials of myth and earlier epics does not simply mean that the interest in individual personalities is removed and that 'characters' are as traditional as their names, nor does it mean that the characters of tragedy, despite the evident variety of Electras, say, are straightforward 'creations'. It may be the case that Sophocles 'has drawn his Ajax straight from the *Iliad* . . . emphasizing and developing those characteristics of the Homeric Ajax that contribute to the tragic picture he wishes to create',[39] but the very process of 'emphasizing and developing', the very setting of such a figure in a fifth-century tragedy, is essential to the questioning of the values of both the Homeric poems and fifth-century life that this play sets in operation, particularly through the relation of the scenes leading up to Ajax's suicide, and the arguments over the body that ensue. Even the repetition of Homeric characteristics takes on a new light in this new setting. As literary inventions, then, the characters of Greek drama draw on, define themselves through, and develop in relation to other texts. These characters may not have psychological pasts or futures beyond the texts but they carry around the echoes of their verbal pasts, earlier readings, earlier writings. The boundaries of personality and the boundaries between personalities are continually being transgressed by such defining intertextual differences. Ajax's assertions of self are not understandable even in terms of 'attitude' apart from an ever-widening context of other texts. As much as the interventions of the gods, this very textuality challenges the autonomy of tragic characters in the very moment of their proclaiming their autonomy.

The first stasimon which follows has been well analysed by Winnington-Ingram.[40] He argues that the two major themes of time and sickness interrelate and finally come together in the questioning of the precise development over time of the mental disorder of Ajax. The opening strophe reflects on the wearing effects of time on the exhausted chorus and their desire to escape from their present woes. This leads in the antistrophe to Ajax's sickness: 'for Ajax, ill to cure, sits by, and god-sent madness is his consort'. Winnington-Ingram comments: 'What began as an explanation of his attack on the cattle has now become descriptive of the suicidal mood which derived

[39] Kirkwood 1965, 62.   [40] 1980, 33–8.

from the Judgement of the Arms and his frustrated vengeance.'[41] The term 'madness' no longer applies to Athene's explicit intervention but to his desire to kill himself – though it is still described as 'god-sent', 'holy' madness. They contrast his earlier warrior prowess with the present, where 'he keeps his thoughts' flock in loneliness and grieves his friends' (614–16). The chorus has again returned to Ajax's mind. Ajax couldn't have been in his wits killing the sheep, the chorus had said, but after his first speech on suicide, they had concluded that 'no-one could ever call those words spurious or alien to your mind' (481–2). Now, however, his attitude is described once more as 'madness', as brooding on the solitude of his mind. His being alone is a grief to his *philoi*. Cut off from society, angered by the Atreidae, he is a consort only to madness: now it is his brooding, introspective, anti-social position that constitutes Ajax's transgression of a normal mental state.

Indeed, the chorus continue by imagining how Ajax's mother will weep 'when the news of his mind's ravage is brought to her', and they open the final antistrophe suggesting it would be better for Ajax to die 'now his mind has gone'. For 'he keeps no more the steady heart we knew but ranges outside'. Rather than the fixed *ethos* that Ajax had himself proclaimed for himself, the chorus assert he is beyond the norm, in excess, not displaying the temper to which he had been bred. In both antistrophes of this stasimon the chorus attempt 'a description of the diseased state of the hero's mind. In both he is seen as having placed himself outside a certain range'[42] – outside society's ties, in the confines of his own spirit, beyond the limits of his normal attitudes. There is more than one sort of mental transgressiveness.

If it is difficult to reconcile the different descriptions of Ajax's mind in a consistent picture, as Winnington-Ingram writes, this only goes to increase the questioning both of his mental state and of the relations between his mental state and his actions. It is in this light that the famous deception speech which follows must be read. For in the critics' discussions concerning Ajax's intentions, or, less specifically, concerning his change of attitude, it is precisely that relation between mind and action that is at question. The deception speech continues and importantly develops the discourse we have been discussing.

The deception speech is veined with a series of sustained ambiguities. Many critics have outlined the double senses of Ajax's expressed intention to 'hide his sword where none will again see it', for example, or his desire to find 'safety'. Ferguson goes so far as to assert that 'ambiguity is the theme of the play',[43] and Taplin writes that 'a whole crucial scene is deliberately left unclear and unresolved'[44] (although he believes that it becomes clearer in the

[41] 1980, 34.   [42] Winnington-Ingram 1980, 38.   [43] 1970, 30.   [44] 1978, 131.

future course of the narrative). These ambiguities bear strongly on the way we determine the sense of character in this play. Ajax's opening reflection on the mutability of things – significantly expressed, as we will see, in terms of 'clarity' and 'bringing to light' – moves towards a statement of the mutability of even minds (649–51):

> Strong oath and rigid minds come crashing down.
> For my mood, which just before was strong and fixed,
> no dipped sword more so, now has lost its edge.

The word 'for' marks the first of the explanations proffered in this speech: again and again, Ajax appears to offer the reasoning behind a decision – *ethos* revealing a moral choice. Here he expresses his pity for his wife and child, 'widowed and lost among my enemies' (653), but the conclusion of this explanation doubles back into ambiguity and doubt (654–5):

> But now I'm going to the bathing place
> and meadows by the sea to cleanse my stains.

Not only is the sense of 'cleansing' a source of ambiguity. The connection between the explanation and consequent action is also uncertain. The word translated 'but' can indicate an adversative force, as if the structure of the rhetoric were 'I pity her but none the less I'm going ...' But the connective can also indicate a positive encouragement, a sense lost in the translation: 'I pity her, and so I'll go, then ...' This pattern of proffered explanation blocked by the ambiguity of the syntax as well as the semantics of the remarks following the explanation is repeated in different ways throughout the speech. The rhetoric seems to set up an explanation as if it indicated the emotion, thought, reasoning, of Ajax, only to block such a move from words to mind, returning always to the fencing hesitations of language. So Ajax asks 'Shall I not learn place and wisdom (*sophronein*)?' (677). After the loss of his mind and the doubts surrounding his personality, it may appear that *sophronein* (particularly with regard to its etymology of 'safe, sound mind') is precisely the quality wanted for and wanting in Ajax. And many have taken this question as Ajax recognizing his untenable position in the order of things, or a willingness on Ajax's part to withdraw from the extremism of his attitudes, or an acceptance of the need for such moderation at least for others in society. But it is noticeable that this rhetorical question is set in the future, it is his future knowledge rhetorically placed under question – as he had earlier in the speech stated 'I will learn to yield to the gods and I will know to reverence the Atreidae' (666–7). These futures defer the instantiation of such knowledge; and when we next see Ajax, it is as preparing to kill himself, with curses on the Greek leaders, and with no indication of any hesitations in his extreme attitudes of hatred and regard for his honour. If Ajax has a new and profound insight concerning his attitudes of mind, then his 'death works to evade tragic insight by cancelling the question "with such knowledge, what can be done?" '.[45] Or rather it reopens a question both of the relation of knowledge to action and of the relation of Ajax's words to his mind's order. The rhetorical questions of his possible future knowledge are set in tension with his future actions and future expressions: again the rhetoric seems to set up the terms of explanation but blocks the closure of secure interpretation.

This rhetoric of deception makes Ajax's instructions to Tecmessa all the more strikingly misleading (685–6):

> . . . fervently and continually pray the gods
> to grant fulfilment of my soul's desire.

He seems to mark precisely the difficulty of reading his 'soul's desire' in the veils of his rhetoric. Indeed, the chorus' song of joy that follows dramatizes the misreading of Ajax's speech. This can be seen in an interesting way particularly at the end of their ode, where they echo the beginning of Ajax's speech markedly. Ajax in famous and beautiful lines had said (646–7):

> The long and countless drift of time brings
> all things unclear to light and hides the shown.

This oscillation of clarity and obscurity, which seems to look forward to the veiling rhetoric of Ajax's deception, is picked up and not merely reflected in the chorus' language (714):

> All things great time extinguishes.[46]

Rather than the alternation, the continual change of the hidden and the evident, the chorus see the effect of time as a single action of extinguishing. Their univocal reading of Ajax's double language which leads to their misunderstanding is seen in their simplification of Ajax's imagery of time, in their repression of his complex sense of change. The chorus' remarks throughout have created a commentary on the state of Ajax's mind, a difficult series of readings; now the juxtaposition of their reaction to Ajax's complex language dramatizes the process of finding intention in another person's expressions as a process of misreading, misunderstanding. Once more, the

---

[45] Dollimore 1984, 50.

[46] I read here as O.C.T., Jebb, and Teubner (Dawe). The manuscripts have 'extinguish and set alight', which does not correspond metrically with the strophe as it should. It is normally assumed that 'and set alight' was added to match their remark to Ajax's. If one reads the manuscript text (like Knox and Kamerbeek), then this line is no longer a specific example of the chorus' misreading. This does not affect the general argument that this ode of joy dramatizes the misreading of Ajax's speech.

text's dialectic of expression and reaction focuses on the enigma of mind in language, the difficulty of linking language to intention. Does not this dramatized exchange of veiling rhetoric and misreading question the critics who aim to reduce the exchange, like the chorus, to a univocal reading of Ajax's mind? Even so subtle a critic as Knox attempts to maintain the unity and directness of Ajax's mind by asserting that the deception speech is to be thought of as a monologue – as if being a monologue would clarify the speech's doubleness of sustained ambiguity into a simple singularity of intention. The enigma itself forms a significant part of the problematic relationship between mental attitudes and action around which this play revolves.

The messenger scene which separates Ajax's two long speeches of deception and curse add a further important twist to the language of mind. For through the reported words of the seer Calchas, the recession of views of Ajax's transgressive attitude moves back to his departure for Troy from Salamis. His abnormality has extended from his slaughter of the sheep to his whole behaviour that night, to his suicidal anguish, and now to his words and attitudes before the war in Troy began. The boundaries of action or behaviour constituting the evidence of his abnormal attitudes seem to be continually shifting. For the picture of Ajax setting out for war is drawn as an example of the dangers of 'not thinking (*phronein*) according to human measure' (761). Indeed, Ajax is described as 'mindless' (*a-nous*) 763, 'senseless' (*a-phron-*) 766, and his boast not to need the help of god in war is depicted finally as 'not thinking according to human measure', the same phrase as opened Calchas' speech. 'The receding perspective', writes Winnington-Ingram, 'is now carried back to the furthest relevant point to show us an Ajax already abnormal, already *aphron* and *anous*, already megalomaniac before even he leaves home for Troy.'[47] It is not just his failure to win the arms of Achilles, the slight to his honour, that alone is the cause of his unhinging, but in different ways the same vocabulary of a transgressive attitude of mind has characterized each depiction of Ajax in the narrative – with the two exceptions of Athene's view which described Ajax's earlier self as the most endowed with 'forethought' and ability to 'act with judgment' (119–20), a picture similar to Homer's depiction of the hero,[48] and also the favourable reaction of his *philoi* to his past protection and care. How can these two strands of description be reconciled? How can one repress the conflicts in the depiction of the heroic in fifth-century drama? More than any 'inconsistency of character portrayal' this

[47] 1980, 40–1.
[48] North 1966 and Adams 1955, for example, use Athene's remarks to show Ajax's general nobility despite Calchas' comments.

doubt surrounding the evaluation of Ajax's attitude is an essential marking of the play.

Does Calchas' description imply that Ajax may always be regarded as abnormal, even mad? 'It is', Winnington-Ingram replies, 'a matter of terms.'[49] For sure, but the conflicting interplay of terms seems to work against any simple 'revelation of mind'.[50] Rather we see a questioning of the boundaries between 'normality', 'due human measure' and 'more than human excess', 'transgression', 'madness' in the continual and shifting suggestions of the uncertain place of Ajax's heroic attitudes in society's norms. The 'matter of terms', the problem of definition, is the play's problem as well as the critics'.

The messenger scene with its further questioning of the position of Ajax's attitudes in the order of things is significantly set in the narrative as a prelude to the scene of his solitary self-destruction, where his re-adoption of an ethic of permanent hatred for his enemies seems to question the status of the insights of the poetry of the deception speech. For Lattimore, for example, this suicide speech takes place 'in an atmosphere of unreason, barbarism, primitive passion where logic cannot reach',[51] which must stand in a significant tension with the reflections on yielding and *sophronein* in the deception speech, and with the seer's description of Ajax's earlier attitudes. In terms of such a tension between the deception speech's rhetorical questions of Ajax's future knowledge and the suicide speech's cancelling or questioning of such rhetoric, Ajax's last line offers an interesting comment: 'Of the rest to those below in Hades will I speak' (865). There is a famous scene in the *Odyssey* set in the underworld, where Odysseus sees the dead Ajax and attempts a conversation. Locked in permanent hatred even in Hades, the ghost of Ajax turns his back and stalks away in proud silence. Sophocles' Ajax's final words 'in Hades will I speak' ironically look back to his Homeric counterpart's silence of unchanging enmity.

As a corollary to these discussions of the varying descriptions of the boundaries and transgressions of Ajax's personality, critics have returned again and again to the notion of *sophronein* in this play. In its sense of 'sound of mind', 'self-control', *sophronein* would seem to provide the defining opposite to the transgressive states we have been following. Searching for a positive measure from the tragedy, a common argument has been to compare the 'enlightened humanism' of Odysseus with the excessive heroic emotionalism of Ajax and the rationalistic or mean arguments over the corpse: Odysseus, whose brief appearances on stage frame the action, has been taken as a paradigm of *sophronein* which the play is concerned to evince and which is so

[49] 1980, 41.   [50] 1980, 57.   [51] 1958, 77.

lacking in *Antigone*.[52] Tecmessa too has been thought to offer a female version of such qualities,[53] though Ajax's remark to her, 'Don't probe and question. It becomes you to be restrained (*sophronein*)' (586), seems more of an ironic recognition of the disjunction within the term than a simple exhortation of wifely duty. Even Ajax himself has been praised for his demonstration of *sophronein*: Ajax 'was – and but for an act of gross injustice, still would be – a man of supreme *sophrosyne*'.[54] North[55] also notes Agamemnon's political use of the term, which I will discuss below, and she draws parallels with the conservative and democratic uses of the term as a political catchword in Athens. Each of these interpretations quotes for support the lines with which Athene ends the first scene: 'The gods love (*phil-*) men of steady sense (*sophron-*), and hate the base' (132–3). For Bowra and indeed many others this expression 'comes so emphatically and with so clear a message from man and god that we cannot but accept it as given *ex cathedra* by the poet'.[56] It is certainly an emphatic statement from the goddess, but is it 'clear'? Certainly its syntax and sentiment may at first sight seem straightforward. But *sophronein* is a quality which the play sets at stake throughout in its questioning of the bounds and norms of mental attitudes; it dramatizes the clash over the sense of the term. So the rigid determination of the relation of *philein* which the goddess proclaims is what Ajax's insight and Odysseus' qualities of *sophronein* overturn. For Odysseus, in the final scenes, the determination of 'base' (or 'noble', or 'great') is a moral question through which the value of Agamemnon's hatred is questioned. Athene's statement is emphatically expressed in the very terms which the play puts in doubt: no wonder so many critics quote these lines as supporting their belief in the importance of *sophronein*, while differing so radically as to its sense and instantiation. As in *Hippolytus*, a divine injunction to mankind in mortal language cannot escape the tragic dislocation of that language, the tensions and doubts of sense and usage. Odysseus, the goddess' supporter, if he puts into operation her advice, does so by his rhetoric, which shows the shifting of the terms of the divine warning. The goddess of wisdom herself uses the language of morality which cannot transcend the appropriating, dislocating logic of moral language. As the various critics' use of Athene's remark shows, how can 'soundness of mind' be anything but a term of appropriation?

If the first parts of this play seem to have been largely concerned with Ajax's heroic attitudes and the extremes to which he carries a code of conduct, with the result that there became evident an inherent contradiction in the social and individualistic attitudes of the Homeric *ethos*, the remaining scenes of

[52] See e.g. Kitto 1961 for a strong statement of this view.
[53] See North 1966, 59–69.   [54] Adams 1955, 25.   [55] 1966, 61ff.   [56] 1944, 38.

argument over the corpse of Ajax have been discussed largely in terms of fifth-century characterization. Menelaus and, in particular, Agamemnon seem far removed from their Homeric counterparts, and Agamemnon's argumentation is remarkably similar to Creon's in *Antigone*, where we noted the king's allegiance precisely to fifth-century political attitudes and to methods of contemporary analysis of the social order.[57] Agamemnon's appeals to social order draw on a moral system apparently different from Ajax's or Homer's. It is also the case that many critics have felt that the debates show a considerable meanness and rigidity of attitude, which contrasts with the greatness in excess of Ajax. Bowra, for example, calls Teucer 'intellectually inadequate' and Torrance writes 'Teucer, though our sympathies lie with him, is not a character to command deep admiration. He is too small, too rigid, too vitriolic; he lacks vision and stature.'[58] Menelaus has been called ungenerous, petty, foolish. Both brothers have been termed 'vulgar'. But if these characters have seemed to bear the marks of the fifth-century agora, it is also the case, as we saw in Chapter 4, that the arguments on which they draw depend also on traditional values, such as the maintenance of the moral of 'Do good to your friends and bad to your enemies.' These tensions between fifth-century and Homeric values and attitudes are an important and complex structuring of this text, which is especially evident in the contrast of the scenes before and after Ajax's death. In particular, the paradox whereby in contrast with what follows the unacceptable excess of Ajax has seemed to many to be invested with a sort of grandeur, adds to the complexity of our evaluation of the hero. Moreover, Odysseus' role as mediator at the end of the play develops in contrast to the wranglings and squabblings of the other figures. Nevertheless, despite this complex interplay of characters and their views of Ajax, it is not so much on their clash of attitudes that I wish now to focus. Rather, I wish to look briefly at what happens to the vocabulary of mind in this clash of attitudes. I have already discussed the interesting way in which Odysseus' rhetoric separates the action of permitting Ajax's burial from Agamemnon's attitude of hatred – a rhetoric which we can now see in the light of our discussion of the relations between an action and a mental attitude in this play. I have already discussed the way in which various critics who focus on mental attitudes in this scene have developed the ideal of *sophronein* as a positive value, usually associated with Odysseus and his attempt to reconcile the warring factions. Important to both these much-discussed themes is the changing vocabulary of mental attitudes, which has not received due critical attention in this last scene, particularly with regard to this scene's relation to

[57] See Whitman 1951, 78 for a view of an audience reaction to Menelaus and Agamemnon.
[58] 1965, 279.

the overall structure of the play. As the drama turns more and more around the exchange of words as significant action, even words as weapons,[59] it is, then, the importance of the fractured vocabulary of madness which I wish now to investigate.

Menelaus, for example, in his argument for the need of fear and obedience in the ordering of the state and army, uses precisely the term *sophronein* to express the correct ordering of rule (1075). For him, *sophronein* is the quality of due measure which enables the hierarchical structure of the army to be upheld. So when Teucer reviles him, Menelaus retorts (1120):

> The bowman seems to think (*phronein*) big.

The term for 'pride', 'thinking above one's station' echoes the descriptions of Ajax, but now in the context of this all too mortal wrangle, it seems not quite parallel to the hero's rejection of divine assistance.

Agamemnon, too, appropriates the terms of mind to his arguments. For him, it is the ones that 'think (*phronein*) well' who are the rulers everywhere (1252):

> A man of sense always has the advantage.

The vocabulary of sense and wisdom echoes the terminology of the distortion of Ajax's mind. Indeed, Agamemnon complains (1259):

> Will you not learn moderation?

Where the term for moderation is precisely *sophronein*. Perhaps we realize now the force of Ajax's question 'will I not learn to be moderate (*sophronein*)?'. Such 'moderation' in the language of the Atreidae's hierarchy means knowing one's place of obedience. As in *Antigone*, the language of mind, all the more markedly after the extensive interplay of worries and doubts about Ajax's sanity, is invested with a political and social importance.

The chorus reject both Teucer and Agamemnon in this same vocabulary (1264):

> I wish you both might learn a moderate mind (*sophronein*)

The learning of place in the sense of a 'correct' attitude remains part of the appropriating rhetoric of dissension and aggression of these final scenes. As much as the ending of the play seems to depend on a clash of attitudes illuminating and illuminated by the heroic stance of Ajax, so the vocabulary of attitudes, minds, knowing one's place, develops the disjunctive tensions in the discourse of character.

---

[59] Torrance 1965 notes this emphasis on words and language in the final scenes of the play – as we have seen, a common fifth-century concern.

Although, then, one may find unsatisfactory the notion of an inclusive psychological personality to be discerned behind the words of the text, we have seen that it would be misplaced totally to repress a sense of 'character' in this play. For there is a considerable focus both on states of mind and on the relation of states of mind to action. But we have also seen how the language of mind and attitude questions the boundaries of personality, the alignment of the sense of self. We have seen how the overdeterminism of divine causation for psychological events questions the simple internalization of motivation; we have seen too how earlier texts, particularly Homer, set up a range of expectations and differences in the constitution of character: the characters of Greek tragedy carry such expectations and differences in their very names. Indeed, the tension between the attitudes of heroic grandeur carried to a point of excess and the attitudes of those squabbling over Ajax's body form an essential dialectic of this play, essential to the understanding both of the internal contradictions of Ajax's individualism and of the relations between attitudes and actions. Moreover, as the characters cannot be separated from the textual world of language and previous stories, so the very language of the play seems both to provoke a reading focusing on terms of mind but at the same time to block a move through language to the revelation of thought, intention, mental life – not only in the deception speech's ambiguities of syntax and wording but also in the receding perspective of Ajax's excess. The conflicting depictions of the limits of his transgression set up a series of questions about the language of mind in a social context which is continued in the debate over the body. The chorus, Tecmessa, Ajax, Agamemnon, Menelaus, Teucer and Odysseus offer differing perspectives on attitudes of mind in a social setting. The discourse of character, as one may call this essential marking of the play, is developed by and through the different characters' discourses: the attempt to understand Ajax's mental attitude in the deception speech is woven into the discourse of the play (not least by the chorus' misreading of its ambiguities) and is not simply a critics' problem. For through this discourse of character, this play dramatizes the fracturing and dislocation of the language defining the boundaries of the self in the tensions of tragic conflict.

Judgements of Greek tragedy which derive from or are delivered to illuminate the profound and eternally fixed verities of human nature are commonplaces of Victorian and post-Victorian criticism. One need not read far in the secondary material on the *Ajax* (or in the *Ajax* itself) to discover opinions supported by appeals to a generalized 'human nature', 'what any person feels, is'. But 'human nature' is not a cross-cultural 'essential truth' though the way that 'nature', 'human nature' attract the idea of essential truth may make this difficult to grasp. The unquestioning naivety of critics who rely on what they think must be 'human nature' or 'natural' in discussions of character cannot but distort both the specific different attitudes to the self in a different culture's texts, and also the transgressions and dislocations of the self that tragedy effects. If 'character', 'mind', 'human nature' are simply dismissed from critical study or simply taken as the self-evident *données* of a discussion, such discussion cannot expect to do justice to the complex workings of Attic drama. For it is precisely through the splits and tensions in the discourses of 'nature', and 'man' with his limitations and transgressions, of the interplay of changing mental attitudes in a society in flux that the tragedies of fifth-century theatre are set in motion. To rewrite Foucault, human nature is an invention, and Greek tragedy and its criticism highlight the power and distortions of that invention.

8 · BLINDNESS AND INSIGHT

Der Frevel des Wissens.
                    HEGEL

Throughout the fifth century, Athens provided a focal point for the discussion, dissemination and development of the ideas that make up what has been called the fifth-century enlightenment. Travelling sophists, rhapsodes and teachers and artists of all sorts gravitated to Athens, whose self-proclaimed hegemony was cultural as well as political, and whose society offered the most extensive opportunities for intellectual pursuits. 'To sum up' says Pericles in Thucydides,[1] 'I declare our city is an education to Greece' – a paradigm and a school – and throughout Thucydides' history the Athenians are explicitly distinguished by their allies and enemies alike for their intellectual originality and precociousness.[2] For Herodotus, it is a commonplace that the Athenians are renowned for their intelligence;[3] Athens is the *prytaneion*, the 'council-chamber', of the wisdom of Greece[4] – the meeting-place for ideas and debate.

The intellectual revolutions of the fifth-century enlightenment are a highly complex subject which will be considered in the next chapter, but it will prove necessary for the argument of this chapter to mention briefly some specific factors that I intend to discuss in greater depth later. Now Guthrie argues that one of the distinguishing differences between fifth-century and earlier philosophers is the increased 'concentration on human affairs'.[5] Although early writers certainly show considerable interest in human society and behaviour, and indeed the presocratic philosophers, for example, also investigate such topics as the reliability of the sense perceptions, none the less, argues Guthrie, the extended political, ethical and legal debates that dominate so much of the fifth-century enquiry constitute a major shift in the paradigms of intellectual activity, a new focus on the interactions of human intercourse. This leads to an interesting development in the relations between man and the processes of enquiry or understanding. For unlike, say, the Hesiodic texts, fifth-century

---

[1] 2.41.   [2] Cf. e.g. Thuc. 1.71; 1.144; 2.40 ff.   [3] 1.60.
[4] Plato, *Prot.* 337d – a comment in the mouth of the visiting sophist, Hippias.
[5] 1962–81, Vol. III, 15.

writings develop a particular self-projection or image of human endeavour that offers an extraordinary optimism with regard to human capabilities and achievements, particularly with regard to scientific and philosophical investigation. For example, the author of the medical treatise *On Ancient Medicine* writes:[6] 'Medicine is not like some branches of enquiry in which everything rests on an unprovable hypothesis. Medicine has discovered a principle and a method through which many great discoveries have been made over a long period and what remains will be discovered too if the enquirer is competent, knows what discoveries have been made and takes them for the starting-point of his enquiry.' However this passage relates to actual medical practice, it shows not merely a self-confidence in man's possibilities but more specifically a belief in the procedures of rational enquiry, a belief in the capabilities of man to ask and to answer the questions of his world. It offers a vision of man's continual progress towards an end of complete knowledge and control of things – a progress through precise intellectual endeavour.[7]

This sense of confidence in the power of man's rational activity is reflected also in the widely different area of political history and in the self-projection of the Athenians. Thucydides' Pericles demonstrates a 'magnificent self-confidence'[8] in his political exhortation: 'Not courage alone therefore but an actual sense of your superiority should animate you as you go forward against the enemy. Confidence out of a mixture of ignorance and good luck, can be felt even by cowards; but this sense of superiority comes only to those who like us have real reasons for knowing that they are better placed than their opponents. And when the chances on both sides are equal, it is intelligence that confirms courage – the intelligence that makes one able to look down on one's opponent and which proceeds not by hoping for the best ... but by estimating what the facts are and thus obtaining a clearer vision of what to expect.'[9]

For Thucydides, towards the beginning of his narrative of the Athenian empire's defeat, it is the Athenians' special power of intellect, their ability to calculate fact and chance, the 'real reasons for knowing', that create a sense of superiority and confidence. It is in the citizens' individual and collective capabilities for rational investigation and reasoning that the possibility of control is rooted.

At the same time, as there develops this confidence in the powers and progress of humankind – which could be shown in many different ways – the important role of man in the process of intellectual enquiry also leads to a

---

[6] *V.M.* 2. On the polemic contemporary stance of this treatise see Lloyd 1963, and Festugière 1948, especially xv–xviii.

[7] Festugière writes (1948, xvi): 'It is the author of *On Ancient Medicine* who demonstrates the true qualities of a man of science' (my translation).

[8] Knox 1957, 71.   [9] Thuc. 2.62.

specific philosophical questioning of the security of such investigations. Protagoras wrote 'Man is the measure of all things', and if Plato and Aristotle are right,[10] he meant by his apophthegm to suggest an important relativism in the process of determining values – for which the position of man is again central. Protagoras also proposed a position of agnosticism with regard to the divine: 'Concerning the gods, I am unable to discover whether they exist or not, or what they are like in form; for there are many hindrances to knowledge, the obscurity of the subject and the brevity of human life.' This logically argued doubt develops a similar terminology of enquiry to that of the author of *On Ancient Medicine* but leads to a very different conclusion. Protagoras' relativism and agnosticism offered a challenge to the certainty of some contemporary moral and political debate – how could a man claim to know? – but in no way hindered his rise as a famous teacher of political and moral subjects.[11] Such scepticism about man and the objects of his knowledge is often extreme. Gorgias, for example, turns his brilliant rhetorical flair both against Parmenides' famous argument on what is, and also against the security of the central position of man in contemporary debate, when he argues that nothing exists, and if it did exist, one could not comprehend it, and if one could comprehend it, one could not express it to anyone else. This comprehensively self-defeating argument – reminiscent of Heraclitus' opening remark that men always prove not to understand the logos – still vexes scholars: is it a clever *reductio* or foolish rhetorical game?[12] Indeed, the self-confident brilliance of sophistic rhetoric often serves to work against the security of man's position in moral, political, epistemological discussion. My first point, then, is that in the fifth century there develops a specific focus on the relations of man to the world and to knowledge, a focus which is reflected both in positions of extreme confidence in the progress of rational discovery and in new rhetorical arguments against the security of such self-confident assertions.

Central to any discussion of the fifth-century enlightenment is the rise of rhetoric as an object of study and teaching. Both Gorgias and Protagoras were famed as proponents of rhetoric. Protagoras was notorious for his claim to make the weaker argument the stronger[13] (notably satirized in Aristophanes' *Clouds*),[14] and Gorgias was praised by the ironic Plato for claiming to teach

[10] This has been much debated. See Levi 1940a; 1940b; Kerferd 1981, 83–110; Moser and Kustas 1966; Versenýi 1962; Guthrie 1962–81, Vol. III, 164–192; and particularly Burnyeat 1976a and 1976b.
[11] An apparent paradox discussed in Plato's *Protagoras*. See Guthrie 1962–1981, Vol. III, 64ff.; Burnyeat 1976b.
[12] See Segal 1962a, Calogero 1957; de Romilly 1973.
[13] DK A21. See e.g. Kerferd 1981, 83ff.   [14] Cf. above, Chapter 1.

people only how to be better speakers and not professing to teach virtue.[15] As in his arguments above, Gorgias shows an evident and ironic awareness 'of the peculiar nature of the communicatory medium qua medium',[16] and was said to be the first to bring 'rhetoric' as a subject to Athens. The importance of language, persuasion, debate in the institutions and hierarchies of society meant that 'skill in *logos* was the road to supreme power',[17] and the fifth-century teachers professed to ease that road to power by the technical training they offered. Both Gorgias and Protagoras, despite their apparently sceptical and agnostic arguments, offered the possibility of control through the conscious manipulation of the force of language. They taught how to speak for advantage, for profit. The training offered in linguistic, rhetorical and literary studies became a necessary prelude for many intending a life involved in the Assembly and courts, and the profusion of rhetorical text-books and manuals,[18] and the rise of professional speech-writers testify to the extent and importance of the change in attitude towards the use of words in this period. My second point, then, is to mark the importance of the role of rhetoric – the control and manipulation of words – in both the sense of confidence in rational progress, and in the sense of relativism, loss of traditional order, that characterize fifth-century discourse.

These senses of confident human progress through rational investigation, of newly developed skills and training, and of a professionalism in the study of such fields as rhetoric, are interconnected in several ways. The notion of *technē*,[19] for example, provides an important link between different areas of change. It implies a 'skill', a 'learned art' or 'field of study', a 'device' – it is the term from which are derived the English terms 'technology', 'technique', 'technical'. Although it occurs in Homer, say, to describe the work of men and gods,[20] in the fifth century it becomes an especially important value in numerous discourses. It is the word used to describe the new art of rhetoric and the textbooks on it, and the new advances of medical science, and also the various areas of human expertise such as farming, sailing, handicrafts. It is also applied to the political skills taught by the sophists, 'statecraft'. It can also be used with various negative qualifying adjectives to imply the 'art of deception', a 'device' in the sense of cunning guile. Plato often opposes *technē* to true knowledge – a learnt skill or device as opposed to the true understanding that comes from the philosopher's dialectical search for truth. Indeed, doctors, sophists, rhetoricians are often depicted as vying with one another

---

[15] *Meno* 95c. As often with Plato, this remark is difficult to evaluate. Cf. Harrison 1964, especially 188ff.

[16] Segal 1962a, 109.   [17] Guthrie 1962–81, Vol. III, 271.   [18] See Lloyd 1979, 81ff.

[19] See Heinimann 1976.

[20] Cf. e.g. *Od.* 3.433; 6.234; *Il.* 3.61.

both in *technē*, in 'skill', 'achievement', and in their ability to teach that *technē*.[21] But like the word 'science' in the eighteenth and nineteenth centuries, *technē* in the fifth century becomes a key term in the expression of man's attitude to knowledge and the world. It is through *technē* that man's progress is achieved, that man's superiority is conceived.

These specific factors selected to give a skeletal picture of a period of complex change will need considerable qualification and expansion in the next chapter. But it will become clear during this chapter why this sketch is a necessary prelude to my particular investigation of Sophocles. I have already mentioned in Chapter 4 the famous 'ode to man' in the *Antigone*, which lauds the extraordinariness of man culminating in his finest achievement, the *polis*. It is possible to see how this ode draws expressly on a particular fifth-century set of ideas. The opening stanza (331–41) concentrates on man's success in sailing over the seas and in ploughing the soil to grow food. Mastery over these two elements is a traditional sign of civilized achievement. Odysseus, for example, in the *Odyssey* remarks at length on how the Cyclops, a monster of wild savagery, does not know how to build ships or to till the soil, with the result that an island near to the Cyclops' own, despite its fine fertility, is left unutilized.[22] In Sophocles' ode such achievements are followed in the second stanza (342–52) by man's supremacy over the beasts of air, land and sea through hunting and through herding, the taming of the yoke. Man is described as 'extremely careful' and 'gaining power through his contrivances', 'his resourcefulness' (347–8). Although such a description of agriculture, hunting and sailing is likely to reflect traditional cultural elements, it is relevant here that, as many commentators have noted, this narrative also follows a series of accounts prevalent in the fifth century which chart man's forward progress from savagery through the gradual acquisitions of technical expertise towards the foundation of cities. One of the most important[23] of these accounts is from Protagoras, who is depicted by Plato – the work itself is lost[24] – as telling a myth in which Zeus sends down to the world 'justice' and 'respect' (*dikē* and *aidōs*, two words I have already discussed as principles of social order), precisely because men had before lacked the necessary political *technē* to live together.[25]

The connections of the chorus' ode and contemporary arguments become clearer in the third stanza (353–64):

[21] See e.g. Lloyd 1983, 118–19, 166, 208–9.
[22] *Od.* 9.116ff. See Austin 1975, 145ff.; Vidal-Naquet 1981b, especially 84f.
[23] See Kerferd 1981, 44.
[24] For some of the difficulties of the second-hand nature of the evidence, see Guthrie 1962–81, Vol. III, 64 (especially n.1 for a survey of the scholarship).
[25] For a fuller account, see Kerferd 1981, 138ff. It will be discussed below.

Language and thought like the wind
and the impulses that make the order of the town
he has taught himself, and shelter against the cold,
refuge from rain. He has every resource. Resourceless
no future prospect he faces. Only death
he cannot find an escape from. But he has contrived
a refuge from cureless diseases.

Man has 'taught himself' – the self-reliance and confidence seen in the passages I quoted earlier from Thucydides and the medical writers – and the essential human characteristics of language and thought have worked towards the order of the town as a shelter against the force of nature. The juxtaposition of the two adjectives 'with every resource' and 'resourceless' once more emphasizes the role of man's inventiveness, his ability to find a way or route out of difficulties – man can reach the answer. Indeed, only death provides a limit. Where one might expect the limitations of mortality to be the concluding note of a tragic argument, it is here a foil to the success in conquering sickness, the success of medicine in defeating 'cureless', 'impossible' diseases. Man's intellectual endeavours have brought the achievements of progress, of growing control over the order of things. The ode to man is also a hymn to progress through the intellect.

This sense of achievement is summed up at the beginning of the fourth stanza with, however, an added note of caution (365–7):

Clever beyond expectation
the inventive craft he has,
which may drive him one time or another to well or ill.

The final general expression for man's 'craft' here is *technē*, with the sense I have discussed of rational, intellectual, scientific attainment. The word translated 'inventive' is a positive form of the negative adjective applied to diseases in the previous stanza – 'cureless', 'without the possibility of finding an answer' – and implies the successful search for a device, a stratagem to overcome an apparent difficulty. The first word of the stanza is *sophos*, 'wise', 'clever', 'intelligent', the term from which 'sophist' and 'philosopher' derive. It is a key term in the depiction of 'the man who knows' in Greek culture, applicable particularly (though not exclusively), to poets, seers, doctors, political leaders – those who possess a particular *technē*. *Sophos* and its cognates form an essential articulation of the notion of 'master of truth' and in the fifth century in particular, where the possession, dissemination and realignment of knowledge lead to tensions and upheavals in the traditional structures and strictures of society, the sense of 'wisdom' as expressed by *sophos* and its cognates becomes an important object of uncertainty and appropriation. The chorus' general expression of man's abilities, then, draws on the vocabulary and narrative of specifically fifth-century views of the progress of man. Here at the end of the stasimon, however, the possibility that such achievements of intellectual progress may lead also to the disasters of misuse is expressed first in the general remark 'one time or another to well or ill' and then in the charged opposition of 'high in his city', and 'cityless' that I have discussed earlier. The ambiguous value of the opening expression of man's strangeness, his extraordinariness, comes down to the polarization of transgression and order in terms of the city and its ideology. The sense of progress brings with it a sense of going too far, of transgression. This ode relates importantly to the *Antigone*, then – which, as I have argued, articulates a series of questions about order and transgressions, tradition and innovation, self-reliance and community values in the context of the *polis*.[26] In the *Antigone*, the ode to man's progress and achievement is a prelude to the destructive tragedy of human assertiveness.

As a paradigmatic narrative of civilization, the ode to man offers an interesting prelude to the *Oedipus Tyrannus*, on which I wish to focus for the remainder of this chapter. For 'no figure in Greek drama more powerfully and tragically embodies the paradoxes of man's civilizing power than Oedipus'.[27] By virtue of solving a riddle, Oedipus conquers a monster, the Sphinx, and becomes leader of the city; he demonstrates the intellectual vigour, flair and precociousness of a man endowed with the attainments of fifth-century *technē*: rhetoric, intelligence, statecraft. Yet Sophocles' text depicts these attainments leading towards a final discovery of Oedipus' untenable position in the order of the city, his personal outrageous negation of the norms and boundaries of the structures of civilized society.

The figure of Oedipus is constructed through a series of metaphors which parallel the ode to man's narrative of progress: 'Oedipus is . . . presented as helmsman, conqueror of the sea, ploughman, conqueror of the land, and hunter, pursuer and tamer of wild nature.'[28] The search for the killer of Laius is portrayed in terms of a hunt: in response to the first expression of the god's command to find the murderer, Oedipus exclaims 'Where would a track of this old crime, difficult to trace, be found?' (108–9). The same term 'track', an animal's trace or spoor, occurs as the king announces his decision to search: 'For I should not be far upon the track if I alone were tracing it . . .' (220–1). When Teiresias finally accuses Oedipus of being his own prey, as it were, Oedipus angrily responds 'How shamelessly you started up this taunt' (354).

---

[26] On the relation of the ode to the play, see Segal 1964.
[27] Segal 1981, 207.   [28] Knox 1957, 111.

The expression 'started up' is the term for 'to flush out game'. When Creon too faces Oedipus' accusations, it is as one who stupidly attempts 'to hunt down royal power without the people at your back or friends' – the only means 'to capture' a crown (541–2). The pattern of search and accusation is imaged in the language of the hunt. As I argued in Chapter 5, hunting offers a means of representing man in relation to the wild and the city, part of a logic of self-definition. Oedipus' search, which turns out to be inverted as the king is finally traced as the object of his own investigation, significantly draws on the vocabulary of a system of order and categorization to express the disorder that Oedipus' uncategorizable self-definition uncovers.

A similar pattern of inversion or perversion of imagery which draws on inherent values of natural and cultural order, can be traced in the two other networks of images that parallel the opening stanzas of the ode to man, the languages of the sea and of agriculture. The city is described as the ship of state: 'reeling like a wreck / already; it can scarcely lift its prow / out of the depths, out of the bloody surf' (22–4). Oedipus is the man who 'piloted the state' (104) and who 'steered the country I love / when she was crazed with troubles' (694–5) and who may now 'prove a fortunate guide' (696). Jocasta prays to the gods because of Oedipus' fear in terms of his role as 'helmsman': 'Now when we look to him we are all afraid; / he's the pilot of our ship and he is frightened' (922–3). The king's disaster is described finally by the chorus as a stormy sea: 'See him now and see the breakers of misfortune swallow him' (1528). The traditional language of a 'sea of misfortune' takes on a specific new significance in the network of the play's language. Indeed, beyond the reversal of the helmsman tossed in the rough waves, the imagery of disastrous sailing has a specific sexual connotation. Teiresias warned 'Shall there be a place which will not be a harbour to your cries . . . when you shall learn the secret of your marriage, which steered you to a haven in this house – haven no haven after a lucky voyage' (420–3). The journey which Oedipus made to escape the curse, but which led him to the very site of transgression, will lead him finally to a wandering in which each and every place will prove 'a harbour' now to his shrieks and cries. The inescapability of Oedipus' cursed journey back to his mother is ironically heightened by the use of the language of control over the sea. The mastery of seafaring is not reflected in Oedipus' journey, which turns his own home into a false harbour. Moreover, the sexual implications of this imagery of sailing – it is his marriage which undoes the haven of the house – is explicitly marked by the chorus later, when Oedipus' sexual relations are made clear: 'O Oedipus, the famous prince, / for whom as both father and son, / the same great harbour suffered for generation' (1207–9). Jocasta is a 'harbour' to and from which Oedipus has sailed. The imagery of control and order in travelling is turned to the expression of an overdetermined arrival in the place of departure.

The use of agricultural terms to express sexual relations is a commonplace of Greek literature as in English ('fruit of the womb', 'seed of the loins' etc.) and in this play this language 'is pushed to the limits of its capacity'.[29] The chorus' horror at the shared 'great harbour' continues 'how, O how have the furrows ploughed by your father endured to bear you . . .' (1210). The woman is a field ploughed and sown by both Oedipus and Laius: 'O marriage, marriage / you bred me and you who had planted / raised my own seed . . .' (1403–5). The taunt that Antigone will bear is that her father 'ploughed the woman who bore him, where he was sown' (1497–8). The language of sowing leads to a notable ironic ambiguity in Oedipus' first expression of his relation to the dead Laius, an ambiguity difficult to translate (but not even hinted at by Grene). Oedipus proclaims that he now possesses Laius' bed and his wife, whom he calls *homosporos*, which means apparently here 'sown with seed by both of us'; though Laius' seed, continues Oedipus, bore no fruit. But commonly the word *homosporos* means 'sibling' – that is, 'sown by the same parents'. Teiresias repeats the word in a further odd way when he foretells that the murderer will be *homosporos* of his father: 'sowing seed in the same place' (460). It not only picks up Oedipus' own strange expression of his relation to Laius and thus indicates the truth of the royal search but also points to the specific doubleness of Oedipus, who is both son to his father and co-husband to his wife, both father and brother to his children. The language of agriculture, which should express man's civilized and civilizing role in the world, strains to express the distortion of Oedipus' sexual relations. The adjective *homosporos*, both active and passive, expresses precisely the paradox of sowing and sown in Oedipus' generation.

Thebes is afflicted, moreover, in the opening scenes of the play with a plague that afflicts the generation of crops, animals, and children (25–7):

> A blight is on the fruitful plants of the earth,
> a blight is on the cattle in the fields,
> a blight is on our women that no children are born to them.

The normal and interrelated cycles of procreation and fruitfulness have been disrupted by the plague caused by the unpunished crimes of Oedipus. The disruption of the language of agriculture is not merely metaphorical. Oedipus' distortion of the boundaries and structures of civilized order affects the totality of civilized generation.

The plague which opens the drama also constitutes Oedipus as a healer, a

[29] Knox 1957, 114.

doctor. Because of Oedipus' former success in ridding the city of the Sphinx, the priest approaches the king for succour. Oedipus' response is couched in the language of medical curing: 'I know you are all sick . . . on examination, I found only one remedy and that I took' (59–68). Although there is not necessarily a specialist, separate technical terminology of medical science at this time, none the less many of the terms central to the medical texts are used by Sophocles in this play, as Knox has shown.[30] But this vocabulary too turns back on itself as the healer is found to be sick, as the saviour blinds himself, wounds his own senses, when he discovers his 'sickness too great to bear' (1293). Indeed, some sense of his sickness is hinted at even in his first remarks on the city's disease: 'I know you are all sick, yet there is not one of you, sick though you are, that is sick in an equal way to me' (60–1). Not only will this rhetorical statement of Oedipus' suffering at his citizens' plight turn out to be true when he is discovered in his violent transgressions to be the cause of the plague – the sickest man of all – but also the expression of 'equality', 'sameness' – 'sick in an equal way to me', 'in the same way as me' – will return when the king discovers himself 'equal' to, 'the same as' his children in his confused genealogy – 'he begot you from the same place as he sprang' (1498–9) – and when the king fulfils Teiresias' prophecy that 'you will establish a grim equality between you and your children' (424–5). Oedipus' expression of sickness ironically hints both towards himself as a sick man and towards the nature of his sickness.[31]

Moreover, the notions both of man teaching himself – the 'secular' notion of human progress through rational discovery – and of the resourceful man, finding his answer, are essential to Oedipus as they are to the ode to man. Faced with the riddle, Oedipus found the answer which saved the city: 'this you did in virtue of no knowledge we could give you, in virtue of no teaching' (37–8). Although it is suggested that men believe it was with the god's assistance that Oedipus became the city's saviour, none the less it is to Oedipus again, the 'noblest of men', the 'most masterful in all men's eyes' that the priest has turned. Indeed, from the moment that Creon returns with the god's command to seek out the murderer, Oedipus proceeds, despite the warnings of Teiresias, Jocasta and the herdsman, to search out for himself first the circumstances of the murder and then the truth of his own engendering – the two searches coincide horrifically at the moment of Oedipus' recognition – and his investigation proceeds through a process of rational deduction

---

[30] 1957, 139–47. See also Collinge 1962.
[31] On 'equity' see further Goldhill 1984c; Segal 1981, 212ff. Knox 1957, 147ff., considers that the language of numerical reckoning constitutes Oedipus as mathematician – another pattern of civilized achievement subverted.

conducted by his own force of examination. It is a self-motivated, self-conducted search.

Knox's analysis of the terms of this enquiry is again instructive.[32] 'The action of the tragedy, a search for truth pursued without fear of the consequences, to the bitter end, mirrors the scientific quest of the age.'[33] This mirroring is seen in the vocabulary used for Oedipus' search. In particular, Knox has emphasized the use of scientific, legal and philosophical terminology. 'Search', 'investigation', 'examination', 'evidence', 'deduction', 'inference', 'teaching', 'learning'[34] are all words which are used throughout Greek writing but which in the fifth century are being appropriated to the processes of intellectual humanist enquiry in particular. The knowledge of Oedipus is part of the pattern of inversion and reversal. A man of domineering intelligence and powerful scrutinizing mind is forced to confess to the truth of his own dismissive description of himself as 'Oedipus who knew nothing' (397). He found the answer to the Sphinx's riddle 'by my wit alone. Mine was no knowledge got from birds' (398) but the present riddle that he works so hard to solve, has an answer which is equally self-reflexive, but which constitutes Oedipus as previously ignorant especially with regard to himself, his self. Jocasta, after desperately trying to prevent Oedipus from finding out what she has just realized, can only say 'God keep you from the knowledge of who you are' (1068), and Oedipus, dismissing the queen's distraught exit, promises he will not hesitate finally 'to search out the secret of my birth' (1085). His 'passion for the disclosure of being'[35] will solve the riddles of the play in the coincidence of answers that turns King Oedipus into the opposite 'in every aspect – social, religious, human – . . . of what as leader of the city he seems to be'.[36] For Oedipus, recognition is *peripeteia*, knowledge confirms not status but lack of status, not a position of power but an untenable, unnameable position. The resources of the king lead to the collapse of order, his solution to his own undoing. In this light, the final remark of Creon is highly charged (1522–3):

> . . . Do not seek to be master of everything;
> for the things you mastered, did not follow you throughout your life.

Man, in the ode to man, was 'of every resource'. Oedipus had sought to investigate 'every . . . account' (291), to 'do everything' (145) to 'try all means' (265), in his search for the murderer. He was indeed called the 'man of utmost mastery' (46): even the man of utmost mastery cannot have mastery or control

---

[32] 1957, 116–38.   [33] 1957, 116.
[34] *zetema, skopein, historein, tekmairesthai, gignoskein, manthanein, didasko*. See Knox 1957, 116ff. for an extended analysis of these terms in the play.
[35] Heidegger 1959, 107.   [36] Vernant and Vidal-Naquet 1981, 92.

in all things. It is precisely the possibility of such total, all-embracing resourcefulness or knowledge or mastery that is challenged at the end of this drama. It is the uncertain siting of man in the narratives of progress and the acquisition of knowledge that Oedipus' reversal avers.

Oedipus, then, undergoes a reversal of an extreme nature: from Corinthian stranger to Theban citizen, but from first citizen to exile; from dispenser of justice to criminal; from clairvoyant and saviour of the city to blind riddle, bringer of plague to the city; from best, most powerful, wealthy and famous to most unfortunate, worst of men, a defilement and horror. From being in the topmost position in the city, a leader who ordered and righted the state, he becomes a wandering exile, unclassifiable, untouchable, unable to share with anyone the rites and duties of city or household. Oedipus lives through the final tension of the ode to man, between *hupsipolis* and *apolis*, between 'high in his city' and 'cityless'. Oedipus' recognition and *peripeteia* define the extremes of involvement with, and estrangement from the city.

Indeed Vernant has argued with some force that in this play which is 'itself constituted as a riddle', it is the combination of Oedipus the *tyrannos*, the 'king', and Oedipus, the swollen-footed defilement who must be expelled (*pharmakos*) in one figure that constitutes the poles, the tragic doubleness essential to the structure of reversal. 'Divine king and *pharmakos*: these are the two sides of Oedipus that make a riddle of him by combining within him two figures, the one the reverse of the other, as in a formula with double meaning.'[37] Indeed, Vernant argues in a subtle exposition that the two categories of *tyrannos* and *pharmakos* are symmetrical, complementary and representative of an important structure of ideas in Greek culture. The suprahuman and subhuman categories are aimed at 'giving a more precise figure of the specific features of the field of human life as defined by the body of *nomoi* (laws, norms) that characterize it'.[38] The suprahuman and subhuman provide the extreme limits, boundaries within which man is comprehended and contained. But in Oedipus the suprahuman and subhuman meet and become confused. In Oedipus, a model for man (1188–96), 'the boundaries that contained human life, and made it possible to establish its status without ambiguity are obliterated'.[39] This double vision of Oedipus is essential to the structure of ambiguity and reversal. 'Both the reversal of the action and the ambiguity of the language reflect the duality of the human condition which, just like a riddle, lends itself to two opposite interpretations.'[40] For Vernant, Oedipus offers what would be called neither a psychological nor a determinist model; rather the play offers a specifically tragic vision of man divided against

[37] Vernant and Vidal-Naquet 1981, 103.   [38] 1981, 103.   [39] 1981, 110.   [40] 1981, 93.

himself, of man as a being impossible finally to describe and define, of man as 'a problem, a riddle the double meanings of which are inexhaustible'.[41]

One particular element of the ode to man that needs further elucidation with regard to the *Oedipus Tyrannus* is the opening of the third stanza: 'Language and thought like the wind . . .' The swiftness of Oedipus' powers of thought is easily demonstrated. The priest's supplication finds Oedipus remarking that he has already put in motion the one solution he has conceived, and the chorus' suggestion to call Teiresias has also been anticipated: 'Even in this, my actions have not been sluggard' (287). The speed with which he arrives at the conclusion of Teiresias' conspiracy with Creon is remarkable. Whitman comments 'I think the lively Athenians would . . . approve of his shrewdness in smelling a plot',[42] and Knox would seem to agree – despite the disastrous results such swiftness leads to in this tragedy.

As with the *Oresteia* or *Hippolytus*, say, the role of language and man's position in language are fundamental to the tragic structures of ambiguity and reversal. 'No play is more about language than the *Oedipus Tyrannus*.'[43] Oedipus is the man whose rise to greatness depended on his ability to decode a duplicitous riddle, but whose limitations are sealed by Apollo's oracles. The riddle offered a hidden meaning to be solved; the first oracle (that he would sleep with his mother and kill his father, 789–93) gives a terrifying explicitness which drives Oedipus from Corinth ironically to fulfil the prophecy in Thebes, and the second oracle, 'Drive out the pollution nurtured in the land' (97), concealed a relevance specific to Oedipus and caused Oedipus to curse himself to a cityless, outcast future. Reading – and misreading – the signs are an essential part of Oedipus' narrative. The riddle with its double or hidden meanings and postulated answer is a prime model for the search and solution of the structure of this play, but the way that a riddle, like a metaphor or pun, offers more than one meaning for a series of signs also challenges language's role in the process of definition and differentiation, the separation and determination of meanings, categories, notions. Language, rather than being an instrument of order, becomes a network of imperfections and gaps. The potentiality for doubleness in language has already been seen in, say, Oedipus' taunt of Teiresias when he claims that it was he, 'Oedipus who knew nothing', who solved the riddle. In his rhetorical sarcasm, Oedipus unwittingly unveils the truth of the status of his knowledge of his own identity. So, too, Teiresias, forced by Oedipus' accusations to speak out, offers a veiled version of the truth of events. His general third-person revelations – 'this murderer . . . he is here. In name he is a stranger among citizens but soon . . . will be shown to be a citizen, true native Theban, and he'll have no joy of the discovery . . .' – are

[41] 1981, 94.   [42] 1951, 268 n. 31.   [43] Segal 1981, 241.

spoken to the king, who fails to link himself with the person described in the prophecy. Indeed, although Oedipus in his accusations of treason is swift to read between the lines of the seer's remarks, his interpretation notably misreads the hidden sense. The veils and doubleness of Teiresias' prophetic language, like the Delphic oracle, require a reading of the signs, but, like the Delphic oracles, open themselves to a dangerous misreading.

The dangers of misreading the riddles of language are depicted notably in the figure of the Sphinx, who is called 'the hooked-taloned maid of riddling speech' (1200), the 'cruel singer' (36), the 'riddle singer' (130), the 'rhapsode dog' (translated as 'dark singer' by Grene, which loses the irony of likening the riddles of the Sphinx to the poems of the rhapsodes). Each person who misread the Sphinx's riddle was sent to his death. Oedipus found the answer, which killed the Sphinx. The Sphinx was a monster, part human, part animal, and her riddle asked what being was two-footed, three-footed and four-footed at the same time. The monster joins in one form the different biological categories of bird, lion, woman, and her question links in one creature the different generations of man. The riddle and answer is relevant to Oedipus not only in that the answer, like the answer of his later investigation, is himself, man, but also in that the perversion of the trigenerational structure of man's life is precisely what Oedipus' sexual relations effect in making his mother his wife, his children his siblings. The truth of the Sphinx's riddle is on more than one level. Like the oracles, it offers an essential insight into Oedipus' identity and position as much as it forms an essential factor in the narrative of his rise and collapse. 'Riddle and oracle come increasingly to look like mirror images of one another. Both when properly "solved" ... spell Oedipus' doom.'[44] The Sphinx's riddle, which blocks Oedipus' path to the fulfilment of the oracle in Thebes, also marks out Oedipus' overdetermined passage to disaster.

This mirroring of prophecy and riddle is marked in the final exchanges of Teiresias and Oedipus:

> Oedipus: What riddles, what unclear words you always speak!
> Teiresias: Are you not most skilled in unravelling riddles?
> Oed.: Yes. Taunt me where you will find me great.
> Tei.: It is this very fortune that has destroyed you.
> Oed.: I do not care, if it has saved the city.

Teiresias' prophecies are like riddles, and Oedipus, the riddle-solver, is mocked with his inability to find the solution to this enigma. Oedipus retorts that his skill is the source and nature of his greatness, and Teiresias, stressing the paradox of Oedipus' doubleness, comments that it is precisely this

[44] Segal 1981, 238.

fortune, this luck that has destroyed the king. Oedipus' reading of the Sphinx's riddle, like his reading of the Delphic oracle, despite the apparent safety, apparent solution, has in fact led to precisely the horror of the present, a horror marked explicitly in the oracle and implicitly in the riddle of the Sphinx. Yet his destruction is not a source of concern to Oedipus if he saves the city. The fine rhetoric of the yielding of the self to the dictates of the *polis* points also to the paradox of the *tyrannos/pharmakos*, the great figure whose expulsion as extreme defilement will indeed save the city. Oedipus' answer to the Sphinx leads to his present position as saviour and king of the city, as it leads to the city's pollution through plague. The removal of the figure of Oedipus who transgresses the city's order will indeed be the city's salvation.

Teiresias' prophetic speech oscillates between revealing and veiling the truth, as he himself is at first unwilling to be drawn to express a prophecy (315–50), and refuses to explain, but finally allows himself to tell his message. As he speaks out, it is with an exhortation never to use words again: 'I warn you faithfully to keep / the letter of your proclamation and / from this day forth to speak no word of greeting / to these nor me; you are the land's pollution' (350–3). His refusal to speak is not simply an unwillingness to tell of the horror of Oedipus' fate but also seems to be a more general fear of the misprision and misuse of words: 'I see that even your own words / miss the mark; therefore I must fear for mine' (324–5). Oedipus' opening remarks to the prophet hint towards this interplay of silence unwillingly broached, the dangers of words and the doubleness of prophetic language: 'Teiresias, you are versed in everything, things teachable and things not to be spoken' (300–1). In the scene that follows, Teiresias will first declare his truth not to be spoken but will conclude by offering Oedipus a lesson which is not received. Oedipus, once more, ironically hints towards an unforeseen future in the polarities of his language. The expression 'things not to be spoken', the 'ineffable', is normally applied in a religious context to the secrets of the Mystery religions or to crimes which cannot be spoken out of horror – the very word would pollute the speaker. This term for things not to be spoken recurs as the chorus, after Teiresias has exited, wonder who the murderer could be: 'Who is the man proclaimed by Delphi's prophetic rock as the bloody-handed murderer, the doer of deeds that are the unspeakable of unspeakables?' (463–6). The term is recalled by the messenger also in his question about the oracle which Oedipus has mentioned: 'Is it speakable? Or does the sacred law forbid another to have knowledge of it?' (993). The oracle is indeed relatable and when Oedipus tells it, the messenger is able to release Oedipus from fear – and precipitate the disasters of knowledge. The apparently proper or standard question about the right uttering of a religious expression points precisely to these interrelations of speaking and holding back in Oedipus' narrative. The oracle itself had been delivered because of Oedipus' desire to be absolutely sure about a drunken stranger's chance utterance. It is Oedipus' passion to speak out and to have everything said that leads to the understanding of the unspeakable horror of his self. Indeed, at the moment of recognition and *peripeteia*, the truly unspeakable nature of Oedipus' position is marked in the second messenger's report (1287–9):

> ... He shouts
> for someone to unbar the doors and show him
> to all the men of Thebes, his father's killer,
> his mother's – no, the word is unspeakable,
> it is unholy ...

As Oedipus comes out of the palace, he questions 'Where is my voice borne on the wind to and fro?' (1310–11) and his terrible darkness is called an 'unsayable visitant' (1314). Oedipus, who compelled Teiresias to speak out what he did not wish to say, who misread the unspoken in riddles, oracles, others' remarks, utters and performs the unspeakable.

The sense of 'the unspeakable', however, involves more than merely a general notion of horror. For, as Clay (1982) has shown, in the fourth century and almost certainly in the fifth also the utterance of particular words concerned with violence in the family or the killing or disgrace of a fellow citizen was banned by a law against personal abuse. The prohibited terms included words for the perpetrators of patricide, murder, incest – Oedipus' transgressions. Among the Athenians, 'constrained by the tight bonds of family and *polis*, they [these words] were sticks and stones'.[45] There is a power in the aggressive use of such terms that is sufficiently dangerous to be guarded against by the city's law. What must not be said is a categorization of social control over the possibly subversive forces of language. Before the moment of recognition when Oedipus finally declares himself publicly in explicit language to be a convicted father-killer, the term 'father-killer' has been continually 'framed but not pronounced',[46] hinted at but never explicitly stated.[47] And even at the moment of public self-abasement Oedipus' action with his mother remains inexpressible. The horror attached to the expression of Oedipus' deeds, then, is also specifically related to the use and misuse of language in the city. Oedipus' crimes are 'unspeakable' precisely in terms of the civic, legal discourse of the *polis* before which his drama is enacted.

Oedipus' willingness to press his questioning to the end, to search without hesitation for an answer to riddles, chance utterances, oracles, to have the

---

[45] Clay 1982, 283.   [46] Clay 1982, 285.   [47] See Clay 1982, 284–8.

unspoken said, is in contrast not merely to Teiresias' reticence, or Jocasta's and the messenger's desire to hold back from bringing into light the discovery of Oedipus' identity; but also to Creon's careful attitudes. Faced by Oedipus' accusations, Creon responds 'I don't know, and when I don't know I am wont to hold my tongue' (569) – a marked difference from Oedipus' rapid and forceful enquiries into the darkness of his ignorances. The language of this self-defence of Creon is significantly recalled, however, in Creon's and Oedipus' exchange at the end of the play. Oedipus is begging for exile. Creon has said he will wait to hear the god's command. Oedipus says he is most hateful to the gods and Creon has concluded – without a promise – that Oedipus will then quickly obtain his prayer. Oedipus questions 'You consent then?' and Creon responds 'When I don't know I am wont not to speak in vain' (1519). What might have seemed a futile self-defence against Oedipus' angry examination is now seen as the saving hesitation of a survivor. It is Creon's unwillingness to speak out, his unwillingness to press forward with a self-confident, self-motivated decision that is in contrast to the figure of the blinded abomination Oedipus, whose very refusal to avoid investigation and speaking out when he didn't know has been a motivating force of the narrative. The dangers of speaking out, the risks of knowledge are stressed in Oedipus' passage to recognition and *peripeteia*.

'The unspeakable', however, is not just an expression of the proper social horror at Oedipus' crimes. Rather, the confusion of kinship terminology that his sexual relations involve leads finally to the interchangeability of terms. Differentiation is lost. Language can no longer denominate accurately: 'O marriage, marriage ... you created fathers, brothers, children, a blood kinship, brides, wives, mothers' (1405–7).[48] His marriage is indeed a 'no marriage' (1214) and his wife 'no wife' (1256). The words 'brother', 'children', 'wife', 'mother' can no longer adequately delimit the relationships within the house. Oedipus' situation is indeed 'unspeakable'. The first words of the play are Oedipus' regal address to the citizens: 'Children ...' From the start, Oedipus asserts a paternal role. His final exchange with Creon has the defiled king in his last line beg to keep his children (1521–2):

> Creon: Let go the children, then and come.
> Oedipus: Do not take them away from me.

The passage of the play is towards the loss of those that Oedipus can simply call 'children', the loss of the simplicity of the opening scene of nomination. The king, the father to his people and household, is left begging to keep the

---

48 A line is unaccountably left out by Grene here! The phrase translated 'a blood kinship' could also be translated 'the blood of kin', i.e., the murder within the family.

children who are his brothers, and to be exiled from the citizens whose city he has polluted as father. Oedipus can no longer express himself or be expressed in the city's normal language of kinship and sexuality.

The queen as she leaves the stage for the last time points towards this disruption in naming (1071–2):

> O, O, wretched; that is all I can call you
> and the last thing that I shall ever call you.

The moment of the queen's recognition is her recognition also that Oedipus can no longer be named except in and for his wretchedness. Grene's addition of the name 'Oedipus' to his translation ('O Oedipus, unhappy Oedipus that is all I can call you . . .') seems particularly insensitive to the language of the play. For it has been precisely the name, the word 'Oedipus', around which some of the most ironic twists of definition have been enacted. As we saw in Chapter 1, the name offers a predictive insight. Not only is the process of naming the medium of social categories and distinctions – 'one never names, one classes',[49] or, as Plato put it, 'The name is a tool for teaching about and for separating the various parts of reality'[50] – but also the personal name itself constitutes an omen, an oracle of identity. The naming by the father can constitute an attempt to control or predict through predication the future life of the child. Here, however, the explicit moment of naming is by a surrogate father, and, as we will see, the name, like much that comes from the father in this play, is a dangerous gift (1034–8):

> Messenger: I loosed you – the tendons of your feet were pierced and fettered.
> Oedipus: My swaddling clothes brought me a rare disgrace.
> Mess.: So that from this you're called your present name.
> Oed.: Was this my father's doing or my mother's? For god's sake, tell me.
> Mess.: I don't know but he who gave you to me, has more knowledge than I.

The messenger's loosing – Oedipus' undoing[51] – explains Oedipus' name. This refers to the etymology of the name as 'swollen-foot' (the word *pous* means 'foot', and *oideō* 'swell'). His name marks him for his casting out, the 'rare disgrace' of his earliest days. This etymology from 'foot' is echoed at various points in the play in significant ways.[52] Teiresias, for example, prophesies that 'a terrible-footed curse shall drive you forth' (418). 'Terrible-footed' (*deinopous*) itself looks forward to the messenger's significant knowledge that Oedipus' feet provide the clue to his identity, as the curse will refer not only to Oedipus' edict of banishment but also to the earlier curse whose

---

[49] See Lévi-Strauss 1966, 161ff., especially 185.
[50] *Cratylus* 388b13–c1.
[51] On loosing, untying and solving, see Segal's analysis 1981, 232ff.
[52] Cf. Vernant and Vidal-Naquet 1981, 96; Hay 1978 passim.

signs he carries in his swollen feet. The riddle of the Sphinx, too, expresses man in terms of 'feet': 'what being is two-footed, three-footed, four-footed . . .?' Oedipus' 'swollen foot' may be thought to indicate his confusion of that generational division, but the word for 'two-footed' is *dipous*. *Oidipous* ('Oedipus') can also be etymologized as 'alas, two-footed' (*oi-dipous*). Oedipus' name carries a sign of the grief and distortion of his position as a man in terms of the riddle that he himself solved.

Oedipus desires passionately ('For god's sake tell me') to know from the messenger whether it was his mother or father caused that mark of disgrace. The messenger's reply, however, in its very denial of knowledge ironically points to further etymologies of the king's name. For his expression 'I don't know' (*ouk oida*) points back to a series of plays on the king's name based on the word 'I know', *oida*. This is marked strongly, as the messenger enters, with a series of untranslatable puns. Grene translates the three lines as follows: 'Might I learn from you, sirs, where is the house of Oedipus? Or best of all, if you know, where is the king himself?' (924–6). The three lines, however, each end with a strange rhyme which becomes apparent when transliterated: *mathoim' hopou* ('might I learn where'), *Oidipou* ('of Oedipus'), *katisth' hopou* ('you know where'). The drama, as Vernant put it, is constructed as a riddle; it sets in play a series of searches for knowledge, a series of reversals and inversions of man's language of the acquisition of learning, and here Oedipus' name is offered the suggestive etymology 'know where' (*oid-(a) pou*). The status of Oedipus' knowledge and place are sounded in his very name. The sarcastic remark of the king to Teiresias which I have quoted already, 'I, Oedipus who know nothing' (397), beyond the irony of his unrecognized ignorance, also plays on the king's name as proclaiming his own knowledge.

When the priest at the opening of the drama, however, asks for the king's help, he says to Oedipus 'Perhaps you know something from a man . . .' (43). The phrase 'perhaps you know' (*oistha pou*) points towards a different sense of the etymology '*oida pou*'. For the word *pou* with an accent means 'where' (hence the etymology 'I know where'), but without an accent, as in the priest's remark, means 'somewhere', 'perhaps', 'I suppose'. The etymology of the king's name also questions the assertion of knowledge. As much as the narrative and the language of investigation inverts and overturns the search for and proclamation of understanding, so the etymologies of the king's name constantly qualify the assertion of knowledge and place with the recognition of uncertainty and supposition. There is an indeterminability at the heart of Oedipus' name as an expression of knowledge.

The game of the name is not played out yet, however. (As Stanford comments drily, 'The Greeks sometimes played with words to excess.')[53] The messenger's explanation of the reasons for Oedipus' name ends with his statement of ignorance, which like so much information that he generously, naively offers, leads to further, unexpected disastrous knowledge: 'I don't know, but he who gave you to me has more knowledge than I.' The first part of the line, transliterated, brings a further suggestive resonance to light: *'ouk oid' ho dous.'* 'I know; the giver', *oid ho dous*, seems to echo the name of Oedipus (*oidipous*) as the king's naming and its sense are being explicitly discussed. 'I (don't) know; the giver knows' points to a major cause of doubt in the narrative. Again and again in the process of exchange in this drama the giver – of information, answers, names, life – is shown to have been unaware of the full significance of his action. Can a giver be sure in his knowledge? But there is yet another significant echo here. For the syllables *ho dous* also spell the word 'roads' in Greek. 'I (don't) know the roads' is relevant to Oedipus' story not only in his failure to recognize the significance of the murder at the cross-roads, but also in his decision to take to the road to avoid the possibility of incest and patricide only to find the road he takes leads precisely to those outrages. Oedipus' failure to read the roads, to read the significance and direction of his travel, is spelt out in the messenger's unwitting pronouncement.

These multiplying senses of the name of the king could be extended.[54] The name or noun (*onoma* in Greek, like *nom* in French, has both meanings), rather than constituting a stable means of reference, classification, differentiation, in Oedipus' case mirrors the uncertain status of the king himself. The name of the king is overdetermined, excessive in its signification. Oedipus is the solver of riddles and questions, the reader of signs and messages: he claims to want to investigate 'every *logos*' (291) in his search for the murderer. But one word at least which Oedipus cannot read is his own name. The king cannot read the different, ambiguous signs of his ambiguous identity that are set in play by his name. The king's uncertain status is marked in the uncertainty of his name. Sophocles' questioning of man's relation to knowledge and truth is acted out in the elusiveness of the *onoma*.

The terminology for knowledge in Greek is closely related to terms for sight. The word I know (*oida*) is from the same root as the word 'I have seen' – to quote the standard dictionary on *oida*: '*I have seen* or *perceived*, i.e. *I know*'.[55] Many of the terms for investigation are similarly connected to the process of looking and seeing, as they are in English from 'insight' to 'theory'.

[53] 1939, 61.
[54] See Goldhill 1984c; Hay 1978. Hartman writes 'The anxiety raised by language as language is that this echoing movement cannot be economized' (1981, 111).
[55] LSJ *εἴδω BI.

In Chapter 1, we saw that in the *Oresteia* it was not the case that the language of the text simply associated the values of sight and knowledge in a positive value of 'clarity', 'light'; rather there was also a considerable degree of uncertainty about the faculty of vision applied to knowledge, centred around the terms of 'illusion', 'dream', the falseness of 'appearance'.

In the *Oedipus Tyrannus*, this language of sight and knowledge plays an essential role in the dynamics of ambiguity and reversal. The belief and claims of 'clarity' are often repeated in particular by Oedipus in his search for a precise and certain knowledge. Oedipus promises he will 'bring to light' (132) what had been left as 'unclear' (131), as Jocasta promises she will 'bring to light' (710) proofs of the failure of seercraft. The king swears he will 'bring to light' (1059) his origins, since he has such proofs of his identity. Teiresias foretells that the murderer 'will be brought to light as Theban-born' (453), although Oedipus finds the seers' prophecies 'unclear' (439) and challenges Teiresias as a 'clear and certain prophet'. (390). At the moment of recognition, Oedipus movingly concludes his search for clarity and certainty in dismay: 'O, O, O, everything has come out clear' (1182).

But at this moment of clarity, the king continues: 'Light of the sun, let me look upon you no more after today, I who have been brought to light as born from whom I should not have been . . .' (1183–4). The clarity of his knowledge leads Oedipus to blind himself. He blinds himself in order that he cannot see or be seen (1273–5, 1369–90), so that the faculty of recognition, the possibilities of social acceptance of greetings are destroyed. He doubles his anguish of memory with the analogous horror of darkness and forced blindness (1313–20). This blindness of Oedipus recalls his accusations of the seer, as well as his search for clarity (370–5):

> Oedipus: [Truth] has no strength for you because
> you are blind in mind and ears as well as in your eyes.
> Teiresias: You are a poor wretch to taunt me with the very insults which
> everyone soon will heap upon yourself.
> Oed.: Your life is one long night so that you cannot
> hurt me or any other who sees the light.

The association of 'truth' and 'clarity' – 'characteristic of all ages of enlightenment' as Knox remarks[56] – means that Teiresias' blindness, extended from his eyes to his mental and aural capacities, debars him (in Oedipus' view) from the protection of truth. For Teiresias, however, such an insult is merely a prophecy of Oedipus' own end, and indeed Oedipus will finally assert that if there were some way 'to choke the fountain of hearing I would not have stayed my hand from locking up my miserable carcase, seeing

[56] 1957, 133.

and hearing nothing' (1386–9). To Teiresias here, however, Oedipus reasserts his power in terms of the strength of seeing the light as opposed to the seer's life as night. From the blindness of his faith in the clarity and enlightenment of his deductive powers, Oedipus will be turned to a man of knowledge blinded. The reversal is announced by the blind Teiresias: 'with darkness on your eyes, that now have such straight vision' (454); but beyond the pattern of reversal of the king's fortunes, the blinding of Oedipus dramatizes the reversal of his language of sight, the reversal of his discourse of self-confident enquiry. Oedipus' self-mutilation on the discovery of the perverted nature of his self enacts the destruction of the basis of the language by which he formerly defined himself as a rational, powerful, controlled and controlling human. His blindness strikes at the terms of his claims to knowledge and insight. In a reversal of Oedipus' language of knowledge and enquiry in the terminology of sight and enlightenment, recognition requires blindness.

Moreover, as Oedipus enters in his blinded state, the second messenger cries 'You will see a sight to waken pity even in the horror of it' (1295–6) and the chorus reply 'This is a terrible sight for men to see ... I pity you but I cannot look at you, though there's much I want to ask and much to learn and much to see' (1297–1305). As Oedipus speaks of his darkness and asks where his voice is being carried to, the chorus respond 'to a terrible place whereof men's ears may not hear, nor their eyes behold it' (1312). Oedipus requests, indeed, to be thrown out 'to be forever out of your sight' (1412). Oedipus, in this theatrical spectacle, is a pollution not to be seen. The unspeakable in Oedipus has had its reserve of silence broached and the pollution that must not be looked at is displayed to the sight of the chorus and of the spectators in the theatre. In its challenge to the security of the language of sight as a basis for knowledge or enquiry, the *Oedipus Tyrannus* seems to question also the security of the position of the audience or spectators in the theatre – the 'place for watching'. The *Oedipus Tyrannus* questions not only the fifth-century faith in the controlled study of language, science, rhetoric – the progress of knowledge – but also the terminology of sight and language in which the theatrical experience itself is formulated. What does it mean for a spectator to watch or listen to a play which seems to equate sight and ignorance, to associate language with hidden danger and overdetermined significance, and to deprecate tellingly the world and words of illusion? Seeing what one sees and hearing what one hears cannot be regarded as simple processes by the audiences of this text.

Nor is the critic beyond the paradoxes of this work. The sort of questions with which a critic approaches a play must determine the sort of answers he finds, and the circularity of this procedure is uncannily mirrored by Oedipus' search, which searches out the searcher. Indeed, critic after critic mimics Oedipus' language of insight and clarity to hope like the king for 'control in all things', as if there were no need for caution or at least for a recognition of a certain irony in asserting the progress, certainty or absoluteness of knowledge and understanding of a play which so forcibly dramatizes the failures, uncertainties and underminings of humans' progress towards insight, and which in its ambiguities, excesses and transgressions so notably challenges the possibility of absolutely rigorous or exhaustive interpretation. Can the most recent editor of the play do more than repeat the play's rhetoric of misplaced faith, unwitting arrogance and failed knowledge when he rhetorically claims for one of his most polemic interpretations 'we may be sure of this . . .'?[57]

In the interplays of speaking out and reticence, of arbitrary interpretation and ironic hidden truths, of insight and blindness, the *Oedipus Tyrannus* offers a paradoxical paradigm of man and his knowledge that challenges not only fifth-century or modern claims for the rigour, certainty and exhaustiveness of man's intellectual progress, but also the security of the reading process itself with its aim of finding, and delimiting, the precise, fixed and absolute sense of a text, a word. Athenian tragedy questions again and again the place and role of man in the order of things; and in its specific questioning of man's status with regard to the object and processes of knowledge and intellectual enquiry, the *Oedipus Tyrannus* instigates a critique relevant not only to the fifth-century enlightenment and its view of man's progress and achievement but also to the play's subsequent readings and readers. 'In some sense', writes Dodds, 'Oedipus is every man and every man is potentially Oedipus.'[58] He quotes Freud, who wrote 'Oedipus' fate moves us only because it might have been our own.' The model of Oedipus as interpreter of signs and solver of riddles, of Oedipus as the confident pursuer of knowledge through rational enquiry, of Oedipus as the searcher for insight, clarity, understanding, indeed provides a model for our institutions of criticism. It is as readers and writers that we fulfil the potential of Oedipus' paradigm of transgression.

---

[57] Dawe 1982 on 873, challenged even on its own terms by Austin 1984.
[58] 1966, 48.

9 · SOPHISTRY, PHILOSOPHY, RHETORIC

What happened to the truth is not recorded.

JULIAN BARNES

'Personally I hold that the sophist's art is an ancient one, but that those who put their hand to it in former times, fearing the odium which it brings, adopted a disguise and worked under cover. Some used poetry as a screen, for instance Homer and Hesiod and Simonides; others religious rites and prophecy ... some even gymnastic physical training ... Music was used as a cover by ... many others. I myself, however, am not of their mind in this. I don't believe they accomplished their purpose, for they did not pass unobserved by the men who held the reins of power in their cities, though it is on their account that these disguises are adopted; the mass of people notice nothing, but simply echo what the leaders tell them ... I ... have always gone the opposite way to my predecessors. I admit to being a sophist and an educator.'[1]

This quotation from Plato's depiction of Protagoras provides an excellent introduction to the range of problems involved in discussing the sophists, to whom I have often referred in this book as a major factor in understanding fifth-century thought and drama. In Chapter 6 I discussed the conception of the poet having privileged access to truth and forming the education of the citizens. I argued that one of the reasons for Plato's extended hostility towards poets and poetry was the sense of philosophy's rival claims to be a master of truth, a conflict which is still being worked through. One of the commonest adjectives used to describe this special poetic knowledge and the people who demonstrate it is *sophos*, which is the root of the term 'sophist' and 'philosopher', and which is often translated 'wise', 'clever', 'intelligent'. The possessor of any special skill or knowledge from carpentry to rhetoric could deserve the title '*sophos*'. When Socrates in the *Apology* describes his attempts to discover who is *sophos*, he goes first to a series of professional wise men, seers or teachers, men well-known in the city for being *sophos*; then, he goes to the poets; finally, to the craftsmen.[2] Each group of people provides an example of a possible claim to be *sophos*, which are all surpassed in the famous conclusion that Socrates was the wisest of men in that he knew nothing. *Sophos*, as I

---

[1] Plato, *Prot.* 317a–b.   [2] *Apo.* 20d6ff.

argued in the previous chapter, is a key term for expressing the uncertain and conflicting claims of knowledge and its place in society, that are so forcefully instantiated in Socrates' trial and execution, as well as in many of the tragedies.[3] From the fifth century onwards, the word 'sophist' is applied to a series of people who have knowledge beyond that of ordinary people, and in particular to poets, seers, diviners and sages, including the canon of the 'Seven Wise Men'.[4] In the passage quoted above, Protagoras is depicted as claiming affinity with such a tradition. He claims a status which aligns him with Hesiod, Homer, Simonides – the poets as educators and controllers of knowledge – and with the world of gymnastics and music, the two other aspects of Greek education I discussed earlier. Like religious prophets and cult founders too, Protagoras as sophist offers access to a different and special lore. Both Hippias and Gorgias are said to have delivered their rhetorical showpieces robed in purple, the traditional dress of the rhapsodes, as if to stress this link with the ancient methods of disseminating the knowledge of *sophos*.[5] It is both in their contribution to the intellectual developments of the fifth century and in their social role as teachers that the sophists are essential to our understanding of Athens and its theatre. It is to the titles of both sophist and educator that Protagoras lays claim.

It may seem at first sight surprising that Protagoras declares that he has always openly proclaimed himself a sophist – he goes on to say that he has taught and been respected for some forty years – and at the same time to assume that the word 'sophist' brings as a matter of course 'odium', and further that Homer, Hesiod and many others are all sophists under the skin. Is Protagoras speaking with self-deprecating irony? Is he depicted as siding with poets, gymnastic and music teachers in order to facilitate Plato's determination of philosophy as the pinnacle of procedures in the attainment of virtue? Does this picture in any way represent an historically accurate or even possible argument of the sophist? Such questions and hesitations plague the study of the sophists. For the most continuously awkward problem in discussing these writers and teachers stems from the sort of material that must be used as data for our understanding. There are only a very few of the sophists' shorter treatises and some fragments of arguments that survive, and several of these are anonymous. The most extensive source of information about the sophists is in other writers' reactions to or descriptions of their work. The greater part of our information comes through the filter of second- or third-hand quotation. Plato himself writes extensively about the sophists, but it is precisely

---

[3] *Sophos* is especially discussed with regard to the *Bacchae*. See Segal 1982, index *sophia, sophos*, and his references, 27, 77, 226 and especially 229.
[4] See Kerferd 1950.   [5] See DK 82A9.

Plato's – and Aristotle's – well-known continuous and damning hostility that has been a basic element in the evaluation of the role and importance of the sophists in both fifth-century history and the development of philosophy. In several dialogues, Plato attacks the arguments, aims and methods of the sophists; in general, he denigrates their work as at best mere clever-seeming rhetoric, and at worst dangerous pandering to the prejudices of the mob, disguised as a technical skill. In the dialogue known as the *Sophist* he offers seven definitions of the term 'sophist' all of which, with one possible exception, are highly derogatory.[6] More importantly, all seven definitions are concerned with rhetoric and the sophists' misuse of their educational role with the young. There is no mention of the extensive range of subjects actually discussed, created or expanded at this time, for example, mathematics, medicine, physical science, astronomy, geography, anthropology and literature. Plato strives to reduce his opponents to mere manipulators of rhetoric. Above all, he denies the sophists' work the title of philosophy – and many critics have followed Plato's interpretation.

The problem of evaluation, however, stems not merely from the fact that our major sources are notably prejudiced in their dislike for and arguments against the sophists, but also from the fact that the dramatic dialogue form with its dialectic of artful description and philosophic argumentation allows for more than one level of polemic. To what degree are the arguments put into the mouths of the sophistic characters in Plato's dialogue fair or truthful indications of what a sophist said or wrote? To what degree are the scenarios of Socrates arguing with different sophists in themselves designed to support Plato's case? Without even the possibility of any extended comparison of a sophist's work with its Platonic version, the criteria for evaluating the degrees of distortion remain in themselves matter for argument.

The cumulative effect, however, of Plato's literary skill and philosophic power has resulted in a devastating attack which has been repeated in each generation since. The sophists have been said 'to have poisoned and demoralized by corrupt teaching the Athenian moral character'[7] – and many attempts to retreat from the extremism of such a view have felt constrained to agree with Jowett that Plato's criticism and aggression were at any rate reflecting in philosophical guise contemporary responses to dangerous new ideas, or with Hegel that the particular ideas of sophistic writing were a necessary stage in the development of western thought, but necessary in that they existed to be transcended by Plato and Aristotle – a historical narrative which mirrors

---

[6] Socrates says he is unsure, but *elenchus*, a particular form of questioning, has some value in pointing out to a person his flawed knowledge. There has been much discussion of how Socratic *elenchus* might differ from sophistic *elenchus*. See Vlastos 1971, especially 78–157.

[7] Grote 1888, Vol. VII, 52 – he is quoting a view he disagrees with, of course.

Plato's and Aristotle's view of their work as the point towards which earlier philosophy was attempting to travel. In recent times, Guthrie,[8] Classen[9] and Kerferd[10] represent extensive attempts to rehabilitate the sophists as offering substantial and serious contributions to a crucial period of intellectual history. But among many literary critics, especially with regard to Euripides' particular attachment to sophistic rhetoric, further rehabilitation is needed.

There is a further aspect that fuels Plato's aggression. Plato's teacher was Socrates, who was executed by the Athenian courts, and much of Plato's work is concerned radically to separate Socrates from his sophistic contemporaries. Indeed, Scorates is a figure who neatly focuses the problem of evaluation and representation. Plato depicts him as the arch-enemy of the sophists and what they stood for. And indeed through Plato's depiction Socrates over the centuries has played an essential role in the iconography of martyrdom, a central figure in the representation of defending a principle, of questioning the powers that be, of taking an intellectual stand against force, ignorance and prejudice.[11] A martyrdom requires a hagiography and it is Plato who writes that major constituting narrative.[12] None the less, Socrates was put to death by the Athenian jurors for exactly the sort of crimes laid at the door of the sophists – not believing in the city's gods and corrupting the young. Aristophanes' comedy, the *Clouds*, depicts Socrates as a leading sophistic teacher, taking pay and running a school – two practices Plato is particularly keen to deny for his master – and Aristophanes' play ends with the violent destruction of the school building and its inhabitants. Indeed, in Plato's work too Socrates is seen often in debate with leading sophists and their pupils. Xenophon's *Memorabilia* offers in his recollections of Socrates a further more staid view of the philosophical and social aspects of Socrates' didacticism. It may seem evident from the wide range of alternative pictures that Plato's, Aristophanes' and other contemporary or near-contemporary accounts involve a certain degree of distortion, prejudice and picture-painting, even if, like Guthrie, one wants to deny that these accounts 'were actually never intended to be anything but fictions'.[13] But it is precisely the difficulty of determining the exact 'degree of distortion' which has led to the most extensive disagreement. Socrates must be viewed 'as squarely set in his contemporary world of the sophists'[14] but in Plato's generally attractive, ironic, self-deprecating portrait of his master, it is not possible to outline the relations between Socrates and the sophists without constant hesitations and

[8] 1962–81, Vol. III, passim.   [9] 1976.
[10] 1981. For bibliography, see Classen 1976, 641–710.
[11] I have learnt from Dr H. Elsom on this.
[12] Not only Plato, however. See e.g. Xen. *Mem.* passim.
[13] 1962–81, Vol. III, 326.   [14] Guthrie 1962–81, Vol. III, 325.

uncertainties. The literary and philosophical representation of an ironic questioner of received truth itself must be questioned and requestioned in its truth of representation.

It is, then, not merely the difficulty of evaluating arguments repeated in shortened and distorted forms that makes it peculiarly hard simply to describe or evaluate sophistic writers. It is also the fact that much of this material is passed to us through the literary and philosophical prisms of the dialogue form in whose multiple voices Plato speaks. Despite these difficulties in interpretation caused in part by Plato's and Aristotle's marginalization of the enterprise of the sophists, none the less it is the sophists' importance in Athens from the fifth century onward which requires our attention.

As the opening quotation of this chapter indicated, it is as teachers that the sophists are first important. Their revolutionary influence on the control, formulation and dissemination of knowledge is felt in many different areas of society. The sophists were travelling teachers, though many seem to have gravitated to Athens and stayed as foreigners in the city for some years. Their services were paid for, and could be bought by anyone with the fee. Although poets could be paid for their honorific poems, and doctors and craftsmen took money for their services, the sophists' fee-taking and general availability as teachers are regularly a source of complaint in contemporary writers, and Plato, as I have said, stressed that Socrates took no payment.[15] In part, the complaint may be conservative distaste for the process of money-making often expressed in a society with a strong hereditary aristocratic basis. Where wealth and social status are interlinked, the possibilities of gaining wealth from sources outside the traditional means of land ownership constitute money-making as a perceived cause of social mobility or disorder. It is certainly the case that sophists drew many of their pupils from the wealthier and traditionally more conservative areas of society. But the particular complaints about the connection of sophists and money-making may also reflect the specific doubt about the relation between teaching and money. In the most traditional form, education may be thought to offer a sense of continuity and order. Not only were values, trades, knowledge passed from father to son, but also the wider educational processes of poetry, music and gymnastics, as I discussed in Chapter 6, were largely community affairs: a group of young people taught by a member or members of the community in the shared world of the community. Education forms a way of socializing young men into the community. The professionalization, as well as the sceptical new studies, of the sophists can be seen to disrupt that procedure. The teachers are no longer

---

[15] In the fourth century, there is less worry about making money, though it is still possible to accuse others of making too much! See Isoc. 15.155ff; 13.3ff.

members of the community disseminating the cultural values of the community, they are outsiders. The basis of the relation between teacher and taught is, at first level, financial rather than social. According to many sources, what was taught went under the same name as before – virtue, excellence – but it was a private lesson which separated its learners from the previous norms of social duty. The sophists were blamed for teaching young men to overthrow the old values in religion, politics, argument. The relations between power and knowledge are disrupted by the selective, ill-controlled infusion of innovation. The conservative distaste for money-making by the sophists is also an expression of the fear and uncertainties of a period of rapid social change.

The young men who went to the sophists might expect a wide curriculum of learning, which I shall outline later, but first it is important to investigate the aim of such learning. For this too will help us understand the social impact of the sophists. For the varied political studies of the sophists are to prepare a man for political life. Their theoretical works develop a vocabulary for the understanding and discussion of the affairs of society; the rhetorical skills train a man for perfomance in the city of words, its legal and political arenas; the ethical and social discussions direct not only argumentation but also social actions and programmes. The extensive fifth-century debates on civic constitutions are paralleled by extensive activities of reform, conflict and even revolution, and provide a theoretical basis for those activities – political studies and political practice interact with and promote each other. Athens experienced two brief coups by oligarchic forces: in 411, and by the Thirty Tyrants at the end of the Peloponnesian war. Critias was one of the most bloodthirsty of the Thirty Tyrants, whose political expertise and opinions were regarded as being founded on sophistic training.[16] As an explanation of despotism or psychopathic behaviour it is no doubt insufficient, but the stories told do emphasize the close connection perceived between theory and practice in the political world. The new education offered by the sophists was seen to result in new and different techniques for approaching the procedures of democratic authority. Indeed, 'young men in the fifth century consorted with the sophists chiefly in the hope of becoming political leaders,'[17] that is, of gaining success and power in and through the political and legal arenas of Athens.

It is not merely young men about to embark on their adult involvement in the political life of the city on whom the sophists exercise a formative influence, however. Pericles himself seems to have spent much time with theoretical writers, notably with Anaxagoras who taught him, and also with

16 See e.g. Guthrie 1962–81, Vol. III, 298–304.   17 Wilcox 1942, 131.

Protagoras too.[18] While it is easy to see that enemies of Pericles would be happy to spread accounts of him being too close to foreign advisers, the stories of Pericles' involvement with and positive encouragement of studies of statecraft have not been seriously doubted by scholars.[19] There are even further stories of Anaxagoras being prosecuted as a way of attacking Pericles himself.[20] So too Callias, at whose house Plato's dialogue *Gorgias* is set, is depicted as spending great amounts of money to hear various sophists talk and teach, and more general patronage among the wealthy may be joined to specific teaching assignments or lectures as one of the means of gaining a livelihood for a sophist. Public performances too provided a source of income and publicity. The delivery of set lectures or speeches, or speeches in answer to questions from an audience on various topics, were occasions for bravura demonstrations of rhetoric or even for competition between sophists – and no doubt involved a considerable degree of crowd entertainment. Contact with sophistic rhetoric was not only through the rhetorical handbooks or formal arenas of court or assembly. These demonstrations (*epideixeis*) form for Aristotle one of three types of rhetoric and their influence on the lengthy speeches of the tragic *agon* is marked. When, for example, Euripides' Orestes in *Electra* delivers a discourse on nobility and birth – which I mentioned in Chapter 6 – he follows a series of argumentative moves developed by the sophists and uses a series of terms which recur again and again in sophistic language. Indeed, Orestes' opening assertion of the uncertainty of the notions of manliness or nobility are formed specifically in the structures of parallelism and reversal which are endemic in sophistic rhetoric:[21] the noble can show a poverty of spirit, the poor a nobility of soul. The argument develops with the desire for the accurate division of ideas and a series of alternatives offered to be rejected: is wealth an adequate criterion? Or poverty? Or fighting strength? This technique of searching for apparent exhaustiveness through a range of possibilities each of which is systematically refuted is a standard approach of sophistic rhetoric too,[22] as are the terms for 'division', 'accuracy' and indeed the specific subject of debate – man's nature in relation to social behaviour and evaluation. This passage is not merely repeating a sophistic argument for fashion's sake, however.[23] The failure of Orestes to realize the applicability of these arguments to his own behaviour and noble birth offers a typically

---

[18] See Plut. *Per.* 4[vi]–6; 8[i]; 16[vii–ix]; Isoc. 15.235; Plato, *Phaedr.* 270a; *Alc. Mai.* 118c. On Protagoras, see Plut. *Per.* 36.[v].

[19] See e.g. Kerferd 1981, 18–19; Davison 1953; Guthrie 1962–81, Vol. III, 21, 78, 263; Ehrenberg 1954, 92ff.

[20] On attacks on intellectuals, see Dover 1975.

[21] The fullest account remains Gomperz 1965.   [22] See Solmsen 1975, 10–46.

[23] Wilamowitz deleted the lines. Reeve 1973 and other editors delete much of this speech. It is defended in Goldhill 1986.

Euripidean sardonic comment on the distance between words and the world. The young man educated in the modern ways turns out to be the example of his own argument.

The sophists, as well as teaching and demonstrating the arts of political science, also took an active part in the affairs of state and not only as advisers to leaders such as Pericles. Gorgias' most famous trip to Athens was as an envoy for his own city of Leontini, and it was in his speech to the Athenian assembly on that political occasion that rhetoric was said first to have come to Athens. Hippias also boasts, according to Plato's representation, of being a regular ambassador for his city of Elis, and Protagoras drew up the laws for the foundation of the new colony at Thurii;[24] the debate on the status of the laws and on the correct nature of society was not merely of philosophical moment but also of political application. The layout of the streets of this new colony was designed by Hippodamus, a political theorist and planner who was also responsible for the grid pattern of streets in the Piraeus, the port of Athens. The sophists' influence could reach all levels of political life.

So far I have stressed the extensive social impact of the sophists from the fifth century onwards. This is important not just because a large proportion of material written on the sophists tends to stress the philosophical matter or irrelevance of the sophists, with little concern for the relation of those teachers and rhetoricians to the fabric of city life (unless to assert or deny that the sophists were a cause or symptom of Athenian moral decline). It is also important in order to emphasize that the interrelations between tragedians and sophists are not merely a question of 'philosophical influence' on a literary author, as if one were talking of the intellectual impact of Bergson on Proust; still less a question of the amusement of mere fashionable novelty on the part of the sophisticated Euripides, as is sometimes suggested. For while both sophist and tragedian – and there are many like Hippias who were both sophist and tragedian – are committed by their arts to an awareness of the techniques of language and argument, it is their shared response to the question of the relations of man and the city, their shared response to the problems of the language in which the discourse of those relations is formed, that link the various 'wise men' and 'teachers' who lay claim to the title of 'educator of the city'. The sophists and tragedians share the intellectual life of fifth-century Athens not as proponents of high art and low rhetoric but as parallel investigators of the position of man in language and in society.

Our understanding of the social impact of the sophists, however, is largely formed through more or less contemporary reactions to their arguments and

---

[24] On Thurii, see Ehrenberg 1948; on Hippias, see Guthrie 1962–81, Vol. III, 269ff.; on Gorgias, see Guthrie 1962–81, Vol. III, 280ff.

argumentative methods, and it is to the intellectual basis of the impact of the fifth-century sophists that I wish to turn. Now so far I have been referring to the sophists as if they formed a coherent and unified group. While it is true that there is on occasion a tendency in Plato and other hostile writers to generalize about a series of individual and different teachers as if their ideas constituted a unified programme, there are also important and significant differences between the various teachers and philosophers, and it would be totally out of place to think of the sophists as constituting a 'school'. Indeed, it is clear that such a general identification and definition of 'A Sophist' as Plato offers is certainly more argumentative construction than simple description. As we have seen, many men – doctors, scientists, mathematicians, polymaths, poets as well as rhetoricians – are involved in the intellectual activities that could lead to being called a sophist. None the less, in the space available to me here I intend to direct my attention to a series of problems shared among several writers, and if the necessarily broad outline results in a certain occlusion of the interrelations between different sophists and of the specific twists of individual writers' approaches to these problems, the picture offered will, I hope, help to develop an understanding of the complex intellectual activity of fifth-century Greece and especially Athens.

I have already mentioned as part of the range of sophistic interests the 'correctness of names' – the study of the precise and proper forms, usages and references of words. I have discussed too the growth of study of literature and in particular of rhetoric as an essential shift of approach to the uses of language. In Chapter 1, as an example of the 'linguistic turn' of the fifth century, I referred to Aristophanes' satire on the idea of making the weaker argument the stronger in his debate between 'just *logos*' and 'unjust *logos*'. I want first to investigate this sense of opposed *logoi*. For the claim to make the weaker argument the stronger is not just an expression of the rhetoric teacher's claims of power but is related to a series of discussions on the nature of language and rhetoric that are essential to the various sophists' enterprise. 'To give a *logos*', as well as implying to make a speech, or to tell a story, or deliver an argument, has a more specific meaning that is especially relevant for philosophical discourse, namely, to give an explanation, definition, account or rationale of something. The ability 'to give a *logos*' is for Plato too an essential part of knowledge, a factor in determining understanding. Protagoras, one of the earliest and most influential of the sophists, claimed 'that there are two *logoi* concerning everything, these being opposed to each other',[25] and wrote two books called '*Antilogies*' which presumably demonstrated or illustrated this principle. Protagoras' remark sounds a keynote for much fifth-century

[25] DK 80A1.

discussion. Earlier philosophers such as Heraclitus had been concerned with the possibility of contradiction, particularly in the evaluation of the physical world, and how properties of the physical world could be seen or expressed in different ways: how could the same object appear cold to one man and hot to another? Both the nature of sense perceptions and the nature of the phenomenal world were called into question. Protagoras inherits these questions and appears to have asserted, as we have seen, a relativism based on man's different perceptions of things.[26] The claim that there are two opposed *logoi* concerning everything and that they are opposed to each other, however, seems to make a further more precise point about the relations between man and the objects of the phenomenal world. For earlier philosophers such as Zeno the possibility of applying seemingly exclusive opposite predications such as 'cold' and 'hot' to the same object is an essential problem in an argument concerned with determining a principle of non-contradiction. For Protagoras, man in his use of language as a way of relating to the phenomenal world is necessarily involved in the opposition of different *logoi*, necessarily involved in difference and contradiction. There is a scission inherent in man's attempts to give a *logos*, an explanation or rationale of things.

The implications and ramifications of this notion are numerous. Its influence can be seen particularly in the sphere of public rhetoric, the development of new argumentative techniques in, say, the lawcourts, which is the reason in the *Clouds* for going to a sophist for education. Again, the development of sophistic interest interacts with the social and moral developments of fifth-century society. In the public arenas, there develops a sense of the possible reversibility or doubleness of arguments which realigns the criteria of truth, probability and proof. Antiphon's *Tetralogies* are an interesting example of this process. Each of the *Tetralogies* consists of a set of four speeches: the speech of the accuser, the reply of the defendant, and then a second speech on each side. The second *Tetralogy* discusses the question of blame when a boy, a spectator at a gymnasium, is accidentally hit by a javelin, a topic which Pericles and Protagoras were said to have spent a whole day discussing to find the most correct *logos*.[27] Is the boy to blame, for not taking due care in where he walked? Is the thrower to blame, since he threw the javelin? The paired positions form an example of types of argument for the learner, as well as a test-case study of cause and responsibility. The sophistic teacher constructs and discusses the system of opposed *logoi*.

This sense of doubleness, however, does not result in confusion. The

---

[26] The precise nature of this relativism is much discussed. See e.g. Versenýi 1962; Moser and Kustas 1966; Sinclair 1976; Levi 1940a; 1940b; Burnyeat 1976a; 1976b.

[27] DK 80A 10.

further claim to make the weaker argument the stronger points to the (scandalous) sense of the power of rhetoric to reverse the normal order of things, to use language to get an upper hand. This famous claim of Protagoras not only marks the force of willing paradox associated with sophistic rhetoric – one of Socrates' most renowned apophthegms is the apparent paradox that no-one does wrong willingly – but also stresses that the doubled, opposed *logoi* also result in the search for control through *logos*. The structure of polarity and reversal I called endemic to sophistic rhetoric is not simply a surface effect but an argumentative strategy.

Clearly it is not the case that the sophists are the first to deal with opposing arguments, nor indeed with the logic of polarities: their interests grow from earlier philosophy and rhetoric; and respond to a need in the society of fifth-century Athens.[28] But it is the sophists who illustrate in the strongest and most developed manner the notion of opposing *logoi* as a principle linking philosophy and rhetoric. For, as Plato comments (*Phaedr.* 216c4ff.), the technique of opposing *logoi* is not confined to lawcourts or to public speeches but applies to whatever things men talk about. It is, for example, an essential development in the political discussion of Thucydides' histories, where there are major set-piece debates of opposed parties, arguing from different principles or positions about political strategies, ethics or aims. Both the vocabulary and argumentation of these debates show extensive parallels with the arguments developed in sophistic rhetorical training.[29] In ethical discussion, too, the possibility of determining correct action by determining what is good becomes a debate marked by the force of opposed arguments, opposed predications. Plato's own choice of the dialogue ('*dialogos*') as argumentative form constructs a philosophy from the dramatization of opposed *logoi*. In tragedy, the formal debates of the *agon*, as we will see, again and again reflect the rhetoric of legal and political institutions and the training provided for them. In each of these spheres, as in the sophistic, rhetorical and philosophical training, the logic of Protagoras' remark on the twofold, opposed *logoi* is felt.

The effect of this new rhetorical study on intellectual investigation in the fifth century could be summed up in most general form as 'a realization that the relationship between speech and what is the case is far from simple'.[30] 'If', writes Gorgias, 'it were possible through *logoi* to make the truth about reality pure and clear to the hearer, judgement would be easy as simply following from what was said; since it is not so . . . '[31] The relation between *logoi* and the

[28] See the comments of Guthrie 1962–81, Vol. III, 181 n. 3. For the history of the use of polarity, see Lloyd 1966.
[29] See Solmsen 1975; Macleod 1983, 52–158, especially 68–87.
[30] Kerferd 1981, 78.   [31] DK 11A35.

world is contested in various ways.[32] In the search for 'correctness of names' we see a project that moves close to a form of 'naturalism', linking words in a natural and proper way to things. But there are many methods of argument to which Plato, for example, objects because of the uncertainty that they necessarily introduce between words and the world, and because of the challenge to the hope to understand reality through language. The value placed on likelihood and probability rather than truth, for example, is a specific argumentative strategy attacked by Plato.[33] In the case of a prosecution for assault, the two sides are argued by Antiphon as follows: the weaker and smaller man claims that it is not likely that he would assault a man clearly stronger than himself since he would be beaten; the stronger and larger man asserts he would not plausibly assault a man clearly weaker and smaller than himself since the blame would be so likely to fall on him. In both sides of these opposed *logoi*, the argument is not concerned to prove what did happen but what ought to have happened in all likelihood. The philosophical hypotheses behind such assertions may be the illusory nature of claims to truth and knowledge, but for Plato such arguments constituted a rhetorical veil that would not merely help to conceal the truth but also would prevent the search for truth.

This use of the probable and likely to construct an argument is seen clearly in a speech like Hippolytus' defence against the charge of rape in Euripides' play. He is unaccustomed to having 'to give a *logos* in public' (986), but under the circumstances he must hazard an attempt.[34] After asserting plainly his chastity and righteousness, the young man proceeds to an argument which has sometimes seemed bizarre to modern readers, but which in the light of sophistic strategy seems more readily explicable: 'You must demonstrate in what way I was corrupted. / Was it because her body was the most beautiful / of all women in the world? Or did I hope when I had taken her / to win your place and kingdom for a dowry / and live in your house? I would have been / a fool, a senseless fool, if I had dreamt it. / Was rule so sweet? Never, I tell you, Theseus, / for the wise ...' (1008–13). Hippolytus bases his argument on the likelihood of his raping his stepmother. He seems to dismiss the suggested possible reasons as evidently absurd. Neither was Theseus' dead wife beautiful enough to seduce him, nor was the possibility of gaining power real. Moreover, no wise man would desire such power as Theseus'. The only motivation he feels the need to gloss further is his own lack of desire for tyranny, though this is perhaps the clearest example of a standard rhetorical

---

[32] See Graeser 1977.   [33] Cf. e.g. *Phaedr.* 267a.
[34] A standard opening remark, which, Barrett 1964 ad loc. argues, would in this case rebound on Hippolytus, whose 'elitism' would cause hostility.

plea – one which Creon in the *Oedipus Tyrannus* also uses. Hippolytus' arguments make little impression on Theseus, and in this dramatic exchange the levels of irony are typically Euripidean in their complexity. The young man who is actually telling the truth appeals unconvincingly to probability in a poorly conceived rhetorical gesture that is necessary because he will not break an oath to tell a different truth that might explain the situation. The lying letter's text, though false, is more plausible to Theseus and brings conviction. Moreover, the pattern of motivation suggested by Hippolytus' rhetoric of plausibility is notably insufficient in the light of the play's different webs of causation and blame. The sophistic argumentation is not merely part of the characterization of the young man, it also constitutes an essential development of the interplay of speech and silence, veiling and revealing the truth, that I have already discussed as factors in the thematic texture of this play – a texture of themes which are themselves closely related to the sophistic interests in truth and probability, the relation between words and the world, particularly with regard to moral imperatives.

The power of *logos* finds its strongest expression in the writings of Gorgias. In his *Encomium to Helen*, he constructs and dismisses four possible reasons for Helen to have left her home and husband to go to Troy with Paris. Can she be blamed for her behaviour? Three of these arguments are readily understandable. First, it was by decree of the gods and fate: a god is by nature stronger than a human, and it follows that the god rather than the human is to blame. A similar point makes up the fourth of his reasons: that it was all the work of Eros. This position is remarkably similar in form to the nurse's words in Euripides' *Hippolytus*, when she argues that as Aphrodite is a goddess it would be a transgression for Phaedra not to give way to the lusts the divinity has sent. In both Gorgias' and Euripides' writing there seems a marked tension between the traditional anthropomorphic picture of the gods as external forces working on men's lives and the rationalistic use of logic in the one case to excuse and in the other to promote what would be in traditional terms a sin. The traditional depiction of the world of the divine is turned against itself in a highly untraditional way. Gorgias' second possibility is that Helen was forced to leave. In that case, she deserves pity not blame and her barbarian abductor should be punished with all due measure. The third of his four possible arguments suggested only to be dismissed in order to free Helen from blame requires more defence from Gorgias. It is that she was persuaded by the force of *logos*. How can it be that 'persuasion' frees from blame a person who has been persuaded to do something wrong? Gorgias' answer to this question is first to stress the immense power of *logos*. *Logos* accomplishes 'divine deeds' (8) and has a divine force.[35] The divine attributes of *logos* not only support the notion of its irresistible force but also link Gorgias' *logos* with the poetic tradition of divine utterance – the privileged access to truth. '*Logos* is almost an independent external power which forces the hearer to do its will.'[36] The *logos* indeed works as a sort of drug on human souls, creating pleasure, pain, pity, fear. It is through this psychological power of the *logos* that Helen may be said to have been forced to act and thus she is free from the blame traditionally attached to her behaviour.

Gorgias, however, also refers to the *logos* as producing 'deception' as well as persuasion. Moreover, this 'deception' does not involve a moral reproach as one might expect. The deceiver is described – with a conscious air of paradox – as more just than the non-deceiver, and the deceived listener as wiser than the non-deceived. In part, this assertion of the deceptive qualities of *logos* draws on the famous claim of Hesiod's Muses to be able to tell both the truth and falsehoods most like the truth. But several scholars have seen the link between deception and language as rooted in a wider philosophical theorizing about language.[37] The *logos* has a certain autonomy: 'Speech is not a reflection of things, not a mere tool or slave of description but ... it is its own master.'[38] '*Logos* is not and can never be the externally subsisting objects that actually are ... It is not even ... speech that displays the external reality, it is the external object that provides information about the logos.'[39] It follows from these reconstructions of Gorgias' ideas that there is a radical gap between words and the world. The relation between speech and what is the case is always fractured. 'If anything exists, it cannot be understood; if it can be understood, it cannot be expressed.'

Language for Gorgias, the rhetoric teacher, can appeal to truth, profess truth, but not attain it. The *logos* remains deceptive, even as it explains its deception. Vernant expressed tragedy's paradoxical message as 'when understood, precisely that there are in the words exchanged between humans zones of opacity and incommunicability'.[40] A similar irony of representation seems to be taken to an extreme in Gorgias' writing. How can one express the gaps and barriers that prevent secure expression? In a *logos*, how can one claim without deception that the *logos* is deceptive?

It is important not to think of Gorgias' arguments as just 'sophistic word play' or philosophically irrelevant. For the interlocking network of Gorgias' – and the other sophists' – interests in *logos* express an essential insight into the

---

[35] See Segal 1962a, 110ff.; de Romilly 1973.   [36] Segal 1962a, 121.
[37] See Segal 1962a; de Romilly 1973; Rosenmeyer 1955; Guthrie 1962–81, Vol. III, 192ff.; Kerferd 1981, 79ff.
[38] Rosenmeyer 1955, 231–2.   [39] Kerferd 1981, 80–1.
[40] Vernant and Vidal-Naquet 1981, 18.

debated issues contemporary with Greek tragedy. The opposition of *logos* to *logos*; the power of *logos* particularly in persuasion and deception; the relation of words and the world; the shifts and controls of meaning and reference; the clash of rhetoric and rhetoric, undermining security of expression and belief; the dangers and powers of language; the use of argument to challenge traditional depiction of morality and behaviour, particularly with regard to responsibility and causation; all are topics to which I have turned again and again in this book. But the sophistic movement does not simply constitute 'philosophical' or 'intellectual' background to the literary work of tragedy any more than the legal language of tragedy simply reflects contemporary litigiousness. Rather, in the period of rapid change experienced by fifth-century Athens, the sophistic movement represents both a symptom and a cause of a division and a divisiveness in the discourses of fifth-century civic society, to which tragedy also attests. As Saïd puts it, 'The moment of the *Tetralogies*, which is also that of tragedy, is in effect the moment when the gaps (*écarts*) and the oppositions between the sphere of piety ... and that of legality ... are most forcefully felt.'[41] The clashes between old and new ways of approaching the world and in particular the place and use of language in the city are expressions of the tensions within the languages of the city. For the fifth-century conservative the sophists may appear to be the willing corruptors of modern generations who seem all too happy to accept their entertaining and serious lessons; for the third- and fourth-century philosophers, they may appear to be word-playing relativists, a danger to the idealist programme; but it is precisely in their awareness of the uncertainties of language and of man's social and ethical position with regard to *logos* and the traditions of the past, and also in their confident and powerful explication of these problematics, that the sophists and tragedians are linked as the 'wise men' of fifth-century Athens.

Euripides, in his *Troades*, which I said I would come back to in this chapter, has often been blamed by critics for writing a play to show off a series of scarcely linked set-piece rhetorical arguments. I have already mentioned Cassandra's argument, where she debates the claim of the defeated – the weaker argument – to be regarded as better off than the victors (a fine sophistic reversal). In the latter part of the play, Hecuba and Helen in front of the judging Menelaus argue Helen's involvement in responsibility for the Trojan war – precisely the topic of Gorgias' famous *Encomium*. Indeed, both Helen and Hecuba argue in set rhetorical form with suggested reasons for and evaluations of Helen's behaviour put forward and dismissed, with clashing claims of responsibility and morality. Helen begins 'since you regard me as

[41] 1978, 191. My translation.

your enemy, perhaps you will not answer my arguments, however sound or unsound you may think them. But I think I know what charges you would bring against me in debate, and I shall arrange my answers correspondingly, your charge against mine, mine against yours' (914–18). As if she were in a lawcourt, Helen uses the formal rhetoric of opposition to construct an opening speech of defence. Hers will be a point-by-point argument, which proclaims its own logic, and her speech is constructed as if she had used Gorgias for her rhetoric training. First she offers Hecuba, her opponent, as the true cause of the Trojan war, as she gave birth to Paris. Secondly, Priam, who failed to kill the cursed Paris, was to blame. The traditional narrative of the Trojan war follows from these two starting-points. So, like Gorgias, Helen lays the blame for her adultery on Aphrodite. She claims her own personal disaster has proved a great benefit for the Greeks in that it has enabled them to record a great victory over the barbarian Trojans. She claims moreover, like Gorgias, that after the death of Paris she was prevented by force from returning to the Greeks as she had wanted. Thus, she concludes, she cannot justly be punished. 'On the one hand I was married against my will, on the other hand my services to my own people have earned me bitter servitude instead of a victor's prize. So be stronger than the gods if you want to, but it's a foolish thing to want' (962–5).

Hecuba offers a powerful and brilliant point-by-point response. She challenges the whole divine mechanism of Helen's argument. First, with a *reductio* based on a principle of likelihood she questions the standard myths on which Helen draws. Why should the goddesses have argued over beauty? Could Hera have expected a better marriage than with the king of the gods? Why should Aphrodite have come to Sparta when she could have brought Helen to Troy without leaving heaven? Why, if she was forced, did Helen offer no resistance nor try to get any help? Moreover, she challenges Helen's whole argument of divine causation as a fabrication to conceal lust – 'every lewd impulse in man passes for Aphrodite' (989): Helen was in fact an opportunist with an eye for the extravagant luxuries of life in the east. So, Hecuba concludes, justice demands Helen's death as an example for all women. 'And make this law for all other women: the woman who betrays her husband dies.'

Helen is given several of Gorgias' arguments to exculpate herself; the echoes of his intellectual rhetoric are essential to the tone of her defence of her adultery. But she is defeated by Hecuba's superior reason, superior use of rhetorical manipulation. Helen could claim the gods were to blame for leading her astray, but Hecuba could claim such an argument is a mere rationalization for willing sin. This exchange, however, is not merely Euripides offering the

Athenians a modern and entertaining piece of rhetorical posturing. Nor is it sufficient to note 'a sophistic influence' as if that answered the question. For it is the parallel concerns with the relations between action and responsibility, with the morality and traditional models and explanations of behaviour, with the language to express ethical and social responsibilities, that make significant the links between Euripides' and the sophists' representations and uses of the inherited stories of the Trojan war. As we have seen, for many fifth-century readers of Homer – including Aeschylus and Sophocles – his explanations of behaviour and associated morality seem no longer self-evident. The traditional ethical stances are insufficient for the life and attitudes of the city. Euripides dramatizes that clash as aggressively as possible by forcing the old stories and old characters of the Homeric poems into the form of a dramatized debate in sophistic terms and strategies. His willing anachronism in the traditional, retold stories sets in play changing attitudes to war, punishment, responsibility and rationalism – and to sophistic arguments, too: Gorgias' reasoning in the mouth of Helen is judged to be defeated by Hecuba's sarcastic rationalism, but that rationalism itself is set in tension with the opening scene of the play, where the divinities Athene and Poseidon plot to effect disaster for the victorious Greeks.[42] It is not merely indebtedness to rhetorical studies that is important in the debate of Helen and Hecuba, but an attitude to the questions of social and ethical behaviour, how to discuss matters of norms and transgression.

Indeed, despite regular accusations by their detractors of being both immoral and the cause of immorality, the sophists appear to have been concerned with a wide range of ethical and social debates of some importance to our understanding of tragedy. There are two topics, in particular, that I wish to consider here. The first is the question 'Can virtue be taught?' This problem was debated with considerable urgency in the fifth century and is closely related to several of the subjects I have mentioned in this and earlier chapters. The word translated traditionally as 'virtue' could be glossed more usefully as the qualities of a man that make a good and successful person, or that are displayed by a good and successful person, and it is often translated as 'excellence' and 'ability'. It is also used of horses, ships, land, fountains etc. to express their distinctive fine qualities. The debate on teaching virtue has marked social implications. In traditional or conservative terms, as summed up by Theognis in the sixth century, 'virtue' was imparted by association; his general advice is 'consort with the good' (27). 'Virtue' was the property of a

---

[42] There is an open-ended irony about Hecuba's victory and her forebodings about Menelaus' promised punishment. For Homer depicts Helen and Menelaus living happily together in Sparta nine years after the end of the Trojan war. The promised punishment stands in tension with the expectations formed by literary tradition. (Mrs Easterling reminded me of this point.)

particular class, and the qualities that made up the behaviour of a good man were identified strongly with the interest of that class. The sophists claimed to teach precisely 'virtue', that is, the qualities that enabled a man to succeed in society. This claim was 'to the conservatively minded profoundly shocking'.[43] What was previously a selective and personal process now became open to anyone who had the fee. The question of teaching 'virtue' arises specifically with the growth of the democratic city. The debate on education is to be seen as part of the political struggles in society as to who should have access not simply to knowledge but to status and power.

The arguments brought to bear on this debate are varied and numerous. Some of them are recounted in basic form in the minor sophistic treatise *Dissoi Logoi* ('Twofold arguments'), which regards as untenable the position that virtue cannot be taught – as one might expect from someone writing in support of the new teachers.[44] Plato's development of the topic, however, is also one of the main reasons for its continuing interest. The *Meno* begins 'Can you tell me, Socrates, whether virtue can be taught? Or is it a matter of natural aptitude or what?' For Socrates, first of all, the answer must be approached through the further enquiry as to what is meant by 'virtue', and the dialogue is concerned first with the question of definition of 'virtue', a prime term of moral and social vocabulary. In the *Protagoras*, however, the question of teachability is foremost, as Protagoras offers a brilliant and lengthy speech to justify his role as teacher of political virtue. Much has been written on this famous passage, which I have referred to before in Chapter 8, but one specific element of the structure of this argument leads to the second topic of ethical and social debate that I wish to discuss in this chapter. Protagoras tells a story of the earliest times of man in the natural state to explain the growth of the values of the city – as Meno had asked 'Is it a matter of natural aptitude or what?' For one of the major structuring oppositions of sophistic debate is the polarity *nomos* and *phusis*.[45] *Nomos* we have already discussed, particularly in Chapters 3 and 4, as the principle of law so important to the city. Its range of meaning is wider than the merely legal, however, and it involves the notions of 'conventions', something agreed upon within a culture, and different from culture to culture, a principle open to discussion and change but always with a normative force. *Phusis*, connected to the Greek verb 'to grow', is usually translated 'nature' and, like the English word 'nature', *phusis* connotes both the structure of the world as it is (often with the normative sense of the charged opposition 'natural/unnatural'), and also the more specific sense of the

---

[43] Guthrie 1962–81, Vol. III, 250.
[44] See especially Chapter 7. See e.g. Kerferd 1981, 132ff.
[45] For this opposition, see Heinimann 1945; Pohlenz 1953. See also Guthrie 1962–81, Vol. III, 55ff.

inherent form of a particular being or thing. The opposition of *nomos* and *phusis*, then, has certain similarities with the modern critical vocabulary of 'nature/nurture', 'nature/culture'.

In the debate on the teachability of 'virtue', this opposition is often used in a strictly polarized fashion as a structuring force of argument. At one extreme, 'virtue' is considered purely a matter of breeding. It is unteachable because it is a matter of natural character, which is a matter of birth. This argument is given a neat (sophistic) twist by Plato's Socrates, who claims that this is not just the conservative principle it may at first sight seem, but is actually an underlying tenet of Athenian direct democracy.[46] For the democratic state uses specialists for matters requiring expertise, such as shipbuilding, but for matters of general policy, which require 'political virtue', it allows anyone to have a say. Therefore virtue in a direct democracy must be thought of as a generally, naturally possessed characteristic. At another extreme, man's character and value, it was argued, may be trained and educated by a programme of study to prepare a man for taking his role in the city's affairs. If modern interpretations of Protagoras' great speech in Plato's *Protagoras* are right, the sophist is arguing that while to a certain degree the qualities that constitute an ability to live together in the city are innate in man, those qualities can be developed and bettered by the teaching he offers.[47] Even if the capability for 'justice' (*dikē*) is a necessary condition of existing together in a city, a man can be made 'more just' by education. For Protagoras, it would appear that the opposition of *nomos* and *phusis* leads to a dialectical relation rather than a rigid polarization.

The opposition of *nomos* and *phusis* structures numerous political and ethical arguments and has been discussed at length by critics.[48] The views of Thrasymachus in Plato's *Republic* are famous particularly in the catch-phrase 'Might is right.' His position, however, is based on the view that it is natural for the stronger to have and to use power, which is readily opposed to the dictum of restraint implied by conventional justice. A similar argument recurs in a directly political setting in Thucydides, where first in the Mytilenean debate (III 38–48) and then in the Melian dialogue (V 85–111) the Athenians are depicted as arguing for, and in the second case implementing, the mass execution of the men of a rebel city. The arguments used are based on the self-interest of the Athenians as imperial power, and in the Melian dialogue the principle of self-interest is accepted by both sides, with the result that the Melians are forced to argue that it is not in the interest of the Athenians to

[46] Plato, *Prot.* 319ff.
[47] See above n. 26. Protagoras allows for some exceptions – men who are for some reason devoid of such qualities and who must be kept from a city.
[48] See above n. 45.

deny conventional justice to the weaker. The Athenians are unconvinced. It is, they claim, a law of nature to rule if one has the power: 'This is not a *nomos* that was made by us nor were we the first to use it when it had been made. We are merely acting in accordance with it after finding it already in existence, and we shall leave it to exist for ever in the future. We know that you or anyone else with the same power would act in the same way.'[49]

This frightening justification of imperialist violence is not merely an 'immoral' or 'amoral argument', as it is sometimes claimed. Rather, it is putting forward a position which rejects a traditional morality based on *nomos* in favour of a morality based on what is perceived as a dictum of nature, *phusis*. There is a sanction in acting according to nature, which is opposed to the sanction of *nomos*. Once more it is evident that the terminology and argumentation of the sophistic writers are not merely influential in philosophical or literary matters but are also at work in the depiction, enaction, conception of the pragmatics of political life. Thrasymachus' arguments are not merely the ground-clearing opening section of a Utopian scheme.

The oppositions of *nomos* and *phusis*, which function as an essential explanatory principle both in Thrasymachus' arguments in Plato's philosophical dialogue and in Thucydides' depiction of the political rhetoric of his time, appear in a wide range of arguments and in numerous discourses. On the one hand, particularly in such spheres as medicine, ethics or investigations into society, geography, history, the boundaries between the two categories were actively debated. What corresponded to 'nature' and what to 'law', 'convention'? What authority did 'nature' or 'law', 'convention' possess – or should either possess? What was the relative influence of each in the development of the *polis* and its arts? These were all questions returned to again and again. On the other hand, *nomos* and *phusis* are also often used as if the two terms presented an exhaustive choice. In the lawcourt – and other spheres of public rhetoric – the appeal to the self-evident requirement of obeying *nomos* is exclusively opposed by the assertion of the self-evident claims of *phusis* as an overriding principle. When involved in a defence of one's own or someone else's behaviour or attitude, or when attempting to explain events or policies, or when committed to investigation, assertion or criticism, the writers of the fifth century revert again and again to the exclusive opposition of *nomos* and *phusis* as a structuring of argument and language. It becomes a way of seeing the world.

The opposition of *nomos* and *phusis*, which could be discussed at far greater length, is particularly important for the tragic texts, not only as a recurring rhetorical trope, particularly in Euripides, but also as a structuring expression

[49] 5.105.4ff.

of the position of man in the order of things.[50] The extensive debates on the relations between *nomos* and *phusis* with regard to man's behaviour and status are specifically concerned not merely with the determination of the sense and order of the vocabulary of social life – *dikē*, *aidōs*, *nomos* itself etc. – but also with the possibility of defining norms and transgressions. As much as the sophists debate and set at risk the traditional pattern of social thinking through the opposition of *nomos* and *phusis*, so too tragedy, working through similar concerns and similar vocabulary, challenges and questions the position and nature of man and his civilized order. Tragic drama again and again dramatizes the social world of the city at risk from the force of man's behaviour as it approaches the extremes of wild transgression and desire for law and order; again and again, tragic texts, like the sophistic writings, return to the vocabulary of civic relations, to the terminology of norm, error, punishment; again and again, like the sophists, the tragedians depict concern with the definition of a human and his behaviour.

In drawing these connections between the sophistic and tragic critiques of the dominant ideology of the city, I am not intending to efface the differences in terms of social function as well as mode of presentation between sophists and tragedians. Tragic theatre is performed in a civic festival and is constituted in terms of dramatic or religious licence – a delimited freedom to transgress. There are stories of outrage associated with performances of certain plays,[51] but the city supports and attends the festival. Sophists, often from beyond the city, deal with private individuals, and whatever the degree of acceptance among certain classes or groups of citizens, sophists have a less prescribed and more dangerous allowance. Euripides may have shocked, but it is Socrates who is prosecuted and put to death. Whatever the motivations or intentions of the prosecution or verdict, the charges – not believing in the city's gods, introducing new divinities, and corrupting the young – indicate an ostensible social and moral argument against Socrates as a citizen. Although the social and moral effect of the theatre is constantly asserted, it is the perceived relation between a sophistic training and the men involved in the challenge to the city's social order that in part prompts a certain hostility to the sophists. Theatre dramatizes but sophistic programmes are enacted. The sophistic challenge to the norm of a traditional order through education provoked both revolutionary notions and extreme reactions.[52]

Indeed, the senses of danger, of scandal, or disorder seem regularly to have been attached to the sophists since their appearance in the fifth century. But as

[50] This is a major argument of Segal 1981 with regard to Sophocles.
[51] E.g. Euripides' first *Hippolytus* (*Hippolytos Kaluptomenos*); Phrynichus' *Sack of Miletus*, which so moved the audience that the author was fined and the play banned.
[52] See Dover 1975 on such reactions.

Sartre wrote of a later critical movement, which provoked similarly hostile reactions, 'These authors . . . far from being afraid of creating a scandal want to provoke one as strongly as possible, because scandal must bring with it a certain disarray'[53] – and it is in such disarray that change (decline) and enquiry (outrage) are rooted . . .

In this chapter, then, I have tried to offer a brief outline of the social and intellectual importance of the series of individuals known as the sophists for our understanding of the fifth century and in particular of the ideological picture of the fifth-century Athenian *polis*. I have been unable to deal with anything like a full range of sophistic arguments or topics – the open-mindedness and diversity of interests of the sophists are remarkable – still less with a full history of the people or of the problems of historiography. But through this broad outline of some major subjects – the attitudes to *logos*, the question of 'virtue' and its teaching, the opposition of *nomos* and *phusis*, together with the focus on relativism of values and the confidence in rational investigations that I introduced in the previous chapter – I have attempted to show how the sophists do not merely constitute an intellectual background or influence on the literary world of tragedy. Rather, tragedy and sophistic writing both attest to a radical series of tensions in the language and ideology of the city of fifth-century Athens. An understanding of sophistic writings helps us to focus the range and nature of the uncertainties and claims about the role of man in the society and language of the *polis* and to understand the social and intellectual impact of such questioning.

Plato's *Symposium* depicts the story of a party at the house of Agathon, the tragedian; the guests include Socrates, Aristophanes, and Alcibiades, the young aristocrat who enjoyed immense political influence. They debate love, the soul, the self and desire, notions particularly close to twentieth-century determinations of what it means to be a human in society. The dialogue is constructed to lead towards Socrates' philosophical exposition of the subject, but the representation of the discussions of tragic and comic poet, young man at the height of political influence, as well as a doctor, Agathon's young lover, and a disciple of Socrates, offers a convenient metaphor for the interplay of languages in the discourse of the city. The separation of literary, sophistic and philosophical languages and programmes demanded by Plato is demanded in part because of their interpenetration in the world of fifth-century Athens. That some sophists wrote tragedies[54] and tragedians manipulate sophistic rhetoric is not a casual overlap of interest. In fifth-century Athens, what it meant to be a human being living in a city was a (democratically) shared problematic.

[53] 1973, 65.   [54] E.g. Hippias, Critias.

10 · GENRE AND TRANSGRESSION

Horváth: Brecht always liked people to be aware that they were in a theatre. I said to him. 'But Brecht, what makes you think they think they're anywhere else?'

HAMPTON

The innovative late works works of Euripides have given rise to dissension among critics and readers since their first performances. Aristophanes' characterization of Aeschylus in the *Frogs* pillories Euripides for bringing on stage royal figures dressed in rags, and Euripides' 'deglamorization'[1] of tragedy has continued to provoke strong reaction. In particular, the intellectual stance of his plays, his turning to sophistic rhetoric for his agonistic debates, his sheer cleverness have been seen by critics as elements for reproach or regret. So Collard has recently written: 'the poet is guilty of self-indulgent digression for the sake of rhetorical display at the loss of dramatic continuity and relevance',[2] and Winnington Ingram has described Euripides as 'capable of resisting everything but temptation – the temptation to be clever'.[3] There is indeed an institutionalized tradition of strictures on Euripides' innovativeness.[4] I have tried particularly in the previous chapter to show how the connection between the sophists and tragedy is not to be seen as a matter of the regrettable influence on poetry of a rhetoric of tricks or an improper intellectualism, but rather as an important indication of the radical tensions that draw together sophistic and tragic questions about man's place in the order of things. In this chapter, I am going to consider a further major area of innovativeness in tragic theatre that has proved instrumental in the evaluation and appreciation particularly of Euripides' *oeuvre*, namely, the poet's self-conscious marking and manipulation of the conventions of the genre of tragedy. For Euripides' innovativeness is developed not merely in the new material of his plots, the experimental use of lyric, or his 'deglamorization' of myth, but also in his tragedies' self-reflexive sense of theatre as theatre.

This self-reflexiveness has often been associated with the end of tragedy as a genre, and Euripides has often been regarded even as the destroyer of classical

---

[1] Arnott's term, 1981, 181.   [2] 1975, 59.   [3] 1969, 138.
[4] Cf. Arrowsmith 1968, 29–33; Vickers 1973, 17–23.

drama: critics arguing from a principle either that 'art is to conceal art', or that the true subject of the true art is real people and profound emotions, have found the late plays at best 'problematic', but all too often simply 'bad' or 'decadent'. More recent critics, however, developing the prevalent twentieth-century interest in the self-reflexive qualities of literary texts and also the growing sense of the workings of literary tradition that I mentioned in Chapter 6, have attempted a more sophisticated description and evaluation of Euripides' sense of genre. Zeitlin writes of the common basis of the various critics' descriptive vocabulary: 'Ironic, decadent, "modern", even "post-modern": these are the labels usually applied ... and they are all correct in that they insist in one way or another on the self-conscious awareness of a tradition which has reached the end of its organic development.'[5] In these final two chapters, I am going to discuss this self-reflexive awareness of Euripidean theatre with special regard to two late plays: first, the *Electra*, which has met with an extreme range of critical reaction, despite – or perhaps because of – the fact that it is less extreme an example of 'aesthetic boldness ... self-conscious-ness and authorial extravagance'[6] than, say, the *Orestes* or the *Helen*;[7] secondly, the *Bacchae*, Euripides' final masterpiece, which has escaped the general strictures of the other late plays, indeed which has proved central to numerous critics' understanding of tragedy and been used by writers of many disciplines. In the final chapter, I shall consider particularly through the use of the chorus in the *Bacchae* the role of performance in the theatrical experience and the question of stagecraft; in this chapter, my first consideration is with the sense of genre in the *Electra*.

From the opening speech of the farmer, Euripides' *Electra* marks its difference from the tradition in which it is placed. The prologue is defined by Aristotle as the words and action before the first entrance of the chorus;[8] however, in the form of a speech delivered by a dramatic character which is regarded primarily as a means of exposition of the dramatic situation, the prologue is a device associated with the development of Euripidean technique that looks forward to the formal prologue of New Comedy.[9] Like many Euripidean prologues, this speech of the farmer proclaims both its inno-vativeness and its status as work of literature. Unlike the prologues to the *Bacchae, Hippolytus, Troades*,[10] the speaker's identity is not made clear in the

[5] 1980, 51.
[6] Zeitlin 1980, 51.
[7] On the *Orestes*, see Wolff 1968; Arrowsmith 1964; Zeitlin 1980. On the *Helen*, see Zuntz 1958; Podlecki 1970; Segal 1971.
[8] *Poet.* 1452b19ff.
[9] See Schadewaldt 1926, 105ff.; also Hamilton 1978, and now Erbse 1984.
[10] Plays discussed in this book; one could add *Suppl., Her., Iph. in Aul., Phoen., Hec., Ion.*

opening few lines. Rather, the farmer begins with a simplified version of the Trojan war – the departure of Agamemnon, the sack of Troy, the return and regicide, perpetrated by the queen's trick and Aegisthus' force (as in Homer), and Aegisthus' accession to the throne (as in Homer). He turns (14) to the children, Electra and Orestes, and here too the story begins in a simple and not unexpected way. Orestes is sent to Phocis and Electra stays at home. The tale focuses on Electra and on Aegisthus' treatment of her. The usurper's motivations – particularly his fear that Electra may manage secretly to conceive a child – may hint at the coming narrative's tone, but it is not until line 34, where the speaker introduces himself and his marriage to Electra that the radical alterations Euripides has made to the dramatic situation are made clear.

As is evident from the way that the farmer's opening address and narrative pass into his own story, his own moral comments and indeed Electra's entrance, it would be wrong to regard this prologue as entirely or distinctly separate from the dramatic action. Even in a play like *Hippolytus* where Aphrodite does not appear again on stage, the prologue is linked to the action that follows not only as a paradigmatic exposition of events,[11] but also by the discussion of the correct treatment of the goddess that the servant and Hippolytus have in the first short scene and by the powerful sense of Aphrodite's divine force that runs through the play's narrative of passion and disaster. The Euripidean prologue is not a formal opening speech addressed to the audience like the prologue in, say, Shakespeare's *Henry V*.

Many critics have argued that the prologue functions primarily as a way of quickly setting out the situation of the play and its place within a mythological background, and, indeed, here the novelty both of Electra's arranged marriage and of the rustic setting of the tragedy is strongly emphasized by the delayed expression of the identity and role of the speaker, the new twist of Euripides' version thrown into contrast with the highly conventional narrative of the opening lines. But despite its evident links with the play, a prologue seems also to distance itself from the ensuing action. Unlike the opening of the *Antigone*, say, where the dialogue of Ismene and Antigone sets us in the middle of dramatic action and 'dramatic illusion', the device of the prologue – spoken to no-one but the audience in the theatre[12] – acts also as a marker of the conscious siting of the play within a particular theatrical tradition. It's a

---

[11] See Fitzgerald 1973; also Hamilton 1978.

[12] The farmer's speech is addressed, if the text is correct, to the rivers of Argos. Many prologues do not even have an address in this manner. None, however, explicitly acknowledges the audience's presence (as happens in comedy). See Bain 1975, especially 22–3, though as Hunter (1985, 25) notes, this does not mean that an audience could not regard the lines as addressed to them.

theatrical device. The prologue formalizes and draws attention to the conventions of offering necessary information to the audience. It stresses that the play is a written object, composed with regard to other plays, other myths. The expression of Euripides' innovative plot in his innovative use of prologue declares the Euripidean drama to be written in and against a theatrical and mythological tradition.

In Chapter 6, I discussed at some length the intertextuality of Euripides and Homer in the telling of Orestes' story. The interrelations between Euripides and Aeschylus' *Oresteia* are also extremely important to an understanding of *Electra*, and strongly emphasize this sense of composition with regard to the theatrical tradition. It is in the recognition scene that these interrelations are brought most strongly to the fore. For when the old man comes to Electra with his belief in the secret arrival of Orestes, he offers three signs which correspond exactly to the three signs that Electra in the *Choephoroi* uses so bizarrely to prove to her own satisfaction the presence of her brother. First, as in the Aeschylean play, the old man provides a lock of hair found on the tomb of Agamemnon. Like Electra in Aeschylus, he rejects the possibility that it could be an Argive who offered it, and continues 'Look at the lock of hair, match it to your own head, / see if it is not twin to yours in colour and cut. / Often a father's blood, running in separate veins / makes two bodies almost mirrors in their form' (520–3). Both the language and the argument echo Aeschylus' emotional recognition scene: Electra: 'Yet here it is and for appearance matches well ... with my own hair. It is almost exactly like ...' Orestes: 'Now lay the severed strand against where it was cut / and look how well your brother's hair matches my head' (174–6, 229–30). But Euripides' Electra is far from willing to make the leap of faith. First, she rejects the possibility that her brother, so 'bright and bold', would return in secret as if afraid. She goes on (527–9): 'Besides how could a lock of his hair match with mine? / One from a man with rugged training in the ring and games, / one combed and girlish.' What's more, she concludes, many people who are unrelated have similar hair. Electra seems to be appealing to a criterion of fifth-century rationalism in her point-by-point rejection of the likelihood of there being any similarity between her hair and her brother's. The young woman dismisses with scorn the attitude of an earlier Electra in the mouth of an old man. But as events turn out, her confidence both in her brother's heroic ideals and in her powers of deduction will be shaken by the recognition of the indecisive Orestes. The scene does not merely mock the Aeschylean passage by treating it with an 'improper' attitude of liberalism or logic – a different construction of the realities of recognition – but also mocks the mocker for the false conclusions her logic induces.

The old man continues (532–3):

> At least go and set your foot in the print of his hunting boot
> and see if it is not the same as yours, my child.

This instruction parallels the second proof the Aeschylean Electra uses: 'Footprints are here; / the feet that made them are alike and look like mine ... / I step where he has stepped, / and heelmark and the space between / his heel and toe are like the prints I make' (205–10). The old man's advice makes sense only as it tracks the narrative of Aeschylus.

Electra is equally dismissive of this sign: not only would rocky ground leave no footprints, but of course her brother's footprint – he is a man – would be larger. How could she hope to step into her brother's shoes?

Finally, the old man turns to the third proof of the Aeschylean recognition scene (538–40):

> Is there no sign then, if your brother should come home ...
> of loom or pattern by which you would know the cloth
> you wove, I wrapped him in, to rescue him from death?

Electra once more dismisses the logic of the tokens from an earlier play (541–4):

> You know quite well Orestes went away in exile
> when I was very small. If a little girl's hand
> could weave, how could a growing boy still wear that cloth
> unless his shirt and tunic lengthened with his legs?

Once more, Electra's rationalism turns with dismissive humour on the old man. She even questions the basis of his suggestion that she could weave at all when Orestes was exiled. The old man's faulty chronology makes his idea ridiculous.

This apparently parodic scene has caused some critical confusion, and Fraenkel went so far as to delete the whole passage and the corresponding lines in the *Choephoroi* as tasteless interpolations.[13] Is Euripides merely mocking his predecessor? 'Aeschylus was fair game .... It was clever to score points at the expense of the archaic technique of the older poet.'[14] Is it an example of the influx of sophistic rationalism, misreading the profound moment of an earlier tragedy with 'apparently incongruous intellectual content'?[15] Is it part of a Euripidean 'obsession with realistic evidence'?[16] Both the faith of Aeschylus' Electra in her brother and Orestes' own heroic stance play an essential role in the *Oresteia*'s developing sense of what it means to be a member of an *oikos* and, as I showed in Chapters 1 and 2, the *Oresteia* constructs the role of the

---

[13] His arguments are criticised in Lloyd-Jones 1961.   [14] Winnington-Ingram 1969, 129.
[15] Collard 1975, 63.   [16] Gellie 1981, 4.

oikos in terms of the *polis*. The Aeschylean matricide is to be seen as part of the determination of the relations between the sexes in the developing civic discourse. Euripides' play in its questioning of the relation of the Orestes story to contemporary attitudes and morals both challenges the ethical status of Orestes' revenge and in particular rewrites the interrelations within the family and culture of the avengers. As I will argue later, the poet's irony is focused on the different characters' perceptions of their roles within the family and within the myth. Euripides is not just mocking Aeschylean practice in this scene. His ironic rewriting of the moment of recognition shatters the possibility of the 'symbolical as well as real identification of the *family*'[17] in Aeschylean terms. The humorous questioning of the Aeschylean devices of recognition is also a serious questioning of Aeschylus' manipulation of the Orestes myth in its widest implications as played out in the recognition scene. 'What chiefly interested him was less the indictment of tradition, though that was clearly essential, than the *confrontation*, the *dramatic juxtaposition* of the split in his culture.'[18]

I shall return to the role of the recognition in the wider thematic issues of he *Electra*, but first I want here to stress the way this scene develops its sense of genre. For the intertextuality with Aeschylus, the transposition of the recognition tokens of the *Oresteia* into a different narrative, not only emphasizes the generation of Euripides' play within a theatrical tradition – it has a specifically dramatic genealogy through which it derives its sense and force – but also brings to the fore the *conventionality* of the devices of recognition. For although Electra's reasoning demolishes the logical connection between the signs and the old man's argument – as if she were demanding an Aristotelian logic of dramatic cause and effect – none the less the old man's conclusion proves correct. We are left with a characteristic Euripidean juxtaposition – 'mutual criticism . . . mutual exposure'[19] – of the arbitrary assumptions of the old man which make sense only as they advance the traditional norm of myth,[20] and the logical requirements of Electra which fail to account for the truth. As Euripides forces awareness of the incongruity and arbitrariness of the Aeschylean recognition tokens, he also marks the conventionality involved in the recognition process itself. He displays the recognition of long-lost relatives as a literary, theatrical theme, a game complete with rules and conventions. For conventions to function, they must remain unrecognized, but it is precisely recognition that Euripides' writing enforces.

Indeed, the way that the narrative of recognition has been marked by its

[17] Mejer 1979, 119.   [18] Arrowsmith 1968, 20.   [19] Arrowsmith 1968, 19.
[20] On the force of myth constraining its characters, see King 1980; Kubo 1966; Zeitlin 1980, especially 70ff.

hesitations emphasizes the manner of final recognition all the more.[21] Orestes, although he has recognized Electra and ascertained her support and that of the chorus, maintains his disguise of the false messenger – a role adopted by Aeschylus' Orestes in the more pressing circumstances of the hostile palace. He nearly gives himself away when he 'momentarily forgets his assumed role'[22] in talking to Electra of her husband, but continues to deceive his sister.[23] Even when the old man calls him Orestes, the prince withholds his acceptance of the title until Electra's acceptance makes it almost impossible to deny. It is the most conventional[24] sign of all – a hunting scar, like the device used to recognize Odysseus in the *Odyssey*[25] – that convinces the disbelieving Electra and allows the unwilling Orestes to be drawn from his disguise. A brief six lines covers their expression of shared joy, which is also quite different from the lengthy, ecstatic reunion of brother and sister in the *Choephoroi*. Euripides' revengers need the old man and his Aeschylean tokens to prompt the recognition, as indeed he brings the necessary information to advance the matricide. The progress of the revenge depends on its previous tellings.

The examples of the significant resonances of the *Oresteia* in Euripides' *Electra* can be multiplied. Electra's entrance with a water-pot parodies her entrance in Aeschylus with religious offerings for Agamemnon – the title *Choephoroi* means 'libation-bearers'.[26] Clytemnestra's entrance in a chariot with Phrygian captives parallels Agamemnon's entrance for the carpet scene. The religious language of the *Oresteia* is echoed and distorted in the *Electra*.[27] Orestes, since the *Odyssey*, is conceived as a paradigmatic figure, and the *Oresteia* was concerned with expressing moral and social imperatives through the myth. Euripides not only fractures the Orestes myth's status as model, but in these echoes and twists of the *Oresteia* specifically marks his play as a literary rewriting of that earlier model. The game with Aeschylus is not simply literary cleverness but essential to the serious functioning of this tragedy.

Euripides' explicit marking of the conventional elements of his genre is seen in many other places in the play. After Orestes has left to join Aegisthus at the sacrifice, the chorus sing an ode on the misery in the house of Atreus, and, as they conclude, off-stage sounds are heard. The chorus and Electra worry about the outcome. Electra despairs, but the chorus tell her to hold back until she knows for sure. Electra's response is interesting (759):

[21] See especially Solmsen 1967. [22] Denniston 1939, ad 262.
[23] Many suggestions have been made as to why he maintains his disguise so long. See Donzelli 1978, 73–135.
[24] It is, of course, an innovation in the representation of Orestes' and Electra's recognition. See Tarkow 1981.
[25] The contrast with the hero Odysseus is also significant. See Tarkow 1981.
[26] It is not known when the title *Choephoroi* was first used, of course.
[27] See Zeitlin 1970, especially 659ff.

Not possible. We are beaten. For where are the messengers?

The connective 'for' specifies the logic of her remark. The plan must be foiled because 'the death of a king in tragedy cannot fail to be followed, promptly, by a messenger's speech'.[28] Electra's reply depends on a recognition of the conventions of the genre in which she is performing. Two lines later, however, enter a messenger. 'My message is that Orestes has won ...' (762). Once again, Euripides stresses the formal aspects of theatre as theatre as they are utilized. It will indeed be the traditional element of a messenger scene that advances the play now.

The tension between the old man's use of the Aeschylean tokens of recognition and Electra's rationalist arguments against their probability has often been expressed in a more general form as, e.g., an 'antithesis between the tragic-mythical and the realistic'.[29] This contrast is particularly marked in the play's choric odes, which have sometimes been regarded even as totally irrelevant to the action.[30] I have already discussed in Chapter 6 how the Achilles ode, sung after Orestes enters the farmer's hut, far from being irrelevant, significantly juxtaposes a picture of a heroic world replete with splendour, gold, nymphs and warriors, to the opening scenes of the play with their far from glamorous situation, behaviour and surroundings. This juxtaposition is emphasized by certain points of contact articulated between the ode and the dramatic action. The ode 'foreshadows the violence to come; it presents mythical paradigms of Orestes' hunt; and it introduces the Gorgon',[31] with which Aegisthus' corpse will be compared. This dialectic between heroic past and dramatic present informs the evaluation of the play's actions: 'the ode's vision of glamorous superhuman heroes leads inexorably to the unglamorous vision of human victims; so in the real world of Electra and Orestes, unholy acts ... and utter misery are the result of accepting as paradigmatic the traditional heroes of the past'.[32] The paradigm of heroic behaviour not only provides an image of lost glamour, of disinheritance, but also, when taken as a model for the characters of the play, leads to the dangerous results and morality of the avengers' actions.

But there is a further aspect to this description of a work of art within a work of art that relates closely to my concern with the self-reflexiveness of Euripidean drama. For, as Walsh argues (using the terminology of Brecht[33]), the contrast between play and ode develops 'something like the *Verfremdungseffekt* [alien-

---

[28] Winnington-Ingram 1969, 132. See also Arnott 1973, especially 51ff.
[29] Gellie 1981, 7.
[30] The technical term for such breaks in dramatic action is *embolima*. See Arist. *Poet.* 1456a 25ff.
[31] O'Brien 1964, 25 – following a suggestion of Sheppard.   [32] King 1980, 210.
[33] Brecht's terms are discussed also in Bain 1977, 1–6, with regard to tragedy.

ation effect]. Dramatic illusion, which allows an audience to become clearly involved with stage events, must be disturbed by an ode that offers a strikingly different illusion of reality.'[34] The contrast between dramatic action and the ode, like the prologue's slide into the opening scene, or like the explicit mention and dismissal of Aeschylus' recognition tokens, does not allow the audience to develop a single, coherent level of reality. 'Because ode and play evoke different realities, the spectator may not assume that any part of what he sees represents a single, simple reality.'[35] The drama does not construct a neat and bounded opposition between a 'world of myth' and a 'world of reality' but sets in play a variety of 'reality effects',[36] different 'illusions of reality'. It is simply not the case that the 'elements of the actions . . . are all subjected to a literal minded and prosaic naturalism'[37] or that 'the cause/effect structure of the play may seem as nearly as possible an imitation of the life around him [the average hard-headed audience member]'.[38] Not only is the action to be understood through its literary predecessors, but also the interplay of different levels of constructed literary reality challenges precisely the naive assumption of a naturalistic mimesis. Electra's entrance in rags is upsetting not because it represents reality but because it represents reality in a way which transgresses the conventions of dramatic representation, indeed the representations of reality constructed elsewhere in the play. 'Realism', a self-conscious literary mode that cannot be simply reduced to a transparent reflection of the world, is part of a multiplicity of literary voices in the text. Indeed, the farmer's recognition that Electra's rags, dirt and labour – her 'realism' – are unnecessary but a desired part of Electra's self-dramatization of her situation points precisely to a still further 'illusion of reality'. The multiplicity of voices in Euripidean drama constructs a multiform image of a multiform reality. 'The *propter hoc* structure required by Aristotelian drama is in Euripides everywhere annulled by *created* disorder and formal violence. What we get is *dissonance, disparity, rift, peripeteia*; in Euripides a note of firm tonality is almost always the sign of traditional parody; of the false, the unreal or lost innocence remembered in anguish.'[39] The belief that Euripides was striving to create a 'realistic drama' can be maintained only by extracting one strand from the text and ignoring its relation to the other voices of his theatre.

Through the explicit and innovative use of theatrical device, the bold intertextuality with other plays, through the explicit marking and undercutting of the formal elements of tragedy, through the aggressive subversion of expectation and rapid variation of levels of reality, Euripides constantly forces

[34] Walsh 1977, 278–9.   [35]Walsh 1977, 289.   [36] The phrase is Barthes'.
[37] Gellie 1981, 6.
[38] Gellie 1981, 2.   [39] Arrowsmith 1968, 17.

awareness of his theatre as theatre. But these numerous elements of the self-reflexive and transgressive manipulation of the conventions of genre are not simply the symptoms of a precocious innovativeness (or degenerate *fin de siècle* aesthetic). Rather, they are deeply interwoven in the play's thematic texture. The farmer's remark that he has asked Electra before not to do the work she does amid groans, and that the spring is not far away, immediately introduces a hesitation in our evaluation of Electra's self-description. So, too, her refusal to join the chorus in the festival of Hera and to borrow the necessary clothes – participation in a public festival is 'both an obligation and a cherished privilege for a member of the community'[40] – marks her alienation from her community and her continued willing maintenance of that alien-ation. The description of her life that she offers to Orestes – forced to live with the farmer, spending her time weaving, carrying water and unable to take part in religious festivals (307–10) – seems to contradict or misrepresent these earlier exchanges. In a similar way, Electra's expectations of her brother draw directly on a tradition of heroic myth in her picture of his 'bright and bold' return to Argos, but it is an illusory trust in his heroic qualities. She herself will have to drive him to commit the matricide as he hesitates before the outrage (961ff.), and indeed he has slipped over the frontier in disguise, ready to flee. Electra describes Aegisthus as a drunken abuser of her father's grave (326ff.), a tyrant and bully. The messenger speech presents him as a respectably generous host, properly sacrificing to the Nymphs. So too Electra's exchange with Clytemnestra, who is also motivated by the demands of ritual propriety, has left many critics ill at ease with her dismissal of her mother's arguments and overtures. Does Electra's description of the queen as hated monster coincide with the figure on stage?[41]

This suggestion of a variety of ways of viewing people and actions – a plurality of *logoi* – is developed by the focus on the question of judging character. The farmer's opening speech describes his unwillingness to have sexual relations with Electra. He concludes (50–4):

> Whoever says that I am a born fool to keep
> a young girl in my house and never touch her body,
> or says I measure sense by a crooked line
> of judgement, should know that he is as great a fool as I.

The word for 'sense' is *sophron*, which, as I considered in Chapter 5 with regard to *Hippolytus*, is a key fifth-century term, related not only to general behaviour or attitudes but also to specifically sexual behaviour. The question of judging the boundaries and norms of behaviour raised by the farmer's position is seen in terms of other people's contrary opinions; which the farmer amusingly inverts in his final remark. Anyone who calls him fool can have the same title.

The measurement or judgement of character and behaviour is brought further to the fore in Electra's and Orestes' opening exchange. The disguised Orestes questions Electra at length not only to find out the conditions of her life but also to discover the motivations and behaviour of her husband. Why has he not slept with his wife? The stichomythia sets the young man's expectations of behaviour against Electra's description in a way that marks the variety and error in judging personality and intention (254–61):

> Electra: He is a poor man but well-born and he respects me.
> Orestes: Respects? What does your husband understand by 'respect'?
> El.: He has never been violent or touched me in my bed.
> Or.: A vow of chastity? Or he finds you unattractive?
> El.: He finds it attractive not to insult my royal blood.
> Or.: How could he not be pleased at marrying so well?
> El.: He judges the man who gave me had no right to, stranger.
> Or.: I see – afraid Orestes might avenge your honour.
> El.: Afraid of that, yes – he is also decent by nature.

At each point, Orestes' suggestions reveal his expectations of behaviour and attitude, which differ markedly from Electra's explanations. The disjunction between his almost comical question 'he finds you unattractive?', 'unworthy?' and the princess's reply, 'He finds it attractive not to insult my royal blood' stresses the plurality of value systems set in motion by the different strands of this play. Indeed, Electra's final comment, which once more corrects Orestes' oversimplification of the farmer's motivations, picks up the farmer's own opening remarks. The word translated 'decent' is *sophron*, and the suggestion that the farmer is *sophron* by nature – a remark which draws on the opposition of nature and nurture discussed in Chapter 9 – looks towards Orestes' long speech precisely on the problem of evaluating characters and the possible tests for distinguishing man's worth (367–8):

> Alas,
> there is nothing accurate for testing manly worth.
> The characters (*phusis*) of mortals hold confusion.

As I argued in Chapter 9, this speech works through the interlocking moral and social categories of wealth and nobility to challenge, in a sophistic manner, the hierarchy of traditional values. The applicability of his 'penny philosopher'[42] argument to the speaker himself is emphasized in the short scene

[42] O'Brien 1964, 28.

between the farmer and Electra that follows. Electra complains that they can't possibly entertain noble guests in their hovel. The farmer retorts (406–7):

> Why? If they are gentlemen as they seem
> Will they not respect the small and great alike?

The possibility that people are not what they seem, particularly that the external signs of nobility – as opposed to the farmer's natural qualities – may be counterfeit is all too relevant to the strangers in the house.

The exchange between Electra and Clytemnestra is similarly important to this sense of motivation and character evaluation. Clytemnestra (1011–50) constructs a complex picture of why she killed Agamemnon, outlining the build-up of her reasons. Her final personal motivation – the arrival of the adulterous Agamemnon with his second 'bride' – leads to an interesting generalization (1035–8):

> Women are fools; deny it I shall not.
> But since this is the case, when husbands choose
> to despise the bed they have, a woman is quite willing
> to imitate her man and find another friend.

She uses the same term, 'fool', to describe the female sex and their lack of sexual restraint, as the farmer had used to describe people's possible reproach of his chastity. As the farmer turned the word back on its users, here the queen reverses her argument: women are only imitating men, who make the mistake of giving their wives the cause and opportunity to 'find another friend'.

Electra significantly rejects this argument in terms of her mother's attitude of mind, 'How I wish your mind were healthy!' (1061), and in terms of the queen's false representation of her adultery. Clytemnestra, who painted her face and set her curls by the mirror, looked only for an excuse for killing her husband (1066–8): 'You brought ruin on the finest man in Greece and screened it with the argument that for your child you killed your husband. The world knows you less well than I.' It is the screen of arguments that Electra wants to pierce in order to represent the truth of her mother's motivation.

The queen's response to her daughter's venom is to resort to an explanation based on 'human nature' (1102–4):

> My child, from birth you always have adored your father.
> This is part of life. Some children are always for
> the male, some love their mothers more closely than their father.

Clytemnestra's words – a parody of the arguments in the trial scene of the *Eumenides* – attempt to deflect the aggressive *agon*. The specificity of Electra's argument is understood – or suppressed – as an example of a character trait which fits into a well-known pattern of behaviour.

The echoes and rewritings of the Aeschylean and Homeric Orestes together with this regular focus on the question of character and the judgement of motivation are essential to the understanding of Euripides' version of Orestes' and Electra's place in the myth. For sure, Euripides depicts Orestes' character and actions as falling short in terms of earlier heroic models of nobility, and indeed the poet also questions how acceptable the morality of a myth of just matricide can be. But the dramatist also opens to scrutiny the criteria for making such evaluations of nobility and the paradigms involved in the choice of action and behaviour. Time and again, characters behave or hold opinions or are described according to a model – of behaviour, values, expectations – which is itself undermined in the text of the play. Electra, the 'most ostentatious martyr in Greek tragedy',[43] characterizes and dramatizes her own situation, her brother, her mother according to a vision of things that is questioned by the action and characterization of the drama. Orestes' expectations and intellectualism are quite insufficient in evaluating the farmer – or himself. The queen's expression of her motivation is challenged by Electra's version of events, which itself seems far from a privileged expression of the truth. With Euripides, the myth and the characters of myth are fractured in a series of competing *logoi*, different readings, different paradigms for behaviour and understanding. The different illusions of reality set in play by the text's self-reflexive awareness and transgressions of theatrical conventions also provide a model of the characters' manipulation and distortion of self-image and of the rules of conformity. Euripides' play is as concerned with questions of correct behaviour and is as paradigmatic and didactic as Aeschylus' *Oresteia*, but it is the instability of competing moral paradigms, the dangers of fitting events and behaviour into an over-rigid paradigm, that the play dramatizes.

This uncertainty surrounding paradigms for behaviour and particularly the paradigmatic status of myth is forcefully illustrated by the chorus. They have just rehearsed the tale of how the sun fled in horror at Thyestes' crimes – an apparently straightforward example of a choric song which deepens the moral sense of the dramatic action, and which again manipulates a contrast between the heroic world and the present inheritors of family violence.[44] But their final stanza begins (737–41):

---

[43] O'Brien 1964, 28.   [44] On the golden lamb in this play, see Kubo 1966; Rosivach 1978.

Thus it is always told.
I am won only to light belief
that the sun would swerve or change his gold
chamber of fire, moved in pain
at sorrow and sin in the mortal world, to judge or punish man.
Yet fearful myths are gifts
which call men to the worship of god.

After the tale of the golden lamb and the sins of the brothers, Thyestes and Atreus – grandfather and great uncle of Orestes and Electra – the chorus with characteristic Euripidean alienation distance themselves from their own story. The *logos* is as they've told it but it brings even for the tellers scant belief. This lack of belief, moreover, is turned in their final remark to an open intellectual scepticism that has disturbed many critics. Myths which inculcate fear have a certain usefulness in turning people to religion – though this remark in itself is far from certain in tone in view of their own disbelief and since the worship of the gods in this play is scarcely invested with moral certainty. The chorus proclaim that a tale's lack of truth does not affect its didactic value. Clytemnestra, they conclude briefly, did not heed the warnings of such myths when she killed Agamemnon (744–5).

The poet's traditional protestation of the truth of his words authorizes his function as educator of the citizens (in which the chorus plays a fundamental role).[45] But here the Euripidean chorus, while maintaining the didactic value of myth, challenge the traditional connection of ideas underlying such didacticism when they deny that a tale's truth guarantees its value. How, then, are we to read Euripides' telling of the Orestes myth? An unbelievable tale of fear? To turn men to the gods? The chorus' ode questions the status of the play itself as myth. The effect of the chorus' alienation is to prevent the unrecognized working of myth's ideological power to underpin a moral and social discourse. Rather, the ideological functioning of myth is held up to view, a recognition of its use is forced into the light, its value and manipulation as a paradigm is laid open to question.

This stanza, then, illustrates in a bold fashion the connection between the self-reflexiveness of Euripidean theatrical technique and the thematic considerations of the *Electra*. The chorus tell their story and deny their belief in it: once more, a level of reality is developed in order to be dismissed. The alienation of the chorus from its song points towards and transgresses the conventions of telling myths in theatre. But in the suggestion that such myths still have some value as exemplary tales, the choric ode also points towards the theme of the complex relations between paradigm and behaviour, between a

45 See above, Chapter 6.

myth and the people who live it out. The self-reflexiveness and the intel-lectualism of the Euripidean chorus also highlight and develop the themes of the play.

The recognition scene has already been discussed in terms of its intertextua-lity with the *Oresteia*, how it develops a sense of competing paradigms of explanation and behaviour – which are important for the way the *Electra* fragments and disturbs the moral and social focus of the *Oresteia*'s para-digmatic use of the Orestes story. But it also develops the formulation of Euripides' thematic interest in judgement and evaluation in a different way. For the scene constructs the problem of evaluation as a problem of the interpretation of signs. What is the conclusion to be drawn from the signs the old man offers, how are they to be read? This process of judging from marks, signs applies to the recognition of people also. When Orestes appears on stage, the old man circles round him – to Orestes' surprise – 'as if he were analysing the stamp on a coin' (558–9). And when the old man declares the stranger to be her long-lost brother, Electra asks (572) 'What stamp have you seen to persuade me?', and from the proof of the scar she admits she is persuaded (577–8) 'by the tokens you show'. The word for 'stamp' or 'mark' is *charakter*, which comes in later Greek to be used for 'the type' of a personality. The face of Orestes is like a coin whose value can be read, or rather, the image of the coin serves also to mark the problem of human evaluation, since, unlike a coin, the value of a personality and the judgement of a person's worth or behaviour cannot be discovered simply from the external indications of worth.[46] The relations between people's internal life and the external attitudes and attributes, the problem of competing explanations of motivation, compet-ing comprehension and expressions of reality, become through the recognition scene a problem of the relation between signs and what they signify.

The image of the face as coin is linked, then, in a more than superficial way with the interest in wealth and value in Electra. As we saw in Chapter 6, the traditional Greek associations of wealth, moral worth and social position are challenged specifically by the juxtaposition of the farmer and Orestes. The play questions the conventional means of judging a man in terms of his external or material attributes, and the image of the coin recalls the con-testation that wealth is a deceptive guide to value, as it marks the difficulty of interpreting signs. As Gellie writes, the theme of the *Electra* is 'How do you read the signs?'.[47]

This question of how to read the signs – essential to the maintenance and challenging of both morality and conventionality – is also an important strand of *Hippolytus*, where in particular the disjunction between a person's words as

[46] See Tarkow 1981, 151.   [47] 1981, 5.

external signs and his mind as the inward site of intention and desire is summed up in Hippolytus' scandalous remark 'My tongue swore but my mind is unsworn.' But this disjunction between inwardness and external signs has also been linked by several influential writers specifically to the self-reflexiveness of Euripides' late drama. John Jones has written on how Euripides' characteristic interests in the contrast between illusion and reality, between external signs and inwardness, between secrecy and revealing demand a recognition of the possibility of a disjunction between a mask and its wearer. Euripides' 'penetrative enquiry, ... precisely because it forces attention behind the surface show, threatens to destroy the masking convention'.[48] The mask, he writes, 'can present all manner of versions of the human self ... But it is vulnerable at one point. It cannot maintain itself against the thought that all presentational modes are inadequate to the truth.'[49] It is precisely the relation between 'presentational modes' and the truth that is put at stake by the various conflicting voices and manners of representation in Euripidean drama. For Jones, Euripides threatens the convention of masking, by treating it as a cover over a hidden inwardness.

Indeed, Zeitlin describes this fragmentation of Euripides' theatre as 'the creation of a turbulent text',[50] where the past is seen as a 'closet of masks' to be raided by characters in search of a role. 'Words, gestures and acts can be drawn out of the original contexts for the purposes of play, distortion, and dissonance, for reduction of meaning, for parodistic echo and above all for a kind of treasonous, deliberate misunderstanding.'[51] She quotes a remark of Hartman, which seems especially applicable to the vision of the *Electra*. He writes of the situation 'when men, distorting rather than exploring art's commonwealth, its link with an interpretable fund of roles, fall back on narrow concepts of manliness and re-enact those tragedies of revenge which society was founded to control'.[52] For Zeitlin and Jones, like Hartman, the disturbance of dramatic form is a function of a view of man in his culture. It is 'the disruption caused by his way of apprehending the human self'[53] that is constantly implied in Euripides' self-reflexive disruption of theatrical convention. It is Euripides' view of the crisis of culture, the crisis of self-representation in culture that is instantiated in the crisis of form which his plays enact.

The 'whole range of mask piercing and ... mask exploiting effects'[54] culminates in the use of masks in the *Bacchae*, a play which is often regarded as a return to a more traditional form, even a recantation by Euripides, but which provides an extremely important example of the self-reflexive awareness of

---

[48] 1962, 260.   [49] 1962, 45.
[50] 1980, 57. 'Turbulence' is Arrowsmith's term also, see 1968, 13.
[51] 1980, 57.   [52] Hartman 1975, 107.   [53] Jones 1962, 241.   [54] Jones 1962, 270.

genre. Dionysus, the patron god of the drama festival, speaks the prologue to the *Bacchae* in which he announces that he has come in disguise to Thebes to enforce his recognition. The god of theatre appears on his own stage, in costume and in disguise, and he will be honoured in the play by the chorus of Dionysus' worshippers – actors trained for the festival in order to honour Dionysus. Divinities in Homer and elsewhere, particularly when asserting their power over mortals in easy deception, are often depicted as smiling, and the mask of Dionysus is fixed in a smile.[55] Emphasis is laid upon Dionysus' disguise, but the smiling mask identifies him for the audience precisely as a divinity in disguise. The prologue makes it 'quite clear to the audience that the speaker whom they accept as a god will be accepted as a man by the people on stage'.[56] As Foley puts it, 'the audience sees by his mask that the stranger is a god, but Pentheus has no such theatrical cues by which to recognize him ... One mask represents two meanings in a manner that captures the central irony of the dramatic action.'[57] But it is not only in the element of disguise that the mask of Dionysus plays a double role with regard to its representation. For 'the god's mask remains smiling, but the visual effect of this smile does not remain consistent'.[58] The smile of the stranger who allows himself to be captured with ease and who brings a relaxed harmony to his adherents, by the end of the play's violence may seem 'a divine sneer, a ghoulish expression of inappropriate glee at a vengeance too easily executed'.[59] Rather than the convention whereby a tragic mask represents one character and one meaning, the smiling mask of the god of dramatic illusion becomes ambiguous. The smile of Dionysus becomes inscrutable. How are the destructive and benign forces of the god to be linked in the single sign of the smiling mask?

This suggestive exploitation of the mask as a mask, that is, as a possible symbol or disguise, is closely linked to the religious sense of the *Bacchae*. As I will consider in more depth in the next chapter, the possibility of directly perceiving or comprehending Dionysus is undermined by the constant questioning of Pentheus' vision of the multifaceted god who controls representation. Dionysus, as Foley has argued, is seen particularly through his maenads or in the miracles which distort vision: 'The action demonstrates the god's divinity indirectly and symbolically and denies that we can adequately "see" Dionysus with human eyes.'[60] The recognition of Dionysus is also, then, partly a recognition that the god's mysterious divinity and power is finally beyond the control of human knowledge, and it is precisely the perception of the dramatic convention of the mask which draws attention to

[55] See Rosenmeyer 1963, 106–10; Foley 1980, 126ff.; Segal 1982, 223ff.
[56] Dodds 1960, ad 53–4.
[57] 1980, 128.   [58] Foley 1980, 129.   [59] Foley 1980, 129.   [60] 1980, 132.

the barriers between the god and man. 'Euripides makes his anomalous, "untragic" mask become the central mocking image of what we as men can understand of a force that cannot be fully captured by human vision.'[61]

Pentheus, the man who struggles to capture the god, is himself finally reduced to a mere mask (1277–8):

> Cadmus: And whose head do you hold in your arms?
> Agave: A lion's, or so the hunters said.

The word translated 'head' is *prosopon*, which also means 'face' and in particular 'mask'.[62] What Agave holds represents to the audience and Cadmus the character Pentheus. He has become only a mask. To Agave under the influence of Dionysus, Pentheus' mask seems to be that of a lion. The mask is the locus of illusion. But this mask, too, has a further double countenance. It demonstrates on the one hand the successful punishment of the hubristic Pentheus. The chorus prayed (1020–1) 'O Bacchus come, come with your smiling mask/face (*prosopon*). Cast your noose about this man who hunts your Bacchae', and the fulfilment of this prayer is made doubly effective with the contrast of the smiling *prosopon* of Dionysus and the bloody *prosopon* of Pentheus.[63] But on the other hand, it also represents the horror of child-murder into which Agave has been lured.[64] The queen is drawn by Cadmus' words to recognize her son – as she had failed to do on the mountain when he himself had attempted to throw off the maenad's disguise – and in so recognizing the mask in her arms she attests to the two faces of Dionysus' power. As Pentheus saw two suns, two cities, two sets of gates (918–19), seeing double is the mark of Dionysus' influence.

Pentheus' journey to the mountain is preceded by an extraordinary scene in which Dionysus compels the king and hoplite to change his costume and become the god's player and worshipper, as a maenad, a woman. The external marks of recognition shift under Dionysus' manipulation of representation as once more Euripides suggests a split between inward and outward signs of personality. The costume Pentheus is to adopt is described in detail, and when it is put on, Pentheus fusses carefully about the proper wearing of the robes for his new role (928–38):

> Dionysus: One of your curls has come loose from under the band,
>   where I tucked it.
> Pentheus: It must have worked loose
>   when I was dancing for joy and shaking my head.

---

[61] Foley 1980, 133.
[62] Segal 1982, 248 n. 33, notes that there is no unambiguous use of *prosopon* as 'mask' before Demosthenes and Aristotle.
[63] Cf. Segal 1982, 249.   [64] Cf. Taplin 1978, 98–100.

Di.: Let me be your attendant and tuck it back. Hold still.
Pe.: Arrange it. I am in your hands completely.
Di.: And now your strap has slipped, yes,
    and your robe hangs askew at the ankles.
Pe.: I think so. At least on my right leg.
    But on the left the hem lies straight.

Dionysus, ironically calling himself Pentheus' attendant as if the roles of god and man were reversed, helps Pentheus prepare himself to be a victim. Pentheus is indeed in his attendant's hands. The illusion in Pentheus' mind caused by the power of Dionysus is reflected in the dramatic illusion of the change of his costume according to Dionysus' instructions. The god of theatre uses 'theatrical weapons'[65] to destroy Pentheus, and, in the costuming of Pentheus as maenad, the delusion of madness overlaps with the illusion of staging. The costuming by the god, the madness of Pentheus and the theatrical illusion of the play all fall under the aegis of Dionysus and his control and shifting of representation.

This 'play-within-the-play'[66] effect of costuming a character on stage to play a part in the action – which, as we will see in the next chapter, is also described in theatrical terms – has been prepared for notably in two earlier passages. When Pentheus is faced first by the captured Dionysus, he threatens to take the curls and wand of the stranger in a grimly prophetic manner (493–5):

Pentheus: First, I shall cut off your girlish cirls.
Dionysus: My hair is holy. My curls belong to the god.
Pe.: Second, you will surrender your wand.
Di.: *You* take it. It belongs to Dionysus.

Pentheus will indeed take up the curls and wand of Dionysus in order to play his part in the worship of the god – as victim. As he threatens to abuse Dionysus here, so Dionysus with mocking kindness helps him dress in the costume he despised.

Pentheus' first rejection of Bacchic costume, however, is in the first scene, where Teiresias, the seer, and Cadmus, the founder of Thebes, prepare to go to the mountain and honour the new god. They are the only men who are 'right thinking' (195–6). The spectacle of the two old men, dressed as women, preparing to shake their white locks for the god, has often been regarded as comic, particularly in juxtaposition to the chorus of female, Asiatic worshippers of the god – although the precise degree of humour is often disagreed on.[67] Indeed, Old Comedy often manipulates for comic effect the scenario of a character attempting a task which seems quite out of character, and costume

[65] Foley 1980, 113.   [66] Both Foley and Segal use this phrase.
[67] See Seidensticker 1978, 1 ff., for a survey of views.

change, particularly involving a change of sex, is often used for the misunder-standings and parodies of farce. The introduction of this apparently comic technique into the *Bacchae*, as with the opening scenes of the *Electra*, transgresses the expectations of tragic genre. 'From the point of view of traditional tragedy nothing is more strikingly novel than the Euripidean fusion and contrast of comic and tragic effects.'[68] But as with the *Electra* the manipulation and disruption of convention is not simply to draw attention to the work of art as a work of art, or for mere cleverness or wit. For not only do the old men present an approach to Dionysus which is markedly in contrast with Pentheus' and the chorus' attitudes, but also the suggestions of comedy in this tragedy significantly draw together the two genres of Dionysus' theatre. Both comedy and tragedy are theatres of transgression. In both, boundaries and norms are subverted. In comedy, misunderstanding, manipulation of levels of reality in fantasy or farce, even violence and aggressively anti-social behaviour are received with laughter. In comedy 'the consequences are minimal, temporary and certainly not deadly'.[69] In the *Bacchae*, however, Pentheus' misunderstanding and violence prompt a terrible divine punish-ment, which turns comedy's licence to a grimly rejected potentiality. 'The identical theatrical techniques expose with accelerating horror the inadequacy of man to understand or control either himself or his environment. Dionysiac madness becomes the dark double of comic befuddlement.'[70] Euripides' drama articulates a closeness between the tragic and comic transgressions of man's illusions. It is in part that Pentheus' recostuming offers a painfully serious parallel for the old men's posturing which makes the level of laughter in the first scene so disagreed on.

   The critics' disagreement, then, is not just because of the apparently inevitable subjectivity which is involved in trying to answer a question framed in the form 'How serious/comic are the late plays of Euripides?' For the instability introduced into dramatic form by Euripides' mixing of tragic and comic elements challenges precisely the security of the reader or audience of his dramatic texts. In subverting an audience's expectations, which are formed by the conventions of the genre, Euripides forces awareness also of the conventions of interpreting drama, the role of one's conventional expectations in reading. This constant disruption of the audience's stable development of a sense of form, a pattern of narrative, a mode of expression, constantly works to alienate the reader or audience from the appropriation of the work into a ready-made structure of conventional response. The reader or audience member is implicated in interpretation, and forced to recognize in such involvement the challenge to his/her paradigms and conventions of under-

[68] Arrowsmith 1968, 22.   [69] Foley 1980, 116.   [70] Ibid.

standing. The self-reflexive theatrical devices of Euripidean drama also function to challenge the reader's awareness of his self.

I will return in the next chapter to the *Bacchae*'s sense of theatricality, which I have begun to outline here. But I have sufficiently indicated, I hope, the way that Euripides' last masterpiece, so often considered almost Aeschylean in its formal structure, also shows the concern with theatre as theatre that I have stressed in this chapter – both Euripides' sense of genre and his willingness to transgress the conventions and forms of the drama he inherited. This self-reflexivity is not the collapse of a noble genre into an embarrassed or embarrassing self-consciousness; rather, the continually experimental pushing of the formal aspects of genre to and beyond its limits is closely linked with other key elements of Euripidean theatre. The interest in the relations between inward and outward signs and attitudes of behaviour, and how to read those signs; the awareness and questioning of the place of paradigms in behaviour and moral choice; the role of the past in the determination of the present; the role of representation and of self-image in culture; are all implicated in Euripides' self-reflexive drama. The divisiveness, fragmentation, ironies and dissonances of his theatre stem from and express an attitude to man's beliefs and actions in a complex society. Above all, Euripides in forcing awareness of the conventions of writing tragedy also forces recognition of the conventions of approaching tragedy as a reader or audience. The constant disruptions of expectations of form, narrative or expression are aimed at the reader and audience of tragedy and constantly disrupt his/her security. The awareness of the literary or theatrical status of these plays does not produce simply a sense of the work of art as monument, but a sense of the instability of man's place in society as a reader of signs.

11 · PERFORMANCE AND PERFORMABILITY

> The end and the beginning were always there.
>
> T. S. ELIOT

The *Bacchae* is a particularly fitting work with which to end my study of Greek tragedy. Not only is it one of the latest extant plays – Euripides' final masterpiece – but also the dense texture of image and theme in this extraordinary drama recalls so many of the ideas I have explored in the previous chapters. It is a text concerned with a man and a city and relations with the divine (embodied in the disguised Dionysus), and the work has often been read as a fundamentally religious statement, either in terms of a defence of Dionysus (justified divine vengeance); or an attack on the malicious element of destruction and disorder in Dionysiac or similar cult attitudes; or in terms of a recognition and demonstration of the necessary place of the irrational in man.[1] As Foley has recently written, 'the text undeniably raises questions about the nature of divinity and reflects the precariousness of social and political life in late fifth-century Athens'.[2]

This precariousness of social and political order is reflected precisely in the terms in which I have been discussing the transgressions and subversions of tragedy. The young man and new ruler Pentheus is faced by a threat from the outside – Dionysus from the east. This threat, however, is instantiated in the behaviour of the women of the city, who have deserted their places inside houses and inside the city to run wild in the wilds of the mountains. There, they veer between living in an atmosphere of uncanny calm amid the bountifulness of nature, and practising a savage parody of a hunt, in which they rip apart animals with their bare hands. Pentheus attempts to maintain order in the face of this overthrow of normal behaviour. He refuses to accept Dionysus as a divinity and reviles Teiresias and Cadmus, his grandfather, for dressing in the cult's female dress of fawn-skin and dancing for the god. He attempts to bind the disguised god and threatens to take his army out against the women. But Dionysus overcomes Pentheus in a grimly horrific way.

---

[1] This is the most prevalent view. See Dodds 1960; Winnington-Ingram 1948; Segal 1982; Foley 1985.

[2] 1985, 205–6.

Pentheus is tormented with images and distorted visions under the influence of Dionysus; and finally he is persuaded to dress like a Bacchant and to go to spy on the women's rites. The god helps him into his costume and leads him out of the city. In the mountains Pentheus completes his horrific devotion to the god as a victim of *sparagmos*, a violent dismemberment at the hands of the women led by his mother. Like a returning victor or hunter, Agave brings home her son's head on a stake. In the final scenes of the play, the queen is led out of her illusion and into a recognition of her grievous state by her father, Cadmus. Dionysus announces he will continue his journey through Greece demanding recognition.

The clash between the smiling god in his desire for recognition and the human ruler in his attempt to maintain social order is played out, then, in many of the oppositions and images we have seen in the course of this book. The opposition of male and female roles is subverted not only by Dionysus' influence on the women of the city, but also in the figure of Dionysus himself, a male described as looking like a woman, with effeminate hair and appearance. Pentheus, the male ruler and soldier, is led out of the city in woman's garb to be destroyed by the bare hands of female hunters. Before his violent end, however, Pentheus tries but fails to restrain the god, whose verbal and visual deceptions continually undermine the king's attempted control. As I have already pointed out, the *Bacchae* returns obsessively to the values of *sophia* (wisdom, intelligence) in its depiction of divinely induced madness. In these clashes of human and god, male and female, Greek and barbarian, inside and outside, city and mountain, sense and madness, indeed, order and instability, the *Bacchae* develops the threat to the institution of the city in terms of the discourse of the city. Dionysus works to invert the oppositions by which the city defines itself, undermining differences, forcing a 'crisis of symbols',[3] bringing the city face to face with a sense of the other.[4] We saw in Chapter 3 how Dionysus' festival was a festival of transgression. In Euripides' play, which brings on stage the patron of the festival, the drama itself also depicts Dionysus' overturning of social norms.

It is not surprising that such a closely interwoven network of imagery and ideas has provoked a wide range of critical response – including some of the finest contemporary studies of Greek drama. In particular, the *Bacchae* has provided a key text for writers from disciplines outside the mainstream of classical criticism, particularly psychoanalytic[5] and anthropological studies,[6] and although it is such a late play, the *Bacchae* has also been taken as an important document not only for Dionysiac religion in general, but also for the

[3] Segal's phrase.   [4] See Vernant 1985.   [5] See Green 1969; Sale 1977.
[6] See Girard 1977; Segal 1982; Dodds 1951; and the useful introduction of Foley 1985.

specific relation between Dionysus and the tragic festival.[7] The *Bacchae* is the play which most often has prompted classicists to move beyond the confines of their discipline, and it would be difficult now to imagine what a reading of the *Bacchae* might look like without the valuable input of these varied traditions of scholarship. But rather than using the insights and methods of the previous chapters to produce a reading of the *Bacchae* that would stand as a sort of summary or summation of my previous arguments, I want in this final chapter to turn to a subject which many contemporary critics would put first in a discussion of tragedy, namely, the question of performance and stagecraft. In the previous chapter, I considered briefly some ways in which the *Bacchae* has been seen as a text particularly concerned with the theatrical experience as such. In this chapter, I wish to investigate further the relations between this self-reflexive concern with representation and the performance and performability of the tragic text.

There are special circumstances surrounding the first production of this play, and special characteristics of the drama in terms of stagecraft that make it a particularly interesting example through which to consider the questions of performance, but first I want briefly to look at a topic which is always a major concern for a modern viewer or producer of Greek tragedy, primarily because of the difference between modern and ancient theatrical conventions: that is, the chorus. In Chapter 6, I mentioned the important role of choruses in sixth- and fifth-century educational attitudes and I quoted Plato's remark that a person was not educated without the experiences of dancing and singing in the chorus. In the same chapter, I also referred to Vernant's influential comment that the tragic chorus offers 'an anonymous and collective being whose role is to express through its fears, hopes and judgements, the feelings of the spectators who make up the civic community'. It is clear that there is more at stake in discussing the chorus than the awkwardness felt by a modern audience, used to the illusion of intimacy and personal revelation in theatre, when faced by the continual presence on stage of a group of people other than the actors.

Modern critics have only very rarely supported the untenable view that the chorus simply represents the authorial voice – the views of the poet – but it is also the case that the varying degrees of characterization and involvement of the chorus in the action make it difficult to accept Vernant's remarks without considerable qualification. For although a chorus in Greek drama often expresses and reverts to traditional morality or the statements of a civic ideal, there are many exceptions to this general trend, and great differences in the utilization of such ideas or norms. The Erinyes in Aeschylus' *Eumenides*, for example, play a major role in the trilogy, arguing a case and a position which

[7] See Dodds 1960, introduction ix–xxxiii; Seaford 1981.

are seen as transcended by the male, civic order. Similarly, the choruses of Aeschylus' *Persae* and *Supplices*, a group of Persian elders, and fifty half-Greek virgins respectively, can scarcely be said simply to represent the 'feelings of the spectators'. The chorus in plays like the *Eumenides* are also major participants in the action, but even in the *Agamemnon* and *Choephoroi* the chorus plays a significant role in events, not merely as an interlocutor or commentator on the action in their odes. It is the chorus of the *Choephoroi*, for example, which persuades the nurse to change the message she takes to Aegisthus. So too in Sophocles' extant dramas, the chorus has often seemed to critics to be carefully characterized and to play a significant role in the development of the action not just in the deepening of the mythic and moral background of the events on stage in the choric odes, but also in their reaction to and involvement in the business on the stage. The chorus of the *Ajax*, Ajax's own sailors, while offering little that could not be regarded as traditionalist morality, are also closely involved in Ajax's fate as his dependants. Even in the *Antigone*, where the chorus of *polis* elders might be expected to demonstrate clearly *polis* morality and concerns, the attitude of the chorus to Antigone and Creon is sufficiently uncertain to have prompted considerable critical discussion[8] – which may in itself indicate the difficulty of fitting the tensions set in motion by Antigone's and Creon's violent debates into the discourse of the *polis*. One may also mention that both ancient and modern critics have seen already in Euripides signs of the development of Greek drama towards the use of choric odes as decorative songs between acts but without specific relevance to the action. It is also worth recalling that in Chapters 9 and 10 we saw how the criterion of relevance has all too often been used without the care necessary for appreciating Euripides' writing. The *Bacchae* itself, however, provides a special case for Euripidean drama. For 'in no other extant Greek play since Aeschylus . . . is the chorus so prominent'[9] and, moreover, 'their songs are clearly of fundamental importance for an understanding of the play'.[10] In respect of the chorus, too, then, the *Bacchae* is an important example of Euripidean dramaturgy.

If this variety of characterization and use of the chorus make it difficult to regard the chorus simply as representing civic values, is there any generalizable status or position that we may accord the group in the orchestra? There is one fascinating specific opportunity opened by the use of the chorus in ancient drama which seems especially important, as well as helpful in restressing Vernant's insight about the functioning of the chorus in relation to the hero. The presence of a group separated spatially and conceptually from the hero on

---

[8] See e.g. Winnington-Ingram 1980, 137ff. and his bibliography there.
[9] Winnington-Ingram 1948, 2.   [10] Ibid.

the stage introduces a series of relations between an individual and a wider body that are essential for the public functioning of Greek drama. For sure, at moments when the chorus exhort a heroic character in the language of the city's moral imperatives, it is easy to see the chorus as mediating the fifth-century audience's reaction, or as dramatizing the disjunction of a particular individual like Ajax from his surrounding society. But there are many variations of the dialectic of individual and group made possible by the chorus as institution that stress in different ways the importance of the group to the conception of human interaction in these dramas.

The three dramatists' portrayals of Electra point to the variety of inter-relation effectively. In the *Choephoroi*, Electra is separated from the chorus to prepare for the libations and recognition. In the dialogue before the prayer that accompanies the libation, we saw how Electra's questioning about the correct language of prayer distinguishes her concern for the morality of the case from the chorus' direct desire for revenge. For Electra, a family tie with Clytemnestra necessarily affects the position she adopts before the recognition and the *kommos*. As the matricide with its focus on son and mother approaches, Electra is returned to silence within the house – the daughter's position. The chorus of women pray and await the outcome of the conflict of mother and son with a direct, if less problematic, concern for the house of Atreus.

In Sophocles' *Electra*, however, a play which constantly echoes Aeschylus' drama, the position is reversed as the chorus fail to match up to the passionate intensity of Electra's hatred. They join her in lamentation, in expectation, and finally they stand together outside the house waiting and listening as the matricide is perpetrated. But the chorus' songs cannot equal Electra's single-minded loathing of Clytemnestra and her lack of any scruple in desire for vengeance. Unlike the *Choephoroi*, where, as the matricide takes place, a choral ode is sung about the narrative leading up to the revenge, explaining, justifying, qualifying Orestes' action, in Sophocles' *Electra* we see Electra still on stage with the chorus, the focus of the action, waiting, exhorting matricide. The picture of Electra still outside the closed door of the house pleading for the blows to be struck again marks the shift of emphasis in the depiction of the daughter of Agamemnon, particularly through the different relation of individual and group, actor and chorus.

Euripides' *Electra* comes closest to Vernant's description of the chorus and their civic values. The chorus on their way to the Argive festival, as we have seen, offer a picture of socialization and religious behaviour denied to Electra, at least in part by her own attitudes. The interplay of actor and chorus, of individual and group, rather than the violent disjunction of Ajax and the world around him, suggests with characteristic Euripidean irony the complex interweavings of self-projection and social norms.

In each of these three plays, the connections and disjunctions of chorus and actor are essential not only to the characterization of the players but also to the development of the ideas and form of the play. The public sense of character or behaviour that must constantly be recalled in the reading of these plays is developed by the constant interaction of individual not merely with other individuals but also with a group constituted as a group, the chorus.

This sense of the interrelations of an individual and a notion of group is especially important in the light of the wider tensions of Greek tragedy. We have often seen how concern for personality is expressed in terms of conflicting ties of household and *polis* and how the obligations of the individual to the community are a tenet of radical democracy explored in different ways in many of these dramas. This sense of the interrelations of individual and family and state is developed in particularly clear fashion by the ties and conflicts of actor and chorus: Antigone's position of antagonism towards her uncle's rule is focused more sharply by her relation to the chorus of noble statesmen. Aeschylus' Electra's attitudes to and status in the house of Atreus are defined in complement with and contrast to the chorus of household slaves. The chorus of civic elders in Sophocles' *Oedipus Tyrannus* constantly places the turmoil of the house of Laius in the context of the city of Thebes. The dramas of the civic festival through the state-financed chorus – being chosen to produce a play for the festival was referred to as being 'granted a chorus' – express again and again through their structuring an individual action in terms of a wider group depicted as a group in the chorus. A comparison with a modern play like Anouilh's *Antigone*, which keeps a chorus, but as a single actor, shows the importance of the group as such, in developing the social, political, and ethical attitudes of Greek drama. In Anouilh, the chorus becomes another actor, a ringmaster, a master commentator on the action, a mediating figure between the audience and the action, but without the sense of wider social formation (which is completely subsumed into Creon's arguments about the state). The increased sense of individualism, of personal conscience, in Anouilh's version of *Antigone* is seen directly in the voice of the chorus as individual, if privileged, commentator. The chorus constantly provides for Greek tragedy the possibility of a wider social and political context and of regarding the individual in such a context. The possibilities of form offered by the chorus work always to extend the drama from an interest in the individual *per se*.

The drama festival also included a competition for boys' and mens' choruses, and this reminder of the extensive role of the chorus outside the context of tragedy or comedy points to another important function of the chorus in drama. For the chorus, as I have already said, in its educative role may be seen to preserve, transmit and explore the values of society specifically through the telling and retelling of myth, and the chorus of tragedy often works to place the action within different mythic traditions and values (which need not coincide with 'civic values'). As much as the dialectic of individual actor and chorus is essential to the development of the social sense of character, so the dialectic of action and choric stasimon often develops significantly the sense of the events portrayed on stage in relation to a more generalized collection of traditional values and stories. The chorus functions to extend the intellectual and normative context of the dramatized events. The use of the chorus outside drama, then, also helps us recognize the special status of the chorus within drama both as a characterized group within the world of the play and also as a commentator, expander, mediator between the actors and the audience.

This dual status is important to maintain. Victorian critics and their modern heirs have been keen to view the chorus as a source of privileged access to the views of the poet, or, far more commonly, to the meaning of the drama. But as we have seen many times in this book, the chorus' role is often important rather for its insufficient understanding of events, for its failing attempts to offer complete explanations, for the juxtaposition of the passionate individualism of the hero to a less extreme, more traditional attitude. In the previous paragraphs, I used the word 'dialectic' to express the relation between individual and group, story and mythic or traditional expression precisely in order to suggest that meaning in tragedy is produced *in the relation between* actor and chorus, scene and stasimon (rather than that the chorus offers a hypostasized, privileged commentary on the action). It is this dialectic, this play of *difference*, that is in part the reason why tragedy is a genre apparently most given to generalization and didacticism, and yet so difficult to tie down to a consistent, finalized 'message'. For this dialectic can scarcely be reduced to any simple, closed model of generalization and example. Moreover, it is the range of forms this dialectic takes that also makes it hard to view the chorus simply as representing civic values, despite its group status and generalized utterance.

The chorus of the *Bacchae* offers a particularly interesting example of the problematic status that a chorus can maintain. On the one hand, this is one of the few choruses in extant tragedy that is unfriendly towards the royal house central to the action. The chorus are foreign devotees of the god, eastern women, dressed in maenads' costume. They are dependent on Dionysus and under threat of imprisonment or punishment at the hands of Pentheus. Their joyful reaction to the news of his death surprises the messenger who announces the horrific story of the mountain violence (1031–5):

Chorus: All hail to Bromius! Our god is a great god.
Messenger: What is this you say, women? You dare to rejoice
                at these disasters which destroy this house?
Ch.:   I am no Greek. I hail my god in my own way.
                No longer need I shrink with fear of prison.

This dialogue clearly marks the way in which this chorus is certainly no simple civic representative. They remain strangers to the city of Thebes, not sharing in the house's or city's grief, barbarian females.

On the other hand, as several critics have recently pointed out,[11] this band of women in their long odes which dominate so much of the play also offers a series of 'remonstrances or warnings derived from the vast store of Greek traditional wisdom',[12] and it has even been described as 'throughout the play ... an apologist for bourgeois morality'.[13] Indeed, particularly in the beautiful lyrics of the *parodos* and the first, second and third stasimon, the chorus not only depict a peaceful, harmonious world of Dionysiac worship, but also seem to base their moral pronouncements on the simplest and most traditional of Greek values – resistance to excess, rejection of proud thoughts, and perils of desire etc. So they conclude the first stasimon (430–2):

But what the common people do,
the things that simple people believe,
   I too believe and do.

In the relation between the third and fourth stasimon (862ff., 977ff.), the strange doubleness of this chorus is especially marked. The two odes are separated only by sixty-five lines and have certain formal similarities,[14] but whereas the third ode sings of escape,[15] the fawn's joyous flight to the hills, the fourth sings of bloody vengeance. The appeal to the 'slow but unmistakable might of the gods' (882–3) becomes the appeal for *dikē* to come and 'stab through the throat that godless man' (1014). The chorus summon up 'the hounds of madness' (977) with fierce hunting cries: their earlier exhortations of 'to the mountain, to the mountain' take on a grimly different aspect. This difference is crucial to the chorus' performance in demonstrating not only their dual status as actor in the drama and repository or exponent of a standard wisdom (a dual status strongly and strangely emphasized by the chorus' female barbarian characterization and the moral position they often espouse), but also what I have called the two faces of Dionysus' power. For it is also the

[11] Especially Arthur 1972. See also Vernant 1985; Segal 1982, 242–7.
[12] Arthur 1972, 145.   [13] Arthur 1972, 147.   [14] See Arthur 1972, 166–7.
[15] On Euripides and escape, see Padel 1974.

shift from the beneficent aspect of Dionysus' worship to the horrific violence of *sparagmos* that the chorus' two odes mark. The chorus' repeated terms and images used to such different effect fracture the stability of the choric language, as under the influence of Dionysus the women are transformed 'from quiet submission to violent opposition'.[16] The chorus itself in its odes enacts the destabilizing, ambivalent force of Dionysiac religion. Bystanders and instigators, barbarians with Greek ideals, who shift from hymns of peace to hunting cries of hate, the chorus demonstrates well what happens to the poles of difference in categorizations when Dionysus is in play.

The chorus of the *Bacchae*, then, 'focuses the paradoxes and problems of Dionysiac worship',[17] the ambivalence between the horror and the beauty of the wild beyond the city, the uncertain tensions between the potentials of human reason and order, and the potential for destruction, violence and madness in human society. But it is the women of the city who are forced to live through the full horrors and glory of maenadism. It is they who experience the uncanny, miraculous production of water, milk, honey and wine, and who suckle gazelles and wolf-cubs (689–713), and it is they who assault and defeat, first the herdsmen and the herds, ripping apart animals with their bare hands, and then Pentheus himself. This is in contrast to the chorus' passive fear of imprisonment. The power of reversal and doubleness is seen in an extreme form in the women of the city which tried to resist him. They, too, honour Dionysus in a chorus or with a chorus (eg. 220, 1109). The two old men, Teiresias and Cadmus, who try to accept the god (the former by a fine piece of sophistic rationalization (266ff.)), dress as maenads and prepare to form a chorus (e.g. 190, 195). The multiplication of formations of a chorus in honour of Dionysus constructs a multiplicity of attitudes to Dionysiac worship, both in the characters' different expressions of views and in the variety of performances for the god. How do the old men dressed as women on stage relate to the chorus of barbarian women (Athenian citizens playing the woman's role) or to the representation of the females of Thebes on the mountain in their secret rites of worship? The inherent self-reflexiveness of a theatrical chorus in a festival to honour Dionysus playing a chorus of Dionysiac worshippers is also to be seen within this wider series of men playing women, adopting another role, the role of the other (as 'woman' is fragmented into a variety of male representations). The variety of attempts to respond to the force of Dionysus by such role reversals not only stresses Dionysus' potential to make humans different from their normal, controlled selves, but also emphasizes the way in which theatre itself is an essentially Dionysiac experience, where men play roles of others and enact in the

[16] Arthur 1972, 170.   [17] Segal 1982, 245.

transgressions of tragedy and comedy the reversal or subversion of the norms of social behaviour. The interest in the theatrical experience itself and the self-reflexive concern with representation in the *Bacchae* cannot be separated from the question of self and other, of self-projection and self-definition within social norms and their transgression that has been the focus of so much contemporary criticism of the *Bacchae*.

The chorus of the *Bacchae*, then, which has to some critics seemed in the importance and length of its role to look back to the older tradition of Aeschylean drama, scarcely plays a traditional choric role. The response to Dionysus by the citizens with or in the chorus is a major problematic of the play and the chorus itself is an essential focus of this concern. Moreover, the chorus is certainly constructed with the typically Euripidean self-awareness of genre and willingness to test the limits of generic norms. As we will see when we turn to the so-called 'palace-miracle scene', the complexities of representation involved with this chorus have important implications for the questions of stagecraft.

Pentheus is also dressed as a maenad, but unlike the old men, the chorus, or the women of the city, the opponent of the god desires merely to observe the women's rites. 'Would you like to *see* their assembly on the mountain?' (811) is Dionysus' first question in Pentheus' final move towards destruction. 'I would pay a great sum' (812) replies Pentheus in instant agreement. 'Of course', continues Pentheus (814) 'I'd be sorry to *see* them drunk.' 'But for all your sorrow, you'd like very much to see them' (815) insists Dionysus. Indeed, when Pentheus hesitates at the prospect of necessarily dressing as a woman ('they would kill you, if you were seen there, a man' 823), Dionysus leads him towards acceptance with the question (829) 'Then you are no longer keen to be a spectator of the maenads?' The word for 'spectator' is *theates* which is from the same root as the word 'theatre' (*theatron*), and is used precisely for those in the theatre at the festival.[18] Pentheus hopes to be a spectator, watching unobserved what the messenger had described (700) as an 'awesome spectacle (*theama*) to see'.[19] But like the spectators in the theatre who find their own values, attitudes, definitions implicated and questioned in the actions and words of others on the stage, Pentheus, the actor who wants to be a spectator, will be forced to participate in the Dionysiac rites he watches. Indeed, as the king is dressed in a disguise to observe the women, so he will throw off his

---

[18] See e.g. Taplin 1978, 2.

[19] Bain 1977, 209 writes 'Theatrical imagery would be most surprising in tragedy' and claims to find no example of 'what might be termed play with the illusion in fifth-century drama'. While it is true that we do not find the explicit commonplace comparisons between life and the stage frequent in Elizabethan drama ('All the world's a stage' etc.), it is most surprising that Bain does not consider the wider vocabulary of theatrical experience.

disguise in the hope that recognition will preserve him from his mother's violent assault. But his despairing cry (1118) 'I, mother, am your child Pentheus' is ignored by his mother in her mad frenzy (1122ff.) and she wrenches off his supplicating arm at the shoulder. Ironically enough, disguised or not disguised Pentheus is the object of a deluded gaze. The use of the language of sight and in particular of 'spectacle' or 'theatre'[20] to express the different interrelations of humans and Dionysus draws together once more the deluded action of the drama and the illusions of the performance of the play.

Indeed, when Pentheus first comes on stage dressed as a maenad it is precisely to experience himself the distorted vision of Dionysiac influence. Dionysus leads him out (912–16):

> Pentheus, if you are still so curious to see
> forbidden sights, so bent on evil still,
> come out. Let us see you in your woman's dress,
> disguised in maenad's clothes so you may go and spy
> upon your mother and her company.

Pentheus' continuing desire to see forbidden sights, to be a spy on the women, results in him being displayed to the sight of others (including the spectators) as a woman. As he enters in his different costume, he sees the world differently (919–21):

> I seem to see two suns blazing in the heavens
> and now two Thebes, two cities and each
> with seven gates. And you – you are a bull ...

Richard Seaford[21] has shown how seeing double is not merely a symptom of (Dionysiac) drunkenness, but an element specifically drawn from the initiation rites of the cult of the Dionysiac mysteries. Dressed as a devotee of the god, Pentheus is enacting his initiation into the god's religion – in a way which will be horribly distorted in the final *sparagmos*. The illusions and delusions of sight are an essential part of Dionysiac involvement. So Dionysus responds to Pentheus' vision here (923–6):

> The god, who was previously hostile, accompanies us
> in truce. Now you see what you ought to see.

Pentheus' vision is now divinely distorted. This distortion in representation is further emphasized as the dialogue continues. 'What do I look like?' (925–6) asks Pentheus, 'Like Ino or my mother Agave?' The god replies with notable irony (927):

[20] The word 'theatre' itself does not appear in Greek tragedy, as Bain notes (1977, 208).
[21] 1981, passim.

> I seem to be seeing them themselves when I see you.

The god himself speaks as if he were a victim of the illusions of representation that he has enforced for Pentheus' destruction.

This scene looks back to Pentheus' earlier clash with the disguised god, where the king's disbelief in the divinity of Dionysus also focused on sight, knowledge and the Mysteries. First, Pentheus asks of the origins of these new rites; did the god come to the stranger at night in a dream, or clearly seen? 'Seeing the seeing' replies Dionysus (470) (inadequately translated as 'face to face' by Arrowsmith). Pentheus also wants to know what the god looked like (477–8):

> Pentheus: You say you saw the god clearly. What was he like?
> Dionysus: What he wanted. I gave no instructions on this point.

Dionysus is the master of representational forms, and his fluidity refuses the clear answer demanded by Pentheus.

The question of sight returns towards the end of the exchange (500–2):

> Dionysus: He is here now and sees what I endure from you.
> Pentheus: Where is he? He is not clear to *my* eyes.
> Di.: With me. As you are irreverent, you do not see.

As in Sophocles' *Oedipus Tyrannus*, the confident human sight of a ruler is faced by a claim of access to a world beyond mortal, physical sight. Indeed, not only does the god distort sight and function through illusion and delusion, but also, as we saw in the last chapter, the possibility of directly perceiving Dionysus in an adequate manner with human eyes is challenged throughout the action of the play from the disguised god's entrance to his final, ambivalent epiphany.[22] The god's control and manipulation of representation in the illusions and delusions of madness, masking and disguise, ignorance and ecstasy are constructed in the shared language of vision, which is so marked in the vocabulary of both the play and its critics.

The subjects under discussion so far – the chorus and its role in the drama, the shifting plays of representation, particularly through the language of sight and theatrical experience – are central to the lines on which I wish to focus for my most explicit discussion of stagecraft (in the sense of the script's realization in staging), namely, the 'palace-miracle scene'. The *Bacchae* is a play 'taut with overwhelming visual effects'[23] and it holds a unique place in the tragic corpus for the range of information about staging that the text appears to offer us. We are apparently told of the mask of one of the leading characters, the costumes of the chorus, the old men, Dionysus and, for his last scene,

---

[22] See Foley 1980, passim and on the epiphany especially 131–3; also Segal 1982, 228ff. Oranje 1984, 131ff. tries to classify the god's epiphanies.
[23] Segal 1982, 316.

Pentheus. We are told what the god in human form looks like to Pentheus (453ff.). We know what musical instruments accompany the chorus. We know what props the old men and Dionysus carry, and for the last scene, the further important props of the mask or head of Pentheus, and the collected parts of his body. We know that at one point the chorus fling themselves to the ground (604–5), and there are other significant suggested actions (Cadmus' and Agave's final embrace at 1364ff., the loosing and binding of Dionysus at 451ff., 493ff.). If we assume that these references in the text offer stable access to a representational staging, the drama which itself so stresses the devices of theatrical experience seems also to determine certain moments and aspects of enactment.

Yet we should be careful before we assume we have controlled the representational element of this drama of Dionysus. For it is precisely the representation of a miracle of the god that has prompted some of the most extensive discussions of and disagreements on staging. Towards the end of the second stasimon, after Dionysus has been bound and led into the palace, the voice of the god is heard (576–8): 'Ho, hear me! Ho Bacchai! Ho Bacchai! Hear my cry!' As the chorus learn who is shouting, they appeal for an epiphany (582–4): 'O lord Bromius, Bromius come to our company now!' And in response to Dionysus' next utterance the chorus cry out (586–92):

> – Look there how the palace of Pentheus is collapsing!
> – Look the palace is collapsing!
> – Dionysus is within. Adore him!
> – We adore him – Look there!
>   Above the pillars, how the great stones gape and crack.
>   Listen, Bromius cries his victory.

Dionysus summons up the fire of lightning to burn the palace, and the chorus respond again with an injunction to see (596):

> Ah! Ah! Do you not see the fire?

And the maenads throw themselves to the ground before the mighty god. Dionysus' entrance, however, seems far from the chorus' excited lyrics (604–6):

> Women of Asia, were you so overcome with fright
> you fell to the ground? I think then you must have seen
> how Bacchus shook the palace of Pentheus. But come, rise.

Dionysus goes on to explain how he – the stranger – escaped, and again it is through the power of illusion (618–25):

> Inside the stable he intended as my jail, instead of me
> he found a bull and tried to rope its knees and hooves.

> He was panting desperately, biting his lips with his teeth,
> his whole body drenched with sweat, while I sat nearby
> quietly watching. But at that moment Bacchus came,
> shook the palace, and touched his mother's grave
> with tongues of fire. Imagining the palace was in flames,
> Pentheus went rushing here and there, shouting
> to his slaves to bring him water.

The god describes his own intervention in the third person – 'Bromius came' –
as he tells of Pentheus' deluded passion. But this explanation fails to clarify the
action. Was it a real bull or a Dionysiac phantom? Did the palace really shake
and tremble? Or was it, like the burning palace, an 'imagining'? Indeed, as
this narrative continues, the uncertainty of the boundaries between illusion
and reality (an uncertainty focused on the question of representation) is
strongly emphasized (629–35):

> And there Bromius, as it seemed to me – I give you guesswork –
> made a phantom in the courtyard. Bursting in,
> Pentheus thrust and stabbed at the thing of gleaming air, as if he were
>   slaughtering me.
> And then, once again, Bacchus humiliated him.
> He razed the palace to the ground. All is shattered
> for him who saw a bitter end to my imprisonment.

The god describes his own action as that of someone else – he is in disguise
still. He offers his seeming guesswork of the appearance of a phantom – taken
as reality by Pentheus. And the word translated 'guesswork' is the normal
Greek for 'a (mere) opinion', 'fancy', 'image', 'illusion'. The ironic distance
Dionysus puts between himself and the action seems to veil precisely what
happened, in a recession of representational levels. The total destruction of
the palace is also described as the humiliation of the king by the god, but it is
also in terms of the sight of Pentheus. In the ruins of the house, Pentheus –
chaser after phantoms – *sees* the bitter end of the stranger's imprisonment. The
disguised Dionysus' pretence of ignorance not only obscures the clear
understanding of what happened or what is to be thought to have happened in
the palace, but also once more develops such uncertainty through the language
of sight and the distortions of representation.

So is the palace really to be thought of as tumbling? Does fire really rise from
the altar on stage? Indeed, is there any representation of these events on stage
(beyond the chorus' words)? Some critics have argued that indeed the house
could be ruined on stage. Arrowsmith's stage direction has Dionysus enter
'lightly picking his way among the rubble', and Pentheus enters 'stamping
heavily, from the ruined palace'. But after Dionysus' speech that I quoted
above there is no further mention of the ruined palace by any of the characters,

and although it has been seen as explicable in terms of the conventions of Greek drama that neither Pentheus nor any other character should need to comment on the ruins of the palace,[24] both the problems of staging such destruction of the backdrop and the way that such an apparently climactic event is not treated as of further relevance to the drama, have been rightly seen as difficulties for the assumption that the chorus' ecstatic language is simply reporting to the audience what the audience themselves are seeing on stage.

Other critics have suggested that although the earthquake is to be thought of as actually taking place, there need be no attempt at a representation of such disasters except in the words and music of the chorus: 'the chorus sing and dance in frenzy as an earthquake strikes the palace, lightning fires it and a flame springs up in the extinguished pyre of Semele (I doubt there was any attempt to represent these lightning effects and I very much doubt the earthquake was conveyed in any way less effective than the choreography and the words themselves)'.[25]

Some have suggested a sort of compromise between these two positions, arguing that 'the stage business ought to include a minor but conspicuous and threatening alteration of the . . . building's facade, accompanied, no doubt, by violent choreography and music'.[26] A symbolic representation of the destruction of the house, it is suggested, 'would emphasize the assault on the house as an assault on a symbol of Pentheus' pretensions to power and status, namely, his royal palace'. 'The discrepancy between what is said and what is seen forces us to recognize the symbolic nature of what is enacted on stage.'[27]

Still further critics have suggested that the miracle is a miracle of illusion and the chorus in the ecstasy, like Pentheus under the influence of Dionysus, see what is not there, and their intense emotional reaction to an illusion is the demonstration of the power of Dionysus. For Dionysus, as he enters, may be thought to speak with his customary irony when he says (605–6) 'You perceived, as it seems, the house being shaken' (the opposition between the uncertainty of perception and the certainty of reality is a commonplace), and, indeed, the idea of the house being fired (which Taplin seems to be placing among the 'real events') is explicitly described (624) as a delusion of Pentheus. Thus we move from this climactic delusion to further distortions of representations and visions as Pentheus proceeds towards his punishment.

The varieties of suggested realizations, and the significance in a thematic sense for such realizations make this a fascinating problem for the analysts of stagecraft. The repeated injunctions to 'see' can only emphasize the

---

[24] See the comments of Dodds 1960, ad loc.   [25] Taplin 1978, 119.
[26] Castellani 1976, 82. So, too, Dodds 1960, ad loc.
[27] Segal 1982, 220.

uncertainty of the object of vision. What is the audience faced with? If there is no representation beyond the music, words and dance of the chorus, the disjunction between the words of the chorus and the god, and the stability of the stage-building introduces a series of questions for the audience. Are they to imagine (by theatrical convention) the event not portrayed as taking place? The audience come directly under the power of Dionysus' theatrical illusion, as they experience in some way what has not really occurred. The scene thus becomes an expression of the linkage of Dionysiac ecstasy and the theatrical experience, in which the audience – the chorus' double – is directly implicated in the functioning of the text.

If there is some representation of the sort suggested by Dodds or Castellani – a flaring of the flame on Semele's monument, the partial collapse of an architrave – there is still a disjunction between the description of total destruction and its portrayal on stage which invokes a different set of questions. What is the relation between chorus' and god's description of headlong ruin and the brief physical action on stage? Again, the audience is being required to make distinctions between levels of illusion and reality, and representation, where neither the stage conventions nor the words of the play adequately allow such distinctions to be clearly made. As Winnington-Ingram has stressed, 'there is a vagueness, a phantasmagoric quality about the whole episode'.[28] The staged events – including the noise and violent dance that most critics assume without discussion to accompany the scene – suggest something real is taking place, yet the events are also miraculous, portentous and described in the language of a religious ecstasy of divine epiphany. There is a symbolic function to the 'palace-miracle', then, not for the chorus or the god or Pentheus, but for the audience.

If the palace – the stage buildings or backdrop – totally collapses (a view less often adopted by critics),[29] further implications come into play. The conventional perceptions of the limits of theatrical space are shockingly undermined. Euripides' physical breaking of the boundaries of the generic norms again challenges the audience's passive perception of the play as a play. The frame-breaking device is especially relevant in this work, where, as we have seen, the strangeness of bringing Dionysus on stage in the festival of Dionysus leads precisely to a series of questions about the involvement of the audience in the theatrical experience.

This brief look at three of the major possibilities of staging brings us to the key moment in the issue of stagecraft. First, the question 'What is the

[28] 1948, 182.
[29] Though I have seen this possibility brilliantly staged in the fine production of the *Bacchae* at the Old Vic in London in 1973.

audience faced with?' cannot receive an answer that does not interestingly implicate the audience, that does not affect and change the nature of the audience's response – participation – in this scene. In each case, the audience is actively involved in the production of meaning, and that involvement is importantly interwoven with the play's discussion of Dionysus' influence on mortal life. As Foley writes, 'How does the participant and spectator of myth and festival draw boundaries between himself and these events?'[30] Secondly, although it is necessary to consider the physical conditions and organizations of space in the ancient theatre, it is not sufficient for the discussion of stagecraft. For each of these stagings not only has implications for the meaning of the play but is also evaluated in terms of its meaning for the play. 'Stagecraft' cannot be an objective or dispassionate enquiry into what happened on a day in the theatre in the fifth century but must revert to the questions and doubts of interpretation and semantics. Thirdly, the question of the role of sight and understanding, illusion and fantasy, is a recurring problematic of Greek enquiry, not only in drama. The relation of vision and meaning – all too often assumed by analysts of stagecraft to be simple and direct – is considered in a variety of ways in the fifth-century theatre. As I argued with regard to the opening scene of the *Ajax*, and as is also the case with the 'palace-miracle' scene of the *Bacchae*, the most complex scenes of confused sight which are also the most problematic scenes in terms of staging are in a fundamental way interwoven in the thematic texture of the drama precisely in terms of the vocabulary of sight, knowledge, illusion. 'Significance' and 'vision' are not terms to be taken for granted with regard to the ancient theatre. The plays, and especially the *Bacchae*, challenge precisely the assumption that the link between sight and knowledge or understanding is an immediate process, that is somehow beyond the perils and shifts of interpretation.

There are, then, significant ambiguities in the 'palace-miracle' scene which produce the varied possibilities of staging. Indeed, it would be difficult to imagine a text of a play without such ambiguities or potentialities – though perhaps few plays demonstrate such a brilliant interweaving of theme and image and such recessions of self-aware, ironic, representational possibilities as the *Bacchae*. A producer or director, however (the model to which the analysts of stagecraft subscribe[31]), cannot both make the palace collapse and at the same time have no physical movement on stage. Consequently (the stagecraft argument runs), in analysing the plays in terms of performance, the necessary delimitations of staging mean that the aim must be to find the correct terms in which The Performance is to be constructed. Stagecraft

[30] 1985, 239.   [31] See Taplin 1978, especially 172ff.

resolves the ambiguities of the text in the clarity of a single performance. There may be an ambiguity in the text but in performance only one staging is possible. The fact that there could have been only one staging in the one performance of the festival results in the critical requirement that one single staging must be determined.

But how can the aspects of that performance be determined apart from the critic's reading and interpretation of the ambiguous text? What criteria of evaluation can be developed? In general terms, certain sorts of restrictions may be felt to follow from the nature of the theatre of Dionysus, the organization of its space, the number and masking of its actors etc. – throughout this book I have tried to view tragic drama in the specificity of its fifth-century production and there have been recent interesting studies in the spatial dynamics of Greek theatre.[32] But the particulars of each play's realization – music, dance, gesture, entrance, exit, costume etc. – are almost completely unknown, and what little is known is gleaned solely from the texts themselves, precisely by the critic's reading and interpretation.[33] Is it possible to avoid the problematic circularity that arises from the process of discovering a staging from the ambiguity of a text to remove the ambiguity of the text? Can a staging represent the ambiguous text, or merely repress or resite the ambiguities of the text? Is not a performance necessarily only a selection from among the plural potentialities of the text? In what ways is the critic's assertion of the discovery of the true, proper and necessary staging more than a strategy in the rhetoric of criticism? Could a staging of the 'palace-miracle' scene aspire to be more than *a* performance from *a* critical reading? Are all or none or one of the suggested possibilities of staging of the 'palace-miracle' scene 'true to the text' (in its ambiguousness)? Can a performance ever exhaust all the potentialities of a text?

The important implications of such complex questions for theatre and for reading and performing dramatic texts are effaced in the rhetoric of stagecraft by an appeal to the criteria of the 'author's intended meaning' and 'the original performance'.[34] Because Greek plays were generally produced and directed by the author for a single festival performance, because actors' delivery and staging, it is argued, would therefore correspond to a direct authorial instruction if not intention, our problems of reading are false to the facts of theatrical production. Even if it is agreed that there is no possibility of final certainty in determining the author's meaning or the facts of the original

[32] See Foley 1982a; Padel forthcoming; Taplin 1977, especially 34off., has interesting comments on doors.
[33] Vase paintings may give a general indication of the sorts of costume (though they are little help for specific plays).
[34] See Taplin 1978, 1–8 and 172–81.

performance from today's knowledge, nevertheless the discovery of such original authorial sense remains for the stagecraft analyst the necessary goal of dramatic criticism. It certainly remains a standard aspect of the critical rhetoric.

In the twentieth century there have been numerous critics and numerous arguments from many different angles that have been brought to bear on the criterion of authorial intention and indeed on the authenticity of the original performance, which make the often naive reliance of the rhetoric of stagecraft on such terminology somewhat surprising and indeed difficult to accept.[35] But there are also special circumstances surrounding 'the original performance' of the *Bacchae* which may lead towards further insight into this subject. For the *Bacchae* was written by Euripides in exile in Macedonia, or so the story runs,[36] and it was discovered among his papers after his death by either his son or his nephew. It was then brought back to Athens and produced, winning one of Euripides' few first prizes. What does this mean for its stagecraft? There can have been no direct authorial instructions for the staging of the 'palace-miracle' scene or for the delivery of those lines. Indeed, the play may even have been written without the prospect – intention? – of performance. The original production of the *Bacchae* faced similar problems of reading to those of all its subsequent stagings. There never has been an authorized production of this tragedy.

It is not merely the unique circumstances of the first production of the *Bacchae* which undermine 'the author's intention' and 'original performance' as expressions of critical order and control. The story of the *Bacchae*'s genesis points to the way that a text, words forming a text, in their very existence as text, are separated from the controlling order of an author. A text exists apart from its author and his intentions. This has important implications for the sort of communication that takes place in theatre. The dramatic interchanges fragment an author's voice between various speakers. There is no 'neutral', 'unstressed' reading. Each actor reads his lines as an interpretation – with the overseeing of a director or even the author, who may also offer an instructive reading, an interpretation for the actor. The actors' interrelations on stage are subject to the constructive interpretation of the audience. As we have seen again and again, especially with the *Bacchae*, the spectators are implicated in

---

[35] A huge bibliography could be given. Philosophically, Anscombe 1957; Cavell 1976; Searle 1983 map out some territory for discussion. Wimsatt and Beardsley (in Wimsatt 1954) remain the starting-point for literary critics. Barthes 1977 has been influential. In terms of cultural studies, see Foucault 1972; 1979. Generally, Derrida 1976 and 1977 are a brilliant analysis of ideas of intentionality based on 'speech act theory'.

[36] See Dodds 1960, introduction xxxixff. The evidence for this story is such that to deny its validity would seem to suggest no circumstantial evidence for the production of plays in the fifth century could be safely retained.

the development of meaning. From each point, the author's text is subject to reading (in its widest sense); at each point, the text requires reading. Dramatic experience at all levels from directing to watching involves a series of readings, of interpretations. Performance, then, cannot be adequately thought of as removing the difficulties of reading a text, of excising the problems that are inherent in the text as a text. Performance does not merely instantiate a finalized and complete text but is a process of interpreting the text and opening the text to the interpretation of an audience. To put it most apophthegmatically, performance does not efface the textuality of drama.

Indeed, a performance rather focuses the question of representation, of adequate realization, of determined meanings. This can be well demonstrated in one of the most remarkable moments in Greek drama. As Pentheus prepares in his rage to arm and to attack the maenads in the hills, he is stopped and diverted by Dionysus who says (810–11) 'Ah. Would you like to see their revels on the mountains?' Pentheus immediately gives up his plan as Dionysus' question instantly prompts an eager assent. How are we to understand the monosyllable, 'Ah' (translated by Arrowsmith as 'Wait!', which seems quite insufficient)? It stands outside the metre and it appears to be a highly significant interjection, yet it is difficult to judge in tone, impact or sense. Its delivery will certainly alter the understanding of this crucial scene. How does an analyst of stagecraft approach it?

What then are we to make of Dionysus' 'ah' ($\bar{a}$) at 810? Is it an 'ah' of surprise, of protest, of confidentiality, of readjustment? I find it impossible to pin down any single emotion or tone; all one can say is that the delivery must capture the tension of a turning-point which means death for Pentheus ... In performance, this should be obvious in a change of atmosphere – in some ways a relief that the suspense is over and the sentence passed, in some ways pity for Pentheus, in some ways fear of Dionysus' latent power. The 'ah' means death; and yet it epitomizes Dionysus in this play that this terrible moment should be conveyed coolly, enigmatically, monosyllabically.[37]

This is an interesting reading of Dionysus' interjection which shows well the difficulties and strengths of stagecraft analysis. Taplin begins by noting the impossibility of pinning down the force and value of the ambivalent monosyllable, although an actor must deliver it to 'capture the tension of a turning-point' (however that might sound). He proceeds to determine from the structure of the play the function of the interjection (to mark a turning-point[38]) and uses a possible staging to show how to clarify the scene. 'In

---

[37] Taplin 1978, 120–1.
[38] Against this, Oranje 1984, 82 (who does not appear to have read Taplin 1978) writes 'On the stage the poet does not present the process by which Pentheus loses his senses as the happening of a moment.' Oranje goes on, however, to recognize the shock of Pentheus' change of attitude at 812. How one thinks of this 'turning-point' or 'process' will depend on one's view of the

performance, this should be obvious...' Thus he can conclude, after the assertion that it is 'impossible to pin down any single emotion, or tone' that the moment (apart from being enigmatic and monosyllabic) is 'conveyed coolly'. That is, the possible alternatives which he claimed impossible to pin down 'surprise ... protest ... confidentiality ... readjustment' (one could add 'astonishment', and 'pain' from Dodds) have come down precisely to a determination of tone, 'coolly'.

The tension between recognizing the powerful and significant ambiguity in Dionysus' intervention and determining the delivery for performance is strongly marked, then, in the development of Taplin's argument, and, indeed, it is a tension played through every time the line is delivered in performance. How can the necessary determination of delivery adequately or absolutely represent the range of impossible-to-pin-down tones? The critic who tries to pin down the ambiguous utterance of Dionysus finds himself uncannily mirroring Pentheus' attempt to bind the god, and, like Dionysus, the word eludes control, or offers only an illusion of control. As with the variety of possible stagings for the 'palace-miracle' scene, the significant range of delivery for this monosyllable shows how a performance, as representation, realizes but cannot hope to exhaust or comprehend the text. The performance of a text, like the reading of a text, must be partial.

Classicists with roots in the positivism of Victorian scholarship have been particularly resistant to the notion of the open-endedness of the texts of tragedy. There have been – and probably will be – many critics who believe they have attained a conclusive understanding of the Greek tragic texts, or at least who would agree with one scholar's regret that critics have neither 'come to some unanimity ... in this long time' nor 'found a way for the reader's untroubled enjoyment' of tragedy.[39] I have offered in this book a series of arguments to show why and how the possibility of reaching such a final, fixed and complete reading is continually being undermined in the plays of the Attic stage. It is not merely our ignorance of the events and attitudes of fifth-century Athens that makes the experience of reading these texts finally indeterminate and inexhaustible. For as Pentheus' body, dismembered by the Dionysiac chorus, can only be collected in fragments, but never reconstituted to wholeness, so each person's attempts to comprehend the corpus of tragic texts – through the violence of reading, the selectivity of analysis – can never hope

further complex issue of internal and external motivation with regard to Pentheus. Is the cause of Pentheus' change of attitude Dionysus' influence, Pentheus' own suppressed desires coming out, or some combination of the two? Taplin, however, does not consider the 'turning-point' in this light.

[39] Linforth 1956, 96.

to attain the synthesis which can totally efface the signs of *sparagmos*, the *sparagmos* of signs.

It is because tragedy is not reducible to a simple 'message', because these dramas are not played out or exhausted in a single reading or performance, that readers return again and again to ancient tragedy. The continuing response to Greek tragedy is not simply each generation, each reader or each reader at different times, reaching towards some eternally fixed beauty or immutable truth encapsulated in the glory that was Greek tragedy, but being faced with the problems, tensions and uncertainties that these texts involve. It is in reading and responding to the continually unsettling and challenging questions set in motion by these plays that Greek tragedy is performed and experienced.

BIBLIOGRAPHY

This bibliography contains only the works cited in the text and notes. Further bibliographical information on particular problems is given in the notes. In the case of reprinted editions, the edition cited in the text is the only edition given in the bibliography.

Adams, S. M. (1955) 'The *Ajax* of Sophocles', *Phoenix* 9: 93–110.

Adkins, A. W. (1963) '"Friendship" and "self-sufficiency" in Homer and Aristotle', *C.Q.* 13: 30–45.

Allen, J. T. (1938) *On the Program of the City Dionysia during the Peloponnesian War.* Berkeley.

Allen, R. E. (1980) *Socrates and Legal Obligation.* Minneapolis.

Andrewes, A. (1956) *The Greek Tyrants.* London.

  (1971) *Greek Society.* Harmondsworth.

Anscombe, G. E. (1957) *Intention.* Ithaca.

Ariès, P. (1962) *Centuries of Childhood: a social history of family life.* Trans. Baldick, R. London.

Arnott, G. (1973) 'Euripides and the unexpected', *G. & R.* 20: 49–64.

  (1981) 'Double the vision: a reading of Euripides' *Electra*', *G. & R.* 28: 179–92.

Arnott, P. D. (1959) *An Introduction to Greek Theatre.* London.

Arrowsmith, W. (1964) 'A Greek theatre of ideas', in *Ideas in Drama*, ed. Gasner, E. New York.

  (1968) 'Euripides' theatre of ideas', in Segal, E. (1968).

Arthur, M. (1972) 'The choral odes of the *Bacchae* of Euripides', *Y.C.S.* 22: 145–80.

  (1973) 'Early Greece: the origins of Western attitudes toward women', *Arethusa* 6.1: 7–58.

  (1981) 'The divided world of *Iliad* VI', *Women's Studies* 8.1 & 2: 21–46.

  (1983) 'The dream of a world without women: poetics and the circles of order in the *Theogony* prooemium', *Arethusa* 16.1 & 2: 97–116.

Austin, C. (1984) 'Sophocles' *Oedipus Tyrannus* 873', *C.Q.* 34: 233.

Austin, M. and Vidal-Naquet, P. (1972) *Économies et sociétés en Grèce ancienne.* Paris.

Austin, N. (1972) 'Name magic in the *Odyssey*', *C.S.C.A.* 5: 1–19.

  (1975) *Archery at the Dark of the Moon: poetic problems in Homer's Odyssey.* Berkeley.

Avery, H. C. (1968) '"My tongue swore but my mind is unsworn"', *T.A.P.A.* 99: 19–35.

Bachofen, J. J. (1967) *Myth, Religion and Mother-Right. Selected writings.* Trans. Manheim, R. London.

Bain, D. (1975) 'Audience address in Greek tragedy', *C.Q.* 25: 13–25.

  (1977) *Actors and Audience: a study of asides and related conventions.* Oxford.

Baldry, H. C. (1981) *The Greek Tragic Theatre.* London.

Bamberger, J. (1975) 'The myth of matriarchy: why men rule in primitive society', in Rosaldo and Lamphere (1975).

Barrett, W. S. (1964) *Euripides' Hippolytos*. Oxford.

Barthes, R. (1975) *S/Z*. Trans. Miller, R. London.

(1977) 'The death of the author', in *Image, Music, Text*. Trans. Heath, S. Glasgow.

Bayley, J. (1974) 'Character and consciousness', *N.L.H.* 5.2: 225–35.

Beardsley, M. and Wimsatt, W. K. (1954) 'The intentional fallacy', in *The Verbal Icon*. Wimsatt, W. K. Lexington.

Beck, F. A. (1975) *Album of Greek Education*. Sydney.

Beer, G. (1983) *Darwin's Plots: evolutionary narrative in Darwin, George Eliot and nineteenth-century fiction*. London.

Benardete, S. (1975a) 'A reading of Sophocles' *Antigone* I', *Interpretation* 4.23: 148–96.

(1975b) 'A reading of Sophocles' *Antigone* II', *Interpretation* 5.1: 1–55.

(1975c) 'A reading of Sophocles' *Antigone* III', *Interpretation* 5.2: 148–84.

Benveniste, E. (1973) *Indo-European Language and Society*. Trans. Palmer, E. London.

Bergren, A. L. (1983) 'Language and the female in early Greek thought', *Arethusa* 16.1 & 2: 69–95.

Bourdieu, P. (1977) *Outline of a Theory of Practice*. Trans. Nice, R. Cambridge.

Bowra, C. M. (1944) *Sophoclean Tragedy*. Oxford.

Brown, N. O. (1951) 'Pindar, Sophocles and the Thirty Years Peace', *T.A.P.A.* 82: 1–28.

Brown, W. E. (1965–6) 'Sophocles' Ajax and Homer's Hector', *C.J.* 61: 118–21.

Bulloch, A. W. (1985) *Callimachus: the Fifth Hymn*. Cambridge.

Burkert, W. (1983) *Homo Necans*. Trans. Bing, P. Berkeley.

Burnyeat, M. (1976a) 'Protagoras and self-refutation in later Greek philosophy', *The Philosophical Review* 85.1: 44–69.

(1976b) 'Protagoras and self-refutation in Plato's *Theaetetus*', *The Philosophical Review* 85.2: 172–95.

Calame, C. (1977) *Les Choeurs de jeunes filles en Grèce archaique*. 2 vols. Rome.

Calogero, G. (1957) 'Gorgias and the Socratic principle nemo sua sponte peccat', *J.H.S.*77: 12–17.

Cameron, A. and Kuhrt, A. eds. (1983) *Images of Women in Antiquity*. London and Melbourne.

Castellani, V. (1976) 'That troubled house of Pentheus in Euripides' *Bacchae*', *T.A.P.A.* 106: 61–83.

Cavell, S. (1976) *Must We Mean What We Say?* Cambridge.

La Cité des images: religion et societé en Grèce antique. (1984). Institut d'archéologie et d'histoire ancienne, Lausanne. Centre de recherches comparés sur les sociétés anciennes, Paris.

Cixoux, H. (1974) 'The character of "character"', *N.L.H.* 5.2: 383–402.

Classen, C. J. ed. (1976) *Sophistik*. Darmstadt.

Clay, D. (1982) 'Unspeakable words in Greek tragedy', *A.J.P.* 103: 277–98.

Coleman, R. G. G. (1972) 'The role of the chorus in Sophocles' *Antigone*', *P.C.P.S.* 198: 4–27.

Collard, C. (1975) 'Formal debates in Euripides' drama', *G. & R.* 22: 58–71.

Collinge, N. E. (1962) 'Medical terms and clinical attitudes in the tragedians', *B.I.C.S.* 9: 43–55.

Connor, W. (1971) *The New Politicians of Fifth-Century Athens*. Princeton.

Coward, R. (1983) *Patriarchal Precedents*. London.

Coward, R. and Ellis, J. (1977) *Language and Materialism*. London.

Crotty, K. (1982) *Song and Action: the victory odes of Pindar*. Baltimore.

Culler, J. (1975) *Structuralist Poetics*. Ithaca.

Daube, D. (1972) *Civil Disobedience in Antiquity*. Edinburgh.

David, E. (1984) 'Solon, neutrality and partisan literature of late fifth-century Athens', *M.H.* 41: 129–38.

Davies, J. K. (1977) 'Athenian citizenship: the descent group and the alternatives', *C.J.* 73.2: 105–21.

(1978) *Democracy and Classical Greece*. Hassocks.

Davison, J. A. (1953) 'Protagoras, Democritus, and Anaxagoras', *C.Q.* 3: 33–45.

Dawe, R. D. (1963) 'Inconsistency of plot and character in Aeschylus', *P.C.P.S.* 9: 21–62.

(1982) *Sophocles: Oedipus Rex*. Cambridge.

de Beauvoir, S. (1972) *The Second Sex*. Trans. Parshley, H.M. Harmondsworth.

Denniston, J. D. (1939) *Euripides' Electra*. Oxford.

Denniston, J. D. and Page, D. L. (1957) *Aeschylus' Agamemnon*. Oxford.

de Romilly, J. (1973) 'Gorgias et le pouvoir de la poésie', *J.H.S.* 93: 155–62.

Derrida, J. (1976) 'Signature, event, context', *Glyph* 1: 172–99.

(1977) 'Limited Inc. abc.', *Glyph* 2: 162–254.

Detienne, M. (1967) *Les Maîtres de vérité dans la Grèce archaique*. Paris.

(1972) 'Entre bêtes et dieux', *Nouvelle revue de psychanalyse* 6: 231–42. Trans. in Gordon (1981).

(1979) 'Violentes "eugénies" en plein Thesmophories: des femmes couvertes de sang', in Detienne and Vernant (1979).

Detienne, M. and Vernant, J.-P. (1978) *Cunning Intelligence in Greek Culture and Society*. Trans. Lloyd, J. Brighton.

(1979) *La Cuisine du sacrifice en pays Grec*. Paris.

Dodds, E. R. (1925) 'The AIΔΩΣ of Phaedra and the meaning of the *Hippolytus*', *C.R.* 39: 102–4.

(1951) *The Greeks and the Irrational*. Berkeley.

(1960) *Euripides' Bacchae*. Oxford.

(1966) 'On misunderstanding *Oedipus Rex*', *G. & R.* 13: 37–49.

Dollimore, J. (1984) *Radical Tragedy: religion, ideology and power in the drama of Shakespeare and his contemporaries*. Brighton.

Donzelli, G. B. (1978) *Studio sull' Elettra di Euripide*. Catania.

Dover, K. J. (1973) 'Classical Greek attitudes to sexual behaviour', *Arethusa* 6: 59–73.

(1974) *Greek Popular Morality in the Time of Plato and Aristotle*. Oxford.

(1975) 'The freedom of the intellectual in Greek society', *Talanta* 7: 24–54.

du Bois, P. (1982) *History, Rhetorical Description and the Epic: from Homer to Spenser*. Cambridge.

(1984) *Centaurs and Amazons: women and the pre-history of the great chain of being*. Ann Arbor.

Easterling, P. E. (1973) 'Presentation of character in Aeschylus', *G. & R.* 20: 3–19.

(1977) 'Character in Sophocles', *G. & R.* 24: 121–9.

(1984) 'The tragic Homer', *B.I.C.S.* 31: 1–8.

Eco, U. (1976) *A Theory of Semiotics.* Bloomington.

Ehrenberg, V. (1948) 'The foundation of Thurii', *A.J.P.* 59: 149–70.

(1954) *Sophocles and Pericles.* Oxford.

(1960) *The Greek State.* Oxford.

Engels, F. (1972) *Origins of the Family, Private Property and the State.* Trans. Leacock, E. B. London.

Fehrle, E. (1966) *Die kultische Keuschheit im Altertum.* Giessen 1910.

Ferguson, J. (1970) 'Ambiguity in *Ajax*', *Dioniso* 44: 12–29.

Festugière, A.-J. (1948) *Hippocrate: l'ancienne médecine. Études et commentaires IV.* Paris.

Finley, M. I. (1968) 'The alienability of land in ancient Greece: a point of view', *Eirene* 7: 25–32.

(1972) Introduction to *Thucydides' History of the Peloponnesian War*, trans. Warner, R. Harmondsworth.

(1980) *Ancient Slavery and Modern Ideology.* London.

(1983) *Politics in the Ancient World.* Cambridge.

Fitzgerald, G. J. (1973) 'Misconception, hypocrisy and the structure of Euripides' *Hippolytus*', *Ramus* 2: 20–44.

Foley, H. P. (1978) '"Reverse Similes" and sex roles in the *Odyssey*', *Arethusa* 11: 7–26.

(1980) 'The masque of Dionysus', *T A P A* 110: 107–33.

(1982a) 'The "female intruder" reconsidered: women in Aristophanes' *Lysistrata* and *Ecclesiazusae*', *C.P.* 77: 1–21.

ed. (1982b) *Reflections of Women in Antiquity.* London, Paris, New York.

(1985) *Ritual Irony: poetry and sacrifice in Euripides.* Ithaca.

Forrest, W. G. (1966) *The Emergence of Greek Democracy.* London.

Forrester, J. (1980) *Language and the Origins of Psychoanalysis.* London.

Foucault, M. (1972) *The Archaeology of Knowledge.* Trans. Sheridan, A. M. London.

(1979) 'What is an author?', in *Textual Strategies: perspectives in post-structuralist criticism*, ed. Harari, J. V. Ithaca.

Fraenkel, E. (1950) *Aeschylus' Agamemnon.* 3 vols. Oxford.

Frischer, B. D. (1970) '*Concordia discors* and characterisation in Euripides' *Hippolytus*', *G.R.B.S.* 11: 85–100.

Fuks, A. (1953) *The Ancestral Constitution.* London.

Garton, C. (1957) 'Characterisation in Greek tragedy', *J.H.S.* 77: 247–54.

Gellie, G. H. (1963) 'Character in Greek tragedy', *A.U.M.L.A.* 20: 24–56.

(1972) *Sophocles: a reading.* Melbourne.

(1981) 'Tragedy and Euripides' *Electra*', *B.I.C.S.* 28: 1–12.

Gernet, L. (1981) *The Anthropology of Ancient Greece.* Trans. Hamilton, J. and Nagy, B. Baltimore.

Giangrande, G. (1970) 'Hellenistic poetry and Homer', *A.C.* 39: 46–77.

Girard, R. (1977) *Violence and the Sacred.* Trans. Gregory, P. Baltimore.

Glotz, G. (1904) *La Solidarité de la famille dans le droit criminel en Grèce.* Paris.

Goldhill, S. D. (1984a) *Language, Sexuality, Narrative: the Oresteia.* Cambridge.

(1984b) 'Two notes on τέλος and related words in the *Oresteia*', *J.H.S.* 104: 169–76.

(1984c) 'Exegesis: Oedipus (R)ex', *Arethusa* 17: 177–200.

Gomme, A. W. (1925) 'The position of women in Athens', *C.P.* 20: 1–26.

Gomperz, H. (1965) *Sophistik und Rhetorik*. Stuttgart.

Gordon, R. L. ed. (1981) *Myth, Religion and Society*. Cambridge.

Gould, J. P. (1978) 'Dramatic character and "human intelligibility" in Greek tragedy', *P.C.P.S.* 24: 43–67.

(1980) 'Law, custom and myth: aspects of the social position of women in Classical Athens', *J.H.S.* 100: 38–59.

(1983) 'Homeric epic and the tragic moment', in *Aspects of the Epic*, eds. Winnifrith, T., Murray, P. and Gransden, K. W. London.

Graeser, A. (1977) 'On language, thought and reality in ancient Greek philosophy', *Dialectica* 31: 359–88.

Green, A. (1969) *Un Oeil en trop: le complexe d'Oedipe dans la tragédie*. Paris.

Grote, G. (1888) *The History of Greece, from the earliest period to the close of the generation contemporary with Alexander*. 8 vols. London.

Guthrie, W. K. C. (1962–81) *A History of Greek Philosophy*. 6 vols. Cambridge.

Haigh, A. (1907) *The Attic Theatre*. Oxford.

Hamilton, R. (1978) 'Prologue, prophecy and plot in four plays of Euripides', *A.J.P.* 99: 277–302.

Hands, A. R. (1968) *Charities and Social Aid in Greece and Rome*. London.

Harrison, E. L. (1964) 'Was Gorgias a sophist?', *Phoenix* 18: 183–92.

Hartman, G. H. (1970) *Beyond Formalism*. New Haven.

(1975) *The Fate of Reading*. Chicago.

(1981) *Saving the Text: Literature/Derrida/Philosophy*. Baltimore.

Hartog, F. (1980) *Le Miroir d'Hérodote: essai sur la représentation de l'autre*. Paris.

Harvey, A. E. (1957) 'Homeric epithets in Greek lyric poetry', *C.Q.* 7:206–23.

Havelock, E. A. (1978) *The Greek Concept of Justice: from its shadow in Homer to its substance in Plato*. Cambridge, Mass. and London.

Hay, J. (1978) *Oedipus Tyrannus: lame knowledge and the homosporic womb*. Washington.

Heidegger, M. (1959) *An Introduction to Metaphysics*. Trans. Manheim, R. New Haven.

Heinimann, F. (1945) *Nomos und Physis: Herkunft und Bedeutung einer Antithese im griechischen Denken des 5 Jahrhunderts*. Basel.

(1976) 'Ein vorplatonische Theorie der τέχνη', in Classen 1976.

Hester, D. A. (1971) 'Sophocles the unphilosophical', *Mnemosyne* 24: 11–59.

Hirzel, R. (1966) *Themis, Dike, und Verwandtes; ein Beitrag zur Geschichte der Rechtsidee bei den Griechen*. Hildesheim.

Hogan, J. C. (1972) 'The protagonists of the *Antigone*', *Arethusa* 5: 93–100.

Hopkinson, N. (1984) *Callimachus: Hymn to Demeter*. Cambridge.

Howald, E. (1930) *Die griechische Tragödie*. Munich.

Humphreys, S. C. (1983) *The Family, Women and Death*. London.

Hunter, R. L. (1985) *The New Comedy of Greece and Rome*. Cambridge.

Jakobson, R. and Halle, M. (1956) *The Fundamentals of Language*. The Hague.

Jameson, M. H. (1977) 'Agriculture and slavery in Classical Athens', *C.J.* 73: 122–45.

Jebb, R. C. (1883–1908) *Sophocles: the plays and fragments with critical notes, commentary and translation in English prose*. 7 vols. Cambridge.

Jones, J. (1962) *On Aristotle and Greek Tragedy*. London.

Just, R. (1975) 'Conceptions of women in classical Athens', *The Journal of the Anthropological Society of Oxford* 6.3: 153–70.

Kahn, L. (1978) *Hermès passe: ou les ambiguïtés de la communication*. Paris.

Kamerbeek, J. C. (1963–84) *Sophocles: the plays*. 7 vols. Leiden.

(1965) 'Prophecy and tragedy', *Mnemosyne* 18: 29–40.

Kells, J. H. (1963) 'Problems of interpretation in the *Antigone*', *B.I.C.S.* 10: 47–64.

Kennedy, G. (1963) *The Art of Persuasion in Greece*. London.

Kerferd, G. (1950) 'The first Greek sophists', *C.R.* 64: 8–10.

(1981) *The Sophistic Movement*. Cambridge.

King, H. (1983) 'Bound to bleed: Artemis and Greek women', in Cameron and Kuhrt (1983).

King, K. C. (1980) 'The force of tradition: the Achilles ode in Euripides' *Electra*', *T.A.P.A.* 110: 195–212.

Kirkwood, G. M. (1958) *A Study in Sophoclean Drama*. Ithaca.

(1965) 'Homer and Sophocles' Ajax', in *Classical Drama and its Influence, essays presented to H. D. F. Kitto*, ed. Anderson, M. J. London.

Kitto, H. D. F. (1951) *The Greeks*. London.

(1956) *Form and Meaning in Drama*. London.

(1961) *Greek Tragedy*. London.

Knox, B. M. W. (1952) 'The *Hippolytus* of Euripides', *Y.C.S.* 13: 3 31.

(1957) *Oedipus at Thebes*. London.

(1961) 'The *Ajax* of Sophocles', *H.S.C.P.* 65: 1–39.

(1964) *The Heroic Temper: studies in Sophoclean tragedy*. Berkeley.

(1971) 'Euripidean Comedy', in *The Rarer Action, essays in honor of Francis Fergusson*, eds. Cheuse, A. and Koffler, R. New Brunswick.

(1977) 'The *Medea* of Euripides', *Y.C.S.* 25: 198–225.

Kraut, R. (1984) *Socrates and the State*. Princeton.

Kristeva, J. (1980) *Desire in Language: a semiotic approach to literature and art*. Trans. and ed. Roudiez, L. S. Oxford.

Kubo, M. (1966) 'The norm of myth: Euripides' *Electra*', *H.S.C.P.* 71: 15–31.

Kuenen-Janssens, L. J. (1941) 'Some notes on the competence of Athenian women to conduct a transaction', *Mnemosyne* 9: 199–214.

Kuhns, R. (1962) *The House, the City, the Judge*. Indianapolis.

Lacey, W. K. (1968) *The Family in Classical Greece*. London.

Lattimore, R. (1958) *The Poetry of Greek Tragedy*. Baltimore.

Lebeck, A. (1971) *The Oresteia*. Washington.

Lefkowitz, M. (1981) *The Lives of the Greek Poets*. London.

(1983) 'Influential women', in Cameron and Kuhrt (1983).

Lesky, A. (1965) *Greek Tragedy*. Trans. Frankfort, H. A. London.

Levi, A. (1940a) 'Studies on Protagoras', *Philosophy* 15: 147–67.

(1940b) 'The ethical and social thought of Protagoras', *Mind* 49: 284–302.

Lévi-Strauss, C. (1966) *The Savage Mind*. Chicago.

(1969) *The Elementary Structures of Kinship*. Trans. Bell, J. and Sturmer, J. Chicago.

Linforth, I. M. (1953) 'Three scenes in Sophocles' Ajax', *U.C.P.C.P.* 15.1: 1–28.

(1956) 'Philoctetes: the play and the man', *U.C.P.C.P.* 15.3: 95–156.

Lloyd, G. E. R. (1963) 'Who is attacked in *On Ancient Medicine?*', *Phronesis* 8: 108–26.

(1966) *Polarity and Analogy*. Cambridge.

(1979) *Magic, Reason and Experience*. Cambridge.

(1983) *Science, Folklore and Ideology*. Cambridge.

Lloyd, M. (1984) 'The Helen scene in Euripides' *Troades*', *C.Q.* 34: 303–13.

Lloyd-Jones, H. (1961) 'Some alleged interpolations in Aeschylus' *Choephoroi* and Euripides' *Electra*', *C.Q.* 11: 171–84.

(1971) *The Justice of Zeus*. Berkeley.

(1972) 'Tycho von Wilamowitz-Moellendorf on the dramatic technique of Sophocles', *C.Q.* 22: 214–28.

(1983) 'Artemis and Iphigeneia', *J.H.S.* 103: 87–102.

Loraux, N. (1981a) *L'Invention d'Athènes*. Paris.

(1981b) *Les Enfants d'Athéna*. Paris.

(1981c) 'Le lit, la guerre', *L'Homme* 21.1: 37–67.

McCabe, C. ed. (1981) *The Talking Cure: essays in psychoanalysis and language*. London.

MacDowell, D. M. (1976) 'Hybris in Athens', *G. & R.* 23: 14–31.

MacKay, L. A. (1962) 'Antigone, Coriolanus and Hegel', *T.A.P.A.* 93: 166–74.

Macleod, C. W. (1983) *Collected Essays*. Oxford.

Manville, B. (1980) 'Solon's law of stasis and *atimia* in Archaic Athens', *T.A.P.A.* 110: 213–21.

Marrou, H. (1956) *A History of Education in Antiquity*. Trans. Lamb, G. London.

Mejer, J. (1979) 'Recognizing what, when and why', in *Arktouros*, eds. Bowersock, G., Burkert, W., and Putnam, M. C. J. Berlin.

Millet, K. (1971) *Sexual Politics*. New York.

Moore, J. A. (1977) 'The dissembling speech of Ajax', *Y.C.S.* 25: 47–67.

Moser, S. and Kustas, G. L. (1966) 'A comment on the "relativism" of the *Protagoras*', *Phoenix* 20: 111–15.

Mossé, C. (1979) 'Comment s'élabore un mythe politique: Solon père fondateur de la démocratie athénienne', *Annales* 34: 425–37.

Muecke, F. (1982) '" I know you – by your rags": costume and disguise in fifth-century drama', *Antichthon* 16: 17–34.

Musurillo, H. (1967) *The Light and the Darkness: studies in the dramatic poetry of Sophocles*. Leiden.

Nilsson, M. (1925) *A History of Greek Religion*. Oxford.

North, H. (1966) *Sophrosyne: self-knowledge and self-restraint in Greek literature*. New York.

O'Brien, M. (1964) 'Orestes and the Gorgon: Euripides' *Electra*', *A.J.P.* 85: 13–39.

Onians, R. B. (1951) *The Origins of European Thought*. Cambridge.

Oranje, H. (1984) *Euripides' Bacchae: the play and its audience*. Leiden.

Osborne, R. (1985) *Demos: the discovery of classical Attika*. Cambridge.

Ostwald, M. (1969) *Nomos and the beginnings of Athenian Democracy*. Oxford.

(1973) 'Was there a concept ἄγραφος νόμος in Classical Greek?', in *Exegesis and Argument, studies in Greek philosophy presented to Gregory Vlastos*, eds. Lee, E. N., Mourelatos, A. P., Rorty, R. M. Assen.

Padel, R. (1974) '" Imagery of elsewhere": two choral odes of Euripides', *C.Q.* 24: 227–41.

(forthcoming) *In and Out of the Mind: consciousness in Greek tragedy.*

Parker, R. (1983) *Miasma: pollution and purification in early Greek religion.* Oxford.

Pembroke, S. G. (1965) 'The last of the matriarchs: a study in the inscriptions of Lycia', *Journal of Economic and Social History of the Orient* 8: 217–47.

(1967) 'Women in charge: the function of alternatives in early Greek tradition and the ancient idea of matriarchy', *Journal of Warburg and Courtauld* 30: 1–35.

Peradotto, J. (1969) 'Cledonomancy in the *Oresteia*', *A.J.P.* 90: 1–21.

Pfeiffer, R. (1968) *History of Classical Scholarship.* Oxford.

Pickard-Cambridge, A. (1968) *The Dramatic Festivals of Athens.* (Revised by Gould, J. and Lewis, D. M.) Oxford.

Podlecki, A. (1966a) 'The power of the word in Sophocles' *Philoctetes*', *G.R.B.S.* 7: 233–50.

(1966b) *The Political Background of Aeschylean Tragedy.* Michigan.

(1970) 'The basic seriousness of Euripides' *Helen*', *T.A.P.A.* 101: 401–18.

Pohlenz, M. (1953) 'Nomos und Physis', *Hermes* 81: 418–38.

Pomeroy, S. B. (1977a) 'Selected bibliography on women in antiquity', *Arethusa* 11: 127–57.

(1977b) 'Technikai kai musikai,' *A.J.A.H.* 2: 51–66.

Pucci, P. (1977) *Hesiod and the Language of Poetry.* Baltimore.

Reeve, M. D. (1973) 'Interpolations in Greek Tragedy III', *G.R.B.S.* 14: 145–71.

Reinhardt, K. (1979) *Sophocles.* Trans. Harvey, H. and D. Oxford.

Rosaldo, M. and Lamphere, L. (1975) *Women, Culture and Society.* Stanford.

Rosenmeyer, T. (1955) 'Gorgias, Aeschylus and ἀπάτη', *A.J.P.* 76: 225–60.

(1963) *The Masks of Tragedy.* Austin.

Rosivach, V. (1978) 'The "Golden Lamb" ode in Euripides' *Electra*', *C.P.* 73: 189–99.

(1979) 'The two worlds of the *Antigone*', *I.C.S.* 4: 16–26.

Roudiez, L. S. Introduction to Kristeva (1980).

Rousselle, A. (1983) *Porneia: de la maîtrise du corps à la privation sensuelle.* Paris.

Rudhardt, J. and Reverdin, O. eds. (1981) *Le Sacrifice dans l'antiquité.* Fondation Hardt, *Entretiens sur l' antiquité classique,* 27. Geneva.

Russell, D. A. (1983) *Greek Declamation.* Cambridge.

Ryffel, H. (1949) *Metabole Politeion. Der Wandel der Staatsverfassungen.* New York.

Saïd, S. (1978) *La Faute tragique.* Paris.

Sainte-Croix, G. de (1972) *The Origins of the Peloponnesian War.* London.

Sale, W. (1977) *Existentialism and Euripides: sickness, tragedy and divinity in the Medea, the Hippolytus and the Bacchae.* Berwick, Victoria.

Sansonne, D. (1978) 'The *Bacchae* as satyr play?', *I.C.S.* 3: 40–6.

Sartre, J.-P. (1973) *Politics and Literature.* Trans. Underwood, J. A. London.

Schadewaldt, W. (1926) *Monolog und Selbstgesprach.* Berlin.

Schaps, D. M. (1977) 'The woman least mentioned: etiquette and women's names', *C.Q.* 27: 323–30.

(1978) *The Economic Rights of Women in Ancient Greece.* Edinburgh.

Schnapp, A. (1984) 'Éros en chasse' in *La Cité des images.*

Seaford, R. (1981) 'Dionysiac drama and the Dionysiac mysteries', *C.Q.* 31: 252–75.

Searle, R. (1983) *Intentionality: an essay in the philosophy of mind.* Cambridge.

Segal, C. P. (1962a) 'Gorgias and the psychology of the logos', *H.S.C.P.* 66: 99–155.
  (1962b) 'The Phaeacians and the symbolism of Odysseus' return', *Arion* 1.4: 17–64.
  (1964) 'Sophocles' praise of man and the conflicts of the *Antigone*', *Arion* 3: 46–66.
  (1965) 'The tragedy of the *Hippolytus*: the waters of ocean and the untouched meadow', *H.S.C.P.* 70: 117–69.
  (1967) 'Transition and ritual in Odysseus' return', *P.P.* 22: 321–42.
  (1969) 'Euripides' *Hippolytus* 108–12: tragic irony and tragic justice', *Hermes* 97: 297–305.
  (1970) 'Shame and purity in Euripides' *Hippolytus*', *Hermes* 98: 278–99.
  (1971) 'The two worlds of Euripides' *Helen*', *T.A.P.A.* 102: 553–614.
  (1972) 'Curse and oath in Euripides' *Hippolytus*', *Ramus* 1: 165–80.
  (1981) *Tragedy and Civilization. An interpretation of Sophocles*. Cambridge.
  (1982) *Dionysiac Poetics and Euripides' Bacchae*. Princeton.
Segal, E. ed. (1968) *Euripides: a collection of critical essays*. Englewood Cliffs.
  ed. (1983) *Oxford Readings in Greek Tragedy*. Oxford.
Seidensticker, B. (1978) 'Comic elements in Euripides' *Bacchae*', *A.J.P.* 99: 303–20.
Shaw, M. (1975) 'The female intruder: women in fifth-century drama', *C.P.* 70: 255–66.
Shuttleworth, S. (1984) *George Eliot and Nineteenth-Century Science: the make-believe of a beginning*. Cambridge.
Sicherl, M. (1977) 'The tragic issue in Sophocles' *Ajax*', *Y.C.S.* 25: 67–98.
Silk, M.S. (1974) *Introduction in Poetic Imagery*. Cambridge.
Silverman, K. (1983) *The Subject of Semiotics*. New York.
Simon, B. (1978) *Mind and Madness in Ancient Greece*. Ithaca and London.
Simpson, M. (1969) 'Sophocles' Ajax: his madness and transformation', *Arethusa* 1: 88–103.
Sinclair, T. A. (1976) 'Protagoras and others. Socrates and his opponents', in Classen (1976).
Sissa, G. (1984) 'Une virginité sans hymen: le corps féminin en Grèce ancienne', *Annales E.S.C.* 6: 1119–39.
Slater, P. (1968) *The Glory of Hera*. Boston.
Snell, B. (1953) *The Discovery of the Mind*. Trans. Rosenmeyer, T. Oxford.
Solmsen, F. (1949) *Hesiod and Aeschylus*. Ithaca.
  (1967) 'Electra and Orestes: three recognitions in Greek tragedy', *Med. Konin. Nederl. Akad. van Wet. afd. letterk.* n.r. 20.2: 9–18.
  (1975) *Intellectual Experiments of the Greek Enlightenment*. Princeton.
Stanford, W. B. (1939) *Ambiguity in Greek Literature*. Oxford.
  (1975) 'The serpent and the eagle', introduction to *Aeschylus: the Oresteia* trans. Fagles, R. New York.
Steiner, G. (1984) *Antigones*. London.
Stewart, D. J. (1976) *The Disguised Guest: rank, role and identity in the Odyssey*. Lewisburg.
Stone, L. (1977) *The Family, Sex, and Marriage in England 1500–1800*. London.
Stroud, R. (1971) 'Greek inscriptions: Theozotides and the Athenian orphans', *Hesperia* 40: 280–301.
Sutton, D. F. (1971) 'The relation between tragedies and fourth place plays in three instances', *Arethusa* 4: 55–72.

Svenbro, J. (1976) *La Parole et le marbre: aux origines de la poétique grecque*. Lund.

Tanner, A. (1980) *Adultery and the Novel: contract and transgression*. Baltimore.

Taplin, O. P. (1977) *The Stagecraft of Aeschylus*. Oxford.

(1978) *Greek Tragedy in Action*. London.

Tarkow, T. (1981) 'The scar of Orestes: observations on a Euripidean innovation', *Rh.M* 124: 143–53.

Thomson, G. (1941) *Aeschylus and Athens*. London.

(1966) *Aeschylus: the Oresteia*. 2 vols. Amsterdam.

Torrance, R. M. (1965) 'Sophocles: some bearings', *H.S.C.P.* 60: 269–367.

Tyrrell, W. B. (1984) *Amazons: a study in Athenian mythmaking*. Baltimore.

Vandvik, E. (1942) 'Ajax the insane', *S.O.* suppl. 11: 169–75.

Vernant, J.-P. (1965) *Mythe et pensée chez les Grecs*. Paris.

ed. (1968) *Problèmes de la guerre en Grèce ancienne*. Paris.

(1980) *Myth and Society in Ancient Greece*. trans. Lloyd, J. Brighton.

(1983) *Myth and Thought among the Greeks*. London.

(1985) 'Le Dionysos masqué des *Bacchants* d'Euripide', *L'Homme* 93: 31–58.

Vernant, J.-P. and Vidal-Naquet, P. (1981) *Myth and Tragedy in Ancient Greece*. Trans. Lloyd, J. Brighton.

Verrall, A. W. (1889) *The Agamemnon of Aeschylus*. London.

Versenýi, L. (1962) 'Protagoras' man-measure fragment', *A.J.P.* 83: 178–84.

Vickers, B. (1973) *Towards Greek Tragedy*. London.

Vidal-Naquet, P. (1968) 'The Black Hunter and the origin of the Athenian *ephebeia*', *P.C.P.S.* 14: 49–64.

(1970) 'Ésclavage et gynécocratie dans la tradition, le mythe, l'utopie'. Recherches sur la structure sociale dans l'antiquité classique. (Actes du colloque de Caen 25–6 April, 1969) Paris. Trans. in Gordon (1981).

(1974) 'Les jeunes: le cru, l'enfant grec et le cuit' in *Faire de l'histoire* eds. Le Goff, J. and Nora, P. Paris.

(1981a) *Le Chasseur noir: formes de pensée et formes de société dans le monde grec*. Paris.

(1981b) 'Religious and mythic values of the land and sacrifice in the *Odyssey*,' in Gordon (1981).

(1981c) 'The Black Hunter and the origin of the Athenian *ephebeia*' (revised from Vidal-Naquet 1968) in Gordon (1981).

(1981d) 'Recipes for Greek adolescence' (revised and translated from Vidal-Naquet 1974), in Gordon (1981).

Vlastos, G. (1971) *The Philosophy of Socrates*. Garden City.

Walsh, G. R. (1977) 'The first stasimon of Euripides' *Electra*', *Y.C.S.* 25: 277–89.

Walton, J. M. (1984) *The Greek Sense of Theatre: tragedy reviewed*. London.

Whitman, C. H. (1951) *Sophocles*. Cambridge.

(1974) 'Sophocles' *Ajax* 815–824', *H.S.C.P.* 78: 67–9.

Wiersma, S. (1984) 'Women in Sophocles', *Mnemosyne* 37: 25–55.

Wigodsky, M. W. (1962) 'The "salvation" of Ajax', *Hermes* 90: 149–58.

Wilamowitz, T. von (1969) *Die dramatische Technik des Sophokles*. Zurich.

Wilcox, S. (1942) 'The scope of early rhetorical instruction', *H.S.C.P.* 53: 121–55.

Willetts, R. F. (1959) 'The servile interregnum at Argos', *Hermes* 87: 495–506.

Willink, C. W. (1968) 'Some problems of text and interpretation in the *Hippolytus*', *C.Q.* 18: 11–43.

Wimsatt, W. K. (1954) *The Verbal Icon.* Louisville.
Winnington-Ingram, R. P. (1948) *Euripides and Dionysus: an interpretation of the Bacchae.* Cambridge.
  (1949) 'Clytemnestra and the vote of Athena', *J.H.S.* 68: 130–47.
  (1960) '*Hippolytus*: a study in causation' in *Entretiens sur l'antiquité classique* 6: 171–91.
  (1969) 'Euripides: *poietes sophos*', *Arethusa* 2: 127–42.
  (1980) *Sophocles: an interpretation.* Cambridge.
  (1983) *Studies in Aeschylus.* Cambridge.
Wolff, C. (1968) 'Orestes', in Segal, E. ed. (1968).
Woozley, J. (1979) *Law and Obedience: the arguments of Plato's Crito.* London.
Zeitlin, F. (1965) 'The motif of the corrupted sacrifice in Aeschylus' *Oresteia*', *T.A.P.A.* 96: 463–505.
  (1970) 'The Argive festival of Hera and Euripides' *Electra*', *T.A.P.A.* 101: 645–69.
  (1978) 'Dynamics of misogyny in the *Oresteia*', *Arethusa* 11: 149–84.
  (1980) 'The closet of masks: role-playing and myth-making in the *Orestes* of Euripides', *Ramus* 9: 62–73.
  (1982a) *Under the Sign of the Shield: semiotics and Aeschylus' Seven against Thebes.* Rome.
  (1982b) 'Cultic models of the female: rites of Dionysus and Demeter', *Arethusa* 15: 129–57.
  (1985) 'The power of Aphrodite: Eros and the boundaries of the self in the *Hippolytus*' in *Directions in Euripidean Criticism*, ed. Burian, P. Durham.
Zuntz, G. (1958) 'On Euripides' *Helena*: theology and irony' in *Entretiens sur l'antiquité classique* 6: 201–27.

ADDENDA 1988

Clarke, H. C. (1981) *Homer's Readers.* Newark.
Erbse, E. (1984) *Studien zum Prolog der euripideischen Tragödie.* Berlin.
Euben, J. P. ed. (1986) *Greek Tragedy and Political Theory.* Berkeley.
Gagarin, M. (1986) *Early Greek Law.* Berkeley.
Goldhill, S. (1986) 'Rhetoric and relevance: interpolation at Euripides' *Electra* 367–400', *G.R.B.S.* 27: 157–71.
  (1987) 'The Great Dionysia and civic ideology', *J.H.S.* 107: 58–76.
Hansen, M. H. (1985) *Demography and Democracy. The number of Athenian citizens in the fourth century B.C.* Herning.
  (1987) *The Athenian Assembly.* Oxford.
Pelling, C. (1988) ed. *Characterization and Individuality in Greek Literature.* Oxford.
Vernant, J-P., and Vidal-Naquet, P. (1986) *Mythe et tragédie deux.* Paris.
Vidal-Naquet, P. (1986) 'Oedipe entre deux cités. Essai sur l'*Oedipe à Colone*, in Vernant and Vidal-Naquet 1986.
Whitehead, D. (1986) *The Demes of Attica.* Princeton.
Zeitlin, F. (1986) 'Thebes: theater of self and society in Athenian Drama', in Euben 1986.

INDEX

Achilles, 91, 144–5, 156, 158, 164, 165, 187, 251
Adams, S., 182, 186, 192, 194
Adkins, A., 80, 146
adultery, 19, 24, 127
Aegisthus, 5, 15–16, 21, 38, 45, 79, 147–54, 246, 251, 253
Aeneas, 107
Aeschylus, 1–56, 138, 139, 164, 238, 244, 274; *Oresteia*, 1–56, 59, 77, 79, 83ff., 107, 114, 120, 123, 128, 138, 147–54, 170, 171, 247–51, 256, 258, 267–8, 269, 270; *Persae*, 138, 268; *Supplices*, 268
aidos, 80–1, 83, 87, 134–5, 203, 242
Alcibiades, 64, 243
Allen, J., 75
Allen, R., 95
Amazons, 127
anachronism, 238
Anaxagoras, 227–8
Anaximander, 36
Andrewes, A., 57, 61
Anouilh, J., 89, 270
Anscombe, G., 283
anthropology, 111–13, 137, 266
Antiphon, 95, 97, 231–3, 236
Apollo, 14, 21, 28, 39–40, 46, 48, 59, 152, 163–4
Ariès, P., 112
Aristophanes, 1, 64, 67, 123, 124, 140, 201, 225, 230, 243, 244
Aristotle, 1, 58, 83, 85, 97, 162, 171, 224–6, 228, 245, 261
army, *see* warfare
Arnott, G., 244, 251
Arrowsmith, W., 244, 245, 249, 252, 259, 263, 276, 278
Artemis, 37, 119ff., 152
Arthur, M., 108, 272–3
Athenaeus, 138
Athene, 5, 28ff., 36, 39–40, 44, 46, 48ff., 68, 83, 158, 181ff.
audience, 3, 32, 46–7, 55–6, 76, 89–90, 92, 105–6, 130, 135–7, 173, 179, 183, 220–1, 263–4, 278–86
Austin, C., 221
Austin, M., 57
Austin, N., 203

autochthony, 66–9
Avery, H., 134

Bachofen, J., 51ff., 108
Bain, D., 246, 251, 274, 275
Bamberger, J., 53–4
Barrett, W., 124–5, 134, 135, 233
Barthes, R., 173–4, 252, 283
battle, *see* warfare
Bayley, J., 168
Beck, F., 140
Beer, G., 51
Benardete, S., 97, 102
Benveniste, E., 8off.
Bergren, A., 108
Bergson, H., 229
binding song, 28
Bloom, H., 139
Bourdieu, P., 111
Bowra, M., 179, 194, 195
Bradley, A., 171
Brauron, 122
Brecht, B., 251
Bulloch, A., 138
Burkert, W., 60
Burnyeat, M., 201, 231

Calame, C., 140, 141
Callias, 228
Calogero, G., 201
Cameron, A., 108
carpet scene, 12–14
Cassandra, 25–8, 38, 54, 166, 236–7
Castellani, V., 279, 280
Cavell, S., 283
Cecrops, 67
character, 12–13, 169–98
childbirth, 15, 20, 67–8, 72, 116, 121–3
chorus, role of, 86–7, 140ff., 256–8, 267–74
citizenship, 58ff.
city, 5, 19, 28, 29–30, 31–2, 34, 36–7, 40, 48–9, 51–6, 57–8, 82, 83, 88–107, 109, 113–14, 152–4, 203, 204, 205, 210, 229, 241, 242–3, 265–74
civic duty, *see* city
Cixoux, H., 168
clarity, 17ff., 27, 219ff.
Clarke, H. C., 142